Music and Postwar Transitions
in the 19th and 20th Centuries

Explorations in Culture and International History Series
General Editor: Jessica C. E. Gienow-Hecht

Volume 1
Culture and International History
Edited by Jessica C. E. Gienow-Hecht and Frank Schumacher

Volume 2
Remaking France
Brian Angus McKenzie

Volume 3
Decentering America
Edited by Jessica C. E. Gienow-Hecht

Volume 4
Anti-Americanism in Latin America and the Caribbean
Edited by Allan McPherson

Volume 5
Practicing Public Diplomacy: A Cold War Odyssey
Yale Richmond

Volume 6
Searching for a Cultural Diplomacy
Edited by Mark C. Donfried and Jessica C. E. Gienow-Hecht

Volume 7
Music and International History in the Twentieth Century
Edited by Jessica C. E. Gienow-Hecht

Volume 8
Empire of Pictures: Global Media, the 1960s Cold War, and the Transformation of U.S. Foreign Policy
Sönke Kunkel

Volume 9
Nation Branding in Modern History
Edited by Carolin Viktorin, Jessica C. E. Gienow-Hecht, Annika Estner, Marcel K. Will

Volume 10
Music and Postwar Transitions in the 19th and 20th Centuries
Edited by Anaïs Fléchet, Martin Guerpin, Philippe Gumplowicz, and Barbara L. Kelly

Music and Postwar Transitions in the 19th and 20th Centuries

Edited by
Anaïs Fléchet, Martin Guerpin,
Philippe Gumplowicz, and Barbara L. Kelly

First published in 2023 by
Berghahn Books
www.berghahnbooks.com

© 2023, 2026 Anaïs Fléchet, Martin Guerpin,
Philippe Gumplowicz, and Barbara L. Kelly
First paperback edition published in 2026

All rights reserved. Except for the quotation of short passages
for the purposes of criticism and review, no part of this book
may be reproduced in any form or by any means, electronic or
mechanical, including photocopying, recording, or any information
storage and retrieval system now known or to be invented,
without written permission of the publisher.

Library of Congress Cataloging-in-Publication Data

Names: Fléchet, Anaïs, editor. | Guerpin, Martin, editor. | Gumplowicz, Philippe, editor. | Kelly, Barbara L., editor.
Title: Music and postwar transitions in the 19th and 20th centuries / edited by Anaïs Fléchet, Martin Guerpin, Philippe Gumplowicz and Barbara L. Kelly.
Description: [1st.] | [New York] : Berghahn Books, 2023. | Series: Explorations in culture and international history ; 10 | Includes bibliographical references and index.
Identifiers: LCCN 2022045515 (print) | LCCN 2022045516 (ebook) | ISBN 9781800738942 (hardback) | ISBN 9781800738959 (ebook)
Subjects: LCSH: Music and war—19th century. | Music and war—20th century. | Music—Historiography. | War (Philosophy) | Music—Social aspects—History—19th century. | Music—Social aspects—History—20th century.
Classification: LCC ML3916 .M87265 2023 (print) | LCC ML3916 (ebook) | DDC 780.72/2—dc23/eng/20220927
LC record available at https://lccn.loc.gov/2022045515
LC ebook record available at https://lccn.loc.gov/2022045516

British Library Cataloguing in Publication Data

A catalogue record for this book is available from the British Library

EU GPSR Authorized Representative

LOGOS EUROPE, 9 rue Nicolas Poussin, 17000, LA ROCHELLE, France
Email: Contact@logoseurope.eu

ISBN 978-1-80073-894-2 hardback
ISBN 978-1-83695-656-3 paperback
ISBN 978-1-80758-559-4 epub
ISBN 978-1-80073-895-9 web pdf

https://doi.org/10.3167/9781800738942

Contents

List of Tables   viii

Foreword by Jay Winter   ix

Acknowledgments   xiii

Introduction
Toward a Musical Approach to Postwar Transitions   1
*Anaïs Fléchet, Martin Guerpin, Philippe Gumplowicz,
and Barbara L. Kelly*

Part I. Reconstructing the Music World

Chapter 1
Transitioning from the Turmoil through Music: Withdrawal,
Patriotism, Sublimation: Georges Bizet in the Early 1870s   21
Hervé Lacombe

Chapter 2
Revolutionary Music from War to Peace: Mexico, 1910s–1930s   39
Pablo Palomino

Chapter 3
First Concerts on the International Stage: The British
Comebacks of the Vienna and Berlin Philharmonics in 1947/48   54
Friedemann Pestel

Part II. A Gradual Demobilization: Music, Cultures of War, and National Imaginations

Chapter 4
Discourse on Music and the Postwar Transition: The Case
of France after the Franco-Prussian Conflict of 1870–1871   83
Emmanuel Reibel

Chapter 5
Singing about the Former Enemy: Two Postwar Transition
Periods Seen through the Lens of the Café-Concert and
Music Hall Chanson, 1871–1923 — 102
Martin Guerpin

Chapter 6
War of Taste in Popular and Folk Music: French Chanson,
1940–1942 — 121
Philippe Gumplowicz

Chapter 7
Postwar Transitions and Uses of Music in a Central
European Borderland Region: Tyrol and the Aftermath
of Two World Wars, 1900–2010s — 137
Michael Wedekind

Part III. Memory, Mourning, and Commemoration

Chapter 8
Béranger's Napoleonic Songs: Mourning, Memory,
and the Future — 159
Sophie-Anne Leterrier

Chapter 9
"Will We Return Unscathed?" Paul Hindemith's *Minimax*
and the Trauma of War — 179
Lesley Hughes

Chapter 10
The Construction of a Transatlantic Repertoire of
Resistance and Mourning in the Postwar Years: Sources
Collected by Shmerke Kaczerginski (Vilna, New York,
Buenos Aires) — 194
Jean-Sébastien Noël

Chapter 11
Singing the Unspeakable in Rwanda in the Summer of
1994: Music in the Context of the Genocidal Abyss
through a Portrait of the Artist — 208
Benjamin Chemouni and Assumpta Mugiraneza

Part IV. Music for Peace and Reconciliation?

Chapter 12
Peacemaking and Festivities at the Congress of Paris, 1856 229
Damien Mahiet

Chapter 13
Internationalism and Musical Exchange in Post–World War I
Europe, 1918–1923 246
Barbara L. Kelly

Chapter 14
Music: A Weapon for Peace? The United States, UNESCO,
and the Creation of the International Music Council,
1945–1953 271
Anaïs Fléchet

Afterword
Survival, Desire, Empowerment, and the Absence of
Words: Music in Postwar Transitions, 1800–1950 290
Jessica Gienow-Hecht

Index 299

Tables

Table 4.1. List of French music magazines that resumed publication following the Franco-Prussian War. Table created by the author.   84

Table 5.1. Number of chansons referencing the enemy after the Franco-Prussian War. Table created by the author.   104

Table 5.2. Number of chansons referencing the enemy after World War I. Table created by the author.   105

Table 5.3. Number of reissues of "La Marseillaise" and "Le Chant du Départ" after the 1870 war (period 1871–1913) and the 1914–18 war (period 1919–29). Table created by the author.   109

Table 9.1. The movements in *Minimax*. Table created by the author.   180

Table 13.1. Performances of selected contemporary foreign composers (Bartók, Szymanowski, Stravinsky, Schoenberg) 1921–26. Table created by the author.   256

FOREWORD
Jay Winter

Music is a language of memory. It is also a language in which political and social conflicts are expressed and at times defused. The innovation of this book is in documenting the ways in which musical composition and performance have intersected with the complex process of the disengagement of nations and societies from war since the mid-nineteenth century.

The authors examine three vectors of musical life. The first is institutional; that is, the authors address the question of the social and political space occupied by music at times of transition from war to peace. The second is pacifist; they address the ways music has been used to move away from war, either through individual initiatives or through the diplomatic mobilization of music and musicians. The third is commemorative; they probe the use of music in the liturgy of remembrance, both secular and sacred.

These inquiries significantly advance the conversation in which historians have been engaged over the last thirty years regarding the question of when wars end. In this context, scholars have come to realize that international wars generate all kinds of armed conflicts as their sequelae.[1] Substantial research in the 1980s and 1990s established that along a vast arc from Finland to Turkey, there were at least as many deaths due to armed violence in the period 1918–23 as there were between 1914 and 1918. Part of the source of this second phase of violence were wars of succession in the "shatter zones" of collapsed empires—the German, the Austro-Hungarian, the Russian, and the Ottoman.[2] The use of the term the "Greater War,"[3] adopted by historians Robert Gerwarth and John Horne, has captured the move toward incorporating the immediate aftermaths of military conflicts as an integral part of the phenomena we call war.

Part of the impulse behind this work was the end of the Cold War. The collapse of the Soviet empire in 1989–91 helped liberate historians of World War I from a solely Western European outlook. As archives opened up, it was possible to shift the center of gravity of Great War studies from London to Warsaw and from Paris to Petrograd. Historians in Eastern Europe uncovered the war from the obscurity in which it had been placed by regimes that took for granted that 1917, not 1914, was the foundational moment in twentieth-century history.[4]

Furthermore, initial benign predictions as to the geopolitical benefits of the "end of history" in the victory of liberal (or not-so-liberal) capitalism in 1989[5] faded in the thirty years that followed. The transition to democracy in Eastern Europe and Russia has wound up being hardly a transition at all in many cases. What post-communist regimes have inherited from their communist past is the subject of a substantial body of scholarship. It includes an appreciation of the long-term damage communism did to those sent to the gulag archipelago. The traumatic memories of these people have entered into history, just as have the memories of victims of the Shoah.

Indirectly linked to the end of the Cold War, this research field has benefited from the exponential growth of the field of memory studies. In part a reaction to the collapse of Marxism long before 1989 as a theory of history, the worldwide "memory boom"[6] has helped attract scholars and students to cultural history, even more than political history, in their approach to writing about war in the modern period. Auditory history is one important facet of the history of emotions and the senses, both important subfields within cultural history. The study of the arts of remembrance went global[7] and stimulated an interest in music as being central to the cultural landscape of societies both during and after war.

In 1980 the America Psychiatric Association validated the medical diagnosis and treatment of posttraumatic stress disorder. This was only five years after the end of the Vietnam War. Since then, historians of modern warfare have shown that war-related casualties lingered for decades, or even for entire lifetimes. Many of these conditions were psychological or neurological in character. Consequently, historians helped shift the focus from the damage war did to men in combat to the damage that lingered long after the end of hostilities.

The transition from war to peace remains an important part of historical research. The way historians configure their studies has changed from an emphasis on political history to an emphasis on cultural history. The best work in this field brings the two together.[8] The essays in this volume draw upon these powerful currents in historiography. They also point toward a greater recognition by historians outside of the field of music, that they cannot ignore the contribution of musicians, composers, and their audiences to the way contemporaries over the last two centuries have tried to understand war, and even, at times, to escape from its cruelties.

Jay Winter is the Charles J. Stille Emeritus Professor of History at Yale University. He is a specialist on World War I and its impact on the twentieth century. Winter is the author or coauthor of twenty-five books, including *Sites of Memory, Sites of Mourning: The Great War in European Cultural History*; *The Great War and the Shaping of the 20th Century*; and most recently *War beyond Words: Languages of Remembrance from the Great War to the Present*. In addition, he has edited or coedited thirty books and contributed 130 book chapters to edited volumes. Winter was also coproducer, cowriter, and chief historian for the PBS/BBC series *The Great War and the Shaping of the 20th Century*, which won an Emmy Award, a Peabody Award, and a Producers Guild of America Award for best television documentary in 1997. He has received honorary doctorates from the University of Graz, the University of Leuven, and the University of Paris.

Notes

1. Gerwarth and Horne, *War in Peace*.
2. Bartov and Weitz, *Shatterzone of Empires*.
3. This is the title of a book series launched by Oxford University Press in 2012.
4. Winter and Prost, *The Great War in History*, chapters 9–10 and conclusion.
5. Fukuyama, *The End of History and the Last Man*.
6. Winter, "The Generation of Memory," 69–92.
7. Huyssen, *Twilight Memories*.
8. Horne, "End of a Paradigm? The Cultural History of the Great War," 155–92.

Bibliography

Bartov, Omer, and Weitz, Eric D., ed. *Shatterzone of Empires: Coexistence and Violence in the German, Habsburg, Russian, and Ottoman Borderlands*. Indianapolis: Indiana University Press, 2013.

Fukuyama, Francis. *The End of History and the Last Man*. New York: Free Press, 1992.

Gerwarth, Robert, and John Horne, eds. *War in Peace: Paramilitary Violence in Europe after the Great War*. Oxford: Oxford University Press, 2012.

Horne, John. "End of a Paradigm? The Cultural History of the Great War." *Past & Present* 242, no. 1 (February 2019).

Huyssen, Andreas. *Twilight Memories: Marking Time in a Culture of Amnesia*. London: Routledge, 1995.

Winter, Jay. "The Generation of Memory: Reflections on the 'Memory Boom' in Contemporary Historical Studies." *Bulletin of the German Historical Institute* 27 (Fall 2000).

Winter, Jay, and Antoine Prost. *The Great War in History: Debates and Controversies 1914–2020*. 2nd ed. Cambridge: Cambridge University Press, 2020.

Grande Guerre international research center in Péronne (Stéphane Audoin-Rouzeau, Annette Becker, John Horne, and Jay Winter) on the cultural mobilizations and demobilizations linked to World War I.[10] This was the theme of a 2001 conference at Trinity College Dublin entitled *Demobilizing the Mind, Culture, Politics, and the Legacy of the Great War, 1919–1933*.[11] It is therefore not surprising that the French expression "sorties de guerre" (postwar transitions) appeared shortly after in a 2004 work by World War I specialist Bruno Cabanes,[12] who subsequently formalized it with Guillaume Piketty in an article published in 2007.[13] While this notion was initially adopted by World War I specialists, it quickly transferred to other periods and other types of conflicts.[14]

Studying postwar transitions challenges the chronology of war and peace, which is traditionally based on the signing of declarations of war, armistices, and peace treaties. The official end of a war can give rise to multiple forms of conflictual relations (including low-intensity conflicts) and traumas with infinite impacts.[15] Just like any entry into war, each postwar transition has its own chronology, its own dynamics, its own temporalities, its own music, and its own polyrhythm.

The traces of the conflictual relations that continue to act on a society once a peace treaty has been signed have been considered from a number of angles, and their interconnection now structures the field of postwar transitions studies. A first key theme is reconstruction. It encompasses territorial occupation policies;[16] the return of soldiers, deportees, exiles, and emigrants;[17] urban, landscape, and institutional reconstruction;[18] reparations and restitutions;[19] clean-up of state apparatuses;[20] and transitional justice in the case of societies torn apart by civil wars.[21]

Memory constitutes another major research area in Postwar Transitions Studies. Work in this domain has focused on a range of themes: the persistence and appeasement of individual or collective trauma after a conflict;[22] the way in which mourning is organized or trauma is sublimated collectively through commemorations or war memorials;[23] and the conflicts of memory that can arise after a war.[24]

What are the processes of "*demobilizing* the mind"[25] that ended the use of artistic institutions, artistic works, and discourses on artistic works for a country's war aims? Studying these processes of appeasement implies considering their corollary, namely the persistence of the cultural mobilization of a nation or group after a conflict has ended. The first question was mapped out by John Horne. It concerns the reconciliation of populations through overcoming the antagonisms and hateful representations that have separated them.[26] The second issue concerns reeducation programs. Whether implemented by totalitarian or democratic regimes, these programs closely combine education and propaganda.[27] The third element, which is the most recently developed and least studied to date, concerns the "disarmament of minds," by which we mean the end of the mobilization of the cultural and scientific world for war purposes.[28] Research on cultural demobilization highlights the different forms of disengagement from the violence that is inherent in the culture of war,[29] as well as the persistence or reconfiguration of representations of the enemy, sometimes long after a conflict has come to an end.[30]

Taking all these different issues into account reveals the multiple temporalities of the postwar transition processes—from the appeasement of physical and symbolic violence to the rise of the pacifist ideal—as well as the many domains through which they are played out. The main contribution of Postwar Transitions Studies is therefore to postulate the possibility of a "war in peace"[31] and, more fundamentally, to question the dividing line between these two notions, which in most languages are structured as diametrically opposed, mutually exclusive notions. At what point and under what conditions can we say that a postwar transition process is fully complete? And, more significantly, is it possible to transition fully out of a war?

Bringing Music into the Field of Postwar Transitions Studies

From an anthropologic perspective, music is an active factor in the construction and reconstruction of human communities. By proposing to incorporate music—understood here in the broad sense of repertoires, discourses, practices, and musical sociability—into Postwar Transitions Studies, this book opens up a vast field of study that is situated at the intersection of four domains that have so far received little scholarly attention: the relationship between music and war culture;[32] the commemorative and consolatory dimension of music;[33] migration and exile;[34] and the links between music, cultural diplomacy and propaganda.[35]

Based on a comparative, multidisciplinary approach that brings together historians, political scientists, psychologists, and musicologists working on various geographical areas and musical repertoires (art music, folk music, and popular music), this volume offers the first study of the subject and makes the case that the specificities of postwar transitions are linked not only with specific periods or places but also with types of conflict. This perspective has emerged out of the studies initiated during the colloquia entitled "Music, Nationalism, Transnationalism" (Royal Northern College of Music, Manchester, 2015) and "Music in Postwar Transitions 19th–21st Centuries" (University of Montreal, 2018) and with the "Music et Nation" research program launched by Université Paris-Saclay in 2015.

In these studies, France has served as a starting point for initiating the field of postwar transitions studies. Yet the diversity of postwar transition situations involving the musical world emerges throughout the book. The geographical diversity perhaps stands out most of all, with chapters looking at locations such as Rwanda, the villages of South Tyrol, the Parisian cabarets, and the most prestigious stages of Berlin, Vienna, and London. There is also a diversity of repertoires that extends well beyond art music, with a special focus on chanson, popular, and folk music as vehicles for expression and investment in identity. The chapters cover a diversity of actors, too, including musicians, composers, performers, conductors, and collectors of popular songs, as well as all the cultural intermediaries associated with music, such as concert agents, music publishers, administrators, and music critics, who acted not just as mouthpieces during postwar transitions but as full-blown participators in the context of musical patriotism. In addition to these private actors, the book takes in public actors, who were particularly significant during these reconstruction periods, including international organizations, trade unions, and political states. Finally, there is a consideration of functional diversity in the volume. Music can reflect the postwar transition processes as they happen, and at the same time, can play an active role in these processes. As such, it can contribute to accelerating or slowing down the return to peace. This ambivalent political use of music invites us to go beyond an irenic conception that seems to reduce music to simply being an agent of peace and harmony between peoples.

Aesthetic, Institutional, and Political Reconfigurations

Beyond the diversity of the situations, periods, and regions observed, the study of music in postwar transitions nevertheless reveals common overarching themes, which have been used to structure this book. The first part of the volume considers the aesthetic, institutional, and political reconfigurations that the musical world undergoes in the aftermath of a conflict. What are the mechanisms that operate in musical culture to generate its transformations, resilience, and reactivations (if it had slowed down or stopped during the conflict)? To what extent does war bring about a sudden change?[36] How far can a postwar transition open the way for other music or music practices?

Hervé Lacombe adopts this perspective in his study of Bizet's itinerary in the aftermath of the 1870 Franco-Prussian War. He examines the composer's creative process and the experience of a "postwar transition through music" at an individual level. Bizet's works from the early 1870s bear the marks of the sublimation of defeat and mourning but also a sense of urgency and finitude. As such, the composer contributed to the French musical territory's recomposition, a process that was accelerated in the aftermath of the conflict with the creation of the Société Nationale de Musique and its famous motto *Ars Gallica*.[37] Lacombe concludes that the postwar transition therefore appears to have been a time of aesthetic and political elucidation.

Pablo Palomino's chapter on Mexican musical life in the two decades following the 1910 revolution sheds light on the aesthetic and political crystallization process by focusing on institutions. He shows how the new regime introduced musical policies aimed at reconciling the "many Mexicos" opposed in the civil war. Conceived as a vehicle for national identity, music—along with mural art, education, and public ceremonies—was to promote the regime's unifying discourse. The new institutions that were set up contributed to structuring a professional field that brought together musicians, orchestra directors, impresarios, and music teachers. Palomino writes that the postwar transition coupled with a change of regime gave rise to a varied, new, and modernizing musical order that included village and military bands and choirs, working-class musical associations, urban and rural musical education, conservatoire programmes, and nightlife commercial music.

The reconstruction of musical life was also taking place on an international level, with the resumption of musicians' travels and tours, which had been interrupted by the particular conflicts. Friedemann Pestel focuses on the first international tours of the Berlin and Vienna Philharmonic Orchestras after World War II. What was to be done with these orchestras of undeniable international stature? Many of their musicians had joined the Nazi Party, and both orchestras had been an aural showcase for Nazism. The question of their denazification and return to the international stage was raised. Wilhelm Furtwängler remains the most polemic figure among those who made a controversial return, while the great conductor Bruno Walter's return from exile allowed the Vienna Philharmonic Orchestra to play the victim card. Pestel highlights the role of the "musical tandems" that emerged between the musicians who returned, like Walter, and those who remained in Nazi Europe.

Cultural Demobilization

The second part of the volume analyzes the uses of music for cultural demobilization and the return to peace. The press, and particularly the music press, offers one of the best vantage points for observing these phenomena, as Emmanuel Reibel demonstrates in his chapter on France after the 1870 Franco-Prussian War, a subject that has experienced a real historiographic renewal since the first decade of the twenty-first century. Reibel's study of the publications that reappeared in the two years following the war reveals a tension between, on the one hand, a desire to encourage people to forget the traumatic conflict by reviving prewar practices and discourses and, on the other, a tendency to transfer the war that had just ended on the field of battle into the field of music.

Martin Guerpin's chapter highlights a similar transfer in the domain of French café-concert and music hall chanson repertoires that referenced the enemy—sometimes not without humor—in the wake of the 1870 Franco-Prussian War and World War I. The difference in this case was that these chansons followed on from other works that had been produced *during* the war. A comparative approach to the chronology of the publication of these chansons, their lyrics, and their musical content after each war reveals that the nature of the conflict and their outcomes conditioned the duration and nature of the postwar transition processes, as well as the persistence of enemy stereotypes for a given country.

The question of postwar transition nationalism can also be approached through music from the perspective of aesthetic taste and sensibility. Philippe Gumplowicz examines the loathing that the writers Céline and Abel Bonnard and the musicologist André Coeuroy expressed for variety music after the 1940 armistice, which the vast majority of French people saw as marking the end of the war. Considered immoral, seedy, and cosmopolitan, these popular chansons were totally alien to the song of France's provincial heartland and were thought to have emasculated the populations and thus contributed to France's defeat.

While Martin Guerpin's chapter reveals the possibility that the demobilization of music was not fully complete in the intervening years between the two conflicts, Michael Wedekind's study of Tyrolean folk music repertoires and institutional structures from the 1900s to the present day shows that this absence of demobilization can extend over several conflicts and over a long period of time. Even before the First World War, Tyrolean folk music had been mobilized as a means of ethnic, ideological, and even racial in-group/out-group conditioning. It had been used as a means of disseminating a conservative, antisocialist, anticapitalist, nationalist, and often xenophobic ideology that was rooted in a rejection of urban aesthetics, urban cultural interactions, and the urban lifestyle. The two world wars led to a radicalization of this vision and strengthened the position of its proponents, and the transition periods that followed them did not change this situation. Folk music can thus be seen here as an extension, through other means, of the ethnic conflicts that had shaken the region.

Memory, Mourning, and Commemoration

The third part of this book explores music as a space for the expression of memory, mourning, and commemoration. Among the different topics linked with postwar transitions, this field is the most explored in recent literature, especially by scholars in musicology. Music has been studied as a way to soothe war traumas and injustices thanks to cathartic and therapeutic means,[38] and as an efficient way to reenact traumas and thus construct and reconfigure their memory.[39] The perspective of postwar transitions leads us to question the function of music commemoration as a tool to appease and soothe minds and bodies. Chapters grouped in this section once again cast out one-sided, conciliatory views on music. They show that commemorative repertoires and uses of music can express the failure of reconciliation and perpetuate a state of collective cultural mobilization against a former (or newly constructed) enemy. Sophie-Anne Leterrier sees the corpus of songs created by the "national chansonnier" Béranger in the post-Napoleonic period not only as a weapon in the fight for liberalism but also as a vehicle for feelings, mourning, hope, and the memory of past events and struggles as the songs engaged in a subtle interplay with censorship and the shared memory of the Napoleonic period.

Lesley Hughes's approach is distinctive in being based on a specific work, *Minimax* (1923) by Paul Hindemith (1895–1963). Her analysis of this string quartet is informed by the composer's correspondence before, during, and after the Great War. She reveals a series of parodic devices that make *Minimax* a true satire of German militarism. Hughes thus shows that this musical work served both as an outlet for the anger felt toward the horrors of a war that had ended a few years earlier, and as a means of exorcising through humor and laughter the trauma it may have engendered.

Jean-Sébastien Noël examines the process of constructing a transatlantic musical memory of the genocide of European Jews after World War II that spanned Vilnius, New York, and Buenos Aires. His analysis is based on the itinerary of the poet and publisher Shmerke Kaczerginski, one of the principal collectors of songs written by resistance fighters and Jewish victims of the genocide. Kaczerginski's most influential work, *Lider fun di getos un lagern* (Songs from the ghettos and camps), which was published in New York in 1948, established a repertoire for commemorating the genocide and forms of Jewish resistance. Noël reveals the role of music in the reestablishment of cultural flows and transfers between the main centers of Jewish life from the 1930s to the 1950s. His contribution shows the value of an approach that consists in combining music history and diasporic studies, because the construction of the memory of a conflict through music is a dimension of postwar transitions.

In their chapter on songs composed after the Tutsi genocide, Benjamin Chemouni, and Assumpta Mugiraneza also focus on the impossibility of forgetting a genocide and the difficult reconstruction of an annihilated society. During the Rwandan Civil War (1990–94), song, sometimes under the guise of bucolic invocations of a fantasized Rwanda, created an atmosphere of violence and fear that prepared Rwandans for the annihilation of the other. But what was to become of song in the civil postwar transition, where the genocide was imposed as the new yardstick of Rwandan life? Chemouni and Mugiraneza address this question through a study of the way in which two artists, Suzanne Nyiranyamibwa and Mariya Yohana Mukankuranga, expressed their feelings of paralysis at a country rendered unrecognizable by the "genocide by proximity" and tried to give the victims back the dignity that their deaths had denied them. The voice that rose up through song tried to express the unspeakable and to offer a substitute for revenge.

Music, Diplomacy, and Peacebuilding

The fourth part of the volume concerns the establishment of musical diplomacy in postconflict situations and the mobilization of music to promote peace. The links between music, diplomacy, and propaganda have been the subject of very active research since the publication of Jessica Gienow-Hecht's pioneering book *Sound Diplomacy* (2009). Historians, political scientists, and musicologists have highlighted various uses of music in international relations, during wars or to assert the strategic interests of states.[40] As Danielle Fosler-Lussier has shown, music, often presented as apolitical, could be used as a diplomatic weapon, serving the soft power of the United States and the Soviet Union during the Cold War, through the creation of an "international economy of prestige."[41] As a practice and source of shared emotions, music has also been able to serve great international causes, in postconflict situations, as underlined by Yehudi Menuhin's commitment to UNESCO; or, more recently, that of Daniel Barenboim and the West-Eastern Divan Orchestra for peace in the Middle East, or the Silk Road Project led by the cellist Yo-Yo Ma for the promotion of "multicultural artistic collaborations" beyond the borders and political rivalries that cross the Asian continent. This musical diplomacy, with its share of idealism, as well as the geopolitical approach of states and international organizations, provide many elements for thinking about the role of music in postwar transitions.

"Congresses never work better than when they dance."[42] Repeating this quip made by a journalist during the Paris Congress of 1856, Damien Mahiet looks at the role of music and dance in peace negotiations from the Congress of Vienna (1815) to the mid-nineteenth century. Do balls, operas, concerts, and operettas facilitate diplomatic action, or do they just serve to mask the interests of the various actors involved? Drawing from press reports, histories, memoirs, and diaries, Mahiet retraces the nineteenth-century history of an idea—musical peacemaking and the pursuit of pleasure as a component of congress diplomacy—and examines the sonorous recomposition of the "European concert" and international system. He shows that music and dance not only modeled conceptions of peace but also compounded misunderstandings and, on occasion, enmity. Diplomats mobilized music and musicians at once as instruments of cooperation and communion, and as weapons in the battlefield of salons and media.

Barbara L. Kelly compares the organizations that became the British and French sections of the International Society for Contemporary Music: the British Music Society and London Contemporary Music Centre in Britain, and the *Revue musicale* and Concerts de *La Revue musicale* in France. She explores the overlapping commitments to national promotion and international exchange as well as the tensions between the two positions. The end of hostilities motivated a network of composers, conductors, critics, and performers to promote musical exchange with the aim of promoting peace and cooperation through culture. At the same time, it was also an opportunity for nations to make their mark on the international stage. This was particularly true for Britain as it sought to stimulate interest in its contemporary music both at home and abroad and to look toward France, its wartime ally, rather than to Germany as a model. Wartime attitudes also persisted in the very brand of internationalism, which sought to challenge the historic dominance of Austro-German music within a European framework. While postwar musical culture bore some resemblances to the vibrant internationalism of the prewar period, there were also notable differences in reflecting new power relations and alliances resulting from the experience of conflict.

Anaïs Fléchet retraces the early years of the International Music Council, an organization founded in 1949 in the wake of the United Nations Educational, Scientific and Cultural Organization (UNESCO) to promote "an ideal of peace and universal harmony." Conceived as a forum for exchange between composers, performers, and musicologists, regardless of political borders or rivalries between nations, the organization nevertheless appears to have been closely linked to Washington in the dual context of the end of World War II and the beginning of the Cold War. At UNESCO in the late 1940s, the links between music, diplomacy, and propaganda were being reconfigured because, as the American ethnomusicologist Charles Seeger, who was the International Music Council's main promoter, pointed out, "the arts, without exception, are equally prime fields of competition and for cooperation."[43]

The authors of this book thus explore disruptions to the musical world in the aftermath of a war as well as the influence of prewar cultural, political, and institutional legacies. The relationship between music and postwar transitions is twofold and reciprocal. On the one hand, postwar transition periods are favored times for institutional reconfiguration. On the other, music plays a role in prolonging or ending postwar transition periods. Hence, there are commemorative repertoires that encouraged fraternity between former enemies (John Foulds's 1921 *World Requiem* or post-1994 Rwandan songs, tackled in chapter 14) and songs that perpetuated the stigmatization of the enemy, such as those studied in chapter 5. *Music and Postwar Transitions* offers a first synthesis of all these subjects by situating them in the context of the nineteenth, twentieth, and twenty-first centuries. In so doing, it aims to contribute to the renewal of the history of music by proposing a history *through* music with a double agenda: demonstrating the importance and specificity of music in understanding the cultural continuities and transformations that run through contemporary societies.

No one can deny what so many historians and musicologists have affirmed over the last thirty years: that music is a language through which a community shares feelings, representations, and knowledge. This language, whether it be sounds, songs, or the speeches that accompany them, only takes on its meaning through the concrete situation in which it is produced and received. In each postwar period, particular voices have been raised to express grief, honor the dead, celebrate victories, salute the newfound peace, attenuate passions or, on the contrary, excite them. Musical institutions were reconstituted at the same time as national communities were reformed or projects for democratic conflict resolution were forged. In this volume, the reader will find studies on the management and production of collective emotions that only music can arouse—and this over a span of more than two centuries and three continents.

Notes

1. Bizet, *Correspondance générale*. "Nous sommes entre un monde qui s'en va et un monde qui vient. Nous avons une rude mer à traverser."
2. This introduction was translated from French by Clare Ferguson.
3. Picard, *Wagner*, 299–328; Buch, "Métaphores politiques," 66; Kelly, *Music and Ultra-Modernism*, 85, 166.
4. O'Connell, "Music in War, Music for Peace," 117.
5. O'Connell and El-Shawan Castelo-Branco, *Music and Conflicts*; O'Connell, "Sound Bites."
6. Urbain, *Music and Conflict Transformation*; Wu, "Music's Role in Peacebuilding," 138–43; Dieckmann and Davidson, "Peace, Empathy and Conciliation through Music," 293–99; Urbain, "Overcoming Challenges to Music's Role in Peacebuilding," 332–40.
7. Cusik, "Music as Torture, Music as Weapon."
8. Bergmann, "The Sound of Trauma"; Bergh Arild, "Music and Art in Conflict Transformation"; Becker, *Voir la Grande Guerre*; Guerpin, "*Le Courrier musical* et le premier conflit mondial." 35–57; and Kelly, *Tradition and Style in the Works*

of Darius Milhaud, 1912–1939, 11–15; and Kelly and Moore, *Music Criticism in France, 1918–1939*, 127, 140–49.
9. Dower, *War without Mercy*; Mazower, *After the War Was Over*.
10. Becker, *Les Monuments aux morts*; Winter, *Sites of Memory*; Audoin-Rouzeau and Becker, *14—18: Retrouver la guerre*; Audoin-Rouzeau and Prochasson, *Sortir de la Grande Guerre*; Winter, *War beyond Words*.
11. Horne, "Démobilisations culturelles après la Grande Guerre."
12. Cabanes, *La Victoire endeuillée*.
13. Cabanes and Piketty, *Retour à l'intime au sortir de la guerre*.
14. Pernot and Toureille, *Lendemains de guerre. . .*
15. Creveld (van), *Les Transformations de la guerre*; Cohrs, *The Unfinished Peace after World War I*.
16. Ménudier, *L'Allemagne occupée (1945–1949)*; Knowles, *Winning the Peace*.
17. Cabanes and Piketty, *Retour à l'intime au sortir de la guerre*; Agazzi and Schütz, *Heimkehr: eine zentrale Kategorie der Nachkriegszeit*; Reinisch and White, *The Disentanglement of Populations*.
18. Woolf, *Italia, 1943–1950;* Diefendorf, "Urban Reconstruction in Europe after World War II"; Clout, *After the Ruins*; Castillo (del), *Rebuilding War-Torn States*; Clapson and Larkham, *The Blitz and Its Legacy*; Michonneau, Rodríguez-Lópeza, and Vela Cossío, *Paisajes de guerra*.
19. Barkan, *The Guilt of Nations*; White, *"Making the French Pay"*; Colonomos, "De la réparation à la restitution"; Perrot, "Les biens culturels dans les réparations pour dommages de guerre."
20. Aron, *Histoire de l'épuration*; Virgili, *La France "virile."*
21. Klotz, *Zivile Konfliktbearbeitung*; Rettberg, *Entre el perdón y el paredón*; Priemel and Stiller, *Reassessing the Nuremberg Military Tribunals*.
22. Grossmann, *Trauma, Memory and Motherhood*; Santos, *Memoria de la guerra y del franquismo*; Aróstegui and Godicheau, *Guerra civil*.
23. Becker, *Les Monuments aux morts*; Winter, *Sites of Memory*; Tison, *Comment sortir de la guerre?*
24. Ostriichouk, *Mémoires de conflits, mémoires en conflits*.
25. Horne, "Demobilizing the Mind."
26. Gorguet, *Les Mouvements pacifistes*; Bar-Siman-Tov, *From Conflict Resolution to Reconciliation*; Horne, "Guerres et réconciliations européennes."
27. Pronay and Wilson, *The Political Re-education of Germany and Her Allies*; Mombert, *Sous le Signe de la rééducation*.
28. Rasmussen, "Réparer, réconcilier, oublier"; Dagan, *La Nouvelle Revue française de la guerre à la paix*.
29. Mosse, *Fallen Soldiers*; Hassner and Marchal, *Guerres et sociétés*; Dimitrijevic, "Sorties de guerres et de violence"; Boyle, *Violence after War*.
30. Dower, *War without Mercy*; Jeismann, *La Patrie de l'ennemi*.
31. Horne and Gewarth, *War in Peace*.
32. Watkins, *Proof through the Night*; Audoin-Rouzeau, Buch, Chimènes and Durosoir, *La Grande Guerre des musiciens*; Morag, "On Music and War."
33. Rehding, *Music and Monumentality*; Rogers, *Resonant Recoveries*.
34. Baily, *War, Exile and the Music of Afghanistan*.
35. Gienow-Hecht, *Sound Diplomacy*; Fléchet and Marès, "Musique et Relations internationales," 155–56; Gienow-Hecht, *Music and International History*; Fosler-Lussier, *Music in America's Cold War Diplomacy*.
36. Kelly, *French Music, Culture, and National Identity*.
37. Strasser, "The Société nationale and Its Adversaries," 225–51; and Duchesneau, *L'Avant-garde musicale à Paris*, 16–63.

38. Rogers, *Resonant Recoveries*.
39. Fauser and Figueroa, *Performing Commemoration*.
40. Ahrendt, Ferraguto, and Mahiet, *Music and Diplomacy*; Fléchet and Marès, "Musique et Relations internationales"; Gienow-Hecht, *Music and International History*; Mikkonen and Suutari, *Music, Art and Diplomacy*; Ramel and Prévost-Thomas, *International Relations, Music and Diplomacy*; Dunkel and Nitzsche, *Popular Music and Public Diplomacy*.
41. Fosler-Lussier, *Music in America's Cold War Diplomacy*.
42. "Les congrès ne marchent jamais mieux que quand ils dansent."
43. Seeger, "The Arts in International Relations," 41.

Bibliography

Agazzi, Elena, and Erhard Schütz, eds. *Heimkehr: eine zentrale Kategorie der Nachkriegszeit. Geschichte, Literatur und Medien*. Berlin: Duncker & Humblot, 2010.

Ahrendt, Rebekah, Mark Ferraguto, and Damien Mahiet, ed. *Music and Diplomacy from the Early Modern Era to the Present*. New York: Palgrave Macmillan, 2014.

Aron, Robert. *Histoire de l'épuration* (4 vol.). Paris: Fayard, 1967–1975.

Aróstegui, Julio, and François Godicheau, ed. *Guerra civil. Mito y memoria*. Madrid: Marcial Pons, 2006.

Audoin-Rouzeau, Stéphane, and Annette Becker. *14–18: Retrouver la guerre*. Paris: Gallimard, 2000.

Audoin-Rouzeau, Stéphane, and Christophe Prochasson, ed. *Sortir de la Grande Guerre. Le monde et l'après 1918*. Paris: Tallandier, 2008.

Audoin-Rouzeau, Stéphane, Buch Esteban, Chimènes Myriam, and Georgie Durosoir, ed. *La Grande Guerre des musiciens*. Lyon: Symétrie, 2009.

Baily, John. *War, Exile and the Music of Afghanistan: The Ethnographer's Tale*. Abingdon-on-Thames: Taylor & Francis, 2016.

Barkan, Eleazar. *The Guilt of Nations: Restitution and Negotiating Historical Injustices*. New York: Norton, 2000.

Bar-Siman-Tov, Yacob, ed. *From Conflict Resolution to Reconciliation*. New York: Oxford University Press, 2004.

Becker, Annette. *Les Monuments aux morts. Mémoire de la Grande Guerre*. Paris: Errance, 1988.

———. *Voir la Grande Guerre. Un autre récit. 1914–2014*. Paris: Armand Colin, 2014.

Bergh Arild, Sloboda John. "Music and Art in Conflict Transformation: A Review. Music and Arts in Action." 2, no. 2 (2010): 2–17.

Bergmann, Katrina. "The Sound of Trauma: Music Therapy in a Post-War Environment." *Australian Journal of Music Therapy* 13 (2002): 3–16.

Bizet, George. *Correspondance générale*, ed. Thierry Boudin and Hervé Lacombe, forthcoming.

Boyle, Michael. *Violence after War: Explaining Instability in Post-Conflict States*. Baltimore: John Hopkins University Press, 2014.

Buch, Esteban. "Métaphores politiques dans le *Traité d'harmonie* de Schoenberg." *Mil neuf cent. Revue d'histoire intellectuelle* 21, no. 1 (2003): 55–76.

Cabanes, Bruno. *La Victoire endeuillée. La sortie de guerre des soldats français (1918–1920)*. Paris: Seuil, 2004.

Cabanes, Bruno, and Guillaume Piketty, eds. *Retour à l'intime au sortir de la guerre*. Paris: Tallandier, 2009.

Castillo (del), Graciana. *Rebuilding War-Torn States: The Challenge of Post-Conflict Economic Reconstruction*. New York: Oxford University Press, 2008.

Clapson, Mark, and Peter Larkham, ed. *The Blitz and Its Legacy: Wartime Destruction to Post-War Reconstruction*. Ashgate: Farnham, 2013.

Clout, Hugh. *After the Ruins: Restoring the Countryside of Northern France after the Great War*. Exeter: University of Exeter Press, 1996.

Cohrs, Patrick. *The Unfinished Peace after World War I: America, Britain and the Stabilisation of Europe, 1919–1932*. Cambridge: Cambridge University Press, 2006.

Colonomos, Ariel. "De la réparation à la restitution: trajectoires philosophiques d'une histoire." *Raisons politiques* 1, no. 5 (2002): 157–69.

Creveld (van), Martin. *Les Transformations de la guerre*. Paris: Éditions du Rocher, 1998 [1991].

Cusik, Suzanne. "Music as Torture, Music as Weapon." *TRANS. Revista Transcultural de Música* 10, 2006, http://www.sibetrans.com/trans/articulo/152/music-as-torture-music-as-weapon.

Dagan, Yaël. *La Nouvelle Revue française de la guerre à la paix, 1914–1925, mobilisations et démobilisations culturelles*. Paris: Tallandier, 2008.

Dimitrijevic, Dejan, ed. "Sorties de guerres et de violence." Special issue of *Balkanologie* 8, no. 1 (2004).

Dieckmann, Samantha, and Jane W. Davidson. "Peace, Empathy and Conciliation through Music." *International Journal of Community Music* 12, no. 3 (2019): 293–99.

Diefendorf, Jeffry M. "Urban Reconstruction in Europe after World War II." *Urban Studies* 26, no. 1 (1989): 128–43.

Dower, John. *War without Mercy: Race and Power in the Pacific War*. New York: Pantheon Books, 1987.

Duchesneau, Michel. *L'Avant-garde musicale à Paris de 1871 à 1939*. Sprimont: Mardaga, 1997).

Dunkel, Mario, and Sina A. Nitzsche, ed. *Popular Music and Public Diplomacy*. Bielefeld: Transcript Verlag, 2018.

Fauser, Annegret, and Michael Figueroa, ed. *Performing Commemoration: Musical Reenactment and the Politics of Trauma*. Ann Arbor: University of Michigan Press, 2020.

Fléchet, Anaïs, and Marès Antoine, eds. "Musique et Relations internationales." Special issue of *Relations internationales* 155 and 156 (2013).
Fosler-Lussier, Danielle. *Music in America's Cold War Diplomacy*. Berkeley: University of California Press, 2015.
Gienow-Hecht, Jessica. *Sound Diplomacy: Music and Emotions in Transatlantic Relations*. Chicago: University of Chicago Press, 2009.
Gienow-Hecht, Jessica, ed. *Music and International History in the Twentieth Century*. New York/Oxford: Berghahn Books, 2015.
Gorguet, Ilde. *Les Mouvements pacifistes et la réconciliation franco-allemande dans les années vingt (1919–1931)*. Bern: Peter Lang, 1999.
Grossmann, Atina. *Trauma, Memory and Motherhood: Germans and Jewish Displaced Persons in Post-Nazi Germany, 1945–1949*. Archiv für Sozialgeschichte 38 (1998): 215–39.
Guerpin, Martin. "*Le Courrier musical* et le premier conflit mondial (1904–1923). Propagande, mobilisation culturelle et sortie de guerre." *Revue musicale OICRM* 4, no. 7 (2017): 35–57.
Morag, Josephine G. "On Music and War." *Transposition*, Special issue (2020).
Hassner, Pierre, and Roland Marchal, eds. *Guerres et sociétés. États et violence après la Guerre froide*. Paris: Karthala, 2003.
Horne, John. "Démobilisations culturelles après la Grande Guerre." *14–18, Aujourd'hui, Today, Heute* (2002): 45–53.
———. "Demobilizing the Mind. France and the Legacy of the Great War, 1919–1939." *French History and Civilization. Papers from the George Rudé Seminar* 2 (2009): 101–19.
———. "Guerres et réconciliations européennes au 20e siècle." *Vingtième Siècle. Revue d'histoire* 4, no. 104 (2009): 3–15.
Horne, John, and Robert Gewarth, eds. *War in Peace: Paramilitary Violence in Europe after the Great War*. New York: Oxford University Press, 2012.
Jeismann, Michael. *La Patrie de l'ennemi. La notion d'ennemi national et la représentation de la nation en Allemagne et en France*. Paris: CNRS Éditions, 1997.
Kelly, Barbara L. *Tradition and Style in the Works of Darius Milhaud, 1912–1939*. Aldershot: Ashgate, 2003.
———., ed. *French Music, Culture, and National Identity*. Rochester, NY: University of Rochester Press, 2008.
———. *Music and Ultra-Modernism in France. A Fragile Consensus, 1913–1939*. Woodbridge: Boydell & Brewer, 2013.
Kelly, Barbara L., and Christopher Moore, eds. *Music Criticism in France, 1918–1939: Authority, Advocacy, Legacy*. Woodbridge: Boydell and Brewer, 2018.
Klotz, Sabine. *Zivile Konfliktbearbeitung. Theorie und Praxis*. Heidelberg: Forschungsstätte d. Ev. Studiengemeinsch, 2003.
Knowles, Christopher. *Winning the Peace: The British in Occupied Germany, 1945–1948*. London: Bloomsbury Academics, 2017.

Mazower, Mark, ed. *After the War Was Over: Reconstructing the Family, Nation and State in Greece, 1943–1960*. Princeton, NJ: Princeton University Press, 2000.

Ménudier, Henri, ed. *L'Allemagne occupée (1945–1949)*. Brussels: Éditions Complexe, 1990.

Michonneau, Stéphane, Carolina Rodríguez-López, and Fernando Vela Cossío, eds. *Paisajes de guerra: Huellas, reconstrucción, patrimonio (1939–años 2000)*. Madrid: Casa de Velázquez, 2019.

Mikkonen, Simo, and Pekka Suutari, ed. *Music, Art and Diplomacy. East-West Cultural Interactions and the Cold War*. Routledge: New York, 2016.

Mombert, Monique. *Sous le Signe de la rééducation: jeunesse et livre en zone française d'occupation (1945–1949)*. Strasbourg: Presses Universitaires de Strasbourg, 2002.

Mosse, George. *Fallen Soldiers: Reshaping the Memory of the World Wars*. New York: Oxford University Press, 1990.

O'Connell, John. "Music in War, Music for Peace: A Review Article." *Ethnomusicology* 55, no. 1 (2011): 117.

———. "Sound Bites: Music as Violence." *Transposition*, Special issue 2 (2020).

O'Connell, John, and Salwa El-Shawan Castelo-Branco, eds. *Music and Conflicts*. Urbana: University of Illinois Press, 2010.

Ostriichouk, Olha, ed. *Mémoires de conflits, mémoires en conflits. Affrontements identitaires, tensions politiques et luttes symboliques autour du passé*. Bern: Peter Lang, 2016.

Pernot, François, and Valérie Toureille, eds. *Lendemains de guerre . . . De l'Antiquité au monde contemporain: les hommes, l'espace et le récit, l'économie et le politique*. Bern: Peter Lang, 2010.

Perrot, Xavier. "Les biens culturels dans les réparations pour dommages de guerre, 1919 et 1945, *restitutio in integrum*, compensation et fongibilité." *Revue historique de droit français et étranger* 84, no. 1 (2006): 47–69.

Picard, Timothée. *Wagner, une question européenne : Contribution à une étude du wagnérisme (1860–2004)*. Rennes: Presses universitaires de Rennes, 2006.

Priemel, Kim, and Alexa Stiller, eds. *Reassessing the Nuremberg Military Tribunals: Transitional Justice, Trial Narratives, and Historiography*. New York: Berghahn Books, 2012.

Pronay, Nicholas, and Keith Wilson, eds. *The Political Re-education of Germany and Her Allies: After World War II*. Abingdon: Routledge, 1985.

Ramel, Frédéric, and Cécile Prévost-Thomas, ed. *International Relations, Music and Diplomacy: Sounds and Voices on the International Stage*. Basingstoke: Palgrave Macmillan, 2018.

Rasmussen, Anne. "Réparer, réconcilier, oublier: enjeux et mythes de la démobilisation scientifique, 1918–1925." *Histoire@Politique* 3 (2007): 8–20.

Rehding, Alexander. *Music and Monumentality: Commemoration and Wonderment in Nineteenth Century Germany*. New York: Oxford University Press, 2009.
Reinisch, Jessica, and Elizabeth White, ed. *The Disentanglement of Populations: Migration, Expulsion and Displacement in Post-War Europe, 1944–49*. New York: Palgrave Macmillan, 2011.
Rettberg, Angelika, ed. *Entre el perdón y el paredón: Preguntas y dilemas de la justicia transicional*. Bogotá: Universidad de los Andes, 2005.
Rogers, Jilian. *Resonant Recoveries: Music and Trauma between the World Wars*. New York: Oxford University Press, 2021.
Santos, Juliá, ed. *Memoria de la guerra y del franquismo*. Madrid: Fundación Pablo Iglesias, Taurus, 2006.
Seeger, Charles. "The Arts in International Relations." *Journal of the American Musicological Society* 2, no. 1 (1949): 36–43.
Strasser, Michael. "The Société nationale and Its Adversaries: The Musical Politics of l'invasion germanique in the 1870s." *19th-Century Music* 24, no. 3 (Spring 2001): 225–51.
Tison, Stéphane. *Comment sortir de la guerre? Deuil, mémoire et traumatisme (1870–1940)*. Rennes: PUR, 2011.
Urbain, Olivier. "Overcoming Challenges to Music's Role in Peacebuilding." *Peace Review* 31, no. 3 (2019): 332–40.
Urbain, Olivier, ed. *Music and Conflict Transformation: Harmonies and Dissonances in Geopolitics*. London: I.B. Tauris Publishers, 2008.
Velasco-Pufleau, Luis, ed. *Transposition*, Special issue 2 (2020).
Virgili, Fabrice. *La France "virile." Des femmes tondues à la Libération*. Paris: Payot, 2000.
Watkins, Glenn. *Proof through the Night: Music and the Great War*. Berkeley: University of California Press, 2003.
Wu, Haishang. "Music's Role in Peacebuilding." *Journal of Aggression, Conflict and Peace Research* 11, no. 2 (2019): 138–43.
White, Eugene. "Making the French Pay: The Cost and Consequences of the Napoleonic Reparations." *European Review of Economic History* 5 (2001): 337–65.
Winter, Jay. *Sites of Memory, Sites of Mourning: The Great War in European Cultural History*. Cambridge: Cambridge University Press, 1995.
———. *War beyond Words: Languages of Remembrance from the Great War to the Present*. Cambridge: Cambridge University Press, 2017.
Woolf, Stuart, ed. *Italia, 1943–1950. La Ricostruzione*. Laterza: Roma-Bari, 1974.

Part I
RECONSTRUCTING THE MUSIC WORLD

Chapter 1

Transitioning from the Turmoil through Music
Withdrawal, Patriotism, Sublimation: Georges Bizet in the Early 1870s

Hervé Lacombe

At the end of their 2007 article entitled "Sortir de la guerre: jalons pour une histoire en chantier" (The postwar transition period: Milestones for a history under construction),[1] Bruno Cabanes and Guillaume Piketty note: "There is another research area that calls for an examination of personal journeys, local contexts, the return of conflict participants to the 'intime'[2] and the intergenerational transmission of the memory of the war."[3] Two years later, the same authors published a collective work entitled *Retour à l'intime: au sortir de la guerre* (Return to the "intime": the postwar transition period). For musicians, the priority during postwar transitions is not so much their private lives or the "intime" as the traces, echoes, and impacts of the conflict on their work and imaginations, and the role music should play in a world that has been turned upside down. Rather than giving an account of the postwar transition period based, for example, on a study of musical institutions and their repertoires, this chapter proposes to examine the particular fate, choices, and musical output of Bizet (1838–1875), a composer who was caught up in the turmoil of the Franco-Prussian War, the Battle of Sedan, the collapse of Napoleon III's regime, the Siege of Paris, domestic French power games, the Franco-Prussian negotiations, and the Paris Commune. During France's *année terrible*, the country suffered two con-

---

Notes for this section begin on page 33.

secutive wars: one against Prussia, and the other a civil war. As a result, there was an overlap of two postwar transition periods, each with different enemies. Bizet navigated these events first by trying to understand them and by getting involved on the ground (he was a member of the National Guard), and then by withdrawing and abandoning his position as a committed citizen.[4] In the early 1870s, this withdrawal marked Bizet's final rite of passage as a composer. The political being seemed to give way to the artist. Was the postwar transition period an act of denial for Bizet, an escape from the world, or did music offer him the means to create an autonomous space that was external to the problems generated by the conflicts?

The Question of Withdrawal

For Bizet, the withdrawal process was initiated—from an aesthetic point of view—at the height of the Siege of Paris. On 29 November 1870, he wrote the manuscript for a vocal duet, significantly entitled *La Fuite* (The escape). A month earlier, or more specifically between 5 and 12 October 1870, Henri Duparc (1848–1933) (who, like Bizet, was a member of the National Guard) had decided to set the same poem to music. Théophile Gautier's verse told the story of an "exotic" couple, Ahmed, and Kadidja. Ahmed was reluctant to run away with his beloved Kadidja because he was terrified at the thought of his pursuers' daggers. Both Bizet's and Duparc's melodies can be viewed as imagined responses to imprisonment in besieged Paris. While Duparc's melody was a rather anguished response, Bizet's was more lyrical in nature. For Bizet, the female character was becoming a beacon of emancipation, a mantle that he himself was to take on in different ways in the two exotic operas he composed during the postwar period.

Bizet had always used exoticism to respond to a need for poetry and wonder, to signify a form of escape from a life of constraints, everyday worries, and trivialities and to express an aspiration to new horizons and a place where desires—unrequited love, forbidden love, idealized love—can find resolution through the imagination.[5] He was to revive this theme during the postwar transition period with *Djamileh* (a wonderful orientalizing reverie first performed in 1872) and *Carmen*. In his exotic *La Fuite*, he was escaping the external violence in France by revealing a desire that was subsequently to find its full expression in Carmen's "Là-bas, là-bas" (Over there, over there) and in his celebration of the "intoxicating thing"[6] that is freedom. The war, the National Guard, and imprisonment in besieged Paris were all the antithesis of this outdoor life, whose melody irradiated his ultimate masterpiece. However, taking refuge in the artist's ivory tower and in an imagined space cannot prevent the memory of times of unrest from filtering through to and even influencing the artist's work and subject matter as well as the ways in which they are presented.

The Sublimated Homeland

The return to activities at the Opéra-Comique was marked by the premiere of Charles Gounod's *Gallia* on 8 November 1871 (the work was first performed on 1 May 1871). It should be remembered that Charles Gounod (1818–1893) was Bizet's mentor and probably still exercised some sort of influence over him. The postwar transition period for Bizet meant a resurgence of his desire to take action through music, but this action had now transmuted into a symbolic reconfiguration. A few months after the conflict had ended, he found the perfect vehicle for this in *Patrie*, a piece that would speak to symphonic concert audiences. Rather than just a transposition of emotions, the score of this overture is a narrative. Moreover, this narrative does not just present the lived experience; it is the demonstration of a thesis.

At the beginning of the 1873–74 season, Jules Pasdeloup (1819–1887) ordered an overture from three "jeune école" representatives: Bizet, Ernest Guiraud (1837–1892), and Jules Massenet (1842–1912).[7] The works they produced were first performed over three successive Sundays (15, 22, and 29 February 1874). On 8 March, Bizet's piece was rescheduled for the Concerts Populaires, where it went on to be performed regularly.[8] It was also incorporated with great success into the Concerts Colonne repertoire on 20 December 1874[9] and frequently performed at the Concerts Lamoureux from 1887 onward.[10] It was played at Bizet's funeral on 5 June 1875. The press's announcement of its first performance provided a few details on its subject matter.[11] For example, on 13 February 1874 the *Moniteur Universel* wrote: "*Patrie* . . . Dramatic overture (1st performance), G. Bizet—(Episode in the Polish War—Battle of Raclawa [now called Racławice], defeat of the Russians by Koscuiszko, 1792 [1794])."[12] The same programmatic indication appeared on the *transcrite pour piano à quatre mains* edition produced by Bizet.[13]

Henry Cohen (1808–1880) criticized Bizet's program. He wrote in his review that "only Polish or Russian songs could have justified the title" and called on readers to consider the overture as "some kind of battle set to music."[14] He acknowledged the beautiful orchestral effects and combinations but bemoaned its rambling vagueness.[15] When Albert Wolff (1825–1891) saw the concert posters, he instantly spoke out. He asked whether it were possible to reasonably claim, first, that the Polish character could be musically conjured up and, second, that the scene was set in Raclawa (and not somewhere else) and in 1792 (rather than, say, 1321).[16] He claimed it was like dangling the notion of program music in front of the wrong end of the spyglass, confusing the spirit and the letter, the musical rendering and the realist narrative. For Bizet, musical patterns could only really be formulated in association with human drama and passion. He defined himself as an artist who was made for the theater,[17] hence his insistence on preserving the title of his symphonic piece. He wrote to his publisher, Antoine de Choudens (1825–1888), saying: "Add the word 'dramatique' after 'ouverture' in the title. I would like to use the following designation: *Ouverture dramatique* [Dramatic overture]."[18] Most of Bizet's output contextualized music and assigned it the role of producing emotions or even (as with *Patrie*) a kind of narrative. He achieved this by manipulating not only contemporary expressive codes and characteristic formulas but also the poetics of instruments established by Berlioz in his great treatise on instrumentation. So, what does this approximately thirteen-minute piece, *Patrie*, tell us?

It is organized into five main parts. The first comprises a dazzling, vigorous, almost aggressive march in C minor that becomes increasingly unstable. It presents a theme that came to be referred to as the *Ennemi* (enemy). In the published program, it was said to represent the Slavic world. The overture's main theme was borrowed from Bizet's grand opera *Don Rodrigue*,[19] which he composed around the same time. On the opera manuscript, there is an eloquent stage direction specifically referencing this theme: "March of soldiers carrying weapons and flags taken from the enemy."[20] The second part (in F major) presents a theme associated with the Poles that we might refer to as the *Patrie*. A transition section introduces a strong dramatization of the enemy threat, comprising a martial call from the brass, drumrolls from the timpani, and tremolos from the strings. A return to the *Patrie* motif is this time accompanied by the drum, which signals either the entry into war, the enlistment of the men, or the looming threat. The tragic aspect here is rendered by a powerful surge with rapid chord successions and then a disquieting silence. This is immediately followed by the third part played andante molto in A minor, which we might refer to as pain of the oppressed. The respected critic of *Le Temps*, Johannès Weber (1818–1902), conjectured that this part represented a "lamentation over the dead."[21] For Victorin Joncières (1839–1903), composer and critic, it was a "melancholic phrase" charged with conveying "with great feeling the immense pain of people oppressed under the barbarians' yoke." The melody, which is given over to the violas, clarinets, and bassoons, creates a sadness "whose plaintive voice is made all the more striking by the mournful accompaniment of the brass"[22] in the bass line. The fourth part (in A major), which we might refer to as a motif of comfort or hope, brings relief with a "soft, comforting character," according to Weber, who wonders whether it might be "communicating the joy of soldiers hugging their mothers, sisters, fiancées or mistresses?"[23] The fifth and final part begins with no transition. It contains two consecutive sections. The first opens with a repetition of the *Ennemi* motif, played in the treble, as if coming from afar, over rumblings from the bass instruments. A secondary thematic element from part one, this time played by the flutes (resembling military fifes), is then superimposed onto the *Patrie* motif played by the strings. A martial call brings the conflict to a close and leads into a repetition of the *Patrie* motif, this time played in 6/8, maestoso moderato (somewhat in the spirit of the Lisztian thematic metamorphoses) and in a strong C major, marking the moment of triumph.

This postwar transition program comprising the enemy followed by the homeland, the threat, hope, the battle, and finally the triumphant homeland that Bizet was proposing to his compatriots is detectable behind the official Russian-Polish program, which euphemized the reactivated memory of that terrible year. France was not a triumphant homeland, however. The overture thus appears to reference something other than a recollection of the conflict just passed. Johannès Weber claimed that the title, the *Patrie*, should actually be accredited to Pasdeloup,[24] who had wanted to call it something more exciting than just a simple, generic "ouverture dramatique," which is what Bizet had suggested. Charles Pigot, the composer's first biographer, revised this claim, proposing instead that Pasdeloup may have chanced upon the word that represented what the artist had wanted to say, but it was definitely the musician's idea originally:

> When writing his "Ouverture Dramatique", the misfortunes of his defeated, surrendered homeland and the anguish of that terrible year were at the forefront of Bizet's mind. All this suffering, all this mourning that had so pained his soul as a patriot had captured his imagination as a poet. He wanted to tell the story of his grieving homeland, which

was mutilated and bleeding but still alive and so dear to its children's hearts. He wanted to tell the story of his homeland rising again from the ashes. But he soon understood that these expressions of pain, these reminders of the days of anguish and tears, would not be appropriate during this time of healing. Using his poet's imagination, he used a well-chosen substitution, a touching, detailed allegory, to conjure up the great shadow of a country (Poland) that was defeated and dying but still standing and whose indelible memory, whose sacred name still lived on in the hearts of its dispersed children.[25]

The overture's subject matter is the despair of the vanquished and the people's love of their homeland. The work also seems to have been an aesthetic response to a dream that Bizet had had in the midst of all the torment, which he related to Ernest Guiraud: "I dreamt last night that we were all in Naples, staying in a delightful villa. The government there was made up solely of artists: Beethoven, Michelangelo, Shakespeare, Giorgione *e tutti quanti*. The National Guard was replaced by a huge orchestra."[26] No more politicians in government. No more National Guard. Bizet's dream was about the sublimation process, and *Patrie* brought this to life. The composer thus avoided the category of direct commemoration. He positioned himself in what Jean-François Lecaillon simply called "the indirect evocation of war" by "dealing with the subject through another war, which, by analogy, referenced the memories that the artist and/or the audience had of the Franco-Prussian War."[27]

Patrie met with great success for a number of years, probably because it offered audiences more than just a slick score, moving tones, and highly inventive orchestral combinations. Both the title and the program resonated with the memories of 1870. Because *Patrie* had historical depth, that particular event in 1870 gained a more universal significance and was able to transition beyond just an acknowledgment of failure. The overture situated the Franco-Prussian War within the grand narrative of a people struggling against an oppressor and, in so doing, gave it both meaning and value. Bizet brought about a change in direction by reviving the myth of the "glorious defeat," which, according to Jean-Marc Largeaud's analysis based on the example of Waterloo,[28] the French had turned into something of a specialty.

The arts contributed in their own way to reviving a feeling of positivity and value among the French population. In 1872, for example, the artist Puvis de Chavanne (1824–1898) exhibited *L'Espérance* (hope) at the Salon (no 1282). This painting shows an allegorical figure of a young woman seated amid ruins and embodying a sense of renewal. As Aimée Brown Price noted in her catalogue raisonné of the painter's work, the oak leaf in the allegorical figure's left hand is a symbol of value, civic pride, and triumph.[29] Placing "Espérance" (hope) on a crumbling, broken wall suggests resurrection and reconstruction, the feelings that Bizet wanted to convey. He was governed not by the spirit of revenge but by the idea of the homeland and its ability to regenerate. Victorin Joncières clearly understood this dimension in *Patrie*: "What has saved Monsieur Bizet from the common pitfall of just being descriptive in style is that he was supported during the creation of his work by one great, elevated, overarching thought, the idea of the homeland. . . . It was only when he could not do anything else, during the battle itself, that his music became imitative."[30] It is striking that none of the chroniclers of the overture's creation made a connection with the Franco-Prussian War. Victorin Joncières, for example, stopped at the general idea of homeland, as if a more direct mention of bruised and battered France had become taboo. In September 1871, *Le Ménestrel* advised the Swedish composer of an orchestral piece entitled *Die Schreckenstage von Paris* (The days of horror in Paris), J. M. Rosen, not to come to France: "The memory of such events would not be welcomed in Paris, not even by the orchestra."[31] This interpretation of Bizet's orchestral piece is confirmed by his attitude toward German musicians, which was completely devoid of any resentment or desire for revenge.

Music and Nationalism: The Relationship with Germany

Music, at least in the nineteenth century, was thought out, learned, composed, played, and appreciated on the basis of traditions, practices, repertoires, local institutions, and genealogies that delimited musical nationalities. Music was not neutral, and the common ground between the German, French, and Italian repertoires served to consolidate the principle of musical nationalities in the imaginations and cultures of each country and each composer. For example, Verdi spoke of his work as an Italian composer and of the work of foreign composers like Wagner and Bizet as German and French composers. While the question of musical nationalities prevailed throughout the nineteenth century,[32] the war came at a time when Wagnerism—understood here as dramaturgical principles (such as literary themes and writing processes)—began to be emulated in France. For artists, the postwar transition was complicated by a tension between two different levels of action and appreciation, namely aesthetic judgment, and patriotic positioning. Postwar art is rarely neutral. Claude Digeon's now classic work *La crise allemande de la pensée française, 1870–1914*[33] gives us an understanding of "how literature presents the complex of defeat."[34]

At the beginning of the Franco-Prussian War, composer and music critic Ernest Reyer (1923–1909) alluded to a situation in which musical admiration and patriotic duty clashed: "Our patriotism cannot be doubted now, although I like German music much better than French music."[35] In September 1870, he added: "Ah, those Prussian scoundrels! I loved them so much for their musical talents, and now I will be forced to exterminate a very large number of them!"[36] The juxtaposition of these two words "love" and "exterminate" strikes a chord. What happens after the war? Do the people affirm their national art and reject the conqueror's art? For a musician of Bizet's caliber, who was drawing on Wagnerian drama and Verdian opera and becoming increasingly aware of polarized musical Europe, German music had seemed, even before the war, to be a high ideal rather than a model to be followed. The war did not mark the beginning of his admiration for German music. Beethoven was a god in his eyes, and his Choral Symphony was "the greatest sheet of music our art has ever possessed."[37] He also agreed with the analysis of some German critics who, in the aftermath of the war, condemned the superficiality of French music. Offenbach's operetta was, to them, emblematic of this, a symbol of moral degeneration.[38] For Bizet, Offenbach's music must be fought against. Its diffusion within the opera market seemed to him to be a threat and his scores closer to naught than to the sublime.[39]

On 8 August 1870, Bizet expressed his feelings to Ernest Guiraud: "I am not a jingoist as you know, but I have had a heavy heart and tears in my eyes since yesterday! Our poor country! Our poor army! Governed and led by a now notorious incompetence!" He was not criticizing the Germans here but, like Ludovic Halévy[40] (1834–1908) and so many others, Napoleon III. Bizet maintained this position throughout the postwar transition period: "We find ourselves alive (only just), standing amid the ruins of our poor France, so culpable but also so unfortunate. We may none of us live long enough to know what the Napoleons have cost us!"[41] The establishment of the Republic following the collapse of the Empire was to console him for a while in terms of the "notorious incompetence" he had denounced. On 26 December 1870, he wrote: "There is no doubt these three months of the Republic have removed the worst of the thick layer of shame and filth smeared on our country by that infamous

Empire. I have a feeling Gambetta is the man we were hoping for. To drive out the Prussians and keep the Republic! It is hard, but my hopes increase with every day that passes."[42] It is clear that even before the war had ended and then during the postwar transition period, there was another process underway, namely the post-regime transition process. The Empire had collapsed, and the people were left to deal with its legacy, especially the sense of shame that was attached to it. Bizet revisited this legacy in April 1871 with an assessment of the state of the Conservatoire, which had been unaffected by the war but marred by the Second Empire and Auber's leadership. Auber's death, in 1871, marked the end of an era. Bizet told his mother-in-law: "Let us hope this upright government that we have just now consolidates its position and reforms the arts that are most in need."[43] This post-regime transition process was also a way of transferring the burden of guilt. It was no longer France that was being called into question but the despised regime. Nevertheless, transitioning into a new Republic was not an easy process, and there was moreover an overlap from one regime to another and from one war to another.

After the Commune, which was pure chaos and madness as far as Bizet was concerned, the composer took up where he had left off and even started a discussion on Wagner with his mother-in-law. In May 1871, he explained his position to her:

> Wagner is not my friend. In fact, I hold him in quite low esteem. But I cannot forget the immense pleasure this innovative genius has given me. The charm of his music is indescribable, inexpressible. It is voluptuousness, tenderness, love! If I played it for you for a week, you would fall in love with it! Also, the Germans, who unfortunately are at least as strong us as at music, have understood that Wagner is one of their most solid pillars. The nineteenth-century German spirit is embodied in this man.[44]

Bizet's comments could not have been more astute. In the same letter, he called on Léonie Halévy (1820–1884) to form her own opinion, detached from nationalist discourses, of the aesthetic condemnations of the French and of Wagner's hateful remarks: "Judge for *yourself*. Forget everything you have heard or read, including the silly, spiteful articles and the malicious book published by Wagner, and you will see."[45] Bizet had managed to make this distinction (which many of his contemporaries found difficult to do) between the man and the artist.

Bizet's choice of exotic settings (Provence for L'*Arlésienne*, Egypt for *Djamileh*, Spain for *Carmen*) were a way of both escaping reality and avoiding Germany's captivating sirens on his journey of self-discovery. This was his main concern. While he wanted to remain a truly French artist, he also wanted to draw on advances in musical language and the evolution of forms, the most influential models for which were coming from Germany. Bizet introduced, as if in a musical slip of the tongue and in homage, a rewrite of the *Tristan* chord[46] to express his Eastern heroine's (Djamileh) pain as she contemplates the possibility of her impending death (from a broken heart).

Any discussion of the history of French musical nationalism would be incomplete without reference to the creation of the Société Nationale de Musique (SNM). Bizet, like Édouard Lalo (1823–1892), was one of the first to join this society, which was officially instituted on 25 February 1871 at the instigation of Camille Saint-Saëns (1835–1921), Romain Bussine (1830–1899), and a few others. This society responded not just to the postwar circumstantial situation and the desire to create an active musical sociability (in the aftermath of the geographic dispersion of the population) but also to a need that had been expressed long before the war[47] to provide a space for French chamber music, which, as Michel Duchesneau has shown, was soon to compete with symphonic music.[48] There has been much written about the SNM's motto, *Ars Gallica* (French art), which has perhaps given it more significance than was originally intended. *Ars Gallica* should be understood here not as the ability to express Frenchness (as distinct from Germanness or Italianness) through music, but rather primarily as art that was thought, written, and played by French people. The purpose was to create a dynamic that was conducive to the emergence of a repertoire of instrumental music previously unrecognized by Parisian music institutions. Gabriel Fauré (1845–1924) (albeit exaggerating somewhat) revealed in an interview: "The truth is, before 1870, I would never have dreamt of composing a sonata or a quartet. There was just no chance of a young musician having such works played at the time."[49] Bizet played at the SNM's second concert on 9 December 1871, and on 23 December 1871 he performed an excerpt from his reduced *Roma* symphony for two pianos as well as *Variations Chromatiques* and some of his melodies.

The first SNM concert, which took place on 17 November 1871,[50] closed with Saint-Saëns's *Marche Héroïque*[51] performed on two pianos. This blatant appeal to patriotic sentiment (which was not as successful as his friend Bizet's later creation) was first and foremost a musical commemorative monument in memory of the painter Henri

Regnault (1843–1871), who had been killed at age twenty-seven on 19 January 1871 at the Battle of Buzenval by a Prussian bullet to the temple. The work's subject matter is not the country but the artist's heroism. An orchestral version of the piece was performed at the Concerts Populaires in December 1871. It was just one of a whole series of musical works that emerged in the aftermath of the war, including *Dieu Sauve la France*, a patriotic piece with music by Augusta Holmès (1847–1903),[52] and *Jeanne d'Arc*, a symphonic poem by Georges Pfeiffer (1835–1908). It may have been during this period that Bizet first planned to compose an orchestral score on the subject of the war.[53] The idea of giving substance through music to the memories and emotions generated by the war or to a need for storytelling never left him. This is evidenced, for example, in *Sainte Geneviève*, which he worked on between 1873 and 1875 but never completed.

Conclusion

At the height of the war, Bizet feared that his dreams of becoming a composer would be shattered along with the rest of civilization. In the postwar transition period, he was acutely aware that it would take months, years even, to give meaning to the momentous succession of events that had shaken France to its core: "We need time to be able to fully grasp this series of episodes."[54] His fear that France might descend into chaos gave him a clear goal, which was "to be useful to the country, to humanity."[55] He had this wonderful saying: "We are stuck between two worlds, one that is on its way out and one that is on its way in. We have a rough sea to cross."[56] Bizet's journey shows how an individual can elude unequivocal interpretation and how their own personal postwar transition can take multiple forms. For Bizet, the post-1870 period meant, in turn, escaping from France and from the terrible memories (*Djamileh*), working through residual recollections, and revaluating (*Patrie*) and configuring the meaning of history through a mythical narrative (*Sainte Geneviève*). A further point worth noting is that Bizet's dual sense, on the one hand, of an urgent need to create and, on the other, of a certain finitude linked to the conflict probably pushed him to externalize an anguish that had haunted him for a long time but which he had not yet been able fully and genuinely to express. Djamileh's wish to die (which is manifested in the harmonic signature of her master, representing Germany), the glorious death of the *Patrie*, Frédéri's suicide in *L'Arlésienne*, and the destructive impulses and dancing with death that punctuate the *Carmen* score (which, moreover, tells the story of a deserter!) are all narratives of the negative forces that inhabit human beings and literally explode in times of war.

Music composed in the aftermath of a conflict can help us comprehend the trauma generated and its impact on sensibility and culture. By analyzing the way in which the musical world is reorganized, the choices and plans made by different actors, and the musical works produced during postwar transition periods, we can gain a better understanding of both the changes brought about by war and this "singular time during which societies [and individuals] disentangle themselves from the violence of war and redefine themselves."[57] Because of the war (or "thanks to the war," as some might say, even though they consider it an unacceptably violent act), a large number of French musicians driven by a common ideal (leading to the creation of the SNM) were able to come together and promote national instrumental music. For Bizet, the situation was especially tricky in this respect. Although he continued to define himself as an opera composer, his desire to write instrumental music intensified; however, he died before he could achieve this aim. He had nevertheless shared with many of his colleagues his belief that the "German" idea of music should be a prerequisite for any French artist seeking a place in the great history of music. He was able to draw on this model while still preserving a strong individuality, which Nietzsche, in a spectacular reversal of circumstances, would use in his criticism of Wagner's philosophical music and all its charms. According to Romain Rolland, there was a "surge of faith and energy that rebuilt French music"[58] from 1870 onward, and "the disasters of war . . . regenerated the nation's artistic spirit."[59] The truth is, the postwar transition period crystalized a process that was already underway in which France's musical territory was being reconfigured, and that music contributed to the country's moral and intellectual recovery.

Hervé Lacombe is a professor of musicology at the Université Rennes 2. He is also a member of the publications committee of the Société Française de Musicologie and of the editorial boards of *Nineteenth-Century Music Review*, and "L'Opéra français" (Bärenreiter-Verlag). A specialist in nineteenth- and twentieth-century music, he has edited or coedited ten collective works and written *Les Voies de l'opéra français au XIXe siècle* (1997), a biography of Bizet (2000), a biography of Poulenc (2013), a study on the globalization of opera,

Géographie de l'opéra au XXe siècle (2007), all published by Fayard. Together with Yves Balmer, he coedited a collective work on the *Histoire intellectuelle de la* Revue de musicologie: *Mutations thématiques et évolutions méthodologiques* (*Revue de musicologie*, 2017 and 2018). He designed, organized and edited a *History of French Opera* in three volumes (2020-22). The volumes are written by an international and interdisciplinary team of nearly 200 authors.

Notes

1. This chapter was translated from French by Clare Ferguson.
2. "Intime" is defined by Cabanes and Piketty (*Retour à l'intime*, 11) as "the space in which our self-image and fundamental relationship with others are constructed through our bodies, gestures, knowhow, filiations (real or imagined), living spaces, representations of self (in private writings, portraits, self-portraits), the objects invested with our memories, and so on." "L'espace où se construisent l'image de soi et le rapport profond aux autres, à travers le corps, les techniques corporelles (gestes, savoir-faire. . .), la filiation (réelle ou imaginaire), les lieux de vie, les objets investis de souvenirs, les représentations de soi (écrit du for privé, portraits et autoportraits)."
3. Cabanes and Piketty, "Sortir de la guerre," 8. "Un autre chantier apparaît alors, qui ferait la place aux parcours individuels, aux études locales. Au retour à l'intime des acteurs des conflits et à la transmission de la mémoire de la guerre, de génération en génération."
4. See Lacombe, *Georges Bizet*, 459–99.
5. See Lacombe, *Georges Bizet*, 728–32.
6. "Chose enivrante," Carmen (Act II, Sc. 5): "Le ciel ouvert, la vie errante, / Pour pays l'univers, pour toi la volonté, / Et surtout la chose enivrante, / La liberté ! la liberté !"
7. According to Pigot (*Georges Bizet*, 216). Bizet gave "September–December 1873" as the composition date on the autograph. See Macdonald, *The Bizet Catalogue*.
8. 1874 (3 times), 1875 (1), 1876 (1), 1877 (1), 1878 (1), 1881 (1), 1882 (1), 1883 (1). Pasdeloup died on 13 August 1887. See Simon, "Concerts Pasdeloup (1861–1887)."
9. See Bernard, *Le Concert symphonique à Paris*.
10. On 30 October and 6 November 1887; 30 March and 4 November 1888; 13 January, 7 March, 23 May, and 10 and 17 November 1889; 4 December 1890, and so on. See Simon, "Orchestre Lamoureux."
11. Cirque d'Hiver concert programs (15 February 1874 program), F-Po, Pro B.94, Opéra C. 315.
12. "Nouvelles des théâtres et des arts." *Le Moniteur universel*, 13 February 1874. "*Patrie* . . . Ouverture dramatique (1re audition), G. Bizet—(Épisode de la guerre de Pologne—Bataille de Raclawa, gagnée sur les Russes par Koscuiszko, 1792 [1794])."
13. *Patrie, ouverture dramatique transcrite pour piano à quatre mains par l'auteur*, Paris: Choudens [1874]. The autograph evidences the late addition of the adjective "dramatique." The title page reads: "To my friend J. Massenet/ Patrie! . . . / Dramatic [in a different handwriting] Overture / for/ Full orchestra/ Georges Bi-

zet/ Op. 19" ("À mon ami J. Massenet/ Patrie! . . . / Ouverture [ajout d'une autre main:] dramatique/ pour/ Grand orchestre/ Georges Bizet/ Op. 19"). The published orchestral score does not give the program but retains the title (*Patrie. Ouverture dramatique pour grand orchestre*, orchestral score, Paris: Choudens, [n.d.]).

14. Henry Cohen, "Revue des concerts," *La Chronique musicale*, 1 March 1874, 220–21. "Seuls, des chants polonais ou russes en eussent pu justifier le titre" and "une bataille quelconque mise en musique," respectively.
15. "The melee of a battle is perfectly expressed here. The cannon is admirably imitated. The bugles and drums combine with all the other instruments to give it a strange, fiery flavor. But what about the melody in all this? It is a rather beautiful, broad, and melancholic melody played in a minor key, which seemed to me to represent the moaning of the wounded. Perhaps I was mistaken? But this motif arrives unannounced and is immediately followed by another that has already been heard. This sequence links two very disparate melodies, neither of which is developed." "La mêlée d'une bataille y est parfaitement exprimée; le canon y est admirablement imité; les clairons, les tambours se mêlant au bruit des autres instruments, lui donnent une couleur ardente et étrange; mais que devient la mélodie dans tout cela? Un assez beau chant dans le mode mineur, large et mélancolique, m'a semblé représenter les plaintes des blessés. Me serais-je trompé? Mais ce motif arrive sans être annoncé; il cesse en s'enchaînant avec un autre motif qu'on a déjà entendu, et cet enchaînement ne sert qu'à lier deux chants très disparates, dont aucun n'est développé."
16. Albert Wolff, "Georges Bizet et la Pologne," *Le Gaulois*, 16 February 1874.
17. Letter from Georges Bizet to Paul Lacombe, end of 1871 or the beginning of January 1872, in Imbert, *Portraits et études*, 194–95.
18. Letter from Bizet to Choudens, February 1874, in *Correspondance*. "Après le mot ouverture faites ajouter dramatique pour le titre. Je tiens à cette dénomination: *Ouverture dramatique.*"
19. *Don Rodrigue*, F-Pn, Ms 477, V, no. 22 Marche et Cortège, mes. 1-4 sq (= *Patrie*, mes. 1-4 sq).
20. "Marche de soldats portant les armes et les drapeaux pris à l'ennemi."
21. Johannès Weber, "Critique musicale," *Le Temps*, 24 February 1874. "Une plainte sur les morts."
22. Victorin Joncières, "Revue musicale," *La Liberté*, 23 February 1874. "Phrase mélancolique," "l'immense douleur du peuple oppressé sous le joug des barbares, avec un grand sentiment," "dont l'accent plaintif," and "est rendu encore plus saisissant par l'accompagnement funèbre des cuivres," respectively.
23. Johannès Weber, "Critique musicale," *Le Temps*, 24 February 1874. "Caractère doux et consolant" and "Exprime-t-elle la joie des soldats embrassant leurs mères, leurs sœurs, leurs fiancées ou leurs maîtresses?," respectively.
24. Johannès Weber, "Critique musicale," *Le Temps*, 15 June 1875: "The title was the brainchild of Monsieur Pasdeloup." "Le titre est de l'invention de M. Pasdeloup." Weber made no mention of this in his previously cited column of 24 February 1874.
25. Pigot, *Georges Bizet*, 217–18. "Bizet avait eu d'abord en vue, en écrivant son *Ouverture dramatique*, les malheurs de la Patrie vaincue et livrée, les angoisses de l'année terrible. Toutes ces souffrances, ajoutait Pigot, tous ces deuils, qui avaient douloureusement ému l'âme du patriote, avaient vivement sollicité son imagination de poète. Il voulait chanter la Patrie en deuil toujours vivante et chère au cœur de ses enfants, la Patrie mutilée et saignant encore, le relèvement futur; mais il comprit bientôt que les chants de douleur, que l'évocation des

jours d'angoisse et de larmes, ne convenaient pas à notre époque d'apaisement; alors par une fiction de poète, par une substitution heureuse, d'une allégorie touchante, pleine de renseignements, il évoqua la grande ombre de la Pologne agonisante, toujours vaincue, toujours debout, et dont le souvenir ineffaçable, dont le nom sacré vit toujours au cœur de ses enfants dispersés."

26. Letter from Georges Bizet to Ernest Guiraud, [end of 1870?], in Bizet, *Correspondance*. "J'ai rêvé cette nuit que nous étions tous à Naples, installés dans une villa délicieuse; nous y vivions sous un gouvernement purement artistique. Le Sénat était composé de Beethoven, Michel-Ange, Shakespeare, Giorgione *e tutti quanti*. La garde nationale était remplacée par un immense orchestra."

27. Lecaillon, *Les Peintres français et la guerre de 1870*, 141. "L'évocation indirecte de la guerre" and "traiter le sujet à travers un épisode d'une autre guerre qui, par analogie, renvoie aux souvenirs que l'artiste et/ou son public entretiennent du conflit franco-prussien," respectively.

28. See Largeaud, "Mémoire et identité."

29. Price, *Pierre Puvis de Chavannes*, 170.

30. Victorin Joncières, "Revue musicale," *La Liberté*, 23 February 1874. "Ce qui a sauvé M. Bizet de l'écueil ordinaire du style descriptif, c'est qu'il a été soutenu dans la conception de son œuvre par une pensée générale, grande et élevée, l'idée de la patrie . . . Ce n'est que lorsqu'il n'a pu faire autrement, dans l'épisode de la bataille elle-même, que sa musique devient imitative."

31. *Le Ménestrel*, 10 September 1871, 316. "Même à l'orchestre, écrivait-il, le souvenir de pareils événements serait mal accueilli à Paris."

32. See, for example, Kelly, *French Music*, and Cheyronnaud, "Éminemment français," 93–108.

33. Digeon, *La Crise allemande de la pensée française*.

34. Tison, *Comment sortir de la guerre?*, 16. "Comment la littérature met en scène le complexe de la défaite."

35. Letter from Ernest Reyer to [Charles Nuitter?], 29 July [1870], F-Po, L.a.s. Reyer 243. "Notre patriotisme, écrivait-il, ne peut être soupçonné maintenant, bien que j'aime beaucoup mieux la musique allemande que la musique française."

36. Letter from Ernest Reyer to Charles Nuitter, Fouday, 13 September 1870, F-Po, L.a.s. Reyer 244. "Ah les gredins de prussiens! Moi qui les aimais tant à cause de leurs vertus musicales et qui vais être forcé d'en exterminer un très grand nombre!"

37. Letter from Georges Bizet to Léonie Halévy, 24 or 29 May 1871. "La plus grande page que possède notre art."

38. See Ehrhardt, *Les Relations franco-allemandes et la musique à programme*, 13.

39. Letter from Georges Bizet to Paul Lacombe, end of 1871 or the beginning of January 1872, in Imbert, Portraits et études, 194–95.

40. See Halévy, *L'Invasion*.

41. Letter from Georges Bizet to Ernest Guiraud, [Barbizon, 8 August 1870], in Bizet, *Correspondance*. "Nous nous retrouvons debout, vivants, ou à peu près, sur les ruines de cette pauvre France, si coupable mais aussi bien malheureuse. Ce que coûtent les Napoléons, nous ne vivrons peut-être pas assez pour le savoir!"

42. Letter from Georges Bizet to Ernest Guiraud, [26 December 1870], in Bizet, *Correspondance*. "Décidément, ces trois mois de République ont enlevé le plus gros de l'épaisse couche de honte et d'ordure dont cet infâme empire avait badigeonné le pays. Je pressens que Gambetta est bien l'homme que nous espérions. Chasser les Prussiens et garder la République! C'est dur, mais mon espoir augmente chaque jour."

43. Letter from Georges Bizet to Léonie Halévy, [Le Vésinet, April 1871], in Bizet, *Correspondance*. "Espérons que le gouvernement honnête que nous possédons en ce moment se consolidera et remoralisera les arts qui en ont grand besoin."
44. Letter from Georges Bizet to Léonie Halévy, 29 May [18]71, in Bizet, *Correspondance*. "Wagner n'est pas mon ami, et je le tiens en médiocre estime. Mais je ne puis oublier les immenses jouissances que je dois à ce génie novateur. Le charme de cette musique est indicible, inexprimable. C'est la volupté, la tendresse, l'amour! . . . Si je vous en jouais huit jours, vous en raffoleriez! . . . D'ailleurs les Allemands qui hélas, nous valent bien en musique, ont compris que Wagner est une de leurs colonnes les plus solides. L'esprit allemand du XIXe siècle est incarné en cet homme."
45. Idem. "Jugez bien *vous-même*, en oubliant tout ce que vous avez entendu dire, en oubliant les sots et méchants articles et le plus méchant livre publié par Wagner, et vous verrez."
46. Some critics denounced the score for its harmonic excesses, which were associated with Wagner's detrimental influence.
47. See Fauquet, *César Franck*, 425–26.
48. See Duchesneau, *L'Avant-garde musicale à Paris*, 22. In 1886 the society expanded to include non-French repertoires and the repertoires of deceased and nonmember French musicians, which led to Bussine's and Saint-Saëns's resignations.
49. *Le Petit Parisien*, 28 April 1922, cited in Nectoux, *Gabriel Fauré*, 133. "La vérité est, qu'avant 1870, je n'aurais pas songé à composer sonate ou quatuor. Il n'y avait alors aucune possibilité pour un jeune musicien de faire entendre de tels ouvrages."
50. Cesar Franck, *Trio en Si b* op.1, no 2; Théodore Dubois, two melodies for voice and piano; Alexis de Castillon, *Pièces pour Piano dans le Style Ancien*; Jules Garcin, *Concerto pour Violon et Piano*; Jules Massenet, *Improvisation pour Violon et Piano*; Camille Saint-Saëns, *Marche Héroïque* for two pianos. The concerts took place fortnightly between October and May. From 1873 onward, three concerts, with orchestra, were organized annually.
51. Date of composition: November 1870 (version for two pianos). Date of orchestration: November 1871. Dedicated to the memory of Henri Regnault. Gallica: https://gallica.bnf.fr/ark:/12148/bpt6k11638297.
52. First performed at the Théâtre de la Gaîté on 19 December 1871.
53. Tiersot, *Un Demi-siècle de musique française*, 32. On *Patrie*: "There can be no doubt that when he was composing it, Bizet was recalling his memories, still fresh in his mind, of that terrible year." "Que Bizet, en la composant, se soit reporté à ses impressions encore fraîche de l'année terrible, cela ne saurait faire doute."
54. Georges Bizet to Léonie Halévy, [10 March 1871], in G. Bizet, *Correspondance*. "Il faut l'éloignement du temps pour embrasser l'ensemble d'épisodes."
55. Idem. "Être utile à la patrie, à l'humanité."
56. Idem. "Nous sommes entre un monde qui s'en va et un monde qui vient. Nous avons une rude mer à traverser."
57. Tison, *Comment sortir de la guerre?*, 15. "Temps particulier au cours duquel les sociétés [mais aussi les individus] se déprennent de la violence de guerre et se redéfinissent."
58. Rolland, "Le Renouveau: esquisse du mouvement musical à Paris depuis 1870," in *Musiciens d'aujourd'hui*, 209. "Poussée de foi et d'énergie qui a recréé la musique française." This chapter was first published in Berlin by Marquardt in 1904 under the title *Paris als Musikstadt*.

59. Idem., 215. "Les désastres de la guerre . . . régénérèrent l'esprit artistique de la nation."

Bibliography

Bernard, Elisabeth. *Le Concert symphonique à Paris entre 1861 et 1914: Pasdeloup, Colonne, Lamoureux*, PhD thesis, 2. vol. Université Paris 1, 1976.

Cabanes, Bruno, and Guillaume Piketty, ed. *Retour à l'intime: au sortir de la guerre*. Paris: Tallandier, 2009.

Cabanes, Bruno. "Sortir de la guerre: jalons pour une histoire en chantier." *Histoire@Politique* 3, no. 3, (2007): 1–8.

Cheyronnaud, Jacques. "Éminemment français." *Terrain* 17 (1991): 93–108.

Digeon, Claude. *La Crise allemande de la pensée française, 1870–1914* [1st ed., 1959]. Paris: Presses Universitaires de France, 1992.

Duchesneau, Michel. *L'Avant-garde musicale à Paris de 1871 à 1939*. Liège: Mardaga, 1997.

Ehrhardt, Damien. *Les Relations franco-allemandes et la musique à programme, 1830–1914*. Lyon: Symétrie, 2009.

Halévy, Ludovic. *L'Invasion: souvenirs et récits* (Jean-Claude Yon ed.). Paris: Mercure de France, 2013.

Fauquet, Joël-Marie. *César Franck*. Paris: Fayard, 1999.

Imbert, Hugues. *Portraits et études*. Paris: Fischbacher, 1894.

Kelly, Barbara L., ed. *French Music, Culture, and National Identity, 1870–1939*. Rochester, NY: University of Rochester Press, 2008.

Lacombe, Hervé. *Georges Bizet*. Paris: Fayard, 2001.

———. *La Habanera de Carmen: Naissance d'un tube*. Paris: Fayard, 2014.

———. *Les Voies de l'opéra français au XIXe siècle*. Paris: Fayard, 1997.

Lacombe, Hervé, and Yves Balmer, ed. *Histoire intellectuelle de la* Revue de musicologie: *Mutations thématiques et évolutions méthodologiques*, special issue of the *Revue de Musicologie* 1, 2018.

Largeaud, Jean-Marc. "Mémoire et identité: Waterloo et la genèse de la 'défaite glorieuse.'" In *Voies nouvelles pour l'histoire du Premier Empire: territoires, pouvoirs, identités*, edited by Nathalie Petiteau, 283–302. Paris: La Boutique de l'histoire, 2003.

Lecaillon, Jean-François. *Les Peintres français et la guerre de 1870: 1870–1914*. Paris: Bernard Giovanangeli publisher and Metz: Éditions des Paraiges, 2016.

Macdonald, Hugh. "The Bizet Catalogue." 2014. Retrieved 1 September 2019 from http://digital.wustl.edu/bizet/works/Patrie.html.

Nectoux, Jean-Michel. *Gabriel Fauré: les voix du clair-obscur* (2nd rev. ed.). Paris: Fayard, 2008.

Pigot, Charles. *Georges Bizet et son œuvre*. Paris: E. Dentu, 1886.

Price, Aimée B. *Pierre Puvis de Chavannes*. Vol. 2. New Haven, CT: Yale University Press, 2010.

Rolland, Romain. *Musiciens d'aujourd'hui*. Paris: Hachette, 1908.
Simon, Yannick. "Orchestre Lamoureux." *Dezède, 2015*. Retrieved 9 October 2018 from https://dezede.org/dossiers/concerts-lamoureux/.
Simon, Yannick. "Concerts Pasdeloup (1861–1887)." *Dezède, 2017*. Retrieved 9 October 2018 from dezede.org/dossiers/id/249/.
Tiersot, Julien. *Un Demi-siècle de musique française*. Paris: Félix Alcan, 1918.
Tison, Stéphane. *Comment sortir de la guerre?* Rennes: Presses Universitaires de Rennes, 2011.

Chapter 2

REVOLUTIONARY MUSIC FROM WAR TO PEACE
Mexico, 1910s–1930s

Pablo Palomino

In a series of articles on the musical life of Mexico for the newspaper *El Universal Ilustrado* in the 1930s, the music critic and composer Gerónimo Baqueiro Foster (1898–1967) discussed the state of the music scene from the perspective of the armed phase of the Mexican Revolution. During the violent years between 1910 and 1920, he explained, music bands in armies and even police bands crisscrossed the entire country, disseminating and mixing the sounds from the metropolis and the provinces, thereby transforming the musical taste of audiences all over Mexico. These military musicians who traveled "from town to town, like bees flying from flower to flower" spread the seeds of what the revolutionary musical establishment would later define as Mexico's modern "musical nationalism."[1] During the revolutionary war, it was the favor of chiefs, not a test at the conservatory, that promoted music careers. Baqueiro Foster writes:

> "The position of the directors of military bands used to fall on the unprepared, just because they grabbed the opportunity in those days— sad for some and happy for others—of the Revolution, to entertain the fortunate victory..."

But since the postwar transition of the 1920s, "things have changed," he added. Musical careers followed more predictable paths, and "today's directors, without being extraordinary, are at least competent. But, for what?"[2]

Notes for this section begin on page 50.

For what? This question, addressed to the postwar musical establishment, was about the goals they should pursue in further elaborating the musical legacy of the wartime experience. Baqueiro was fiercely critical: he lamented that postwar state bureaucrats did not work hard enough to professionalize those bands, "letting them sleep," abandoning them to a minimal activity, without sponsoring new programs, study, or tours, and paying low salaries. Despite the state's official rhetoric, which praised the worker, actual members of the police force military band were condemned to making ends meet and poverty, all of which resulted, according to Baqueiro Foster, in lower musical quality. Lamentation about state indifference and low salaries is probably inherent to music life across time and space—certainly among those Latin American countries at the time that also animated a modernizing musical activism to catch up with their economic and demographic growth, like Argentina and Brazil. But in Mexico the experience of the revolutionary war gave Mexican musical critics and actors a peculiar "myth of origin" and therefore a teleological framework to organize their ambitions: they assigned themselves the task of channeling the musical maelstrom unchained by a war still fresh in their minds.

The problem—for music critics back then, and for historians today—is that the Mexican Revolution did not have one shared ideology, nor a master plan, let alone an aesthetic program. War occurred within a vast and heterogeneous territory for about seven years (1910–1917), resulting in mass casualties and economic destruction.[3] It began in 1910 as a rebellion against the dictator Porfirio Díaz, continued against Francisco Madero, then against general Victoriano Huerta's federal army, then among the different revolutionary factions, until the victory of the Constitutionalist Army in 1917. But armed conflicts continued and political stability was reached under a new regime in 1920, with Alvaro Obregón first and then Plutarco Elías Calles at the helm of the new "revolutionary state." But violence continued to permeate Mexican life well beyond that year, including a civil war in part of the territory in the late 1920s (although this Cristero War was not part of the Revolution, strictly speaking). Hence, the very chronology of the transition from war to peace is difficult to establish. Also, unlike international wars, the armed phase of the Mexican Revolution opposed the federal army to multiple regional armies, local militias, and political networks, but these actors at different times allied and also fought each other, as the old federal army was disbanded and replaced by a new Constitutionalist one. War happened at different times in different points of the territory;

in some of them a "total war" engulfed entire communities, while in others the battlefield and the home were neatly separated. Local conditions often thwarted national policies before, during, and after the war, as historians of education have shown.[4] (Also, because the Revolution brought about the destruction of many archives, important lacunae in the historiography still hinder the reconstruction of continuities with previous periods.[5]) The Revolution was thus in fact many regional conflicts, involving multilingual indigenous societies, conservative and progressive elites, anarchist unions, middle- and working-class political parties and activists, small ranchers, peasant communities, and agribusiness capitalists. The Revolution was made by "many Mexicos."[6] Because all these actors fought for their views and interests as Mexicans, the postwar musical brokers lacked a non-Mexican enemy repertoire to combat.

A popular-nationalist identity promoted by the emerging political elite became hegemonic during the postwar transition, through mural painting, education, public ritualism, and music. It proposed a unifying meaning that the actors of the Revolution actually had never expressed. In their own teleological narrative, music activists in the 1920s and under the "populist" policies of the 1930s sought to integrate a society the war had proved disconnected, by musically reaching vast swaths of the population through the Secretary of Public Education's (SEP) Fine Arts Department, "Casas del Pueblo" (Popular Houses), Rural Schools, and "Cultural Missions."[7] Their policies had, as I will show, a *centralizing* ambition and were musically *omnivorous*. They were inspired by the official narrative of the Revolution as the fundamental watershed moment that unveiled "the essence of Mexicaness in music."[8] These pedagogical, performative, and ideological operations constitute the most important aspect of the long postwar transition in Mexico.

A brief set of comparisons will help us understand the uniqueness of the Mexican case. All other postwar transitions in Latin America—after the Paraguay, Pacific, Cuban Independence, and Chaco Wars—produced state-sponsored cultural projects, but none as expansive as the Mexican one. The Revolution loosened the oligarchic control of the cultural agencies that dominated in those other cases, and infused in its renewed bureaucracy a conscious critique of the "neocolonial" nature of the region's cultural agencies,[9] with the goal of incorporating not only socioeconomically and politically but musically as well, increasing portions of the urban and rural population into a modernizing welfare state. The Mexican policies were in this sense closer to contemporary nationalizing programs by revolutionary and modernizing state bureaucracies in other corners of the world, such as Soviet Russia and Ataturk's Turkey, also aimed to reshape society through multiple means, including music. But the Mexican musical policies resulted from the negotiation and convergence of interests and views from multiple groups under the leadership of a modernizing elite far more porous, in doctrine and practice, than the Communist and military rule of Russia and Turkey. Last but not least, the Mexican bureaucrats had to build musical institutions in a country deeply imbricated, in music as in everything else, with the United States, in terms of labor, investments, and markets; this proximity forced them to navigate a peculiar mix of private, public, national, and foreign musical actors and aesthetics.[10] This chapter focuses hence on how state and civil musical brokers turned the experience of the Mexican revolutionary war into one of the world's most successful experiments in nationalist musical branding.

"The Revolution Imposed the Art of the Small Towns and Fields"

The postwar musical transition in Mexico was shaped by a series of policies based on what its main actors considered the legacy of the "true" Mexico revealed by the revolutionary war. Their narrative can be summarized in the words of musicologist and composer Daniel Castañeda in 1939: "the Revolution imposed ... the art of the small towns and fields, the art of the masses, the art of the national sadness and the national picaresque turned into melodic and rhythmic line, sung in the undisciplined enthusiasm by the choir of our peasants and workers."[11] The Revolution was seen as the event that violently brought to life, breaking the Europeanist façade of the Porfirian regime, a musical culture shaped by several centuries of pre-Hispanic, colonial, and Independent life. Castañeda made this argument in "La música y la Revolución Mexicana," a paper presented in 1926 at the First National Congress of Music in Mexico City and rewritten in 1939.[12] He argued that the years between 1910 and 1925 radically transformed Mexico's musical life, posing to artists and policy makers a question: *el problema estético de la Revolución*—how to organize a musical legacy that had no aesthetic program.[13] The transnational *Bulletin of Latin American Music* published this article in 1941, consolidating among Latin Americanist musicologists the idea that the Revolution had been *the* fundamental watershed moment in the musical history of Mexico.

The musical myth of the Revolution was powerful because it connected with the actual experiences of popular musicians and their audiences. As Castañeda put it, the Revolution had circulated the truly popular music of the small towns and provinces, bringing it to the "bourgeois" musical culture of Mexico City—for whom "real" Mexican music was then as foreign as Hawaiian music or US jazz bands would be in the 1930s. With the Revolution, the "Italianizing romanza" so fashionable in 1908 was replaced by the "song of the *Bajío*, the *corrido*, or the *huapango*"—popular regional genres that circulated widely during the Revolution. Whereas until 1910, music came from Europe, from 1925 on, "our music is ours, we assimilated the popular lyricism and now we showcase the open secret of our intimate life."[14] Castañeda mentions here the first collections of revolutionary *corridos* published in the 1930s. The Secretary of Public Education also did its part, by ordering in 1935 the printing of five hundred copies of several "Revolutionary Corridos": "Corrido del sol," "La chinita," "La jesuita," "La cucaracha," "Adelita," "La florecita," "Agua que refresca," "El bolerito," "Juga, niño, juega," "El cántaro de Coyotepec," and also "Canto popular ruso" (Russian popular chant) and "En la cuna del niño proletario" (In the cradle of the proletarian boy), the latter two probably added by Soviet-inspired socialist educators.[15] The corrido, a narrative music genre that disseminates actual local stories and their morals through dramatic verses, was popularized by publishers and singers throughout Mexico during and after the Revolution.[16] And well beyond Mexico: Castañeda quotes the adaptation by Catalan anarchists of the famous corrido "La cucaracha" (The cockroach), which I also found it morphed into a Yiddish-Spanish version in Buenos Aires around 1935.[17]

The concentration of artists and performers from all over Mexico in the capital city during the 1920s, bringing to it "the simple truth of the peasant and popular sentiment," was for Castañeda the most important result of the armed phase of the Revolution. Multiple circuits had connected Mexico's towns and regions for over a century, through village and military bands.[18] But it was the Revolution and the years of migrations that followed it that brought to Mexico City music as varied as *mariachis de Cocula*; *trovadores yucatecos*; singers and dancers of *jarabe* and *zandunga*; *orquestas típicas*; groups of *yaqui* soldiers; *pascola* dancers; *trovadores* from Tamaulipas and Veracruz; *Huapango* players from Veracruz; *cancioneros típicos* from Oaxaca; *mariachis* from Guerrero who sang *chilenas*, *gustos*, *sones*, and *malagueñas*; and *cancioneros* from Michoacán. It could be said that their canonization by the broadcasting and recording industries during the 1930s marked the end of the postwar transition.

Classical music artists and critics participated in this process as well. They responded to the call in September 1926 by the newspaper *El Universal* to join the First National Music Congress in Mexico City (Castañeda's text was presented here), where they engaged in a debate on the modernization and definition of "national music." Even if mostly limited to "art" music and musicians, with folk music considered as raw material for erudite translation into European musical language, this was, however, the first "public discussion" about popular musical traditions.[19] The recognition of a specific Mexican folk music tradition was fundamental for the establishment of the National Conservatory curriculum in the following years, and for the cultural atmosphere in which commercial radio started to broadcast "typical Mexican music." But there was another crucial mediator, overlooked in the musical histories of the Revolution and closely linked with the war experience and the postwar transition: the Constitutionalist Army's choir.

From Military Choirs to Children and Workers Choirs

In 1918 the press of the Department of Militarization (within the Secretary of War) published a history of the Orfeón Militar written by the folklorist Rubén M. Campos.[20] This text provides a less teleological view of the emergence of a populist ideology in music when the postwar transition began. For Campos it was the army itself, rather than a vague "popular sentiment," that transmitted to postwar Mexico the musical experience of the Revolution.

Seeking to present the army's choir as a deeply ingrained feature of Mexican musical life, Campos begins by defining collective chanting in Mexico as a continuation of the medieval Gregorian chants present in all repertoires—secular, romantic, and popular—in nineteenth-century Mexico. But the book was devoted to the creation, by the Constitutionalist Army under General Venustiano Carranza in 1915, of a military choir. This *orfeón militar* was at the origins of the postrevolutionary *orfeones*, in which "children marching and singing by the streets of the metropolis . . . in harmony with a people that celebrated the recovery of its freedom" produced the "popular spectacle" of "the union of the people and the young army through music." This military *orfeón* was thus for Campos the inception of a process by which soldiers ended up becoming "the people itself" and instituting choral singing in the schools, to make each student no longer a soldier but a music teacher for the future Mexico.

The founder of this ambitious Orfeón de las escuelas de tropa (military school choir) was Jesús Reynoso Aráoz[21] who, according to his own memoir, created this organization, in fact, by inviting colleagues from an older Mexico City popular choir (Orfeón popular, active from 1907 to 1914). On 15 September (Independence Day) two thousand soldiers from different brigades got together to sing the national anthem in conjunction with a military march, and two weeks later the Orfeón was incorporated to the Troops School. By the end of 1915 they were teaching to thirty-six hundred students in twenty-six barracks; the eight original teachers grew to sixteen.

The Orfeón was reassigned in May 1916 to the Secretary of Public Instruction and Fine Arts, with the task of "militarizing the children." Teaching extended from the barracks to regular schools and some professional schools, and also expanded its roster and upgraded its salaries. On 1 May 1917, at the Condesa hippodrome in Mexico City, its first big choral event featured two thousand children singing "classic Mexican songs, several patriotic chants, and two extensive musical art works."[22] In September, at the same location, twenty thousand children "organized in battalions" made gymnastic exercises while two thousand young children, two thousand nurses, as well as a thousand other performers organized in four bands and played patriotic hymns, peace and war chants, popular songs, and other artworks, in front of the president. These singers, trained by the Orfeón teachers, were musically illiterate, having learned exclusively through auditory methods. The massive scale of celebrations was a novelty. But in 1918 the Orfeón was dissolved. The demilitarization of choral singing was intended, according to Aráoz, to generalize its principles throughout the educational system, now under the name of Canto Coral y Orfeónico.

Between 1920 and 1922, always under the direction of Aráoz, the 1915–18 military *orfeones* became the Orfeón Popular, which functioned within the National University. It became in March 1922 a different institution, the Night School Department of the National Music Conservatory, and finally, in 1924, the Popular Music Night School (EPNM), targeting Mexico City's working-class youth. The crucial 1922 reincarnation was approved by Congress after a proposal by avant-garde composer Julián Carrillo, who wanted the National Music School to be relieved of the less prepared students, for whom a different type of professional training could be provided based on the military choirs—which did not just turn into children choirs but ultimately became a tool in professional training for the working-class youth of Mexico City. The first cohort (the year 1922) was consisted of 1,374 "young ladies, young men, and kids; clerks, professionals, members of the military, workers, school students, etc,"[23] of whom 400 attended regularly, only 182 of them advancing to the second year ("because the rest were not used to taking exams"), but the entire cohort participated in collective singing classes. Curiously, the peasant nationalism that later musicologists saw as the main musical legacy of the Revolution was not obvious in the early years of this night school: the first cohort debuted by singing at the inauguration of the new building of the Secretary of Public Education an Italian version of Richard Wagner's *Tannhäuser*. Students performed at another public concert an oratorio by Lorenzo Perosi (1872–1956), in Latin, and Franz Liszt's *Faust* Symphony, in German.[24] This was still the kind of musical legitimacy a choir like this needed in order to prove themselves. But already in that first year, and under the supervision of José Carrillo, the Mexican youth choirs performed what we may call an "omnivorous" repertoire:[25] music from dramas and comedies, *sainetes*, regional folklore—such as "La pajarera"—Johann Strauss's *The Blue Danube*, the iconic *jarabe tapatío* from Jalisco, *zarzuelas*, and a sixteenth-century piece by Palestrina.

From 1923, under the name of the National Popular School of Music, the former military choir professor Aráoz taught working-class students with the following goals: every night to "keep them from dissolution," "elevate them aesthetically," give them "economic opportunities as music performers," "organize the popular neighborhoods," and create a disciplined and "organized mass of people at official and cultural events"[26] by the revolutionary state. By 1932 more than thirteen thousand students had attended classes, many of them becoming music teachers themselves or performers at bands, orchestras, theaters, film studios, and radio stations. The best among them entered the music departments at the universities and conservatories of music, dance, and dramatic arts.

The debates about the musical orientation of the National Popular School of Music were intense. Some critics argued that it should develop the modernist canon, whereas others demanded an "indigenist" conception of authentic popular music. Aráoz defended the school's aesthetic orientation in terms of improving the cultural and material conditions of the Mexican working class "as it is," neither an idealized indigenous society of the past nor an imagined futurist one:

> The School's mission is to develop the aesthetic and moral sentiments of the working class ... It therefore has to be based on popular songs ... but at the same time has to educate the aesthetic sentiments of the students ... the School has to go from popular songs and then lead the students to ... at least Italian opera and other classic musical forms. It could hopefully lead them also to German opera.[27]

These debates anticipated more ambitious policies. In July 1937 the musical postwar transition was officially over: President Lázaro Cárdenas decreed compulsory and free musical education through choral singing in primary, middle, and normal schools in all the states and municipalities of the Mexican confederation. The military bands, which had originated this movement of popular musical education, were by then in decline. They still played classic marches, double-steps, fashionable popular songs, and sometimes well-known opera overtures and selections, at sport events, bullfights, and horse races, less frequently at school events, and sometimes in the street to attract the public to entertainment halls. But according to Baqueiro Foster, their decadence and lack of creativity was linked to the audiences' increasing preference for the "degenerate" influence of radio programming,[28] which increasingly included jazz, tango, and other foreign styles next to Mexican music.[29]

Music Education against Commercial Music

State officers thought of counterbalancing private interests in the airwaves in many ways—for example, by means of a broadcasting system centralized in the office of the president, who would control the communications of the several branches of the state, such as war, education, agriculture, health, statistics, foreign relations, governors, and the legislative and judiciary powers. The Music Section of the Secretary of Public Education (SEP) also looked for inspiration in foreign models of popular control through music and education, such as the Fascist choral singing program in Italy (the archives contain a copy of the *Inno popolare della scuola fascista*) and the 1931 poll, conducted by the International Institute of Intellectual Cooperation, on uses of broadcasting at the school. More consequential were the education programs intended to unify the country's musical culture. A series of SEP-sponsored musical and anthropological missions were sent to isolated corners of Mexico, to collect and distribute music sheets of folk songs, echoing a hemispheric current of *indigenismo*. Like their colleagues throughout Latin America, cultural state officers in Mexico sought to redefine the notion of "indigenous" music in order to incorporate it into a modernizing nationalist identity. But music education was the key of the musical postrevolutionary activism.

Musicologist Luis Sandi, research head of the Music Section of the SEP in 1933–34, sent a report to his boss at the Fine Arts direction, composer and musical titan Carlos Chávez (1899–1978), describing his work between May 1933 and May 1934. The report starts by pointing out the challenges faced by music teachers: they expected students to read music and to learn school songs, but the basis for both were "nineteenth-century *zarzuelas* and *cuplés*," which presented the students only the "formal and external difficulties" of music and forced them to use compositions of low quality that were also outdated. As a result, primary-school children were not able to read a popular song composition after years of training, detested classical music, and ended up getting used to "the music of the city outskirts" (*un tipo de música extraído de los arrabales de la ciudad*) cultivated by merchants. The youngest children were particularly affected by the despicable quality (*canallesca*) of the "dictators" of radio music; the older generations had at least the habit of attending classical concerts and even modern ones. A "radical change" was thus required, and it consisted, among other things, of putting children and adolescents in contact with "representative works of the diverse cultures of the world, and of the times of Mexican, Inca, and Western cultures," in order to "form an intelligent and active musical audience" (formar un público musical interesado e inteligente) who would form the basis of future music teachers.

Sandi invited a group of young composers to create and propose musical works for the schools. He described the scope of the group's production as follows:

> The group has produced the following works: almost 200 original musical works in pentatonic, Greek, major and minor modes, for kindergarten; 14 original works in those same modes for students in first stage of primary school; "Chuparrosa"–Yaqui chant; "Los Xtoles"–Mayan chant; "Ténabari"–Yaqui chant; "La Estrella Matutina"–Pápago chant; "El Pequeño Hermano"–Pápago chant; "I-coos"–Serí chant; "Canción del Coyote"–Yaqui chant; and "Bura Bampo"–Yaqui chant, selected and arranged for the first level of the second stage; 7 Mexican popular songs selected for the second level of the second stage; "Yo tengo un buen pastel"–Rondel by Adam de la Halle and "Se tu m'ami" by Pergolesi for the first level of the third stage; "Paloma Blanca"–Peruvian chant; "Veyñi amán"–Araucano chant; "Kuriquinga"–Ecuadorian chant; "Muchacha Bonita"–Peruvian chant and "Encantadora Sirena"–Peruvian chant, selected and arranged for the second and third trimesters of the first

level of the third stage; two African chants and an Arab one for the first trimester of the second level of the third stage; "Canto de la Tarde"–Mussorgsky, selected for the second trimester of the second level of the third stage; three original chants in modern style and the "Bestiario" or "Cortejo de Orfeo" by Francis Poulenc for the third semester.[30]

The Music Section organized two traveling concert groups to perform throughout the schools of Mexico, one of them a duo of piano and singer, the other a "Mariachi Quartet" exclusively dedicated to "anonymous popular music." In 1933 an official event was held that combined the performance of selected choirs of schoolchildren who sang some parts of the repertoire they learned at their choral singing lessons; the reconstruction of some indigenous works from the Music Section's archive; and the performance of an orchestra that included instruments from the different regions of the country (this synthesis of regional orchestras was called *Orquesta Mexicana*).[31]

Sandi's report and the Night School programming suggest that the postwar transition consolidated in the 1930s a musical ideology that combined music genres and examples perceived as folkloric with indigenous and a Universalist (European) canon, as well as a paradoxical relationship with music markets—seen as both a professional opportunity for working-class performers and a threat to the national music. The task for revolutionary critics and pedagogues was to teach the "right" songs and techniques in order to foster the incorporation of children and youth into a Revolution born out of a chaotic war, in a programmatic fashion, directed by its artists and experts.

Conclusion

Postwar musical brokers saw their work as an organic continuation of the Revolution: the revelation of Mexico's true musical identity. The reification of this cultural work in state discourses and rituals over many decades turned it retrospectively into a teleology, and even a stereotype.[32] Wartime military bands and choirs became peacetime professional training programs and school curriculum. State music pedagogues concocted nationalist programs based on those repertoires and many other sources, always under the auspice of the Revolution. The expansion of music practice and education fed in turn a growing musical market, which lured audiences to commercial radio and live music that promoted "Mexican music."

The actual experience of the Revolution as well as the symbolic and material rewards that tying their practice to the revolutionary myth brought to all artists and educators, made a huge difference when compared to other cases in Latin America. For example, in Argentina, musical policies in the 1930s were a conservative, catholic, and Hispanicist attempt at combating tango, and in Brazil they were an authoritarian and modernizing but ultimately weak attempt at bridging the vast gap between the population and the state. In Mexico, to the contrary, the Revolution and the ensuing postwar transition infused the expanding state bureaucracy and the modern media systems with both a powerful unifying myth and musical material from all over the country, creating a musical identity that—although questioned, transformed, and coexisting with others—is still very much alive.

Pablo Palomino is an Argentine cultural historian and associate professor of Latin American and Caribbean Studies at Oxford College of Emory University in Atlanta, Georgia. His book, *The Invention of Latin American Music: A Transnational History* (New York: Oxford University Press, 2020, also published in Spanish as *La invención de la música latinoamericana: una historia transnacional*, Buenos Aires: Fondo de Cultura Económica, 2021), reconstructs the history of the transnational musical networks that shaped Latin America during the golden era of the region's cultural nationalisms.

Notes

1. "El derrumbamiento de la Banda de Policía," Archivo Gerónimo Baqueiro Foster. Manuscripts. Centro Nacional de la Música, Ciudad de México.
2. Baqueiro Foster, "Demóstenes," "La música y los músicos entre bastidores: las bandas militares de música" [signed with the pseudonym "Demóstenes"], 11 June 1936, Idem.
3. Knight, "Guerra, violencia y homicidio en el México moderno."
4. Chowning, "Culture Wars in the Trenches?"
5. Bravo, *Gobiernos revolucionarios y educación popular en México*.
6. Simpson, *Many Mexicos*.
7. Vaughan, *Cultural Politics in Revolution*; Vaughan and Lewis, *The Eagle and the Virgin*; Aguirre Lora, "En pos de la construcción del sentido de lo nacional;" Bolaños, *La "invención" de la música indígena de México: antropología e historia de las políticas culturales del siglo XX*; Tortajada Quiroz, "La investigación artística mexicana en el siglo XX."
8. Madrid, "Sonares dialécticos y política en el estudio posnacional de la música," 22.

9. Even if today's decolonial and anti-racist scholarship critically emphasizes the continuity of traditional hierarchies in the postrevolutionary practice and rhetoric, the official embrace of *indigenismo* and *mestizaje* by the Mexican State, in music as in other domains, represented a deeper rupture with the old Europeanism than in those other postwar transitions. See, for example, the ambiguities of the state campaign of children's literature, in Alcubierre Moya and Bazán Bonfil, "José Vasconcelos' Classical Readings for Children."
10. Palomino, *The Invention of Latin American Music*, chapter 3.
11. "Fue ella -la Revolución- la que impuso, como consecuencia de su ideología popular y campesina, el arte de los poblados y de los campos, el arte de las masas, el arte de la tristeza y de la picaresca nacional hecho línea melódica y rítmica, y voceado -en la indisciplina del entusiasmo- por el coro de nuestros campesinos y trabajadores." Castañeda, "La música y la revolución mexicana," 443.
12. Castañeda was coeditor of the music magazine *Música. Revista Mexicana* in 1930–31 and author of the text of numerous music compositions in the 1930s, as well of studies on pre-Hispanic music instruments. He also published in 1941 a *Balance de Agustín Lara*. See Carredano and Picún, "El nacionalismo musical mexicano"; and Madrid, "The Sounds of the Nation."
13. Castañeda, "La música y la revolución mexicana," 438.
14. "nuestra música es nuestra, nos hemos asimilado la lírica popular y empezamos a proclamar el secreto a voces de nuestra vida emocional." Castañeda, "La música y la revolución mexicana," 444–45.
15. "Memorandum," 7 December and 27 December 1935. Archivo de la Secretaría de Educación Pública.
16. Lira-Hernández, "El corrido mexicano," 31–32.
17. *La cucaratxa, la cucaratxa / ja ni amb rodes por anar / Es derrotista, fa espionage / I amb el peu s'ha d'esclafar*, Castañeda, "La música y la revolución mexicana,"445–46; Palomino, "The Musical Worlds of Jewish Buenos Aires, 1910–1940," 39.
18. Ruiz Torres, "Las bandas militares de música en México y su historia."
19. Madrid, "Sounds of the Nation."
20. Campos, *Los orfeones populares en la cultura nacional.*
21. Jesus Reynoso Aráoz, "Apuntes biográficos."
22 Campos, *Los orfeones populares en la cultura nacional*, 19.
23. "Objeto del establecimiento del Departamento Nocturno de la Escuela Nacional de Música, su organización, plan de estudios, resultados prácticos y galardones obtenidos," SEP (Secretaría de Educación Pública), Mexico City, Departamento de Bellas Artes, Box 46, Folder 2.
24. "Objeto del establecimiento del Departamento Nocturno de la Escuela Nacional de Música, su organización, plan de estudios, resultados prácticos y galardones obtenidos," SEP (Secretaría de Educación Pública), Mexico City, Departamento de Bellas Artes, Box 46, Folder 2.
25. Peterson and Kern, "Changing Highbrow Taste."
26. Letter from Jesús Reynoso Aráoz, Director of the Popular Music Night School (EPNM), to Narciso Bassols, Secretary of Public Education, in SEP (Secretaría de Educación Pública), Mexico City, Departamento de Bellas Artes, Box 47, Folder 3.
27. SEP, Bellas Artes, Box 47, Folder 3.
28. Demóstenes, "Las Bandas Militares de Música," 6/11/1936, Manuscripts, AGBF.
29. Palomino, *The Invention of Latin American Music*, 90–91.
30. Report by Luis Sandi on the activities of the Music Section, May 4, 1934. SEP (Secretaría de Educación Pública), Mexico City, Departamento de Bellas Artes, Box 47, Folder 9.

31. SEP, Bellas Artes, Caja 47, Folder 9 (5/4/1934).
32. Pérez Montfort, "Un nacionalismo sin nación aparente."

Bibliography

Aguirre Lora, María Esther. "En pos de la construcción del sentido de lo nacional. Universos sonoros y dancísticos en la escuela mexicana (1920–1940)." *Historia de la Educación* 25 (2006): 205–24.

Alcubierre Moya, Beatriz, and Rodrigo Bazán Bonfil. "José Vasconcelos' Classical Readings for Children and the Making of Childhood in Post-Revolutionary Mexico." *Bookbird* 55, no. 1 (2017): 14–23.

Bolaños, Marina Alonso. *La "invención" de la música indígena de México: antropología e historia de las políticas culturales del siglo XX*. Buenos Aires: SB Ediciones, 2008.

Bravo, Engracia Loyo. *Gobiernos revolucionarios y educación popular en México, 1911–1928*. 1st ed. México, D.F.: Colegio de México, Centro de Estudios Históricos, El Colegio de México, 1999.

Campos, Rubén M. *Los orfeones populares en la cultura nacional*. México D.F.: Secretaría de Guerra y Marina, 1918.

Carredano, Consuelo, and Olga Picún. "El nacionalismo musical mexicano: una lectura desde los sonidos y los silencios." In *El arte en tiempos de cambio, 1810–1910–2010*, edited by Hugo Arciniega, Louise Noelle, and Fausto Ramírez. Ciudad de México: Instituto de Investigaciones Estéticas, Universidad Nacional Autónoma de México, 2012.

Castañeda, Daniel. "La música y la revolución mexicana." *Boletín Latino-Americano de Música* 5 (1941): 437–48.

Chowning, Margaret. "Culture Wars in the Trenches? Public Schools and Catholic Education in Mexico, 1867–1897." *Hispanic American Historical Review* 97, no. 4 (2017): 613–49.

Knight, Alan. "Guerra, violencia y homicidio en el México moderno." *Clivajes. Revista de Ciencias Sociales* 1 (2014). Retrieved 10 August 2020 from https://clivajes.uv.mx/index.php/Clivajes/article/view/827/0.

Lira-Hernández, Alberto. "El corrido mexicano: un fenómeno histórico-social y literario." *Contribuciones desde Coatepec*, no. 24 (2013): 29–43.

López, Rick. *Crafting Mexico: Intellectuals, Artisans, and the State after the Revolution*. Durham, NC: Duke University Press, 2010.

Madrid, Alejandro L. "Sonares dialécticos y política en el estudio posnacional de la música." *Revista Argentina de Musicología*, no. 11 (2010): 17–32.

———. "The Sounds of the Nation: Visions of Modernity and Tradition in Mexico's First National Congress of Music." *Hispanic American Historical Review* 86, no. 4 (2006): 681–706.

Palomino, Pablo. "The Musical Worlds of Jewish Buenos Aires, 1910–1940." In *Mazel Tov, Amigos! Jews and Popular Music in the Americas*, edited by Amalia Ran and Moshe Morad, 25–53. Leiden: Brill, 2015.

———. *The Invention of Latin American Music: A Transnational History.* New York: Oxford University Press, 2020.
Pareyón, Gabriel. *Diccionario Enciclopédico de Música en México 2.* Jalisco, Mexico: Universidad Panamericana, 2007.
Pérez Montfort, Ricardo. "Un nacionalismo sin nación aparente. (La fabricación de lo 'típico' mexicano 1920–1950)." *Política y Cultura,* no. 12 (1999): 177–93.
Peterson, Richard A., and Roger M. Kern. "Changing Highbrow Taste: From Snob to Omnivore." *American Sociological Review* 61, no. 5 (1996): 900–7.
Reynoso Aráoz, Jesús. "Apuntes biográficos del orfeón de la Escuelas de Tropa y Orfeón del Departamento de Enseñanza Militar, con una breve reseña de sus trabajos desarrollados durante los años de 1915, 1916 y 1917, México, January 1918." In Campos Rubén M. *Los orfeones populares en la cultura nacional.* México D.F.: Secretaría de Guerra y Marina, 1918.
Ruiz Torres, Rafael A. "Las bandas militares de música en México y su historia." In *Bandas de viento en México,* edited by Georgina Flores Mercado, 21–44. México, D.F.: Instituto Nacional de Antropología e Historia, 2015.
Simpson, Lesley Byrd. *Many Mexicos.* Berkeley: University of California Press, 1960 [1941].
Tortajada Quiroz, Margarita. "La investigación artística mexicana en el siglo XX: la experiencia oficial del Departamento de Bellas Artes y del Instituto Nacional de Bellas Artes." México, *Cultura y Representaciones Sociales* 2, no. 4 (2008): 169–96.
Vaughan, Mary K. *Cultural Politics in Revolution: Teachers, Peasants, and Schools in Mexico, 1930–1940.* Tucson: University of Arizona Press, 1997.
Vaughan, Mary K., and Stephen E. Lewis, eds. *The Eagle and the Virgin: Nation and Cultural Revolution in Mexico, 1920–1940.* Durham, NC: Duke University Press, 2006.

Chapter 3

FIRST CONCERTS ON THE INTERNATIONAL STAGE
The British Comebacks of the Vienna and Berlin Philharmonics in 1947/48

Friedemann Pestel

Two Orchestras after World War II

Starting in the late nineteenth century, orchestral tours have become a major part of international musical life[1]. Among the European, US, and later Asian ensembles first touring around Europe and the Americas, and after 1945 increasingly on a global scale, the Berlin and Vienna Philharmonics took leading roles. With their artistic prestige, their frequency and scope of touring, and the reach of international audiences both through concerts and records, they set standards for twentieth-century musical performance. Yet perhaps the most distinctive feature of their international presence was its continuity in the face of the political ruptures of the twentieth century. This observation holds particularly true for periods of war, dictatorship, and postwar transitions. During World War I, the two orchestras toured until 1918 and resumed their international activities as early as 1920/21; after World War II, their absence from the international stage between 1944 and 1947/48 lasted only slightly longer.[2]

    Nevertheless, the musical *sorties de guerre* after 1918 and 1945 also differed. Touring in the aftermath of World War I had been marked by the persistence of cultural mobilization and immediate continuities with wartime patterns. The Berlin Philharmonic undertook its

---

Notes for this section begin on page 72.

first tours in the early 1920s to Denmark, Sweden, and Switzerland, counting on the demand for concerts in these neutral countries that had been main targets of German wartime propaganda. The fact that chief conductor Arthur Nikisch, at very short notice, removed works by French composers from the 1920 Copenhagen programs in order to protest against the deployment of Black French occupation forces from Senegal in Frankfurt, however, highlights the persistent politicization of music making.[3] Cultural demobilization was still years ahead.[4] For the Vienna Philharmonic, the end of World War I marked above all a postimperial challenge. As the Philharmonic's tours to Czechoslovakia in 1921 and to Germany from 1924 demonstrate, it was not only Austria's bleak economic postwar situation that made the musicians look for lucrative performances abroad; these tours also triggered debates about Austria's political and cultural orientation after the breakdown of the Habsburg monarchy.

For the period after World War II, musical continuities have importantly been emphasized for German and Austrian domestic musical life. In that light, the trope of a "zero hour," paving the teleological way from the abyss of National Socialism, war, and destruction, to a new order arising from the rubble or marking a turning point between disillusion, void, and openness of the future, needs to be taken as a temporal construct and retrospective narrative.[5] This observation also applies for the Berlin and Vienna Philharmonics, which gave their first "postwar" concerts at home a few short weeks after their last "wartime" appearances—in the case of the Vienna Philharmonic, even under the same conductor, Clemens Krauss. Studies on the music politics of the occupation forces have demonstrated the extent to which cultural engineering and reeducation programs of the Allies relied on the persistent prestige of Austro-German musical institutions and canon that, despite the defeat in war, asserted their standing.[6] The temporary interruption of touring after 1945 related to the different postwar situations in Central Europe. Denazification, occupation, and transportation difficulties impeded musical mobility, as did the Berlin Philharmonic's massive wartime presence in occupied countries such as France where it gave its last touring concert "abroad" in June 1944. The orchestra's international comeback in Britain in 1948, therefore, resulted from a postwar private charity initiative but was catalyzed by early Cold War confrontation when the Soviet blockade of West Berlin increased the political relevance of a tour to the West.[7] In the case of the Vienna Philharmonic, in contrast, international planning resumed as early as 1945. However, a significant number of orchestral members' involvement with National Socialism created considerable obstacles. Whereas about 20 percent of their Berlin colleagues had joined the Nazi Party and those remaining after 1945 had already been denazified before they returned to the international stage, the Vienna Philharmonic counted almost 50 percent former Nazi Party members in its ranks. If they had all been dismissed, the orchestra would no longer have been able to perform.[8] It took until spring 1947 for the occupation powers to grant travel permissions for concerts in Switzerland and France; yet it was its appearance in Britain that marked the Vienna Philharmonic's actual international comeback some months later.

Based on material from the orchestras' archives, the personal papers of conductors, and other collections, this chapter presents a comparative view of the Vienna and Berlin Philharmonics' "first concerts" with Bruno Walter and Wilhelm Furtwängler on the international stage in Edinburgh and London respectively. The concept of "first concerts" is borrowed from musicologist Matthias Pasdzierny who builds upon the category of "first letters" developed by literary exile studies to describe how émigrés resumed correspondences with their homelands after the end of the war. Reappearing on the musical stages they had had to leave after 1933/38 provided Jewish and political emigrants returning to Central Europe after National Socialism with a central means of communication for ending their exile or, at least, reestablishing professional connections and performance occasions in German-speaking musical life.[9] In this chapter, I expand Pasdzierny's concept of first concerts to international musical relations in order to demonstrate that the entanglements between musical mobility, political exile, and remigration also gained relevance beyond domestic contexts of music making. Given the high interest in the international appearances of two European orchestral flagships during but also before and after the war, the Vienna and Berlin Philharmonics' international comebacks serve as a case in point for this constellation. In the following sections, I discuss the political dimensions of music-making alongside the orchestras' and their conductors' dealings with the National Socialist past, as well as strategies of depoliticization relating to ideas of reconciliation or music's alleged autonomy from its political contexts. Against more traditional understandings of state-centered cultural diplomacy focusing on bilateral musical relations, I argue here that the spatial frameworks of musical practices between national self-affirmation and universalist Europeanizing or even global discourses provided the basis for a broad range of meanings ascribed to these concerts by the organizers, performers, journalists, and audiences.

The most important conveyors of these multiple meanings were musical "tandems," which Pasdzierny, with regard to postwar Germany, has defined as postwar "alliances of returnees and those who had stayed home."[10] From the transnational perspective of touring, I invert these tandem relations: I look at musical intermediators who, as Jewish émigrés, political exiles, or national wartime heroes, had impacted concert life beyond the National Socialist sphere of influence. On the international stage, they collaborated with those politically compromised musical actors who sought to rehabilitate their reputations and resume their international careers leaving behind their international isolation or association with Nazi propaganda. By their trajectories of exclusion and persecution, political commitment, and humanitarian self-understanding, (r)émigrés used their moral authority and political integrity as symbolic capital in favor of their German and Austrian musical partners. The Vienna Philharmonic built tandem relations with conductor Bruno Walter, the figurehead of musical emigration, and concert manager Rudolf Bing, who in his British exile had cofounded the Glyndebourne Festival in 1933 and then became the director of the newly established Edinburgh International Festival in 1947.[11] The Berlin Philharmonic relied on the intermediation by Furtwängler's London-based former secretary Bertha Geissmar as well as religious activist John Collins and pianist Myra Hess, an icon of British wartime musical life.

The availability of tandem partners, the presence of musical émigrés, and the continuous performance of Austro-German compositions during the war by the Allied powers was one set of factors that accounts for Britain's pivotal role in postwar musical transitions.[12] Moreover, Britain had neither been an immediate target of Nazi propaganda, let alone occupation, nor suffered war destruction to an extent that severely affected postwar musical life. This constellation made it one of the few destinations in the realm of the Western Allies that could be reached relatively easily in terms of transportation (unlike the United States), was democratic (unlike Spain or Portugal), did not present the risk of political protests (unlike France, the Benelux states, or Scandinavia with still-fresh memories of German occupation[13]), and provided private support as well as public demand for concerts. Finally, both the Vienna and the Berlin Philharmonics were well known in Britain. They had made lasting impressions among British audiences, musical brokers, and administrators with their regular visits between the late 1920s and 1938 that could be reactivated one decade—and one world war—later.[14] Against such long-term patterns, this chapter also discusses the extent to which musical tandems provided new impulses for international musical life beyond their attempts at depoliticization in a period usually characterized as musically and socially conservative and oriented toward the past.[15] It concludes by an outlook toward another transition: from postwar to Cold War touring, from European to intercontinental musical mobility, and from pacifying tandem relations to open political protest.

"A Chapter of World History"? The Vienna Philharmonic and Bruno Walter at the 1947 Edinburgh Festival

It took the Vienna Philharmonic four months after the end of World War II to reconnect with Bruno Walter, the conductor with whom they had the longest lasting collaboration and who had been one of the last to conduct them before the Anschluss in 1938. After 1945, Walter was the major hope for the self-administrating orchestra to facilitate the musicians' return to the international stage in the name of "newly resurrected Austria."[16] In fact, he was one of the few internationally renowned conductors who did not refuse to work with the orchestra in its present state, like Arturo Toscanini, or was not politically compromised, as were most conductors who had remained and performed in the German Reich until the end of the war. To convince Walter to accept leading an international tour, the Viennese musicians affirmed the relationship by awarding him a medal that his more politically malleable colleagues such as Karl Böhm, Wilhelm Furtwängler, Hans Knappertsbusch, Clemens Krauss, and Richard Strauss had already received at the orchestra's centenary in 1942.[17]

The orchestra's representatives and members who had been persecuted by the Nazi regime put particular emphasis on the apology of the musicians' misconduct: "Your deep human feelings will also understand those colleagues who, out of pure idealism, fell prey to the heterodoxy of National Socialism."[18] Such statements are remarkable as they give proof of the strong sense of cohesion inside the Vienna Philharmonic despite different political attitudes and highly contrasting experiences under the Nazi regime. They reflect at least three dimensions of collaboration within the orchestra: the shared Austrian victimization myth I will further elaborate; the musicians' identification with the Vienna Philharmonic as an institution and its long-standing tradition; and their shared economic interest in promoting the orchestra as well as possible in Austria and abroad in order to secure and increase their personal incomes. As this chapter demonstrates, Walter adopted this depoliticizing interpretation on the part of the orchestra, thereby depoliticizing the musicians' international reappearance on his part.

Moreover, the Vienna Philharmonic took great care officially to reinvite Walter before Furtwängler, with whom they had been closely collaborating after the Anschluss, in order not to cast doubt on their political sincerity as the former refused to share the podium with colleagues tainted with "Nazi relations."[19] During his exile, Walter had been turned by international audiences and media into the figurehead of musical emigration, but he only rarely made explicit political statements.[20] Also in 1947, he refrained from commenting on the Vienna Philharmonic's role during National Socialism, but quickly agreed "to give proof of my disposition in full view of the public."[21] He was implying the international public, not the Austrian public, as he only consented to conduct the orchestra on tour but not yet in Vienna.

For this musical tandem, the inaugural Edinburgh Festival provided the ideal stage. In Edinburgh, not only did director Rudolf Bing build on his previous experiences at the Glyndebourne Festival, which had been a joint venture of British arts patrons and German exiles, but he also took inspiration from the Salzburg Festival, the Vienna Philharmonic's traditional summer residence since 1922 and one of Walter's major pre-Anschluss conducting venues.[22] The Viennese-born Bing was convinced that "the presence of Bruno Walter on the podium would in itself denazify the Vienna Philharmonic and guarantee against any kind of political demonstration."[23] With his political integrity and professional expertise, he also could fully justify the participation of an Austrian orchestra as a symbol of newly established international cultural relations, spiritual uplift, and European civilization that since the final phase of the war had been at the core of the ideas discussed for the Edinburgh Festival. He demonstrated this openness by simultaneously inviting the French Orchestre Colonne.

Turning Edinburgh into "the cultural resort of Europe" was also compatible with British and Scottish initiatives of arts promotion in the immediate postwar period and the development of tourism.[24] The Edinburgh Festival profited from the arts support program of Clement Attlee's Labor government. Building on wartime initiatives for public art sponsorship, the government attempted to make culture accessible to broader audiences and to integrate it into the postwar welfare state complementing previous forms of private patronage and commercial enterprise by state subsidies. The British

Arts Council, whose first chair was no other than John Maynard Keynes, was set up parallel to the Edinburgh Festival and provided a substantial grant for the first festival. Given Britain's bleak postwar economic situation, the ongoing food rationing, and the austerity measures taken by the government in other sectors, these attempts toward nationalization and democratization of culture as British strategies of postwar transition were all the more remarkable.[25] The same holds true for the decision to have the quality standards of these new cultural ambitions displayed by the Vienna Philharmonic in Edinburgh and immediately afterward by guest performances of the Vienna State Opera—whose orchestra is made up of the same musicians—in London.

The constellation between the Vienna Philharmonic, Bruno Walter, and the Edinburgh Festival helped by the British occupation authorities in Austria, which facilitated traveling and relations with Whitehall, proved to be politically efficient even before the Edinburgh concerts and the London opera performances. It helped downplay protests from Austrian exiles, left-wing politicians, and the British Musicians' Union, which denounced the predatory competition with foreign musicians as well as the appearances of dozens of former Nazi Party members in Britain.[26] In a parliamentary inquiry, Foreign Minister Ernest Bevin deflected this criticism by referring to the official denazification process operated by the Austrian government, and Prime Minister Attlee cited Walter's agreement to conduct the orchestra as sufficient proof of the orchestra's political integrity.[27]

Moreover, the Vienna Philharmonic counted on the favorable effect that inviting the Jewish cellist Friedrich Buxbaum to play with them in Edinburgh would have on the British audience. Excluded from the orchestra in 1938, Buxbaum had been, as a member of the long-standing Rosé Quartet, an important figure of musical émigré life in London.[28] It was, however, in terms of repertoire that the Vienna Philharmonic and Walter made their most strategic choices: the first set of a series of six concerts opened with Ralph Vaughan Williams's *Fantasia on a Theme by Thomas Tallis* as reference to their hosts and continued with Beethoven's *Pastoral* Symphony as a symbol of Austria's regained national independence.[29] To the Queen consort, who attended this performance, Walter readily explained that the Vienna Philharmonic played it so well because the musicians knew exactly which brook in Heiligenstadt had given Beethoven the inspiration for the symphony.[30] All the other works played in Edinburgh could be presented as specifically Viennese as well—from late Haydn (with a side-glimpse to Britain) to Schubert and Johann

Strauß—though all of these composers had also prominently figured in the repertoire during National Socialism as well as the decades before.[31] Therefore, the most distinctive piece was Gustav Mahler's *Das Lied von der Erde*. Bruno Walter, as Mahler's former student and assistant, had posthumously premiered it in 1911. With regard to the Vienna Philharmonic, Mahler's work marked the most explicit break with Nazi musical politics as Mahler had been one of the pivotal targets facing stigmatization as "degenerated" music.[32] The fact that the solo parts sung in the original German were taken over by two leading British singers, contralto Kathleen Ferrier and tenor Peter Pears, made a further contribution to a credible performance of postwar reconciliation through music.[33]

The Viennese musicians together with the festival organizers used the Edinburgh concerts as a demonstration of musical normality and a return to prewar musical mobility. The listeners even rose without hesitation from their seats for the new Austrian national anthem, although Britain had not yet concluded formal peace with Austria.[34] The experiences of National Socialism, war, exclusion, and exile were completely silenced or turned into the formulistic discourse of reconciliation. At the first reunion with Walter, clarinetist Alfred Boskovsky—the orchestra's vice chairman—declared, "This human and artistic connection was only seemingly interrupted by the tremors of a transforming world, and with you we will prove in Edinburgh to the entire world that the arts can build a bridge across all the separations of the past for the understanding of humankind for a better future."[35]

Given the orchestra's and its musicians' involvement with National Socialism, it is hardly surprising that the Vienna Philharmonic turned into an ardent promoter of the postwar Austrian victimization myth.[36] Already during the war, Austrian exile groups had lobbied the Allied powers to consider Austria "Hitler's first victim" rather than a major responsible actor.[37] Yet Bruno Walter in Edinburgh went much further than lending his humanist goodwill to the orchestra's attempts at re-internationalization and the festival's Europeanizing program. His participation allowed for evoking National Socialist persecution and emigration of individual musicians, but largely left aside the orchestra's active involvement in Nazi cultural politics.[38] Informed in detail about the orchestra members' individual dealings with the Nazi regime, Walter not only rejected any critical question by journalists but fully embraced the orchestra's depoliticizing rhetoric downplaying his own career break after 1938.[39] At the end of the festival, Walter made two influential statements that were widely circulated. To the Vienna Philharmonic, he made a patriotic declaration that the orchestra used as proof of its international rehabilitation: "Do you know what happened in these weeks, what you have achieved? A chapter of world history! . . . You have accomplished a very great mission. You have demonstrated to Edinburgh and the world that Vienna is alive and cannot perish."[40] Along with this statement, he sent an open letter to Austrian president Karl Renner, which was no less explicit in his apology for National Socialism:

> I am convinced that Austria's world reputation in the field of music . . . is now re-established. And the fact that the Philharmonic, throughout the terrible events of the last decade—dangers, sufferings, and deprivations in wartime and postwar times—could maintain itself at the top musical level is a praiseworthy artistic and moral accomplishment that was recognized in England with true enthusiasm.[41]

Not only did Walter instrumentalize the British audience, including the Queen consort, for the political clearing of Austria's name, but, from the background of his transatlantic career, he also spoke politically for the Western world in general, particularly as his allusion to wartime and postwar deprivations served the Austrian self-image of being the double victim of Nazi annexation and postwar occupation by the Allies.[42] Inasmuch as this "chapter of world history" took place in Edinburgh, it was nevertheless compatible with the festival's—and in a broader sense, the British—struggle for postwar international radiance, albeit different from Austrian oblivion.

The Vienna Philharmonic happily used Walter's cooperation for their own purposes. Against persistent reproaches about the orchestra's insufficient denazification from Austria's political left, chairman Rudolf Hanzl, a bassoonist, mobilized the orchestra's "mission" in Edinburgh for closing the ranks in favor of Austria's self-promotion as a "cultural great power": "as the representatives of a country that went through all the horrors of war, oppressed by the heaviest economic misery, poor, and bled to death; a country that is nevertheless determined to mobilize all forces to reconquer its previous rank in the field of arts."[43] Moreover, thanks to Walter's efforts in Edinburgh, further lucrative touring invitations for the private orchestra followed abundantly. When their growing absences from the Vienna State Opera, which had had to close for weeks to make the 1947 Edinburgh and London performances possible, caused tensions with Austria's cultural authorities, it was once more Walter who lent his tandem services to influence Austrian cultural diplomacy:

I believe that Austria has nothing more precious to export than its glorious orchestra. Living abroad myself for so long, I can confirm that there still remains a great unspent capital of enthusiasm in the world for Austria as a country of music, and this promises considerable interest for the future when the orchestra as a nationally grown organism can present anew its maximum performance to the cultural world.[44]

After 1947, this cultural capital linked to the Austrian victimization myth quickly turned the Vienna Philharmonic into a major global player that for the most part successfully eluded its National Socialist past. This postwar capital paid off until the Waldheim affair in the 1980s sparked doubts across the globe about Austria's coming to terms with this apparently smooth postwar transition. In 1986 the election of former UN general secretary Kurt Waldheim, who had been a member of the Nazi organization SA (*Sturmabteilung*) and a Wehrmacht officer serving on the Balkans during World War II, as president of Austria led to the country's widespread international isolation. The international debate about Waldheim also put the Vienna Philharmonic's touring activities under strain and contributed to the gradual inquiry of the orchestra's own role during National Socialism.[45]

The Berlin Philharmonic and Wilhelm Furtwängler in London 1948

Whereas the postwar international comeback of the Vienna Philharmonic represented a challenge the self-governing orchestra largely managed by itself, the initial conditions for Berlin Philharmonic were even more complex. As a public body, the former "Reich's Orchestra" extensively traveling around Europe during the war faced considerable political obstacles for restarting its touring activities. Compared to occupied Vienna, the political tensions among the Allies in divided Berlin were much more conflictive culminating in the Soviet blockade of the city in 1948/49. Finally, it seemed hardly imaginable that the Berlin Philharmonic could give its first concerts on the international stage without Wilhelm Furtwängler, its principal conductor for over two decades.

Soon after Furtwängler had returned to the orchestra in May 1947, immediately following his denazification by the Berlin *Spruchkammer* of the Allied Control Council, he made plans for his large-scale international comeback.[46] He turned to his former secretary Bertha Geissmar, who had been working with the London Philharmonic Orchestra since her emigration from Berlin in 1935, to help him get an engagement with them.⁴⁷ Indeed, during the following months, London became a major anchor of Furtwängler's postwar career. After his concerts with the London Philharmonic Orchestra in spring 1948, he returned for a Beethoven symphonies cycle with the Vienna Philharmonic in October. Its overall negative reception among London's music critics suggests that the absence of musical tandem partners made the acceptance of politically compromised figures more difficult, though.⁴⁸ One month later, Furtwängler led the Berlin Philharmonic on a British tour, together with the orchestra's current chief conductor Sergiu Celibidache.⁴⁹

While the Berlin musicians hoped that Furtwängler would reopen the "world" for them,⁵⁰ allowing them to resume the large Western European tours they had undertaken until 1938, Furtwängler was more concerned with the ongoing international allegations of Nazi collaboration against him and his complicated self-understanding as a "German" musician. As a case in point, a Swiss newspaper commented at that time that though Hitler, Goebbels, Göring, and Rosenberg were all dead, Furtwängler had remained.⁵¹ For the Berliners' opening concert in Britain, scheduled at St. Paul's Cathedral, Furtwängler suggested playing Richard Wagner's preludes to *Parsifal* and *Die Meistersinger von Nürnberg*, the adagio from Anton Bruckner's Symphony no. 7, and the funeral march from Wagner's *Götterdämmerung*. This musical combination referred to ideas of mourning and heroism, of national elevation but also of religion and solemnity.⁵² As an artist who fashioned himself as "unpolitical" but whose musical activities had nevertheless become highly politicized and contested, Furtwängler discarded the fact that these pieces had prominently figured in Nazi music politics. Only three years before, the Bruckner adagio and the funeral march had been played by the Hamburg radio station at the news of Hitler's death—probably Furtwängler's own recordings.⁵³

In Furtwängler's view, the London program was not to mark the transfiguration of the Nazi regime but, through the prism of his own career, to reflect Germany's double experience of victimhood and occupation after 1933 and 1945. For publicity of the Berlin Philharmonic British tour, he instructed Geissmar:

> With regard to Germany . . . I defend the following standpoint: as long as the German public sphere in artistic matters largely remains under the dictate of the occupying powers . . . , it is not possible for me to make a substantial contribution to German musical life. Germany was gagged under Hitler, but intellectual Germany understood itself despite the outside terror [from the Nazis]. Today the terror from outside [from the Allies] has not disappeared but simply changed its direction.⁵⁴

Accordingly, for the first concert of a German orchestra among one of the former war enemies, Furtwängler, looking for a program "that also makes a statement on the situation of Germany,"[55] ended up with this peculiar Wagner-Bruckner combination.[56]

The actual tour, however, differed from Furtwängler's nationalist intentions in nearly all respects. This was the result of a changing international political situation as well as the diverging interests of other actors in the musical field. The first shift came about by a new administrative tandem partner for Furtwängler and the Berlin Philharmonic. Instead of Geissmar, it was the theologian John Collins, dean of Oriel College Oxford, who finally took the lead as he was able to provide the tour with an extramusical message. As a social reformer and Anglican activist, he headed the Christian Action movement promoting reconciliation among the war enemies, a revival of Christian values, and European integration.[57]

In its combination of political, moral, and spiritual values, the agenda of Christian Action was not dissimilar to the ideas that had underpinned the foundation of the Edinburgh Festival. It is therefore not surprising that Collins also sought to pursue his agenda through music. At the invitation of the Foreign Office, he traveled through the British occupation zone in Germany in 1947 and, from his experiences in Berlin, decided to invite the Berlin Philharmonic for a British goodwill tour. This clear postwar orientation was, however, largely eclipsed by the Soviet blockade of Berlin from June 1948 shifting the British-German relations from postwar reconciliation to Cold War solidarity. In terms of ideology, this new context fitted well with Christian Action's anticommunist orientation and ideas of Western European integration as put forward by Winston Churchill shortly before. In terms of logistics, however, the blockade of divided Berlin posed considerable problems. Collins planned to transport the musicians on the return flights of the "Candy Bombers" the Western Allies used for the supply of the cut-off Western sectors of the city. The musicians probably were finally transported on former Royal Air Force planes that had been converted for civilian purposes.[58]

The coincidence of a goodwill tour and the military blockade put the project under financial pressure. As Collins had to rely mainly on private donations and wanted to give the profits to "organizations seeking to assist in the rehabilitation of Europe,"[59] he asked the musicians to play without fees; they would only receive travel allowances. This bypassing of the regular musical market provoked again the opposition of the British Musicians' Union fearing that the rising demand for orchestral concerts, while the economic situation in the United Kingdom remained bleak, would lead to fee evasion by inviting cheap foreign orchestras. The Union therefore sarcastically asked whether Christian Action would next import foreign doctors, teachers, journalists, miners, or bus drivers.[60] In view of these discussions, the tour's "German" character as intended by Furtwängler or its "German-British" orientation promoted by Christian Action was further eclipsed.

To emphasize the cause of reconciliation, Collins also imposed a musical tandem partner on Furtwängler—reluctant as he was to having soloists in his concerts. The choice fell on pianist Myra Hess who combined a Jewish background with her wartime reputation as organizer of the National Gallery concerts in Blitz-weary London. She had collaborated with émigré musicians such as former members of the Vienna Philharmonic, and she was a close relation to the Queen consort.[61] To protests in the United States against her appearance with Furtwängler, Hess reacted by stressing the international quality of music: "Either we close off Germany and exterminate the Germans or we find our common ground again through the arts."[62]

When Hess and Furtwängler finally bowed holding hands in front of the thunderous applause of an audience of six to eight thousand people after Beethoven's *Piano Concerto No. 4,* the atmosphere was, however, very different from the setting Collins had originally imagined. Instead of St. Paul's Cathedral where he had been appointed canon, the inaugural concert took place in Empress Hall in Earls Court. The archdeacon had refused to lend the cathedral for a commercial concert, and the tight tour budget did not allow for a concert without a paying audience.[63] Moreover, instead of performing the "situation of Germany," Furtwängler had to abandon Bruckner and Wagner—because the orchestra did not possess enough horn players and was unable to hire extra musicians in a divided Berlin—in favor of Bach and Brahms.[64] Flower decorations, barely hidden microphones, advertisements for skate rental (Empress Hall normally operated as an ice rink), listeners smoking pipes, and staff listening "noncommittally" to Brahms dissipated all pathos imagined—though in very different ways—by Furtwängler and Collins.[65] Postwar deprivation further impacted the concert: the problematic location, as remarked by the German émigré press, was the direct consequence of the destruction of Queen's Hall, London's finest concert venue, by German bombs in 1941.[66] The austere aspect of the Berlin musicians, who by lack of tailcoats had to perform in simple lounge suits, gave rise to public calls that the audience should also refrain from wearing formal evening attire.[67]

Finally, the British reception of the tour was largely void of "German" interpretations as intended by Furtwängler. Though the press attested his "lack of firmness in political matters," his authority "in things musical," well-documented by his London appearances in the 1920s and 1930s, remained undisputed this time.[68] The reconciliatory rhetoric deployed by Christian Action and British government members around the concerts operated on a transnational scale highlighting music as a symbol for "European civilization" or even "world peace" in a clear Cold War optic. Only the remark later made in Liverpool by Minister of Civil Aviation Frank Pakenham that Britain could learn a lot from Germany in the field of music roughly corresponded to ideas of hegemony.[69] Against this de-Germanizing shift, Furtwängler finally refrained from national undertones and grudgingly declared with regard to his own highly mobile postwar career: "I have no permanent place of work. I belong to Europe."[70]

Tandems as Agents of Postwar Musical Mobility: Some Comparisons

Analyzing the two orchestras' first concerts in postwar Britain, this chapter adds the perspective of international reappearances to the rich literature on musical exile, the transition of musical institutions after National Socialism, and the question of émigrés' reappearances or collaborations with musicians and ensembles from Germany and Austria. The concept of "musical tandems" that has so far been discussed in domestic German and Austrian musical life is also relevant for the international stage in two respects. First, while there was no "zero hour" in domestic musical practices in 1945, the resumption of international musical relations and, importantly, international artistic careers posed a more difficult challenge. The musical topographies shifted from hegemonic and coercive performances of German ensembles in Allied, neutral, and occupied countries during the war to the return to former war enemies. For (r)émigrés like Bruno Walter, such international performances provided a third space that allowed them to resume former musical relations without returning immediately to Germany and Austria and exposing themselves politically.

Second, looking at tandem partners operating on the international stage places their personal agency into musical infrastructures. Tandems were not restricted to performing artists but also involved musical administrators like Rudolf Bing and Bertha Geissmar, who, during exile, managed institutions such as festivals that provided career opportunities for émigrés and politically compromised German and Austrian returnees on the international stage as well as new impulses for musical life in their host countries. The postwar and international agenda of the newly founded Edinburgh Festival is a case in point in that regard. Such a broader view further allows for expanding the concept of tandems to local artists with political or humanitarian commitments as well as activists and politicians promoting postwar reconciliation, spiritual renewal, or European integration in all possible combinations.

While both the Vienna and the Berlin Philharmonic profited from establishing tandem relations, the challenges of their international comebacks differed along their internal structures and dealings with National Socialism. For the self-administrating and self-engaging Vienna Philharmonic, the high percentage of party members among their musicians put clear limits to denazification in terms of artistic feasibility. Though a very lenient purification was finally acknowledged by all the occupying powers in Austria, it posed obstacles for international touring, which was nevertheless of vital economic importance for the independent concert orchestra. The Vienna Philharmonic was therefore looking for a tandem partner whose integrity would, at least, shield it from political reproaches and, at best, enhance its international reputation. Bruno Walter adopted this role to the extent that he even turned into an active promoter of the Austrian victimization myth.

In contrast, the Berlin Philharmonic, with a considerably lower number of former party members, feared less the protests against orchestral players. Their major problem consisted in international reservations against Wilhelm Furtwängler, who was still seen as a former musical representative of Nazi Germany. The political debate on Furtwängler did not terminate with his formal denazification by the *Spruchkammer* and his return to both the German and the international stage—and has not yet ended today. The orchestra put their hopes for an international comeback in his artistic reputation. The challenge consisted in setting up a tandem arrangement that depoliticized his appearance with regard to the destination, the repertoire, and the "message" of the tour. In that respect, John Collins's Christian Action initiative was indeed successful, though one might argue that the Berliners' concerts profited from the Soviet blockade of Berlin much more than from charity and the invocation of Christian and European values. As a consequence, the attempt at postwar depoliticization of music-making intertwined with Cold War repoliticization, silencing the debate on National Socialism.

The geopolitical and local contexts of the first concerts abroad therefore highlight the international frameworks in which the postwar transitions of German and Austrian orchestras were embedded, but also provided symbolic resources for legitimizing national interests. The "world" discourse put forward by Walter and the Vienna Philharmonic in Edinburgh served the Austrian victimization myth. The interpretive shift from "the situation of Germany" to "Europe" in the case of the Berlin Philharmonic facilitated postwar musical mobility from a divided city. Moreover, the internationalist musical discourse linked the guest orchestras and their tandem partners to the imperatives of British postwar musical life: the expansion of musical offerings, the state promotion of the arts, and the struggle for international radiance, which would document national musical ambitions alike. The impact of this agenda was confirmed by the protests of the Musicians' Union. According to this union, musical mobility, public subsidies, and music festivals catalyzed competition, financial interests, and expectations of improving the professional status of British musicians.

In that respect, the controversies around the first concerts point both to the exceptionalism and the normalization of postwar international musical life. Certainly, exceptional was the frequent presence of Central European ensembles in Britain in the late 1940s. For the two orchestras, the 1947/48 tours were complemented by the appearances of the Vienna State Opera in 1947, the Vienna Philharmonic's Beethoven cycle in 1948, another residence with Furtwängler in 1949, all in London, and the Berlin Philharmonic's stint at the 1949 Edinburgh Festival to the extent that the press started complaining about the prolonged absences from home.[71] On the side of musical demand, the orchestras largely profited from the revival and reorganization of British musical life, which made postwar musical transitions a shared Austro-German-British endeavor. On the side of musical offerings, Britain's prominence as a tour destination is indicative for prewar continuities and the lack of alternatives related both to postwar isolation and Cold War confrontation.[72]

Outlook and Conclusion: The Limits of Political Rehabilitation in the 1950s

With their comebacks in France, the Benelux states, or West Germany (for the Vienna Philharmonic), the two orchestras, by the early 1950s, reintegrated their British appearances into larger Western European tours as they had done before the war while largely sticking to their canonical repertoire of Austro-German classics. Even more importantly, the Vienna Philharmonic's "world discourse" of 1947 gradually transformed into "world practices"[73] as the orchestras intensified their extra-European presence starting with tours to Egypt in 1950/51 where postwar transition was not a political problem at all.

The long-term rivalry between the Berlin and Vienna Philharmonics that resonated in all these activities finally broke out in their race for the first appearance in North America. While the Vienna Philharmonic, again counting on the Austrian victimization myth, reached out for the US debut as early as in the late 1940s but only managed to realize this project in 1956, the Berlin Philharmonic, after long quarrels around Furtwängler, first arrived in the United States in 1955. A major obstacle of this tour had been solved by Furtwängler's death in 1954 and he was replaced by Herbert von Karajan. Also, the orchestra had secured the services of another tandem partner—the émigré agent André Mertens from Columbia Artists Management. While Karajan fully satisfied American expectations in artistic terms, he, together with the orchestra, nevertheless faced heavy resistance from Jewish, left-wing, and youth activists. As a result of partly critical press coverage, protestors in front of and inside Carnegie Hall and other concert venues largely overshadowed the tour's original purpose as a demonstration of (West) Berlin's reconstruction, a political assertion against the Eastern Bloc, and a gesture of Berlin's and Germany's gratitude for the American airlift of 1948/49.[74] Postwar and Cold War meanings overlapped far more than the orchestra, Karajan, the Berlin officials, and West German diplomats could have wished for. The US debut of the Berliners clearly demonstrated the limits of political rehabilitation in Europe and the risks of not appearing with a respected tandem authority on the stage.

The Vienna Philharmonic, on their turn, were in a similarly difficult position. With Furtwängler and finally Karajan not being available for them, they finally opted for Carl Schuricht and André Cluytens as conductors—certainly no active tandem partners, but hardly politically suspicious in American eyes though little known to American audiences either. As a consequence, the public impact of the Vienna Philharmonic concerts remained somewhat muted. However, the actual political risk for the orchestra emerged behind the scenes. Before the tour, the orchestra had largely rejected pension claims from their former Jewish musicians who had been excluded in 1938 and by majority then emigrated to the United States. Some of these former members now pressured their former colleagues to divulge unpleasant details about the orchestra's dealings with National Socialism to the American public on the occasion of the tour in case their financial claims were further ignored. Once in America, the orchestra gave in, paid compensation to their emigrated former colleagues, and the tour went smoothly in that respect.[75]

Such cases illustrate how much it is worth looking for the long-term effects of postwar musical transitions. The awareness of musical actors for tandem constellations, the (non)availability of these partners, and their reception extended beyond the first concerts, strictly speaking. Since the international postwar return of German and Austrian orchestras, which, at first, led them back mostly to destinations where they already had performed before the war, passed into intercontinental touring and thereby a new phase of globalizing musical mobility, new challenges emerged. A successful comeback in Britain would, therefore, not safeguard uncontested first concerts in the United States whereas debuts in Egypt or, shortly afterward, in Japan eluded the question of the National Socialist and wartime past. Nevertheless, just as international careers, both of individual artists and orchestras, lasted a long time, so did the controversies about them. The Vienna Philharmonic faced new criticism when the Austrian victimization myth crumbled in the 1980s following the globalizing junctures of world war and Holocaust memory; Herbert von Karajan's American career remained limited and performances in Israel were out of the question throughout his life.

Such divergences, incongruencies, and contingencies were characteristic for global classical musical life in the second half of the twentieth century. Therefore, not all initiators, participants, and profiteers of postwar musical mobility welcomed these transitions, but nevertheless had to cope with them as inevitable challenges of their postwar trajectories. After Furtwängler, starting with his British comeback in 1948, had re-Europeanized his career, had made his debut in Latin America, and was yearningly looking for an occasion to return to North America that would never materialize, he noted in his diary in 1951:

> In times of increased communication, tours by whole orchestras have become frequent. . . . Whether such tours are to be welcomed as an enrichment of musical life or to be deplored as externalism or dispersion remains a question in itself. At any rate, they represent the course of our time; we have to reckon with them.[76]

And such reckoning, we might add from the perspective of musical mobility, included the whole spectrum between artistic affirmation and political rejection.

Friedemann Pestel is an assistant professor in modern European history at Albert-Ludwigs-Universität Freiburg. He is currently completing a history of global tours of German and Austrian symphony orchestras in the twentieth century. He was a research fellow at the German Historical Institutes in Paris and London and at the University of Vienna. His research interests and publications include the French and Haitian Revolutions, political migration, the history of classical musical life in the nineteenth and twentieth centuries, and memory studies. He has published two books: *Weimar als Exil. Erfahrungsräume französischer Revolutionsemigranten 1792–1803* and *Kosmopoliten wider Willen. Die monarchiens als Revolutionsemigranten.*

Notes

1. I am indebted to the Baden-Württemberg Stiftung for the financial support of this research, and I would like to thank Anna Karla and the anonymous reviewers for their comments on this chapter.
2. On the two orchestras, see Haffner, *Berliner Philharmoniker*; Hellsberg, *Demokratie der Könige*; Trümpi, *Political Orchestra*. For concert details, I rely on the databases provided by the *Historisches Archiv der Wiener Philharmoniker* (HA WPh) and the *Archiv der Berliner Philharmoniker* (ABPh). The touring activities of German and Austrian orchestras throughout the twentieth century are the subject of my book project *Global Players: Orchestral Tours and International Musical Life, 1880–2000*, from which the following examples are taken.
3. *Social-Demokraten*, 16 May 1920.
4. On this concept, see Horne, "Demobilizing the Mind;" Guerpin, "*Le Courrier musical*."
5. Sabrow, "Die "Stunde Null' als Zeiterfahrung."
6. Gerhard, "'Vorherrschaft der deutschen Musik' nach 1945"; Janik, *Recomposing German Music*; Monod, *Settling Scores*; Thacker, *Music after Hitler*; Linsenmann, *Musik als politischer Faktor*; Gienow-Hecht, "Culture and the Cold War in Europe," 407; Anderton, *Rubble Music*.
7. On Britain and the Berlin crisis, see Mauer, *Brückenbauer*.
8. Mayrhofer and Trümpi, *Orchestrierte Vertreibung*, 204–22; Rathkolb, "Austriakischer Kulturexport," and "Notes on the 'Denazification.'" For the Berlin Philharmonic, see Aster, *Reichsorchester*, 12.
9. Pasdzierny, *Wiederaufnahme?*, 226; Kettler, "'Erste Briefe' nach Deutschland."
10. Pasdzierny, *Wiederaufnahme?*, 444–47. All translations are my own.
11. Jolliffe, *Glyndebourne*, 15–44.
12. Raab Hansen, *NS-verfolgte Musiker in England*; Morris, "Battle for Music."
13. As an overview, see Levi and Fanning, *Music under German Occupation*.
14. Pestel, "'Ein Programm,'" 161–62; Raab Hansen, "Internierung – Bombardierung – Rekrutierung."
15. Glaser, *Kulturgeschichte*, 247–60; Müller, "Ein fehlender Neuanfang;" Eickhoff, "'Mit Sozialismus und Sachertorte'"; Bartie, *Edinburgh Festivals*, 13–17 and 43–70.
16. Fritz Sedlak to Bruno Walter, Vienna, 30 August 1945 and 21 April 1946 (for the quotation), New York Public Library (NYPL) ZB-2677, reel 10, 620; Rathkolb, "Kulturelle Entnazifizierung."

17. Gottfried von Freiberg to Walter, Vienna, 7 January 1947, NYPL ZB-2677, reel 4, 258; Rathkolb, "Honors and Awards," 6.
18. Freiberg to Walter, Vienna, 4 January 1947, NYPL ZB-2677, reel 10, 620; Karl Maurer to Walter, Vienna, 7 January 1947, ibid.
19. Meeting of the Vienna Philharmonic's administrative committee, 2 May 1947, HA WPh A-Pr-31; Walter to Bing, 26 March 1946, quoted from Shirakawa, *The Devil's Music Master*, 306; Ryding and Pechefsky, *Bruno Walter*, 324.
20. Langenbruch, *Topographien*, 175–87.
21. Walter to Freiberg and Maurer, New York, 17 February 1947, NYPL ZB-2677, reel 10, 620.
22. Bing, *5,000 Nights*, 70; Ryding and Pechefsky, *Bruno Walter*, 311.
23. Bing, *5,000 Nights*, 89.
24. Quotation by John Falconer, the Lord Provost of Edinburgh, in Bartie, *Edinburgh Festivals*, 23; on the Edinburgh Festival, see also Miller, *Edinburgh International Festival 1947–1996*, 1–13.
25. Judt, *Postwar*, 161–63; Bartie, *Edinburgh Festivals*, 8–11 and 26–30; Ehrlich, *First Philharmonic*, 218–19.
26. Austrian Embassy London to Bundeskanzleramt/Auswärtige Angelegenheiten, London, 26 July 1947, Österreichisches Staatsarchiv/Archiv der Republik Vienna (ÖStA/AdR), BKA/AA Abteilung Kultur 1947 7; HA WPh, folder Großbritannien 1947.
27. See the minutes from the parliamentary debate on 23 July 1947 in ÖStA/AdR BKA AA Abteilung Kultur 1947 7; for Attlee, Mayrhofer and Trümpi, *Orchestrierte Vertreibung*, 108; see also the correspondence on the orchestra in the National Archives, Kew (TNA), F.O. 1020/591E.
28. Mayrhofer and Trümpi, *Orchestrierte Vertreibung*, 102–10; Brinson, "'Ein Stück wahrer Kultur"; Levi, "'Those Damn Foreigners,'" 95–96; *The Scotsman*, 9 September 1947. The orchestra formally reinvited all their surviving émigrés to return into its ranks in 1946, but none of them did so.
29. For favorable reactions, see *The Times*, 17 September 1947.
30. *The Scotsman*, 10 September 1947; Boskovsky and Hanzl, *Wiener Philharmoniker*, 10.
31. On the routines of musical life between Central Europe, exile, and the destination countries, see Stahrenberg, "'Such occasions form a poignant link with the past,'" 270–71.
32. Tellingly, Wilhelm Furtwängler refused to conduct this work for his international comeback with the London Philharmonic Orchestra in 1948 as he judged it unattractive for shining as a conductor; Furtwängler to Bertha Geissmar, 22 October 1947, Staatsbibliothek Preußischer Kulturbesitz Berlin (SPK) 55 Nachl 13/A, box 14.
33. *The Scotsman*, 12 September 1947.
34. Hanzl, "Unsere Reise nach England," 312.
35. Boskovsky and Hanzl, *Wiener Philharmoniker*, 25.
36. See Bischof, "Victims? Perpetrators?"; Uhl, "From Victim Myth to Co-Responsibility Thesis."
37. Richard Dove, "Einleitung," 10.
38. *New York Times*, 10 September 1947.
39. Allied Control Authority/Social Administration Division to Walter, 4 August 1947, HA WPh Nachlass Hanzl 4.1; Hanzl, "Unsere Reise nach England," 313.
40. Boskovsky and Hanzl, *Wiener Philharmoniker*, 32.
41. Walter to Karl Renner, Lugano, 20 September 1947, in *Wiener Zeitung*, 28 September 1947.

42. See Lehnguth, *Waldheim und die Folgen*, 61–62.
43. Hanzl, "Unsere Reise nach England," 312. On Austrian identity-building through music after 1945, see Szabó-Knotik, "Mythos Musik in Österreich"; idem; "Selbstinszenierung und Handelsbilanz."
44. Walter to Rudolf Hanzl, Vienna, 12 May 1948, HA WPh A-Briefe W/10.
45. Pestel, "'Special Years'?," 258–59.
46. On Furtwängler's career during National Socialism, which was not without problems in evaluating his role, Prieberg, *Trial of Strength*; Roncigli, "Wilhelm Furtwängler."
47. Geissmar, *The Baton and the Jackboot*.
48. *Daily Mail*, 29 September 1948; *The Times*, 29 September 1948; *Spectator*, 1 and 8 October 1948.
49. Furtwängler, after stepping down from his leadership position during the Hindemith affair, would only resume his full duties in 1952. In November 1934 the conductor had taken Paul Hindemith's defense after the latter's opera *Mathis der Maler* had been banned by the Nazis. Considering Furtwängler's interference as politically inadmissible, the Propaganda Ministry urged his resignation from all his offices, in particular the Berlin Philharmonic, the Berlin State Opera, and the Reich Music Chamber; see Kater, *The Twisted Muse*, 24–25; Haffner, *Furtwängler*, 105–8.
50. Ernst Fuhr and Ernst Fischer (representatives of the orchestra) to Furtwängler, Berlin, 14 July 1948, SPK 55 Nachl 13/A, box 4.
51. *Tagblatt der Stadt Zürich*, 5 June 1948.
52. Furtwängler to Geissmar, Salzburg, 30 July 1948, SPK 55 Nachl 13/A, box 14.
53. *Daily Mail*, 2 May 1945; Fischer, "Wagner-Interpretation im Dritten Reich," 146; Müller, "E- und U-Musik im Zweiten Weltkrieg?," 188. For Furtwängler's intellectual self-understanding Allen, *Wilhelm Furtwängler*.
54. Furtwängler to Geissmar, Clarens, 16 September 1948, SPK 55 Nachl 13/A, box 14.
55. Furtwängler to Geissmar, Salzburg, 30 July 1948, SPK 55 Nachl 13/A, box 14; see also Pestel, "Ein Programm."
56. Furtwängler to Geissmar, Salzburg, 30 July 1948, ibid.; see also Pestel, "Ein Programm."
57. Collins, *Partners in Protest*; program notes Berlin Philharmonic, London, 3 November 1948, ABPh Programme.
58. Allen, *Wilhelm Furtwängler*, X; Collins, *Partners in Protest*, 160–68; Haffner, *Berliner Philharmoniker*, 161; travel diary by oboist Helmut Schlövogt, 28 October 1948, ABPh G Schlö 4 Reisekalender; Kostka, "Mehr als nur der 'Juniorpartner.'"
59. John Collins to Frank Pakenham, Oxford, 17 November 1947, TNA F.O. 938/913.
60. *Die Welt*, 4 November 948; *National-Zeitung, Berlin*, 4 November 1948; *Der Tagesspiegel*, 5 November 1948; *Neue Rheinische Zeitung*, 6 November 1948; *Musical Express*, 12 November 1948; Ehrlich, *First Philharmonic*, 221.
61. McKenna, *Myra Hess*; Allen, *Wilhelm Furtwängler*, XI; Geissmar to Furtwängler, London, 4 July 1948, SPK 55 Nachl 13/A, box 16.
62. McKenna, *Myra Hess*, 225.
63. *Glasgow Herald*, 5 November 1948; Collins, *Partners in Protest*, 188; Christian Action to Cyril Jones, TNA F.O. 936/1279. In fact, the Berlin blockade created an unforeseen deficit.
64. Fuhr and Fischer to Furtwängler, Berlin, 23 August 1948, SPK 55 Nachl 13/A, box 4.
65. Charles Stuart, "Berlin Philharmonic," *The Observer*, n.d., ABPh Presse 1948; *New York Times*, 4 November 1948.

66. *Aufbau*, 24 December 1948.
67. *Northern Daily Mail*, 2 November 1948; *Glasgow Bulletin*, 3 November 1948.
68. *News Review*, 11 November 1948.
69. *Manchester Guardian*, 8 November 1948; *Das Musikleben*, December 1948; see also *Frankfurter Neue Presse*, 6 November 1948; "Forming Bonds of Friendship," *Liverpool Post*, n.d., ABPh Presse 1948.
70. *News Review*, 11 November 1948.
71. See, for example, *Weltpresse*, Vienna, 12 October 1949.
72. In the interwar period, Britain was, by far, the Berlin Philharmonic's most important touring destination (fifty-one concerts). Also for the Vienna Philharmonic, Britain, together with France, ranked on top (twelve concerts in each country).
73. On this distinction, see Osterhammel, "'Welteroberndes Künstlertum.'"
74. Haffner, *Berliner Philharmoniker*, 179–89; Jonathan Rosenberg, *Dangerous Melodies*, 259–70.
75. Mayrhofer and Trümpi, *Orchestrierte Vertreibung*, 236–67.
76. Furtwängler, *Aufzeichnungen*, 322.

Bibliography

Allen, Roger. *Wilhelm Furtwängler: Art and the Politics of the Unpolitical.* Woodbridge: Boydell Press, 2018.

Anderton, Abby. *Rubble Music: Occupying the Ruins of Postwar Berlin, 1945–1950.* Bloomington: Indiana University Press, 2019.

Aster, Misha. *Das Reichsorchester: Die Berliner Philharmoniker und der Nationalsozialismus.* Munich: Siedler, 2007.

Bartie, Angela. *The Edinburgh Festivals: Culture and Society in Postwar Britain.* Edinburgh: Edinburgh University Press, 2013.

Bing, Rudolf. *5,000 Nights at the Opera.* London: Hamilton, 1972.

Bischof, Günter. "Victims? Perpetrators? 'Punching Bags' of European Historical Memory? The Austrians and Their World War II Legacies." *German Studies Review* 27, no. 1 (2004): 17–32.

Boskovsky, Alfred, and Rudolf Hanzl. *Die Wiener Philharmoniker – ein Stück Weltgeschichte: Edinburgh – London 1947.* Vienna: Wiener Philharmoniker, 1947.

Brinson, Charmian. "'Ein Stück wahrer Kultur, ein Stück Wien, ein Stück Leben': Das Austrian Centre und die Musik." In *Wien-London, hin und retour: Das Austrian Centre in London 1939 bis 1947*, edited by Marietta Bearman, 148–74. Vienna: Czernin, 2004.

Collins, Diana. *Partners in Protest: Life with Canon Collins.* London: Gollancz, 1992.

Dove, Richard. "Einleitung," in *Wien-London, hin und retour: Das Austrian Centre in London 1939 bis 1947*, edited by Marietta Bearman, 9–13. Vienna: Czernin, 2004.

Ehrlich, Cyril. *First Philharmonic: A History of the Royal Philharmonic Society.* Oxford: Clarendon Press, 1995.

Eickhoff, Thomas. "'Mit Sozialismus und Sachertorte . . .' – Entnazifizierung und musikpolitische Verhaltensmuster nach 1945 in Österreich." In *Deutsche Leitkultur Musik?: Zur Musikgeschichte nach dem Holocaust*, edited by Albrecht Riethmüller, 85–99. Stuttgart: F. Steiner, 2006.

Fischer, Jens Malte. "Wagner-Interpretation im Dritten Reich: Musik und Szene zwischen Politisierung und Kunstanspruch." In *Richard Wagner im Dritten Reich: Ein Schloss Elmau-Symposion*, edited by Saul Friedländer and Jörn Rüsen, 142–64. Munich: C.H. Beck, 2000.

Furtwängler, Wilhelm. *Aufzeichnungen 1924–1954*. Mainz: Schott, 2009.

Geissmar, Bertha. *The Baton and the Jackboot*. London: Hamilton, 1944.

Gerhard, Anselm. "Die 'Vorherrschaft der deutschen Musik' nach 1945 – eine Ironie der Geschichte." In *Deutsche Leitkultur Musik? Zur Musikgeschichte nach dem Holocaust*, edited by Albrecht Riethmüller, 13–27. Stuttgart: F. Steiner, 2006.

Gienow-Hecht, Jessica. "Culture and the Cold War in Europe." In *The Cambridge History of the Cold War*. Vol. 1: Origins, edited by Melvyn P. Leffler and Odd A. Westad, 398–419. Cambridge: Cambridge University Press, 2011.

Glaser, Hermann. *Die Kulturgeschichte der Bundesrepublik Deutschland. Vol. 2. Zwischen Grundgesetz und Großer Koalition 1949–1967*. Munich: Fischer Taschenbuch Verlag, 1990.

Guerpin, Martin. "*Le Courrier musical* et le premier conflit mondial (1904–1923). Propagande, mobilisation culturelle et sortie de guerre." *Revue musicale OICRM* 4, no. 2 (2017): 35–57.

Haffner, Herbert. *Die Berliner Philharmoniker: Eine Biografie*. Mainz: Schott, 2007.

———. *Furtwängler*. Berlin: Parthas, 2006.

Hanzl, Rudolf. "Unsere Reise nach England." *Österreichische Musikzeitschrift* 2 (1947): 312–14.

Hellsberg, Clemens. *Demokratie der Könige: Die Geschichte der Wiener Philharmoniker*. Zurich; Schott, 1992.

Horne, John. "Demobilizing the Mind: France and the Legacy of the Great War, 1919–1939." *French History and Civilization* 2 (2009): 101–19.

Janik, Elizabeth. *Recomposing German Music: Politics and Musical Tradition in Cold War Berlin*. Leiden: Brill, 2005.

Jolliffe, John. *Glyndebourne: An Operatic Miracle*. London: John Murray, 1999.

Judt, Tony. *Postwar: A History of Europe since 1945*. New York: Penguin Books, 2005.

Kater, Michael H. *The Twisted Muse: Musicians and Their Music in the Third Reich*. New York: Oxford University Press, 1997.

Kettler, David. "'Erste Briefe' nach Deutschland: Zwischen Exil und Rückkehr." *Zeitschrift für Ideengeschichte* (2008), no. 2: 80–108.

Kostka, Bernd von. "Mehr als nur der 'Juniorpartner': Der Beitrag der zivilen britischen Charterfirmen zum Erfolg der Luftbrücke." In *Die*

Berliner Luftbrücke: Ereignis und Erinnerung, edited by Helmut Trotnow and Bernd von Kostka, 89–98. Berlin: Frank & Timme, 2010.

Langenbruch, Anna. *Topographien musikalischen Handelns im Pariser Exil*. Hildesheim: Georg Olms Verlag, 2014.

Lehnguth, Cornelius. *Waldheim und die Folgen: Der parteipolitische Umgang mit dem Nationalsozialismus in Österreich*. Frankfurt am Main: Campus, 2013.

Levi, Erik. "'Those Damn Foreigners': Xenophobia and British Musical Life during the First Half of the Twentieth Century." In *Twentieth-Century Music and Politics: Essays in Memory of Neil Edmunds*, edited by Pauline Fairclough, 81–96. Farnham, Surrey: Ashgate, 2013.

Levi, Erik, and David Fanning, eds. *The Routledge Handbook to Music under German Occupation, 1938–1945: Propaganda, Myth and Reality*. London: Routledge, 2020.

Linsenmann, Andreas. *Musik als politischer Faktor: Konzepte, Intentionen und Praxis französischer Umerziehungs- und Kulturpolitik in Deutschland 1945–1949/50*. Tübingen: Narr, 2010.

Mauer, Victor. *Brückenbauer: Großbritannien, die deutsche Frage und die Blockade Berlins 1948–1949*. Berlin: De Gruyter, 2018.

Mayrhofer, Bernadette, and Fritz Trümpi. *Orchestrierte Vertreibung: Unerwünschte Wiener Philharmoniker. Verfolgung, Ermordung und Exil*. Vienna: Mandelbaum, 2014.

McKenna, Marian C. *Myra Hess: A Portrait*. London: Hamilton, 1976.

Miller, Eileen. *The Edinburgh International Festival 1947–1996*. Aldershot: Scolar Press, 1996.

Monod, David. *Settling Scores: German Music, Denazification, and the Americans, 1945–1953*. Chapel Hill: University of North Carolina Press, 2005.

Morris, John Vincent. "Battle for Music: Music and British Wartime Propaganda 1935–1945." PhD dissertation, University of Exeter, 2011.

Müller, Sven Oliver. "Ein fehlender Neuanfang: Das bürgerliche Musikleben in der Bundesrepublik Deutschland nach 1945." In *Bürgertum nach dem bürgerlichen Zeitalter: Leitbilder und Praxis seit 1945*, edited by Gunilla Budde, Eckart Conze, and Cornelia Rauh, 255–69. Göttingen: Vandenhoeck & Ruprecht, 2010.

———. "Wie national waren E- und U-Musik im Zweiten Weltkrieg?: Musikalische Aufführungen zwischen nationaler Abgrenzung und europäischer Angleichung." In *Geschichte ohne Grenzen?: Europäische Dimensionen der Militärgeschichte vom 19. Jahrhundert bis heute*, edited by Jörg Echternkamp and Hans-Hubertus Mack, 185–93. Berlin: De Gruyter, 2016.

Osterhammel, Jürgen. "'Welteroberndes Künstlertum': Weltsemantik und Globalisierung im Zeitalter von Richard Wagner und Werner von Siemens." In *Gefühlskraftwerke* für *Patrioten? Wagner und das Musiktheater zwischen Nationalismus und Globalisierung*, edited by Arne Stollberg,

Ivana Rentsch, and Anselm Gerhard, 17–35. Würzburg: Königshausen & Neumann, 2017.

Pasdzierny, Matthias. *Wiederaufnahme? Rückkehr aus dem Exil und das westdeutsche Musikleben nach 1945*. Munich: edition text + kritik, 2014.

Pestel, Friedemann. "'Ein Programm, was auch irgend etwas über die Situation Deutschlands aussagt'? Wagner auf internationalen Orchestertourneen (1930er bis 1960er Jahre)." In *Sündenfall der Künste?: Richard Wagner, der Nationalsozialismus und die Folgen*, edited by Katharina Wagner, Holger von Berg, and Marie L. Maintz, 154–73, and 207–13. Kassel: Bärenreiter, 2018.

———. "'Special Years'? The Vienna Philharmonic, Baldur von Schirach, and Nazi Cultural Politics in Vienna." *The Musical Quarterly* 102, no. 2/3 (2019): 256–302.

Prieberg, Fred K. *Trial of Strength: Furtwangler and the Third Reich*. Boston: Northeastern University Press, 1994.

Raab Hansen, Jutta. *NS-verfolgte Musiker in England: Spuren deutscher und österreichischer Flüchtlinge in der britischen Musikkultur*. Hamburg: Von Bockel, 1996.

———. "Internierung – Bombardierung – Rekrutierung: Musiker-Exil in Großbritannien." In *Musik im Exil: Folgen des Nazismus für die internationale Musikkultur*, edited by Hanns-Werner Heister, Claudia Maurer Zenck, and Peter Petersen, 279–96. Frankfurt am Main: Fischer Taschenbuch Verlag, 1993.

Rathkolb, Oliver. "Austriakischer Kulturexport." In *Begnadet für das Schöne: Der rot-weiß-rote Kulturkampf gegen die Moderne*, edited by Gert Kerschbaumer and Karl Müller, 67–73. Vienna: Verlag für Gesellschaftskritik, 1992.

———. "Kulturelle Entnazifizierung und Reorientierung des Musiktheaters nach 1945 am Beispiel der Salzburger Festspiele bzw. des Exilanten Bruno Walter." In *Salzburg: Sounds of Migration. Geschichte und aktuelle Initiativen*, edited by Wolfgang Gratzer, Sylvia Hahn, Michael Malkiewicz, and Sabine Veits-Falk, 95–115. Vienna: Hollitzer Wissenschaftsverlag, 2016.

———. "Notes on the 'Denazification." Retrieved 17 September 2020 from http://wphdata.blob.core.windows.net/documents/Documents/pdf/NS/ns_rath_entnazifizierung_en_v01.pdf.

———. "Honours and Awards (Honorary Members, Rings of Honour, the Nicolai Medal and the 'Yellow' List)", Vien, Wiener Philharmoniker 1842, Retrieved 17 September 2020 from http://wphdata.blob.core.windows.net/documents/Documents/pdf/NS/ns_rath_ehrungen_en_v02.pdf.

Roncigli, Audrey. "Wilhelm Furtwängler, une illusion face au nazisme." *Guerres mondiales et conflits contemporains* 227, no. 3 (2007): 75–93.

Rosenberg, Jonathan. *Dangerous Melodies: Classical Music in America from the Great War through the Cold War*. New York: W. W. Norton, 2020.

Ryding, Erik S., and Rebecca Pechefsky. *Bruno Walter: A World Elsewhere*. New Haven, CT: Yale University Press, 2001.

Sabrow, Martin. "Die 'Stunde Null' als Zeiterfahrung." *Aus Politik und Zeitgeschichte* (2020), no. 4/5 (2016). Retrieved 17 September 2020 from https://www.bpb.de/apuz/303645/die-stunde-null-als-zeiterfahrung.

Shirakawa, Sam H. *The Devil's Music Master: The Controversial Life and Career of Wilhelm Furtwängler*. New York: Oxford University Press, 1992.

Stahrenberg, Carolin. "'Such Occasions Form a Poignant Link with the Past': Die kulturelle Praxis des Konzertbesuchs als Identitätsmarker und Erinnerungsanker im britischen Exil." In *Musik und Migration*, edited by Wolfgang Gratzer and Nils Grosch, 263–74. Münster: Waxmann, 2018.

Szabó-Knotik, Cornelia. "Mythos Musik in Österreich." In *Memoria Austriae*, vol. 1. *Menschen, Mythen, Zeiten*, edited by Emil Brix, Ernst Bruckmüller, and Hannes Stekl, 243–70. Vienna: Verlag für Geschichte und Politik, 2004.

———. "Selbstinszenierung und Handelsbilanz: Die (Re)Konstruktion Österreichs nach 1945 mittels Musik." In *Musik-Wissenschaft an ihren Grenzen: Manfred Angerer zum 50. Geburtstag*, edited by Dominik Schweiger, Michael Staudinger, and Nikolaus Urbanek, 355–82. Frankfurt am Main, New York: Peter Lang, 2004.

Thacker, Toby. *Music after Hitler, 1945–1955*. Aldershot: Ashgate, 2007.

Trümpi, Fritz. *The Political Orchestra: The Vienna and Berlin Philharmonics during the Third Reich*. Chicago: University of Chicago Press, 2016.

Uhl, Heidemarie. "From Victim Myth to Co-Responsibility Thesis: Nazi Rule, World War II, and the Holocaust in Austrian Memory." In *The Politics of Memory in Postwar Europe*, edited by Richard N. Lebow, Wulf Kansteiner, and Claudio Fogu, 40–72. Durham, NC: Duke University Press, 2006.

In *Die Berliner Luftbrücke: Ereignis und Erinnerung*, edited by Helmut Trotnow and Bernd von Kostka, 89–98. Berlin: Frank & Timme, 2010.

Part II
A GRADUAL DEMOBILIZATION: MUSIC, CULTURES OF WAR, AND NATIONAL IMAGINATIONS

Chapter 4

DISCOURSE ON MUSIC AND THE POSTWAR TRANSITION
The Case of France after the Franco-Prussian Conflict of 1870–1871

Emmanuel Reibel

> We look forward to seeing an end to this period of inactivity, which continues to affect the best of our writers and artists[1]. Some, the more sensitive natured, have not yet recovered from the despair of the first few days. Others, more robust in nature, are still suffering from the aftermath of violent and frustrated efforts, of desperate pushes forward. They must let the last remnants of anger drain away, regroup and regain control of their lives.[2]

How should the postwar transition period be defined in the case of the Franco-Prussian War? The armistice may have been signed in Versailles on 28 January 1871, but the establishment of the Paris Commune on 18 March prevented any return to normal life for the people of France. Should we, then, view the transition period as beginning with the election of Adolphe Thiers as president of the new Republic on 31 July? We can see from the reflection cited here, which appeared in the prestigious French music magazine *Le Ménestrel* in November of the same year, that this postwar transition was seen as just part of a much longer temporality because of the psychological dimension. It threatened to be a long, painful period for those who had been defeated. So how long does it take to overcome such trauma? The way in which the discourse on music is structured in the wake of a conflict provides us with a modest but emblematic window into how a population emerges from a war. In order to under-

---

Notes for this section begin on page 96.

stand the role and modalities of the discourse on music during this period of gradual return to normal artistic activities, I have investigated French music magazines in their first year after publication resumed following the Franco-Prussian War.[3]

For these magazines, emerging from the war meant first and foremost emerging from the silence, that is, resuming the publication of their interrupted periodical. All the music magazines in France fell silent during the summer of 1870. Table 4.1 shows that some simply disappeared altogether, while others recovered, with the first among them reappearing after the summer of 1871. These magazines not only had to reconnect with their subscribers and restore the economic equilibrium that had been jeopardized by the conflict; they also had to try to pick up the threads of a disrupted publication run. The case of *Le Ménestrel* is particularly interesting in this respect because it attempted in its own way to resolve this problem as soon as it resumed publication: "The issues appearing from today to 1 December, which is the anniversary of the foundation of our mag-

Table 4.1. List of French music magazines that resumed publication following the Franco-Prussian War. Table created by the author.

MAGAZINE	PUBLICATION CEASED	PUBLICATION RESUMED
L'Art musical	11/08/1870	04/01/1872
Revue et gazette musicale	28/08/1870	01/10/1871
La France musicale	04/071870	–
Le Ménestrel	28/08/1870	03/09/1871
La Chronique musicale	06/1870	01/09/1873
La Réforme musicale	06/06/1870	–
Revue de musique sacrée ancienne et moderne	05/05/1870	–
La Nouvelle France chorale	16/08/1870	16/09/1871
L'Orphéon, moniteur des orphéons et sociétés chorales de France	20/08/1870	01/09/1871
Le Moniteur des pianistes	20/07/1870	–
La Musique populaire: chorale, instrumentale, religieuse	01/08/1870	–
L'Avenir musical	08/1870	09/1875

azine, will bear the dual date 1870–71 in order to avoid any apparent discontinuity in our subscribers' collections."[4]

This chronological sleight of hand was symptomatic of a certain level of unease. The magazines found themselves torn between, on the one hand, wanting to gloss over the discontinuity of the journalistic seriality, as if nothing had happened, and, on the other, a longing to highlight it and fill the media void with articles about the events of the past months. But were these attempts to somehow wave a magic wand of journalistic continuity over the months of silence enough to mark a postwar transition symbolically and culturally? Is it possible for music journalism to return to normal while the conflict is still in everyone's minds and while its economic, psychological, and cultural consequences are still impacting artistic life? I will try to find the answers to these questions first by showing that the musical press intended to play an active role in the postwar transition through specific editorial choices and patriotic acts, and second by studying the specific modalities of reviewing that manifested themselves during this singular period of editorial, aesthetic, and ideological reconstruction.

I have chosen to adopt this thematic approach because despite the differences in format, editors and aesthetic position that characterized them before the war, the different periodicals studied adopt a very similar position after the war (with the exception of their judgements on Offenbach, as we shall see). The chapter will put the hypothesis that the post-war period ends when music criticism resumes after a period of generalized empathy towards a reviving musical life and when the battle shifts from the military to the aesthetic field.

The Press as an Actor in the Postwar Transition: Symbolic and Committed Actions

Obituary columns were a prerequisite in the first postwar issue(s) of these magazines. All of them subscribed to this practice, as exemplified by Léon Escudier in the inaugural issue of *L'Art musical*:

> And, like the soldiers after the battle, we too count how many of us are left. We too note with the most profound sadness the many empty spaces made in our ranks during the months of war, the siege, and then the insurrection.
>
> We do not have the heart to draw up a painful list of martyrs, to line up the names of all those who are missing, all those who could not even be given the sad splendour of a ceremonious funeral because the city was plunged into such mourning and struck down by such dreadful terror! . . . Artists, singers, musicians, composers, young midshipmen, and military leaders.[5]

The Obituary Column as a Journalistic Rite

This type of discourse was developed to a greater or lesser degree depending on the magazine. The obituary columns were filled with two very different types of people.

The first type were musicians who died in battle or during the Commune. Among them were the Italian pianist-composer Genaro Perelli, who "died on 22 January from wounds received at the Battle of Buzenval, where he commanded a free corps,"[6] and the violinist Salvador Daniel, who became Director of the Conservatoire de Paris under the Commune and who was "shot in rue Jacob, after the taking of the barricade on rue Bonaparte."[7] The statements concerning Salvador Daniel, who died during the Commune, remain reserved and unfavorable; on the other hand, the newspapers tended to heroize the actions of those who had fallen in battle and to tragedize those who had lost limbs and thus sacrificed their careers in the name of patriotism. The second type were well-known figures who disappeared during the war but with no direct link to the conflict. These included music critics (the *Revue et gazette musicale* was said to be "painfully tested" by the loss of its "two founders," François-Joseph Fétis and Maurice Schlesinger, and "one of its oldest collaborators," Déaddé Saint-Yves[8]) and musicians, such as Thalberg[9] and Auber, who did not receive tributes in the traditional media. The commemorations of Auber, who died on 12 May 1871 (when none of the music magazines had yet resurfaced), unfolded at length in the musical press and even took on a decidedly patriotic tone. For example, Escudier wrote: "We are duty-bound, in a magazine with the title *L'Art musical*, to say a final farewell to the man who was the greatest representative of contemporary French music."[10]

The obituary column appears to have been a true journalistic rite during this period. As the magazines resumed publication, it represented a symbolic benchmark and vital memorial in their efforts to commemorate French musicians as well as to reconstruct a community of readers who would be united in an inaugural mourning.

Top Music Stories from the Conflict

Once they were back up and running, a second way in which the music magazines could symbolize the postwar transition was to give accounts of the top music stories from the conflict. Some articles were mainly anecdotal, such as *La Nouvelle France chorale*'s report on a German raid, where all the instruments belonging to a group of Sociétés Orphéoniques choirs were seized except one Norman double bass, which was described as "patriotic" for having escaped "the Prussian annexation."[11] However, some articles were presented as real historical essays, published over several issues, such as Mathieu de Monter's series entitled "La musique française sur les champs de bataille" for the *Revue et gazette musicale* and Arthur Pougin's series entitled "Tablettes artistiques 1870–1871" for *Le Ménestrel*. Pougin's well-developed study focused on musical life during the war and the heroic actions of musicians during the fighting, providing lively accounts of the achievements of, among others, Jules Pasdeloup, Ernest Guirault, the Duvernoy brothers, Edmond Moreau, Charles Bernard, and Marius Boullard.[12]

In addition to their commemorative function, these music stories from the war had a dual patriotic and moral function. In *La Chronique musicale*, for example, a study entitled "Les Musiciens allemands pendant la dernière guerre" concluded with this eloquent reflection: "Let us hope that, by publishing this article, we have contributed in some small way to rebuilding our country, whose motto must now be: Never forget, and rely on no one but yourself."[13] Likewise, Arthur Pougin claimed he wrote to "reconnect the links in the chain of time" and to serve France, because after the disasters of the past year, "every one of her children should now have just one thought, one objective: to facilitate her convalescence, hasten her recovery and work toward her salvation," adding that "[France] is getting back up onto her feet and preparing to take up her rightful intellectual and moral place in the world again, to reclaim the trailblazing and civilizing role she has (almost unerringly) always played so triumphantly."[14] History was presented as a healing agent for the social body. The musical press, because it had not directly participated in the war effort, intended to exploit this quasi-medical dimension actively to participate in France's reconstruction.

The News Section: A Messenger of Patriotic and Musical Events

The music magazines generally had a factual news section, which at the time was dotted with information relating to the consequences of the war. It reported, for example, on the reopening of opera houses, such as the Grand-Théâtre de Marseille on 1 January 1872,[15] on the prolonged closure of institutions like the Théâtre-Italien (which had served as an infirmary during the Siege of Paris and was very dilapidated[16]), on the state of the Théâtre-Lyrique, which was to be rebuilt after the fire, and on the Opéra national de Paris's financial problems and its difficulties in reopening because of the many singers exiled abroad. The news section also gave publicity to a wide range of issues, including the damage caused to the great organ in the Église de la Sainte-Trinité,[17] the Société des Auteurs, Compositeurs et Éditeurs de Musique's cash deficit,[18] German legislation concerning literary and artistic property,[19] and the efforts of the Ligue de la Délivrance Nationale.

The most extensive information provided in the news sections related to patriotic acts. These could be editorial projects, like the Comité de l'album patriotique des grands maîtres de l'art musical, which was a committee set up to put together an album of music grand masters whose proceeds were to go toward the liberation of French territory,[20] or the many charity concerts organized throughout France, notably to support the work of the Orphelins de la guerre, a national charity that looked after the war orphans.[21] For example, the *Revue et gazette musicale* was constantly publishing the programs and proceeds from a major tour organized by France's First Lady in aid of the Orphelins de la Guerre.[22] Likewise, *L'Art musical* provided regular updates on a series of concerts organized for the liberation of French territory.[23]

In addition to the news sections during this period, the small ads sections would also publicize patriotic musical works with eloquent titles, such as "ALSACE!," "FRANCE!," and "THE LAST SONGS."

The Involvement of the Music Magazines in Patriotic Acts

Not content with just being the messengers of patriotic acts, the music magazines became more militant still by increasingly adopting provocative standpoints. They challenged the government (through constantly alerting the public authorities to the cuts in subsidies to theaters following the Treaty of Frankfurt[24] or through relaying Arthur Pougin's calls for public monuments to be erected to French composers[25]). They also challenged the music professionals, for example, by urging them to join L'Harmonie Française, the new music society founded by Oscar Comettant (to which *L'Art musical* even provided logistic support by offering it office space[26]). They even called on their readers to be generous with their donations to different appeals. For example, *Le Ménestrel* passed on the vast fund from the Comité des arts for the liberation of French territory. One insert in the magazine dated 11 February 1872 was particularly eloquent:

> We have responded to a call from the honourable editor of the *Moniteur universel*, P. Paul Dalloz, to set up a roll of contributions in aid of the liberation of French territory at *Le Ménestrel*, 2 bis, rue Vivienne and have signed up to a first payment of one thousand francs.
>
> This same sum has just been paid to us, for the same cause, by our great artist Fauré, which comes on top of the 1,000 francs fee he re-

fused to take last Thursday following the performance organized by the Opéra [National de Paris] in aid of the work carried out by the *Femmes de France* to free our territory. We should also mention that Madame Alboni has kindly promised us her valuable assistance for a major concert currently being planned.²⁷

Le Ménestrel thus served as a link between the government agency responsible for centralizing performers' efforts and the music community. It was not content with just being an intermediary, however. It was leading by example by making its own substantial donation, valorizing the generosity of committed musicians, and even organizing a concert in aid of this patriotic act.²⁸

These renascent music magazines were therefore not just a symbol of the reawakening of artistic life in France. Their media power during this period, when benefit concerts played a crucial role and music was taking on a new mission of social and moral regeneration, placed them center stage. But how, beyond the general context of the magazine, did music criticism become so polarized, in particular, with regard to German music? And how did this postwar transition impact the discourse on music, including debates not directly related to the war?

Music Criticism in the Immediate Postwar Period

The fact that the music periodicals had started to reappear did not necessarily mean that criticism practices were just able to pick up where they left off. In retrospective reviews, which reported on concerts or performances that had taken place before publication was resumed, the main aim was to recount rather than appraise: "in the year of the war 1870–1871, the critics explain, music should simply be chronicled, nothing more."²⁹ Even in the first few months after publication resumed, criticism remained seriously limited by the many benefit concerts.

Anesthetized Criticism

The focus was on the proceeds rather than the actual quality of the performances, and the discourse developed into one of patriotic celebration, as in this example: "And after more than two hours of truly 'noble' music dedicated to the liberation of French territory, we all dispersed, still proud to be French, despite the sufferings of our country, the loss of our provinces, and the destruction of our buildings, especially the Vendôme Column."³⁰ During the Théâtre-Italien's relaunch event in aid of the deliverance of the territory, all critical judgment was inevitably suspended. An anonymous reviewer from *Le Menestrel* wrote that:

> The Théâtre-Italien has finally reopened under the *patronage of the Dames de France* in aid of their steadfast work *to liberate our territory*.— The whole of the Salle de Ventadour, which has been in mourning for almost two years, was in festive mood last Thursday. Gone from the foyer were the wounded and the Sisters of Charity. In their place, flowers and lights everywhere! We counted how many of us were still here and were overjoyed to see one another again. Everyone enjoyed rolling back the years a little during the joint performance by Madames Alboni and Menco! . . . We will refrain from passing judgment, solely based on this concert, on the opera singers who were performing there for the first time.[31]

While patriotic duty may have forced the critics to "refrain from passing judgment," it was often through forbearance that they went into standby mode. In normal circumstances, they would have protested against the low artistic standards in evidence on the Parisian stages, but in this postwar transition period they were forced to modify their comments. *L'Art musical* thus explained that Halanzier, "the new director [of the Opéra National de Paris], has found our great operatic scene to be in a sad state, and we must be grateful to him for the efforts he has made thus far to restore this battered and bruised body back to life. We need to help him. We need to support him."[32] The critic was equally understanding about the Opéra-Comique: "On the whole, the performance of *The Clerks' Meadow* was not quite up to the standard of the masterpiece itself, but we must take into account the difficulties faced by Monsieurs Leuven and Du Locle in finding artists amid all the disruptions that have shaken our society."[33]

It is possible, then, to propose the following hypothesis: the postwar transition period ends when music criticism comes out of standby mode and begins properly to evaluate artists' performances again. In the case of the Franco-Prussian War, the magazines did not regain their critical function until the autumn of 1872. While forbearance may have been called for the previous year: "It is different now, we have somehow returned to normality. Companies have had a lot of time to prepare the works and hire the artists. The public has the right to demand more and will probably do so. So the management had better watch out. But they know this and have acted accordingly."[34]

It was time then for a return to high artistic standards. Irritation at the Opéra National de Paris's lethargy in this respect was heightened at the end of 1872, as can be seen in the following comment from Mark de Thémines: "It seems to us that since the subsidies are paid with taxpayers' money, the public should have the right to know what the benefits are for them of this imposed contribution, and the administration seems to deny all responsibility."[35] Hence, the suspended or, at best, empathetic criticism of the immediate postwar period was followed by a gradual return to normality in the exercise of critical judgment. However, this gave rise to a dilemma: should musical works be subject to a political interpretation?

The Difficult Retreat into Art for Art's Sake

Many journalists were tempted to retreat into purely aesthetic considerations, as if, after the horrors of war, music should be nothing more than pure entertainment. Indeed, as early as the autumn of 1871, Parisians seemed to have been overcome with an acute yearning for artistic entertainment. They had rediscovered "this longing for pleasure, this passionate search for enjoyment from music and the stage" and exhibited a "tendency to espouse the *art for art's sake* philosophy."[36] These were the words of Mathieu de Monter, who believed that music should be separated from any kind of politics. A few weeks earlier, in the first issue of *Revue et gazette musicale*, he had written that "for the work of art as well as for its creator, an essential prerequisite for success, for esteem, is to have no interest whatsoever in any political concern."[37] This seemed to be the magazine's official line, which regularly tried to dissociate aesthetic appraisals from ideological issues. For example, it published no negative opinions on Offenbach, who was being lambasted by the rest of the press at the time, during the *Boule de Neige* production in December 1871,[38] and there was no political commentary on Saint-Saëns's *Marche héroïque*, which was also being performed at the Concert Populaire.[39]

However, this seemed to be a difficult position to maintain more generally. For other journals such as *Le Ménestrel* and *L'Art musical*, the production, just like music criticism, could not be separated from the contemporary context. The critic Armand de Montgarde seems to regret this strength of history which he nevertheless finds inevitable:

> Totally absorbed in their work, artists are the last people to want to be caught up in this kind of political cataclysm, but they nevertheless suffer its effects. They do not quite relinquish their citizenship, nor do they completely abandon their beliefs and opinions, which, almost in spite of themselves, are revealed through their works.... Some kind of arena

opens up where all these different parties assemble. They throw their hats into the ring and then fight, wrestle, and jostle one another. Each carries their own flag and tries to take down that of their opponents. This phenomenon, which has been re-enacted fairly regularly since the turn of the century, is especially evident today, when our country has been so cruelly shaken, so deeply disrupted that we are not yet able to foresee when order, peace, and tranquillity will be restored.[40]

From Military Combat to Aesthetic Combat

Music criticism during this period was therefore characterized by a heightened nationalism, which included the glorification of French heritage. The majority of the musical press saw the thousandth performance of Hérold's *The Clerk's Meadow* at the Opéra-Comique in October 1871 as a "triumph for the French school." One critic stated: "Now more than ever we need French art to reveal itself in all its glories. We need it to console and comfort us first and then to inspire us to seek out new glories."[41]

The main way in which this heightened nationalism manifested in the musical press was through a rise in hostile reactions to the German repertoire. The opera *Martha*, which was composed by Friedrich von Flotow, who was "from old Prussian stock," was only tolerated at the Théâtre-Lyrique because its Latin style had cast out "any Germanic qualities."[42] Wagner was more than ever the object of repeated ridicule, and, as in the previous decade but now with increased verve, the principal French productions—Bizet's *Djamileh* and Saint-Saëns's *La Princesse Jaune*—were suspected of Wagnerism.[43] Even Offenbach, who had been the embodiment of the French spirit during the Second Empire, was now sent back to his Germanness. When his *Fantasio* was first performed at the Opéra-Comique in January 1872, *L'Art musical* took umbrage at the fact he was now monopolizing the entire Parisian theatrical space:

> Has the creator of *La Grande Duchesse de Gérolstein* been unjustly cast aside, overlooked, disadvantaged? Hasn't he just given *Boule de Neige* to the Bouffes and *Le Roi Carotte* to the Gaîté? Is he not about to give *Le Corsaire Noir* to the Variétés? Was it really necessary to put his name on yet another poster, this time advertising a work composed by Boïeldieu, Hérold, Auber, Adam, Ambroise Thomas or Félicien David?[44]

Le Ménestrel also condemned the Parisians' blind "Offenbachism" and the fierceness of the composer's ambitions as he took over the capital's premier musical stages:

> Offenbach is everywhere! Our exposure to him is all-consuming, absorbing, daily, weekly, monthly, all year round.

Offenbach has turned himself into a legion, and he is invading us.

Was there perhaps another article added to the Treaty of Frankfurt just for him? An article the public is apparently only entitled to know about through its consequences but whose content seems to have been mysteriously and imperatively made known to all the directors in Paris? ... One theatre, which has the honour of being described as the *théâtre national*, must seek out the highest possible art, especially among national works. The public subsidy has no other purport.[45]

This extract comes from the familiar pen of Gustave Bertrand, who was famous for his book *Les Nationalités musicales*, some excerpts of which appeared in *Le Ménestrel* before it was published in 1872.[46] In addition to the heightened national lens evident in this extract, we note a shift in the use of invasion terminology from the political or military field to the aesthetic field. This was a common feature of music criticism at the time, making a blatant appearance in the titles of some xenophobic studies such as "L'Invasion allemande dans la musique"[47] and surfacing in many articles. For example, Pauline Viardot's return to Paris, "abandoning her villa in Baden to take back possession of her former residence on rue de Douai," was perceived as a "real victory for France over Germany's music scene."[48] Another article demonstrated the same nationalist pride when it reported that "Madame Rosine Stoltz—Baroness of Ketschendorf" bids "farewell to Germany."[49] The inherent violence of this invasion terminology betrays a deep anxiety within a section of the French music criticism world, as demonstrated in the following excerpt from another article by Armand de Montgarde.

On the one hand, we see it as a barbarian invasion, or rather, let's be honest, a German invasion, stampeding through our French school and trying to topple it and take over the throne. It attacks from both above and below. From above, it comes in the form of what is called great music, the grand opera, commanded by Richard Wagner. From below, more modest forms, operettas, parodies, farces, satires, with Jacques Offenbach as the conductor and coryphaeus. ... If we had not been on our guard, we believe the entire French school, which has given us the finest works in our great repertoire and which includes, among all its splendours, this eminently French genre that we call comic opera, the entire French school would have been wiped out. At the top, there would have been the most obscure, the most abstract, the most algebraic Wagnerism, and at the bottom, the most vulgar, grotesque, ignoble peccadillos and poppycock. ... When a gang of murderers and arsonists stampeded through Paris and turned the streets into rivers of fire and blood, the conservatives stayed at home. They let them loot the shops and burn down the buildings. It may have lasted a while, but re-erecting the monuments that now lie in a pile of ruins will take a lot longer.[50]

This was obviously not the first time a xenophobic register had appeared in French music criticism, but the Franco-Prussian War had undoubtedly exacerbated it by giving some critics the impression that they had been "surrounded," artistically speaking. For them, there was no question of adding an aesthetic surrender to the military surrender. At stake was a certain moral idea, which music criticism had created for itself.

Music Criticism Instrumentalized in Aid of National, Social, and Moral Regeneration

The reawakening of music criticism might have seemed trivial given the trauma and humiliation the French had just suffered, but the magazines wanted to demonstrate this was not the case. In *Le Menestrel*, critic Paul Lancôme argued that : "The very nature of this magazine limits us to a discussion of relatively minor matters since its focus can only be on art. But in these times of crisis, this becomes of primary importance because art is perhaps the clearest and most disinterested manifestation of France's true state of mind."[51] Music was therefore clearly perceived as an agent of regeneration. *Le Ménestrel*, for example, wrote that "art can do much to revive the soul."[52] One article written by Mathieu de Monter in *Revue et gazette musicale* nevertheless shows the ambiguity of this regeneration, because while he highlights music's supposedly soothing qualities, with its ability to calm spirits and comfort hearts,[53] he also assigns it the function of "demonstrating that our brain is still intact."[54]

Because it was thought that music could therefore play an active role in identity reconstruction, not to mention revenge, the arbiters of music criticism thought of themselves as agents of reconstruction. In the first issue of *Le Ménestrel*, Gustave Bertrand explained:

> After all our defeats and the ruins with which we have been left, we are still perfectly at liberty to retain our supremacy in matters of the mind and good taste, in matters of sociability. Prussia may have been able to generate a better militarism and butcher a few billion of us, but it cannot claim that Berlin is an attractive city or that its national character is warm and friendly. France is still the master of its own destiny. It just needs to realize this and take control.[55]

The Orphéonic[56] press, whose public were more grassroots and undoubtedly more inclined to patriotism, deployed a rhetoric that was even more fervent and voluntarist:

> Rise up and sing! Sing!—Let your powerful voices, muffled for so long by the hideous howls of battle, begin to soar again, calmly, serenely

and full of hope, from the English Channel to the Mediterranean and from the Atlantic Ocean to the Alps! Tell the sons of the motherland that her soul is not dead! ... Rise up!—For in the great undertaking of patriotic regeneration that must now be in all our hearts, you have an enormous and difficult task. Of all the popular instructional and charitable institutions, yours is perhaps the one that must contribute most effectively to the rebuilding of our country through the distribution of enlightenment.[57]

Conclusion

At the end of this investigation, one is struck by the ambivalence of the musical press in relation to the postwar transition. While the reappearance of the magazines could be seen as a sign of a return to normalcy after months of media silence, this was clearly not the case because the periodicals studied here were in reality being torn in two different and contradictory directions. On the one hand, they sought to leave the war behind through a series of symbolic actions to build a musical memory of the conflict; on the other hand, they wanted to reflect the agonies of a musical world that was still inextricably bound by the consequences of war. They longed to reconnect with critical discourse but had to contend with their current circumstances. They saw themselves as a healing agent for the social body, but at the same time they exacerbated national sentiment. They wanted to draw a line under the conflict, but ultimately they transferred the conflict from the political to the aesthetic field. How can a postwar transition be possible if the music magazine space becomes the new battlefield? At the time, however, according to this medical metaphor woven by Paul Lancôme, France thought it was just going through a simple period of convalescence:

> You know of course that after any major operation, the wound, before it begins to heal over, continues for a long time to reject all harmful elements, to be purified through decay. Well, we're currently in the middle of such a purge. ... As the doctors would say, it's an act of elimination. This painful process will, I hope, result in our social body rejecting the putrefying germs that have laid us so low. But this work takes time. ... Nothing can be done without time. Pain comes quickly, but convalescence is long. ... It would be madness to think the wound might heal overnight and that France would just spring back to life again.[58]

We now know that this ideological intensification in music criticism was to have a lasting impact on the music world for decades to come.

Emmanuel Reibel is professor of musicology at the École Normale Supérieure de Lyon and a professor of aesthetics at the Conservatoire de Paris. His work focuses on music discourses, and a recent article, cowritten with Yves Balmer and published in the 2017 issue of the *Revue de musicologie*, looks in part at musicological issues in a postwar transition context based on reports that appeared in the Société Française de Musicologie's bulletin. He is the author of several renowned works (including *Comment la musique est devenue romantique. De Rousseau à Berlioz*) and is the director of the Dicteco (Dictionnaire d'écrits de compositeurs) program, which he cofounded with Valérie Dufour and Michel Duchesneau. He recently published *Du métronome au gramophone: musique et révolution industrielle* (Fayard, 2023).

Notes

1. This chapter was translated from French by Clare Ferguson.
2. Anon., *Le Ménestrel*, 5 November 1871, 388: "Nous avons hâte de voir rompre cette période d'abstention où demeurent les meilleurs d'entre nos écrivains et nos artistes. Quelques-uns, natures délicates, ne sont pas encore revenus de la prostration des premiers jours; pour les natures plus fortes, c'est la réaction qui suit les efforts violents et déçus, les élans désespérés; il leur faut laisser évaporer les dernières fumées de la colère, se recueillir et reprendre possession de soi-même."
3. The reader is referred here to a similar issue, which I addressed in collaboration with Yves Balmer, concerning the transition period following World War I. See Balmer and Reibel, "Un espace métacritique pour une discipline en construction," 409–50.
4. "A nos abonnés," *Le Ménestrel*, 3 September 1871, 313: "les numéros qui paraîtront de ce jour au 1er décembre prochain, anniversaire de la fondation de notre journal, porteront la double date 1870–71, de manière à ce que nos abonnés puissent collectionner sans solution de continuité apparente."
5. L. Escudier, "Les Adieux," *L'Art musical* [*AM*], 4 January 1872, 1–2. "Et nous aussi nous nous comptons, comme les soldats après la bataille, et nous aussi nous constatons avec la plus profonde tristesse que bien des vides se sont faits dans nos rangs pendant les mois de la guerre et du siège, et pendant les semaines de l'insurrection. Nous n'avons pas le courage de dresser le douloureux martyrologe, d'aligner les noms de tous ceux qui manquent à l'appel et qui ne purent même pas avoir le triste éclat de pompeuses funérailles, tant la ville était plongée dans le deuil ou frappée par d'horribles épouvantements! . . . Artistes, chanteurs, cantatrices, musiciens, compositeurs, jeunes enseignes et chefs d'armée."
6. "Revue nécrologique," *Revue et gazette musicale* [*RGM*], 8 October 1871, 281: "mort des suites des blessures reçues à la bataille de Buzenval, le 22 janvier, où il commandait un corps franc."
7. "Revue nécrologique," *RGM*, 15 October 1871, 289: "fusillé rue Jacob, après la prise de la barricade de la rue Bonaparte."

8. E. Mathieu de Monter, "Revue rétrospective janvier 1870–octobre 1871," *RGM*, 1 October 1871, 272: "douloureusement éprouvée," "deux fondateurs," and "l'un de ses plus anciens collaborateurs."
9. L. Escudier, "Bouts de l'an. Thalberg et Perelli," *AM*, 11 January 1872, 9.
10. L. Escudier, "Les Adieux," *AM*, 4 January 1872, 2: "Nous nous devions de donner un dernier adieu dans un journal qui a pour titre *L'Art musical* à celui qui fut le plus grand représentant de la musique française contemporaine."
11. Alfred Desprez, "Invasion allemande en Normandie," *La Nouvelle France chorale*, 1 October 1871, 3. The two quotations translated from French are "patriotique" and "l'annexion prussienne," respectively.
12. See, in particular, Arthur Pougin, "Tablettes artistiques 1870–1871," *Le Ménestrel*, 8 October 1871, 357.
13. Edmond Neukomm, *La Chronique musicale*, 15 September 1873, 273: "Puissions-nous, en la rendant publique, avoir apporté notre petite pierre à la réédification de notre patrie, dont la devise doit être dorénavant: *Souviens-toi, et ne compte plus que sur toi-même.*"
14. Pougin, "Tablettes artistiques 1870–1871," *Le Ménestrel*, 24 September 1871, 339. The three quotations translated from French are "renouer la chaîne des temps," "chacun de ses enfants ne doit avoir aujourd'hui qu'une seule pensée, qu'un seul objectif: faciliter sa convalescence, hâter sa guérison, travailler à son salut," and "[La France] se remet sur ses pieds et se prépare à reconquérir dans le monde la situation intellectuelle et morale qui lui appartient, le rôle initiateur et civilisateur auquel elle n'a que rarement failli," respectively.
15. *Le Ménestrel*, 7 January 1872, 45.
16. "Nouvelles des théâtres lyriques," *RGM*, 5 November 1871, 313.
17. "Nouvelles diverses," *RGM*, 12 November 1871, 323.
18. "Nouvelles diverses," *RGM*, 8 October 1871, 282–83.
19. "Propriété littéraire et artistique en Allemagne," *RGM*, 31 December 1871, 377.
20. "Nouvelles," *Le Ménestrel*, 31 March 1871, 143.
21. "Nouvelles," *Le Ménestrel*, 15 October 1871, 383.
22. "Nouvelles," *RGM*, 22 October 1871, 298.
23. For example, "most of the theatres in Paris, including the Comédie-Française, the Opéra-Comique, the Théâtre-Lyrique, and the Châtelet, gave performances on Sunday to mark the unfortunate anniversary of Paris's capitulation with proceeds going to the association for the liberation of French territory." *AM*, 1 February 1872, 39: "La plupart des théâtres de Paris, entre autres la Comédie-Française, l'Opéra-Comique, le Théâtre-Lyrique, le Châtelet, ont donné dimanche triste jour de la capitulation de Paris, des représentations au bénéfice de l'association pour la libération du territoire"; "Last Thursday, the Opéra [national de Paris] gave an extraordinary performance for the liberation of French territory, raising 10,638 francs and 50 cents." *AM*, 15 February 1872, 54: "L'opéra a donné, jeudi dernier, une représentation extraordinaire pour la libération du territoire. Elle a produit 10,638 fr. 50 c."; "The Association des Artistes Musiciens will have a mass said by Fr. Charles Gounod next Monday, 8 April 1872, at Notre-Dame, which will include soloists and choirs. . . . The sermon will be given by Dominican Fr. R. P. Ollivier. The collection will go to the deliverance of French territory." *AM*, 4 April 1872, 111. "L'Association des artistes musiciens fera exécuter lundi prochain, 8 avril 1872, à Notre-Dame, une messe de M. Charles Gounod, avec soli et chœurs. . . . Une allocution sera prononcée par le R. P. Ollivier, dominicain. La quête est destinée à la délivrance du territoire"; and "A large concert in aid of the liberation of French territory has just taken

place in Limoges. The proceeds and collection have raised 2,700 francs." *AM*, 6 June 1872, 183: "Un grand concert pour la libération du territoire vient d'être donné à Limoges, la recette et la quête ont produit 2700 fr."

24. Gustave Bertrand, "Semaine théâtrale," *Le Ménestrel*, 3 September 1871, 316; 10 September 1871, 323.
25. For example, a statue of Rameau in Dijon and one of Hérold in Paris were requested (see *Le Ménestrel*, 4 February 1872, 78).
26. *AM*, 18 July 1872, 222.
27. "Comité des arts. Souscription pour la libération du territoire," *Le Ménestrel*, 11 February 1872, 83: "Nous avons répondu à l'appel de l'honorable directeur du *Moniteur universel*, P. Paul Dalloz, en ouvrant au *Ménestrel*, 2 bis, rue Vivienne, une liste de souscriptions pour la libération de notre territoire et en nous y inscrivant pour un premier versement de mille francs. Pareille somme vient de nous être versée, dans le même but, par notre grand artiste Fauré, indépendamment du cachet de mille francs abandonné par lui, jeudi dernier, à l'issue de la représentation donnée par l'Opéra au bénéfice de l'œuvre des *Femmes de France* pour la délivrance du territoire. Nous avons dit aussi que Mme Alboni avait bien voulu nous promettre son précieux concours pour un grand concert projeté par nous."
28. The concert notice was published in the 14 April 1872 issue, the program was published in the 28 April (day of the concert) issue, and the proceeds total was published on 5 May. The concert was also publicized in other music magazines as an act of patriotic solidarity (see *AM*, 18 April 1872, 127; 2 May 1872, 141).
29. Charles Bannelier, "Revue rétrospective de l'étranger. Septembre 1870-Octobre 1871," *RGM*, 8 October 1871: "en l'an de guerre 1870–1871, la musique n'a guère droit qu'à une simple chronique."
30. "Semaine théâtrale (réouverture du Théâtre-Italien)," *Le Ménestrel*, 10 March 1872, 119: "Et après plus de deux heures de 'haute musique,' consacrées à la libération du territoire, on s'est séparé encore fier d'être français, malgré les douleurs de la patrie, la perte de nos provinces, la destruction de nos édifices en général, et en particulier de celle de la colonne Vendôme."
31. *Le Ménestrel*, 10 March 1872, 115: "Enfin la réouverture du Théâtre-Italien a pu s'effectuer, et sous le *patronage des dames de France*, au profit de leur œuvre pieuse *de la délivrance du territoire*.—Toute cette salle de Ventadour, en deuil depuis près de deux ans, était en fête jeudi dernier. Au foyer, plus de blessés ni de sœurs de charité; partout, fleurs et lumières! On se comptait, on se retrouvait avec bonheur, et lors de la double apparition de Mmes Alboni et Menco, comme chacun se plut à se rajeunir de quelques années pour jouir plus complètement de ses impressions d'autrefois! . . . Nous nous garderons bien de juger, d'après le concert de jeudi dernier, les artistes lyriques qui s'y sont produits pour la première fois."
32. "Nouvelles," *AM*, 4 January 1872, 7: "le nouveau directeur [de l'Opéra national de Paris], a trouvé notre grande scène lyrique dans un triste état, et il faut lui savoir gré des efforts qu'il a faits jusqu'à ce moment pour rendre à la vie un corps bien abattu. Aidons-le, encourageons-le."
33. "Nouvelles," *AM*, 4 January 1872, 7: "Dans son ensemble, l'exécution du *Pré aux clercs* n'est pas précisément à la hauteur du chef-d'œuvre; mais il faut tenir compte à MM. Leuven et du Locle des difficultés qu'ils ont eues à trouver des artistes au milieu des ébranlements de toute nature qui ont agité notre société."
34. M. de Thémines, "La saison nouvelle," *AM*, 12 September 1872, 284: "Aujourd'hui ce n'est plus la même chose, on a tant bien que mal repris l'aspect ordinaire; on a eu grandement le temps de préparer les ouvrages et d'engager les artistes.

Le public a le droit d'être plus exigeant, et il est fort probable qu'il le sera. Les directions n'ont donc qu'à se bien tenir. Elles le savent, du reste, et ont agi en consequence."

35. M. de Thémines, "Fin d'année," *AM*, 26 December 1872, 401–2: "Il nous semble cependant que puisque les subventions sont payées avec le denier des contribuables, le public devrait avoir le droit de connaître les avantages qui résultent pour lui de cette charge qu'on lui impose, et l'administration dégagerait ainsi sa responsabilité."

36. E. Mathieu de Monter, "Revue de 1871," *RGM*, 7 January 1872, 9. The two quotations translated from French are "cette ardeur au plaisir, cette recherche passionnée des jouissances scéniques et musicales" and "tendance à mettre en pratique la théorie de *l'art pour l'art*," respectively.

37. E. Mathieu de Monter, "Revue rétrospective janvier 1870-octobre 1871," *RGM*, 1 October 1871, 273: "pour l'œuvre d'art comme pour son créateur, une condition essentielle de succès, d'estime, est de se désintéresser absolument de toute préoccupation politique."

38. Adrien Laroque, "Boule-de Beige, opéra bouffe en trois actes, de MM. Nuitter et Tréfeu, musique de M. Offenbach," *RGM*, 17 December 1871, 361–62.

39. "Nouvelles diverses," *RGM*, 17 December 1871.

40. Armand de Montgarde, "Les deux courants," *AM*, 22 February 1872, 57: "L'artiste, celui-là même qui, tout absorbé dans ses travaux voudrait se mêler le moins possible à ce genre de cataclysmes politiques, n'en subit pas moins les effets; il n'abdique pas complètement sa qualité de citoyen, il ne fait pas un entier abandon de ses croyances et de ses opinions, et, presque malgré lui, il les révèle dans ses œuvres. . . . Une sorte d'arène s'ouvre où ces divers partis se rencontrent, entrent en lice, combattant, luttant, s'entrechoquant, chacun arborant son drapeau et tâchant d'abattre celui de ses antagonistes. Ce fait, assez souvent reproduit depuis la fin du dernier siècle et le commencement de celui-ci, est encore plus patent aujourd'hui que notre pays a été si cruellement agité, si douloureusement bouleversé, qu'on ne peut encore prévoir le moment où il retrouvera l'ordre, la paix, la tranquilité."

41. Gustave Bertrand, "Opéra-Comique. *Hérold*. 1000e représentation du *Pré aux clercs*. Rentrée de Mme Carvallo," *Le Ménestrel*, 15 October 1871, 361: "fête pour l'école française" and "Nous avons besoin, en ce moment plus que jamais, que l'art français nous affirme hautement toutes ses gloires légitimes, pour nous consoler d'abord et nous réconforter, et puis pour s'encourager lui-même à en chercher d'autres."

42. "Semaine théâtrale," *Le Ménestrel*, 17 September 1871, 330: "un Prussien de vieille souche" and "tout élément tudesque."

43. Gaston Escudier, "Djamileh," *AM*, 30 May 1872, 171; L. Escudier, "Théâtre de l'Opéra-Comique, *La Princesse jaune*," *AM*, 20 June 1872, 189.

44. Armand de Montgarde, "*Fantasio*. Opéra Comique en trois actes," *AM*, 25 January 1872, 25: "L'auteur de *La Grande Duchesse de Gérolstein* est-il injustement laissé de côté, négligé, déshérité? Ne vient-il pas de donner *Boule de neige*, aux Bouffes, *Le Roi Carotte*, à la Gaîté, ne va-t-il pas donner *Le Corsaire noir*, aux Variétés? Etait-il bien indispensable de voir figurer son nom sur l'affiche d'un quatrième théâtre, celui de Boïeldieu, d'Hérold, d'Auber, d'Adam, d'Ambroise Thomas, de Félicien David, etc.?"

45. Gustave Bertrand, "Semaine Théâtrale. Opéra-Comique. *Fantasio*, opéra-comique en trois actes, d'après A. de Musset, musique de M. Jacques Offenbach," *Le Ménestrel*, 21 January 1872, 59: "Partout de l'Offenbach! C'est la production dévorante, absorbante, à l'année, au mois, à la petite semaine. Offenbach s'est

fait légion et nous envahit. Y aurait-il en sa faveur un autre article additionnel au traité de Francfort, article que le public ne serait admis à connaître que par ses résultats, et dont la teneur aurait été aussi mystérieusement qu'impérieusement signifiée aux directeurs parisiens? . . . Un théâtre qui a l'honneur d'être qualifié *théâtre national* doit chercher l'art le plus haut possible, et surtout par des œuvres nationales: la subvention n'a pas d'autre sens."

46. *Le Ménestrel* serialized Bertrand's chapter on Berlioz from *Les Nationalités musicales* in the 12, 19, and 26 November 1871 issues. See also M. de Thémines, "Les influences musicales," *AM*, 27 June 1872.
47. Arthur Heulhard, "L'invasion allemande dans la mesure," *AM*, 7 March 1872.
48. "Paris et départements," *Le Ménestrel*, 22 October 1871: "abandonnant sa villa de Bade pour reprendre possession de son ancienne habitation de la rue de Douai" and "vraie conquête faite par la France sur l'Allemagne musicale."
49. "Paris et départements," *Le Ménestrel*, 5 November 1871, 391. The two quotations translated from French are "Mme Rosine Stoltz—baronne de Ketschendorf" and "adieu à l'Allemagne," respectively.
50. Armand de Montgarde, "Les deux courants," *AM,* 22 February 1872, 58–59: "Nous voyons d'un côté comme une invasion de barbares, disons toute notre pensée, une invasion allemande se ruant sur notre école française et essayant de s'introniser en la détrônant. Elle vient d'en haut, elle vient d'en bas: d'en haut, par ce qu'on appelle la grande musique, le grand opéra: Richard Wagner la commande; d'en bas, par la petite, par l'opérette, la parodie, la farce, la charge; elle a pour chef et coryphée, Jacques Offenbach. . . . Si l'on n'y prenait pas garde, l'école française tout entière, celle qui nous a donné les plus belles œuvres de notre grand répertoire et celle qui a parmi ses fastes, ce genre essentiellement et éminemment français qu'on nomme l'opéra-comique, l'école française, disons-nous, y passerait. Nous aurions en haut le wagnérisme le plus obscur, le plus abstrait, le plus algébrique, en bas les fredaines et les calembredaines les plus vulgaires, les plus grotesques, les plus ignobles. . . . Quand une bande d'assassins et d'incendiaires se rua sur Paris et le mit à feu et à sang, les conservateurs restèrent chez eux; ils les laissèrent piller, incendier; c'était aussi un moment à passer. Mais il faudra beaucoup plus longtemps pour relever les monuments devenus des amas de ruines."
51. Paul Lancôme, "Bonjour, bon an. Passé—present—avenir," *AM*, 4 January 1872, 2: "La nature même de ce journal nous restreint à un ordre d'idées relativement secondaires, puisqu'il ne peut y être question que d'art. Mais dans les heures de crise que nous traversons, cette question devient de première importance; car l'art est la manifestation peut-être la plus claire et la plus désintéressée de l'état réel des esprits.
52. *Le Ménestrel*, 5 November 1871, 388: "l'art peut beaucoup pour le renouveau des âmes."
53. de Monter, "Revue rétrospective janvier 1870-octobre 1871," 1 October 1871, 273: "Music is tending, as we can see, to reclaim its role, to exert its calming influence once more in these transitional and troubled times." "La musique tend, on le voit, à reprendre son rôle, à exercer de nouveau son influence calmante, dans les temps transitoires et troublés que nous subissons."
54. de Monter, "Revue rétrospective janvier 1870-octobre 1871," 1 October 1871, 273: "montrer que notre cerveau est intact."
55. Gustave Bertrand, "Semaine théâtrale," *Le Ménestrel*, 3 September 1871, 316: "Après toutes nos défaites et nos ruines, il nous est pourtant loisible de garder cette primauté pour les choses de l'esprit et du goût, pour la sociabilité. La Prusse a pu s'organiser un meilleur militarisme et nous saigner de quelques mil-

liards, mais elle ne peut décréter que Berlin est attrayant ni que son caractère national est accueillant et sympathique. La France a toujours ses destinées dans les mains: seulement, c'est à elle à vouloir et à savoir."
56. The Orphéon movement was a mass (originally all-male) choral movement that flourished in France during the nineteenth century.
57. Henry-Abel Simon, "À l'Orphéon français," *L'Orphéon*, 1 September 1871, 1: "Relève-toi et chante! Chante!—que ta grande voix, si longtemps étouffée par les hurlements hideux de la bataille, recommence à planer calme, sereine, et remplie d'espérance, de la Manche à la Méditerranée, de l'Océan aux Alpes! Dis aux fils de la patrie que son âme n'est point morte! . . . Relève-toi!—car dans l'œuvre de régénération patriotique qui doit être aujourd'hui commune à nos esprits, ta tâche est immense et ardue. De toutes les institutions populaires d'enseignement et de charité, tu es peut-être celle qui doit concourir le plus efficacement à la réédification de la patrie par la diffusion des lumières." On the restoration of choral societies as major elements in the reconstruction, see E. Mathieu de Monter, "Paris, le 19 September 1871," in the 20 September 1871 issue: The Orphéon "will join forces in the efforts to regenerate France and will shape male leisure activities to serve the great undertaking of France's revenge"/ "s'associera aux efforts de la régénération française et formera les loisirs virils du grand œuvre de la Revanche."
58. Lancôme, "Bonjour," 3: "Vous savez bien qu'après toutes les grandes opérations, la plaie, avant de se cicatriser, reste longtemps à rejeter tous les principes morbides, à s'épurer par la décomposition. Eh bien! nous sommes en plein exutoire. . . . Comme disent les médecins, il se fait ainsi un travail d'élimination. Par cette voie douloureuse, notre corps social rejettera, j'espère, les germes pourris qui nous ont mis si bas. Mais ce travail-là demande du temps. . . . Rien ne se fait sans le temps; le mal vient vite, la convalescence est longue. . . . Ce serait folie de penser que la plaie se cicatrise et se revivifie ainsi du jour au lendemain."

Bibliography

Balmer, Yves, and Emmanuel Reibel. "Un espace métacritique pour une discipline en construction. Les comptes rendus de livres du *Bulletin de la Société française de musicologie* (1917–1921)." *Revue de musicologie*, no. 103/2 (2017): 409–50.
Duchesneau, Michel. *L'Avant-garde musicale et ses sociétés à Paris de 1871 à 1939*. Sprimont: Mardaga, 1997.
Jeismann, Michael. *La Patrie de l'ennemi. La notion d'ennemi national et la représentation de la nation en Allemagne et en France*. Paris: CNRS Éditions, 1997.
Kelly, Barbara L., ed. *French Music, Culture, and National Identity, 1870–1939*. Rochester, NY: University of Rochester Press, 2008.
Roth, François. *La Guerre de 1870*. Paris: Fayard, 1990.

Chapter 5

SINGING ABOUT THE FORMER ENEMY
Two Postwar Transition Periods
Seen through the Lens of the Café-Concert
and Music Hall Chanson, 1871–1923

Martin Guerpin

In 1821, during the trial of the famous chansonnier Pierre-Jean de Béranger (1780–1857),[1] the prosecutor, Louis-Antoine de Marchangy, cited the chanson's influence on public opinion as justification for bringing proceedings against him:

> Is it because the chanson is so easily engraved on the memory? So readily reminiscent? So peppered with wit that it is like a firecracker formulated for maximum impact? . . . Is it because it travels quickly, passing through cities and hamlets alike, fully understood by every social class? While the most reprehensible pamphlet can only exert its evil influence within a small circle, the chanson, more infectious a thousand times over, can permeate even the air we breathe.[2]

An uncharted territory of musicology until relatively recently, the café-concert and music–hall chanson of the late nineteenth and early twentieth centuries remains a promising area for musicologists.[3] It also offers a fascinating research topic for cultural historians, because the chanson conveyed widely shared representations and affects. Marchangy had no need to wait for the contributions of musicologists, historians, and sociologists to understand this function of the chanson. His rhetorical questions above are strong arguments for those wishing to use the chanson as a source in the study of the history of representations and opinions tackled from a bottom-up

---

Notes for this section begin on page 117.

perspective and relating to fundamental social and cultural transformations. As a popular genre, the chanson reached a much wider audience than classical music. As an ephemeral genre, the chanson, with a few notable exceptions, was subject to the whims of fashion and current affairs. Finally, as a political genre (when it was not confined to the sentimental register), the chanson both reflected and shaped the map of public opinion and collective representations to varying degrees. This dual role was played out to its fullest during the postwar transition periods under discussion here. Chansons published in the wake of a peace treaty could be both a symbol of and a factor in the perpetuation of the war culture, the demobilization of minds and the memory of the conflict. They contributed to the persistence, disappearance, or transformation of the figure of the former enemy.

In order to examine the diversity of these contributions, this chapter focuses on two Franco-German postwar transitions. The first is the period following the Franco-Prussian War of 1870, which was theoretically ended by the Treaty of Frankfurt of 10 May 1871.[4] The second is the period following World War I, which officially ended on 28 June 1919 with the Treaty of Versailles.[5] There were two reasons for choosing to focus on these two periods. First, the period from the late 1860s to the early 1930s marks the heyday of illustrated sheet music. Studied through the lenses of musical iconography and cultural history, these invaluable sources make it possible to connect the analysis of a chanson's lyrics and music with a study of the visual representations associated with it. Second, a study of these two conflicts offers a comparative perspective. While both periods involved the same warring parties, they differed in their duration (a few months for the Franco-Prussian War, five years for World War I), nature (conventional military conflict for the Franco-Prussian War, total war for the 1914–18 conflict), and outcome for France (defeated in 1870, France and its Entente Cordiale allies were victorious in 1918). A comparative study from the French perspective (a transnational approach would exceed the confines of this chapter), based on a corpus of French chansons referencing the enemy after the signing of the peace treaties, reveals the connection between the specific characteristics of each conflict and the different postwar transition modalities. Three questions will be addressed: What figure(s) of the enemy is/are singled out in the chanson? Why are these enemies denounced after the two wars? How can we explain any observable differences between the roles played by the chanson in the two postwar transition periods? This chapter therefore aims to contribute to the history of the chanson, or rather it aims to contribute to history *through* the chanson.

The Role of the Chanson in Perpetuating the Figure of the Enemy

To ensure rigor, the content-analysis phase of this study was preceded by a thorough study of the existence and importance of chansons that reference the enemy after the signing of the peace treaties for these two conflicts. Four sources were mobilized to build the corpus. The two main sources were the legal deposit archive of sheet music for the years 1871–1913 and 1914–39[6] in addition to the catalog of sheet music held at the Bibliothèque nationale de France. While these two sources are extensive, they are not exhaustive. On the one hand, some chansons may have circulated under the radar and have not officially been declared. On the other hand, it is possible that some scores were not deposited until a year, or even several years, after their actual publication. This means that chansons officially dated 1871 and 1919 must be approached with the utmost caution. Were they published before or after the official end of the conflicts? In order to reduce the risk of imprecision as far as possible, two further sources were included, namely music press,[7] which revealed the chansons' publication dates to within a month, and the lists of chansons examined by the Bureau de la Censure du

Table 5.1. Number of chansons referencing the enemy after the Franco-Prussian War. Table created by the author.

Period	Number of chansons
1871–74	19
1875–79	3
1880–84	17
1885–89	9
1890–94	5
1895–99	2
1900–04	4
1905–09	1
1910–13	5
Total	**65**

Ministère de l'Instruction Publique et du Sous-Secrétariat d'État aux Beaux-Arts.[8]

Two additional precautions were taken when assembling the corpus from these sources. First, only those chansons whose title or lyrics directly or indirectly referenced the figure of the enemy after May 1871 and June 1919 were included.[9] However, the many chansons that contained a single reference to the enemy in one of its verses were not included. Second, if it was not possible to determine whether a chanson dated 1871 or 1919 had been written after the signing of the respective peace treaties, it was not included in the corpus. This collection of chansons does not therefore claim to be exhaustive, but it is sufficiently comprehensive to reveal two fairly clear trends.

The first trend relates to the rhythms and temporalities of the two postwar transitions. It is clear the Treaty of Frankfurt did not put an end to the publication of chansons presenting Germany as an enemy. These chansons remained highly visible from May 1871 until 1874, despite the fact that the censors were instructed to block anti-German works for foreign and domestic policy reasons. Because Paris was declared to be in a state of siege from 1871 to 1874 by Adolphe Thiers and because the last cities to be seized after the Treaty of Frankfurt remained under German occupation until 1876,[10] the French government sought to avoid any flare-up of anti-Germanism that might trigger an intervention from the German army in these cities or rekindle the embers of the Commune. In this context, censor-

Table 5.2. Number of chansons referencing the enemy after World War I. Table created by the author.

Year/period	Number of chansons
1919	9
1920	2
1921	1
1922	1
1923	0
1924	0
1925	1
1926–39	0
Total	**14**

ship was seen as an instrument for fostering calm and encouraging a return to peace, as this record dated 1891 from the Ministère de l'Instruction Publique et des Beaux-Arts shows: "From 1871 to 1874, owing to the state of siege, censorship was imposed under the authority of the military government in Paris. It has never been stricter than it was at that time regarding theatre and particularly café-concert repertoires."[11]

A number of anti-German plays, such as *Le Sergent Hoff*, *L'Espionne allemande*, and *Les Martyrs de Strasbourg*, were banned outright.[12] The fact that nineteen chansons perpetuating the figure of the enemy escaped the censorship regime suggests that many more were actually written (see table 5.1). Chanson production during this time under siege shows that, despite the government's efforts, the café-concert remained a space in which the mobilization of minds was perpetuated. Although there was a notable decline from the second half of the 1880s onward, the production of chansons denouncing the enemy never dried up completely. Thus, by 1914 the demobilization of anti-German minds had not really been fully achieved. Four decades of peace had not managed to quell the conflictual state of society that was still reflected in and even maintained by the chanson production, because the café-concert was widely accessible to all social categories during this period, both in Paris and in other major towns and cities where the repertoires and artistes circulated. In 1908 the chansonnier Paulus (Jean-Paulin Habans, 1845–1908) reported that the chansons that were created at the café-concert circulated very quickly in "the streets and salons,"[13] an indication that France never fully transitioned out of the Franco-Prussian War.

The number of chansons produced between 1871 and 1913 that reference the enemy reveals this period as an example of an incomplete postwar transition—in other words, one from which the population never really emerged. By contrast, chanson production after World War I indicates a transition that lasted only four years (1919–22), with production drying up in 1923 (see table 5.2). This finding confirms the existence of the "forgotten era of violence" (1918–23) identified by historians Alexandre Sumpf and John Horne.[14] However, the low number of chansons published during this period also shows that, unlike in the years following the 1871 defeat, the chanson was not the main vehicle for this "violence."

How, then, do we explain how a conflict lasting only a few months gave rise to a figure of the enemy that lingered on for more than forty years after the guns had fallen silent, while this same figure had disappeared from the chanson four years after a total war that lasted five years and aimed to annihilate the adversary? This paradox is even more striking given that World War I produced a genuine chanson culture in France.[15] There is no doubting the fact that the figure of the enemy remains much more pervasive after a defeat (because the losing party remains mobilized by a collective need for revenge) than after a victory (because the winning party wants to forget about the conflict and celebrate a return to peace). Does this mean, then, that musicology has nothing new to bring to the historiographical conclusions that have long contrasted the revanchism of the post-1871 period with the pacifism of the post-1919 period? This is highly unlikely for two reasons. First, anti-German sentiment did not just disappear entirely from French society in 1923. This is evidenced by a series of vitriolic articles in the French music press known as the "affaire des poisons," which pitted the composer Jean Wiéner against the critic Louis Vuillemin, who accused Wiéner of promoting contemporary "boches"[16] (pejorative nickname for Germans and Austrians) composers. Moreover, several studies have shown that between 1871 and 1914 neither French public opinion nor French political discourse was in any way dominated by belligerent revanchism and that this idea results from a historiographical reconstruction that took place during and after World War I.[17] The second reason relates to the internal dynamics of the French chanson. An often politicized and readily patriotic genre in the café-concert context, which was its main outlet until the first decade of the twentieth century, the chanson became a more unifying genre in the music hall context, its principal venue after 1918. For a more in-depth consideration of these two observations, an analysis of the content of the chansons in the corpus is necessary.

The Identities of the Enemy

The first and very important point to clarify is the identity of the enemy referenced in the chansons. Or rather the *enemies*, because in addition to denouncing Germany and the Germans, French chansonniers launched equally virulent albeit more peripheral attacks at some compatriots, whom they considered to be enemies from within.

In 1871 this figure of the enemy from within crystalized around the French leaders who were linked to the military defeats in the Battle of Sedan and the Siege of Metz, particularly Napoleon III, General Trochu, and Marshal Bazaine. The café-concert chanson portrayed them as absolute traitors for having wanted to "sortir de la guerre" (exit from the war) and precipitate France's surrender. "À

Montfaucon"—a chanson created by Jules Perrin, the star turn at one of the most famous café-concerts in Paris, the Eldorado, from 1865 to 1893—provides a perfect illustration of the ways in which these internal enemies were denounced. Not only are Napoleon III and Bazaine specifically targeted in the score's illustration, but verse upon verse denounces the incompetence and lack of patriotism of the French military intendants, magistrates, and politicians as well as the compromises they made with the enemy. Every last one of them, according to the chanson, should be condemned to death on the gallows for leading the heroic unranked soldiers to their deaths.

The chansons castigating the internal enemy after the Treaty of Frankfurt denounced a war that was only really over on paper. Their lyrics proposed two conditions for a proper transition out of the war. The first was that the memory of the humiliation of the crushing defeat suffered by the French army had to be expunged. As in "À Montfaucon," the chansonniers stressed the heroism of the French soldiers and shifted the blame for the defeat to the leaders (with a few notable exceptions such as General Denfert). Underlying the denunciation of the internal enemy was thus a glorification of the conquered. Transitioning out of the war meant restoring the honor of the French soldiers and, by extension, of the French people and nation. Hence the success of the chansons that lauded the soldiers' exemplary resistance and bravery, such as "Les Cuirassiers de Reichshoffen," which was republished numerous times between 1871 and 1914. The second condition was that the French elites responsible for the defeat—in other words, the Second Empire establishment—had to be regenerated. In 1870 this idea could only be referring to the French Revolution, which had seen the French troops confronted with an internal enemy in 1792, namely the aristocracy.[18] The aristocracy was accused of having dealings with the external enemy, which was itself associated with the European aristocracy rather than with the French people. Hence, there was a postwar boom in reissues of revolutionary songs such as "La Marseillaise" and "Le Chant du Départ," which were regularly published right up until 1914. As with the chansons denouncing the enemy, the number of reissues of these revolutionary songs was much lower after 1918 (see table 5.3).

This difference can be explained by the fact that the chansons published after World War I denounced a different internal enemy. In spite of mutinies against the French command from 1917 onward, the generals were spared because they had ultimately led France to

Table 5.3. Number of reissues of "La Marseillaise" and "Le Chant du Départ" after the 1870 war (period 1871–1913) and the 1914–18 war (period 1919–29). Table created by the author.

Year/period	"La Marseillaise"	"Le Chant du Départ"
1865–69	9	4
1870	55	17
1871–74	16	10
1875–79	44	7
1880–84	57	15
1885–89	31	7
1890–94	24	8
1895–99	10	1
1900–04	11	5
1905–09	12	6
1910–13	21	4
Total (1871–1913)	**226**	**64**
Total (1919–29)	**13**	**3**

victory. The internal enemy was now the *mercantis* (profiteers). In Louis Despax and P. Codini's chanson of the same name, this enemy was denounced as profiting from the war after they had "bâti des fortunes" (amassed their fortunes) selling supplies to the military at exorbitant prices and then creating expensive living conditions after the war. The group now being targeted had profited from the heroic sacrifices made by the vast majority of the French population, both on the battlefield and on the home front. The enemy was no longer the traitor or the political foe but the social parasite who had not played their part in national unity. Transitioning out of the war meant deciding their fate. Like "À Montfaucon," "Les Mercantis" called for them to be sent to the gallows. Hence, in addition to the different postwar transition rhythms, the figures of the enemy that emerge are different, as are the uses of these figures and also therefore the functions of the chansons that contributed to their diffusion. Similar divergences can be detected in the chansons about the Germans, which made up the majority of the repertoires referencing the enemy after the peace treaties of 1871 and 1919.

The External Enemy after 1871: A Political Foil to Promote National Republican Regeneration

Like Napoleon III and Bazaine, the German enemy (and more precisely Kaiser Wilhelm I and the German Army Rabble) portrayed in the post-1871 chansons served as a foil, affirming the need for France to draw on its revolutionary heritage and regenerate. In the 1870s and 1880s, this almost omnipresent theme in the "patriotic chanson" genre was particularly timely for the supporters of the Third Republic.

"Ils n'en ont pas en Allemagne" perfectly illustrates this marshalling of the figure of the external enemy to promote the new regime. This chanson was written by two prominent figures in popular music, lyricist Gaston Villemer (1842–92) and composer Robert Planquette (1848–1903), both of whom embarked on a patriotic mission after 1870. Specializing in chanson and operetta, Planquette also wrote "Le Régiment de Sambre et Meuse" (1867), the most famous French patriotic chanson published between 1870 and 1914. Aiming indirectly to eulogize republican France, "Ils n'en ont pas en Allemagne" portrayed the Germans as arrogant, bellicose oppressors. The Germans might have "de gros canons et de grosses mitrailleuses" (big canons and big machine guns), but they did not have "La Marseillaise." The Germans were led by "sombres généraux" (somber generals), but they did not have Generals Kléber or Marceau, two heroes of the Revolutionary Wars.[19] The Germans were subject to "l'esclavage éternel" (eternal slavery); they did not have the "République." Two other more contemporary republican references, Victor Hugo and the chansonnier Béranger, appeared in the lithograph on the front cover of this score. Although it acknowledged Germany's victory, attributing it to its technical superiority and tyrannical discipline, Planquette's chanson asserted that republican France, the country of heroism and freedom, had not been defeated.

This use of references to the enemy as a foil for a France that embodied an ideal born of the Revolution of 1789–92 can also be seen in the rarer chansons that called for fraternization with the former enemy. One case in point is "L'Appel à l'Allemagne" (1871), which was performed on the stages of the three biggest café-concerts in Paris, namely the Eldorado, the Alcazar, and the Ambassadeurs. As with "Ils n'en ont pas en Allemagne," the figure of the enemy is represented by the "tyrans" (tyrants)—in this case Kaiser Wilhelm I—rather than by the German people. The German people were instead portrayed as the victims, suffering under the "joug" (yoke) of "maîtres ambitieux" (ambitious masters) and forced to go to war against their will. In the chorus, which was performed by a three-voice mixed choir, the French people urged their neighbor across the Rhine to draw inspiration from the Revolution of 1789 and throw off their shackles. "L'Appel à l'Allemagne" is interesting in that it upends the figure of the former enemy, transposing it from an object of hatred into an object of commiseration. In turn, France was reassured, even in defeat, through a continued presentation of itself as a model that should be followed by all peoples in the face of tyrants. As the lithograph on the front cover showed, the French model would ensure peace between the populations by putting an end to tyranny. Some of the post-1871 chansons therefore tended to use the figure of the tyrant to universalize the figure of the enemy by not reducing it to its German nationality. At the same time, these chansons cast France in an almost messianic role. Contrary to the conclusions drawn in press-based research studies,[20] the enemy's role, as defined in 1792 by revolutionary France, thus remained active after 1871. While it had admittedly tended to disappear from the newspapers, it was nevertheless kept alive in the field of the popular chanson.

For the café-concert audiences and those who bought the sheet music (the majority of sheet music cost one franc or less, which equated to less than one-third of an average worker's daily wage in 1872[21]), "L'Appel à l'Allemagne," like many other post-1871 chansons, contributed to a portrait of the enemy that promoted the construction of another figure, that of the heroic vanquished. Chansons referencing the enemy in this way thus played an almost therapeutic role. While "lamenting the defeat,"[22] these chansons helped exorcise the national humiliation and trauma of 1870–71. This heroic vanquished figure also existed in a more intimate version that was more closely connected with daily life than with the revolutionary gesture. This is illustrated by the majority of chansons written by Gaston Villemer (1842–92) and Lucien Delormel (1847–99), particularly those concerning the occupation of Alsace-Lorraine. All of these chansons were popularized by Thérèse Amiati (1851–89), who was the voice of vengeful France in the 1870s and 1880s as well as the star turn at the Eldorado, the Scala, and the Ambassadeurs. These chansons were so successful that in 1885 fifty-four of them were published in a single volume. In "Le Fils de l'Allemand" (1882), for example, a French mother refused to breastfeed a German officer's baby, whose mother had died in childbirth, despite the urgency of the request and the baby's innocence. Citing the atrocities she had suffered at the hands of the German soldiers, who had "[mis] le feu dans [son] hameau" (set fire to [her] hamlet) and "[tué son] enfant dans le berceau" ([killed her] child in the cradle), she declared: "Mes garçons chanteront plus tard 'La Marseillaise' . . . ; Je ne vends pas mon lait au fils d'un Allemand" (My boys will sing "La Marseillaise" by and by . . . ; I am not selling my milk to the son of a German). More than ten years after France had been defeated, the nation's patriotism remained intact in the café-concert chanson.

In addition to prolonging hostility toward the enemy after the war had ended, the post-1871 chansons contributed to reconstructing France's image according to different needs and circumstances, such as promoting a new political regime or exorcising the humiliation felt over the defeat. Hence, the decline from the 1890s onward in the production of French chansons referencing Germany as the enemy owes as much to the normalization of Franco-German relations as to the stabilization of the Third Republic and the development of the French colonial empire, which mitigated the humiliation caused by the loss of Alsace-Lorraine. These two functions of prolonging and reconstructing were to reappear in the years following World War I but in different forms.

The External Enemy after 1918

The chansons published from 1919 to 1923 that referenced the German enemy were a continuation of chansons produced during the conflict. They were born of a genuine war culture, a culture that had not emerged during the 1870 conflict owing to its (shorter) duration and (more exclusively military) nature. As such, they mobilized the "boche" as a foil to exorcize the atrocities of war. The inertia of this war culture after the signing of the Treaty of Versailles was, however, relatively minimal compared to the never-ending postwar transition following the Franco-Prussian War. While the figure of the enemy remained present between 1919 and 1923, it was no longer limited to the German leaders or soldiers but rather generalized to *all Germans*, who were most often described in the collective-singular form as the "boche," but also the "Saxon,"[23] or the "Teuton."[24] The collective-singular, here, conceals a transformation that had taken place between the two conflicts, namely the ethnicization and animalization of the external enemy, as exemplified by the caricatures published during the war.[25] The German invasion was now being systematically portrayed as a horde of "barbares pervers"[26] (perverse barbarians), "pillant et brûlant"[27] (plundering and burning down villages) and squealing like "cochons"[28] (pigs) when defeated.

While references to the German enemy "were often a nod to the memory of 1870"[29] (such as the enduring stereotype of the German as a "voleur de pendules" [pendulum thief]), the post-1919 figure of the enemy differed from that portrayed in the post-1871 patriotic chansons. No longer a political countermodel, the enemy was now excluded from humanity altogether. This may explain the much lower representation of the patriotic chanson genre among the post-1919 chansons referencing the enemy than among those published in the wake of the Franco-Prussian War. The few works contained in this genre were not spared the ethnicized view of the enemy. This is evidenced in the "Marseillaise de la Victoire," a chanson written to the tune of "La Marseillaise." Rather than denouncing tyrants, it focused on the Germans and jeered at a "race immonde" (filthy race) of "monstres sans âmes"[30] (soulless monsters). The post-1871 political enemy had been transformed into an ethnic enemy. The main reason for this transformation was anthropological in nature.

After World War I, the chansons referencing the enemy were intended to provide the French people with an outlet for the trauma they had suffered during the conflict. As noted in research on global and civil conflicts,[31] postwar transition can be seen as a cathartic period, a period of emotional release during which singers could exorcise collectively the atrocities of war through tears and emotion, but also though laughter.[32] After 1871, the collection of chansons referencing the enemy was at first dominated by the very serious patriotic chanson genre, and it was not until 1903 that some "comic," "satirical" chansons were published, most of them focusing on Wilhelm II: "Entrevue de Sarah Bernhardt et de Guillaume II" (1903), "Biographie de Guillaume II" (1904), "Les Alliances de Guillaume II" (1906), among others. While these comic and satirical songs remained an exception to the body of chansons evoking the Franco–Prussian conflict, the majority of French songs referencing the First World War after 1918 tended toward burlesque and satire. Examples include "La Ceinture à Guillaume" (1919) and "Les Joies de l'Occupation" (1919), which were written by one of the most famous chansonniers of the time, Lucien Boyer (1876–1942), who lived in Montmartre and popularized this type of chanson both in Paris and in the provincial music halls of seaside and spa resorts such as Vichy and Arcachon. In "Les Joies de l'Occupation," one French soldier "se paye la gueule des boches" (takes the mickey out of the boche) to the bouncy rhythms of a foxtrot played in a major key. In addition to the different status of the "enemy" after 1871 and 1919, the second reason for the strong presence of more upbeat chansons after 1918 was musical in nature. On the one hand, there was a growing influence of English and American musicalhall songs in France since the 1900s, and the resulting increase in lighthearted repertoires based on Anglo–American dance rhythms in French popular music, such as ragtime and foxtrot. The Americanization of the chanson became even more significant after 1917 and the arrival of the US contingent in France, which provoked the vogue for jazz.[33] On the other hand, and more particularly, French songs from the late 1910s and early 1920s were influenced by American songs about the War, composed in 1917 and 1918, such as Jack Caddigan and Chick Story's "You Can't Stop the Yanks" (1918), a joyful march which denounces the atrocities of war (the "slaughter over the water") in a light way and announces that they will "kick the bottom out of Willie's pants." That comic and satirical songs were more important in the transition periods following the First World War than in the aftermath of the Franco–Prussian war was can thus be explained by a combination of at least three factors: the different status of the enemy, the different outcomes of these conflicts from the French perspective, the different musical, and the stylistic context in which chansons were composed. The very nature of the conflict is another key factor. In the dramatic context of the war and the years that followed, mixing joyful rhythms and melodies with themes of death and war certainly provoked harsh criticism, as did apparently light-hearted works such as Erik Satie and Jean Cocteau's *Parade,* and, indeed, jazz itself (1917).[34] However, upbeat satirical songs were another kind of response to the sense of absurdity and irony which developed within the literary world during the war,[35] and also fuelled Dadaism until the mid-1920s.[36] Whether animalized or ridiculed, the German enemy served to exorcise the collective trauma suffered in France during the war. This function explains the rapid disappearance of the chansons that perpetuated the memory of the war. The real enemy now was the war itself. Hence, while there were only a few isolated examples of the pacifist chanson between 1871 and 1913, the genre developed significantly after 1918. After the Franco-Prussian War, the chanson contributed to the calls for revenge. After World War I, it contributed to the pursuit of peace.

Conclusion

It is possible, for any given country, to find at least one example of a chanson that reflects one or other of the many opinions in circulation from the nineteenth century onward. This poses a risk for the researcher because it means they can support whatever it is they are looking to find in a given period with an example of a chanson without questioning its representativeness in terms of chanson production and its diffusion within the society in question. Hence, it is important to mitigate this risk as far as possible by reflexively building a corpus that addresses these two factors (albeit it is difficult to accurately trace the circulation and reception in Paris and the provinces of every chanson in the corpus). Without such a corpus, it is impossible to map and hierarchize the different trends and opinions conveyed by the chanson and indeed the press.

Constructed with this methodological precaution in mind, the present corpus of chansons perpetuating the image of the enemy in two postwar transition periods leads to two findings. The first is that these chansons were both a reflection (indicator function) and a determining factor (driver function) of the duration and nature of the two periods in question. With regard to duration, the chansons show that the postwar transition after 1870 was never truly complete and that they in fact contributed to this incompleteness. After 1918, by contrast, the rapid disappearance of these chansons evidences a shorter and more complete postwar transition. With regard to the nature of the two postwar transition periods, these chansons reflected the main issues at play and kept them topical. After 1871, the figure of the enemy fuelled not only the revanchism generated by France's partly unexpected defeat but also a negative national identity that was formed through opposing the Other rather than identifying a unifying common denominator. After the Treaty of Versailles, the figure of the enemy served a different domestic purpose, which was to exorcise the atrocities of the conflict and preserve the idea of national unity. A postwar transition period represents more than just a perpetuation of the figure of the enemy for a variable duration; it is also a time of reinterpretation.

The second finding is that these chansons, through the enemies they chose to reference, established a truncated and biased memory of the two wars. For example, not one chanson in the corpus denounced Léon Gambetta, even though there was a groundswell of opposition in France to his *jusqu'au-boutisme* (brinkmanship). Similarly, even though the pacifist movement remained strong in the years following the conflict, none of the chansons condemned the French generals for the butchery of World War I. This finding once again raises the question of censorship and prohibition regarding the chansons as well as the political orientation of the café-concert and music hall repertoires. The post-1871 political chanson disseminated what the historian François Roth called "the republican interpretation of the events of 1870–71,"[37] while the post-1918 chanson promoted Clemenceau's patriotic line. It can therefore be hypothesized that the majority of the café-concert and music hall chansons containing a political message are a musical equivalent of the political caricature—an artwork meant to entertain *and* to circulate political opinions, often with a satirical and political tone. Most of these chansons conveyed a patriotic, republican ideology that was rooted in France's revolutionary past. There was of course a repertoire of pacifist chansons published after 1871 and 1918 as well as a corpus of chansons defending a royalist conception of the nation, but these rarely made an appearance on the music hall and café-concert stages.

Finally, it seems that, in addition to fulfilling its dual function as an indicator and driver, the chanson helped establish and convey stereotypes that were to linger on long after the postwar transition periods had ended. A case in point is Bazaine's betrayal, a cliché that was to be transmitted down the generations through "Le Maréchal Bazaine." This chanson, which was published in July 1871 and written to an 1817 melody that had also previously been used by Béranger, was still frequently being sung as late as the 1960s. This is evidenced by the fact that a version of the chanson was recorded by a singer from the rural département of Nièvre in 2006 as part of a survey on chanson and dance in the period 1930–60.[38] Despite some distortions due to the accumulation of oral transmission phases, Bazaine's betrayal had become one of the main commonplaces in the republican memory of the Franco-Prussian War as a direct result of the chansons written in the postwar transition period. Analyses of postconflict chansons perpetuating the figure of the enemy have the potential to make an original contribution to the study both of postwar transitions and of international conflicts more broadly. Music, like other arts, does not just reflect past history. It is not content to simply repeat what traditional cultural history sources and approaches have helped (and will long continue to help) reveal. Musical works also have another story to tell.

Martin Guerpin is an assistant professor at Paris-Saclay University. His research focuses on the relations between art and popular music as well as on the relationship between music and identities (of the nineteenth, twentieth, and twenty-first centuries). His PhD thesis, entitled "Aesthetic and Cultural Meanings of Appropriations of Jazz in the French Art Music World (1900–1939)," is currently in preparation for publication. He is also preparing a critical edition of Francophone texts about jazz written during the 1920s. His publications have been awarded prizes such as the Socan-Proctor Prize (Canada) and the Marie Skłodowska-Curie Fellowship (European Union). His research has been published in *Revue de Musicologie, Revue musicale OICRM, Cahiers du jazz, L'Histoire,* and *Journal of the Royal Musical Association*, and numerous edited collections. Since 2015 he has codirected the international research network Music and Nation, which investigates topics such as the role of music in postwar periods and the role of the arts in the Americanization of Europe before 1945.

Notes

1. This chapter was translated from French by Clare Ferguson.
2. Béranger (de), *Procès fait aux chansons de P.-J. de Béranger*, 17. "Est-ce parce que la chanson [se] grave aisément dans la mémoire, qu'elle est de facile réminiscence, et que le sel piquant qui l'assaisonne est un salpêtre électrique prompt à ébranler les esprits? . . . Est-ce parce que, circulant avec rapidité, elle pénètre en même temps dans les villes et les hameaux également comprise de toutes les classes? Tandis que la brochure la plus coupable n'exerce que dans un cercle étroit sa mauvaise influence, la chanson, plus contagieuse mille fois, peut infecter jusqu'à l'air qu'on respire."
3. Among the pioneering works in this field, see Klein, *La Chanson à l'affiche*; Pénet, *Mémoire de la chanson*; and Leterrier, *Béranger*.
4. This followed the armistice of 28 January 1871. A particular feature of the 1870 conflict is that the Paris Commune episode (18 March–28 May 1871) straddled the period between the signing of the armistice and the signing of the peace treaty. The chronology of the Commune does not call into question the chronology of the official end of the Franco-Prussian War. It represents a phenomenon that is characteristic of some postwar periods, namely the outbreak of civil conflict following an external defeat.
5. This followed the armistice of 11 November 1918.
6. Mentioned for the first time in a Conseil d'État judgment in 1714, the legal deposit ruling obliged music publishers to deposit a copy of each published piece of sheet music in the Bibliothèque Nationale de France. However, some publishers did not comply with this procedure, either out of ignorance or out of a desire to circumvent it. The legal deposit archive is therefore not considered to be an accurate reflection of French musical production at any given time. See Bodez, Pichon and Sablonnière, "Le dépôt légal de la musique à la Bibliothèque Nationale de France," 236–43.
7. Data were collected from five music magazines: *L'Art Musical, Le Ménestrel, Le Courrier musical, Lyrica,* and *La Rampe.*
8. Archives Nationales, série F/18(I)/33 to 65.
9. The keywords used for this search were *ennemi, guerre, allemande, Allemagne, prussien, Prusse, Boche, Fritz, barbare,* and the names of the key political and military figures associated with each conflict (e.g., Bismarck, Wilhelm II).

10. Lagana, "Un peuple révolutionnaire," 175–98.
11. Ministère de l'Instruction Publique (Archives Nationales, F^{21} 5200). "De 1871 à 1874, la censure s'exerçait, en raison de l'état de siège, sous l'autorité du gouvernement militaire de Paris. Jamais elle n'a été plus sévère qu'à cette époque pour le répertoire des théâtres et surtout pour celui des cafés-concerts."
12. Krakovitch, *Censure des répertoires des grands théâtres parisiens*, 46.
13. Paulus, *Trente ans de café-concert*, 306. "Les rues et les salons."
14. "L'ère oubliée de la violence" was the title of a lecture delivered at the German Historical Institute (Paris) on 16 January 2018 as part of the series of lectures entitled *Les Sorties de guerre. France, Allemagne, Europe 1917–1923*, organized jointly by the German Historical Institute and the Mission du Centenaire de la Première Guerre Mondiale.
15. See, for example, Sweeney, *Singing Our Way to Victory*; Audoin-Rouzeau et al., *La Grande Guerre des musiciens*; Pénet, "Chansons de l'arrière et du front"; Doé de Maindreville and Etcharry, *La Grande Guerre en musique*.
16. Guerpin, "*Le Courrier musical* et le premier conflit mondial (1904–1923)," 35–57.
17. Becker, *Comment les Français sont entrés dans la guerre*; and Joly, "La France et la Revanche (1871–1914)," 325–47.
18. On this subject, see Jeismann, *La Patrie de l'ennemi*.
19. General Jean-Baptiste Kléber (1753–1800) took part in the Vendée and Egyptian campaigns. He was assassinated in Egypt in 1800. General François Marceau (1769–96) commanded the Army of the Sambre and Meuse and died in combat trying to break the blockade at Mainz.
20. See, in particular, Jeismann, *La Patrie de l'ennemi*.
21. Renaud, "Prix et salaires à Paris en 1870 et 1872," 177.
22. Paulus, *Trente ans de café-concert*, 136. "Pleurant la défaite."
23. Claure Réal and A. Fredly, *Gloire à Foch* (Paris: Gallet, 1920). Approximate translation from French "Germain."
24. Charles Borel-Clerc and Charles-Louis Pothier, *Ils ont rendu l'Alsace* (Paris: Charles Borel-Clerc, 1920): "teuton."
25. This transformation has already been well described by Jeismann, *La Patrie de l'ennemi*, 301–8. For a broader perspective, see also Mosse, *De la Grande Guerre aux totalitarismes*.
26. Rolland, *La Marseillaise de la victoire*, 1919.
27. E. Favart, R. Chavance and P. Codini, *Les Peupliers de Saint-Cloud* (Paris: Codini, 1919).
28. E. Jaquinot, Willems, and Dommel, *Fritz est frit* (Paris: Willems, 1919).
29. Roth, *La Guerre de 1870*, 715: "Fait souvent référence à la mémoire de 1870."
30. Rolland, *La Marseillaise de la victoire*.
31. Judt, *Postwar*, 45 and Dirnstorfer and Bahadur, "A Stage for the Unknown?" 131.
32. Stewart. "De la *catharsis* comique," 192.
33. The use of humorous and satirical songs was already observable in 1870, notably with the famous *Sire de Fisch Ton Kan*, which portrayed Napoleon III as an incompetent traitor. From a quantitative point of view, however, there was a far larger representation of comic chansons after 1918 than after 1871.
34. Guerpin, "Why Did Art Music Composers Pay Attention to Jazz?", 5461 and Nichols, *The Harlequin Years*, 38.
35. Fussell, *The Great War and Modern Memory*, 335.
36. Blake, "'Jazz-band Dada'", 72–75.
37. Roth, *La Guerre de 1870*, 578. "L'interprétation républicaine des événements de 1870–1871."
38. "Les Occasions de danser sur le canton de Luzy (1930–1960)."

Bibliography

Audoin-Rouzeau, Stéphane, Esteban Buch, Myriam Chimènes, and Georgie Durosoir, eds. *La Grande Guerre des musiciens.* Lyon: Symétrie, 2009.

Becker, Jean-Jacques. *Comment les Français sont entrés dans la guerre.* Paris: Presses de Sciences Po, 1977.

Béranger (de), Pierre-Jean. *Procès fait aux chansons de P.-J. de Béranger, avec le réquisitoire de Me Marchangy, le plaidoyer de Me Dupin.* Paris: Les Marchands de Nouveautés, 1821.

Blake, Jody. "'Jazz-band Dada'. L'afro-américanisme dans le Paris de l'entre-deux-guerres." *Revue de l'Art* 118 (1997), 6977.

Bodez, Marie-Pierre, Pierre Pichon, and Marguerite Sablonnière. "Le dépôt légal de la musique à la Bibliothèque Nationale de France: état des lieux et nouveaux enjeux." *Fontes Artis Musicae* 58, no. 3 (2011): 236–43.

Dirnstorfer, Anne and Bahadur Saud, Nad. "A Stage for the Unknown? Reconciling Postwar Communities through Theatre-Facilitated Dialogue." *International Journal of Transitional Justice* 14 (2020): 122–141.

Doé de Maindreville, Florence, and Stéphan Etcharry, Stéphane, eds. *La Grande Guerre en musique. Vie et création musicales en France pendant la Première Guerre mondiale.* Bern: Peter Lang, 2014.

Fussell, Paul. *The Great War and Modern Memory.* New York: OUP, 1975.

Guerpin, Martin. "Why Did Art Music Composers Pay Attention to Jazz? The Impact of Jazz on the French musical Field (1908-1927)," in *Eurojazzland. Jazz and European Sources, Dynamics and Context*, edited by Luca Cerchiari, Laurent Cugny and Franz Kerbschbaumer, 4780. Boston: Northeastern University Press, 2012.

Guerpin, Martin. "*Le Courrier musical* et le premier conflit mondial (1904–1923). Propagande, mobilisation culturelle et sortie de guerre." *Revue Musicale OICRM* 4, no. 2 (2017): 35–57.

Jeismann, Michael. *La Patrie de l'ennemi. La notion d'ennemi national et la représentation de la nation en Allemagne et en France.* Paris: CNRS Éditions, 1997.

Joly, Bertrand. "La France et la Revanche (1871–1914)." *Revue d'histoire moderne et contemporaine* 46, no. 2 (1999): 325–47.

Judt, Tony. *Postwar. A History of Europe Since 1945.* New York: Penguin Press, 2005, 45

Klein, Jean-Claude. *La Chanson à l'affiche. Histoire de la chanson française du café-concert à nos jours.* Paris: Du May, 1991.

Krakovitch, Odile. *Censure des répertoires des grands théâtres parisiens.* Paris: Centre Historique des Archives Nationales, 2003.

Lagana, Marc. "Un peuple révolutionnaire: la Commune de Paris 1871." *Cahiers Bruxellois* 1 (2018): 175–98.

Leterrier, Sophie-Anne. *Béranger, des chansons pour un peuple citoyen.* Rennes: Presses Universitaires de Rennes, 2013.

"Les Occasions de danser sur le canton de Luzy (1930–1960)." *Base interrégionale du patrimoine oral*. Retrieved 3 October 2018 from http://patrimoine-oral.org/dyn/portal/index.seam;jsessionid=c046ecb188dcc5cf1abbf9b6237d?aloId=2462&page=alo&fonds=1&cid=462.

Mosse, George. *De la Grande Guerre aux totalitarismes. La brutalisation des sociétés européennes*. Paris: Hachette, 1999.

Nichols, Roger. *The Harlequin Years. Music in Paris (1917–1929)*. London: Thames & Hudson, 2002.

Paulus, *Trente ans de café-concert. Souvenirs recueillis par Octave Pradels*. Paris: Société d'Édition et de Publications, 1908.

Pénet, Martin. *Mémoire de la chanson, 1200 chansons de 1920 à 1945*. Paris: Omnibus, 2004.

———. "Chansons de l'arrière et du front," in *Entendre la guerre. Silence, musiques et sons en 14-18, edited by* Florence Gétreau, 36–51. Paris: Gallimard, 2014.

Renaud, Georges. "Prix et salaires à Paris en 1870 et 1872." *Journal de la Société statistique de Paris* 14 (1873): 177.

Roth, François. *La Guerre de 1870*. Paris: Fayard/Pluriel, 1990.

Stewart, Philip. "De la *catharsis* comique." *Littératures classiques* 27 (1996): 183193.

Sweeney, Regina M. *Singing Our Way to Victory. French Cultural Politics and Music during the Great War*. Middletown, CT: Wesleyan University Press, 2001.

Chapter 6

WAR OF TASTE IN POPULAR AND FOLK MUSIC
French Chanson, 1940–1942

Philippe Gumplowicz

French historian Henry Rousso, and after him the Research Center of the Historial de la Grande Guerre, have identified first years after the 1940 armistice as a postwar transition.[1] For all those who returned to work in the autumn of 1940, France was entering a postwar period. The armistice brought with it difficult conditions imposed by the occupying force, along with damaged reputations for some and new opportunities for others. For the majority, but not Jews, communists, or prisoners, however, life just continued as before.[2] France nevertheless still had to come to terms with the defeat, meaning for those who, politically on the right, had a public voice had to be able to understand and explain it. A discourse of defeat thus emerged from among a stream of regretful observations about the unpreparedness of the French army, the disarmament of the country and its elites, and the lack of vision of the nation's leadership.[3] Both the right and far right as well as the 1930s essayists (many of whom are thought to have espoused collaborationism[4]) were pointing out the responsibilities of the Third Republic politicians, whose ultimate dread would have been the Front Populaire.[5] One of them, the musicologist and critic André Cœuroy, head of the musical column of the ultra-collaborationist weekly *Je suis partout*, will be particularly studied in this article through one of his publications on popular music.

Notes for this section begin on page 131.

This discourse of defeat drew on the same religious register of contrition illustrated by Marshal Pétain in his speech of 17 June 1940: "Since the victory [of 1918], the spirit of pleasure [had] prevailed over the spirit of sacrifice."[6] This national examining of conscience thus indicated an extremely intense general state of mind that is difficult for us to grasp today. There was a need to explain the inexplicable, a convergence of factors that had spanned the political, moral, spiritual, and aesthetic spheres. France had already found itself devitalized, morally disarmed, and unable to defend itself before this. Jean-Pierre Maxence, a nonconformist intellectual who subsequently became involved in active collaborationism, wrote at the end of an essay published in 1939: "France is exhausted from so many beatings, shaken by so much futile anger and broken by so many thwarted hopes. It is like a seriously ill patient, no longer moving and barely able to speak. It just waits, pale, tired, and weary of creating fear. Engulfed by everything that has happened to it, it no longer rises up."[7]

How could this defeat be explained in a country whose memory of the glorious moments of its history, particularly the Great War victory, still burned bright? "The disaster in my country has military, political, economic, and social causes, but we lack the necessary perspective to define and enumerate them exactly,"[8] wrote Georges Bernanos. What France was lacking here was art. Although somewhat distanced from this theater of operations, the world of music commentary was called upon to express its views on this devitalization. André Coeuroy, editor in chief of the *Revue musicale*, had detected the first signs of exhaustion in the musical press as early as 1930, and this exhaustion only increased as the decade went on. After the armistice of June 1940, he was asked by the writer and publisher Jacques Chardonne[9] to draw up a medical image to explain the changing tastes in the field of song: "We need to know the reasons for our ruination, . . . This disaster cannot be traced back to just individual errors or technical accidents. Every organ in France's body was undermined."[10]

Was Chardonne also referring to the vocal organ here? Indeed, he was. The explanation of the defeat of France by arguments which borrowed from the lexicon of organic pathology came from the eugenic thought of the extreme right. The lamentation drew on metaphors from the clinical picture of viral and microbial infection. It depicted a healthy body that had been attacked by viruses. France had been subject to attacks from invisible agents prior to the military invasion, and music was certainly partly responsible for the defeat. Coeuroy spoke for the prosecution in his book *La Musique et le peuple en France*. A better title, one more in tune with its content, would have been "la musique *contre* le peuple en France" (music *against* the people of France). A series of corrosive factors had undone the inner song of the French people, the intangible testimony of an identity that Coeuroy would have wished eternal or, at the very least, unshakable.

Could traditional music reflect the inner soul of a France that, although long since unified under a state centralized by the monarchy, was divided into so many small countries? The anti-republican and nationalist unrest at the turn of the century had prompted the composer and teacher Vincent d'Indy to send his students out to conquer rural France. Michel Faure has noted that folklore had become a "musical obsession among scholarly musicians."[11] The emergence from war in 1940 aroused a renewed interest among music experts in the traditional French chanson.[12] Interest in folksongs, yet present before the war, redoubled in perspective of the ruralist issues of the Vichy regime. But this does not belong just to the extreme right, even if, among musicologists, André Cœuroy can be culturally classified under this category. Among the young generation, Jacques Chailley and Norbert Dufourcq, called to occupy an important place in the post-war musicological world, are in cultural agreement with the theses of the Vichy regime. For his part, Henri Davenson, pen name of Henri-Irénée Marrou for his musicological works, saw himself as a "pure resistant". He was involved during the war in the network "Amitié chrétienne," which made it his mission to save the Jews.

The chanson had largely disappeared in the later stages of industrialization, a phenomenon that was marked by the professionalization and development of the chanson industry. Supported by a task force comprising records, radio, and cinema, the industry had become technically and commercially efficient by the beginning of the 1930s. As regards the work songs, which was ironically described by Henri-Irénée Marrou as "an emanation from the collective soul,"[13] the battle had already been lost.[14] By the 1920s the Lyre et palette group and Les Six were enthusing over the café-concert[15] chanson, the music hall, and the variety show. However, as mass circulation of the chanson increased, the genre became progressively more suspect.[16] According to Louis-Ferdinand Céline (and Coeuroy), folklore had become a recourse: "The world no longer has a melody. We are still lulled by folklore, the last whispers of our folklore. When that has gone, and night comes, so will the Negro's tam-tam."[17]

André Coeuroy: Biographical Sketch

After spending four years in captivity during the Great War, this École Normale Supérieure alumnus, who was born in 1891 and who had been a pupil of the composer Max Reger in Leipzig, gave up his post as a professor to work in the press as an opinion columns editor (initially specialist and then generalist columns). He edited the *Revue musicale* from 1921 to 1937 (formally at least), as well as the music columns of *Paris-Midi* (1925 onward), *Gringoire*[18] (1931–39), and *Je suis partout* (1943 onward—the column had been abandoned by Lucien Rebatet), where he published six specialist articles on music. This journalistic cartography suggests a career that was defined by aesthetic discernment. In the early 1920s Coeuroy was passionate about jazz and the festive aesthetics of the Les Six composers. He commissioned articles on the Second Viennese School and protested against musical regionalism, "which ignored everything outside its own race, idiosyncrasies, and prejudices."[19] The first germs of nationalism appeared in his writing in 1928: "For a long time it was believed that music was an international language. But each race has its own musical style."[20] By the end of the decade, his focus had shifted to musical roots. The lifeblood of folklore would provide the impetus that would revive France and revitalize its music. Classical music was all the better for having been regenerated by folklore. Nonconformist in his early writings, this music writer came to champion a French-style volkism. This movement was espoused by a whole section of the musical world who, in 1940, committed themselves with eyes closed and ears open to the Vichy regime's Révolution Nationale.[21]

There was nothing, however, in Coeuroy's professional activities that had predestined him for this change in direction. As general secretary of the International Institute of Intellectual Cooperation (IIIC), a body attached to the League of Nations (whose management team he had joined in 1928), he supervised the various congresses and symposia on the subject of music and folk art. The IIIC's ethos was one of cultural diplomacy and humanist and scientific cooperation between nations. This "UNESCO before UNESCO"[22] disappeared in the wake of the 1940 defeat. Coeuroy was formally advised of the end of his collaboration on 30 September 1941. While *La Musique et le peuple en France* bears the traces of observations drawn from his professional experience, it also represents his first public siding with the Révolution Nationale after a long professional life spent in a radical-socialist, freemason environment.

"Nothing, Nil, Zero": From Catalyst to Putrefaction

The "inner song" of this defeated nation that Coeuroy put forward was quite dark. With "the generational chain"[23] broken, the folk songs (or traditional songs, as they are known today) of the provinces now only existed as keepsakes, relics, replicas, or archives: "Popular music, chansons, all these melodies said to be eternal that dreamers gather together in volumes and archives . . . The folk song can still be found in texts, but it no longer exists in people's heads. Nothing, nil, zero. . . . The farandoles, the pastourelles, are they really nothing more now than opéra-comique?"[24]

"Popular" is the term that the IIIC had substituted in its publications for "folklore" in the early 1930s. The disappearance of folk songs from France was striking from a comparative perspective. At the IIIC, Coeuroy supervised the "Société internationale de musique populaire," which inventoried and examined methods of collecting (recording or manually transferring recordings), identifying, and classifying popular music.[25] The study trips he undertook after attending an international folk art congress in Prague in 1928 introduced him to traditional songs from Hungary, Tyrol, and Asturias. By comparison, he saw that the folklore of the French provinces was no longer just anemic; it was dead. Coeuroy appointed himself the coroner of what Michel de Certeau was later to describe as the "beauty of the dead."[26] De Certeau carried out an autopsy and concluded that the cause of death was intentional. Its demise was due to an offensive of irony and sarcasm in the eighteenth century against the traditional old songs, and its prodromes could be traced back to the "singing societies, where the bourgeoisie came to sing their romances or to listen to those of their neighbor, a school of individualism."[27] The Société du caveau, which was located in the center of Paris and its most famous dining club in the eighteenth century, was at the heart of this "demolition mindset" and "hedonistic bourgeoisie culture . . . that has strangled us to death." This first offensive had then been followed by the "humanitarian songs with their hoarse-voiced claims," the "merrymakers of the July Monarchy," and the "serinettes, . . . operetta refrains, Offenbach's vogue, Montmartre cabarets." These "leisure pursuits of the gentry who presumed to epitomize Parisian elegance and the French spirit" ultimately led to "the café-concert chanson, which cultivated what it believed to be an art form that lacked inspiration, grace, style, taste, in short, everything." Satirical, bawdy, and bacchic, these songs spoke to the individual rather than to the people: "Popular chanson is for the collective soul. It is not individualistic. It has been toppled by the satirical and personal chanson, which aims not at the social spirit but at the critical mind."

This construction of an "organic" link between a territory, its people, and its music was founded on an ideology inspired by Johann Gottfried Herder (1744–1803). In addition to glorifying nativeness, the rural community was presented as a model of human unity. Tangible musical proof of this unity were the *Volkslieder*. The author and the listener were one and the same person. The music writer André Coeuroy writes : "The herdsmen did not write their poems for the peasants; they were the peasants and recognized each other as such."[28] Only the chansons inspired by work, hardship, celebrations, and traditions deserved to be classed as "popular": "The music that comes out of the people continues to live with the people. This music is real 'popular' music, responding, at any given moment, to the demands of everyday life."[29]

A complete contrast was established between chansons *by* the people and chansons *for* the people. The former emanated from and in turn sedimented a collective identity. The latter dissolved the collective identity through a critical onslaught. A pathogenic triad—politics, pleasure, facility—had spread to the whole social body and was deemed "the cause of our decline."[30] The moral aspect of individualism was linked with aesthetic judgment. Songwriters "knew what people liked. They banked on baseness, and it paid off every time."[31] These rootless, premeditated, formulaic, doctored chansons explained the "void into which the population had been descending for more than half a century."[32] Providing the last link in a chain that was alien to the "musical substance of France,"[33] the music hall welcomed a whole parade of corrupting genres. According to Coeuroy,

> under the influence of international exhibitions, especially that of 1900, the foreign contribution had become a threat at the turn of the twentieth century. Internal mindlessness was joined by external mindlessness. Tangos, maxixes, cake-walks. None of them inherently contemptible, but transplanted, they lost all their meaning. Only the coarse nuances could be understood, and the truly French rhythms disappeared.[34]

A collateral effect of this chanson-based globalization was that many forms of strong regional music (strong because they were rooted in their territories) were misrepresented as "Spanish" or "Viennese," first in the opéra-comiques and then in the music halls. For all those who believe that there is an organic link between a music, a land, and a people, any orchestral arrangement for the theatrical stage, any professionalization of the performers, is considered inauthentic. These musical transfers undoubtedly had a degrading effect. No music could withstand the journey. It is important to consider here the trauma of defeat and the fact that the concrete manifestation of this was the territory's permeability. The German invasion had been preceded by a stealth invasion that had already been noted by theorists of nationalism. Charles Maurras had indicated that the aim of nationalism was to provide a "safeguard for all these treasures, which can come under threat without a foreign army ever crossing the border, without the territory being physically invaded."[35]

A History of Mixed Sounds

Coeuroy had already foreseen, at the beginning of the 1930s, the anthropological upheaval that would result from the mass emergence of mechanical music (radio and phonograph).[36] He had reported in detail on the merging or telescoping of music from far-off lands that had begun to be integrated. New sounds and indecent rhythms could now be heard coming out of 78 rpm records, music halls, and dance halls. This proliferation of mixed sounds accelerated the degradation begun at the end of the Enlightenment and launched an assault on the authority that united the individual with a shared destiny, a spirit of place, or a national community, The mixed sounds were transforming good people into a gregarious rabble. According to Coeuroy, the "here" was becoming open to the "elsewhere":

> It is no longer the village bell tower that tells the countryside folk what time it is. They set their clocks by Westminster's chimes. These villagers dance to the sound of some luxury hotel's orchestra of black musicians. They are given a brief glimpse of Paris, London, the far-off capitals that were previously just a name. With the huge diffuser placed at the corner of the outdated old shop, the village is transformed into a ballroom or concert hall, . . . the intrepid old grandmother, who never before knew the joy of hearing a musical note, will fall into her eternal sleep to the sound of Chopin's funeral march.[37]

Could these mixed sounds nevertheless revitalize the rather anemic scholarly music? Or did they represent a contamination threat? The word "variety" took on its full meaning here. This new cultural variety both disconcerted and deracinated the listener.

By 1936, just as the arrival of Léon Blum's Front Populaire government had prompted a shift of the right to the far right, Coeuroy's antimodern reflections in *Gringoire* had become more radicalized.

He railed against the brackish stream of dining clubs, cabarets, and café-concerts, which he considered to be "low-end products of an urban civilization [that were debasing] a shared sensibility, which was becoming poisoned as a result."[38] The corrupting agent was a passive consumption of chansons that were subject to the whims of fashion, a phenomenon that went hand in hand with the decline of rural France. He wrote that if there were to be a revival, it would come from "folk music, the only music capable of regenerating a musical inspiration that was threatened by formulas and intellectual idiosyncrasies."[39] The change came with the Révolution nationale. The traditional chanson was to be the soundtrack of the land that does not lie, a kind of "peasantry turned art form."[40] In 1941 he wrote: "In short, we are unequivocally still peasants. French art, however subtle and unbridled, is connected to the land. In other words, there is nothing left of your Gossec and your Lesueur or any of the social music of that time, but not one of the chansons collected by Gérard de Nerval has perished."[41]

Coeuroy's aesthetic discernments show an increasing predilection for the murky waters of origins as the decade progressed. Although nothing politically concrete emerges from his writings, there is evidence of cultural fascism. This was the "lead weight" of these dark years. There was a valorization of origins, stigmatization of the enemy, and sacralization of the link between music, a territory, and a people. It was an explosive association (race, land, people), and the Great War had acted as an accelerant. If civilization had led to barbarism, why not use the primitive as a catalyst to refound civilization?[42] It would be useful to compare Coeuroy's shifts in journalistic mindset with his IIIC texts, in which he reflected on the question of folklore and folk art. What was meant by "people"? Was a people defined by citizenship (*demos*) or by land and the dead (*ethnos*)? Unlike his institution, Coeuroy had made his choice.

Spirit of the Times

Coeuroy was not the only one protesting against the mixed sounds of the music hall. Other civil voices could also be heard. Both Céline and Abel Bonnard, the latter being a member of the Académie Française and Vichy minister of education in 1942, were critical of a musical genre that they considered to be not just infected but also highly infectious because of its mass diffusion through radio and records. Like Coeuroy, Bonnard had spent his early school years at the Lycée Louis-le-Grand (he failed the École Normale Supérieure entrance exam). Born a generation before Coeuroy, Bonnard was a contributor along with his younger brother to a column in the weekly newspaper *Je suis partout*. He also demonstrated the same repulsive reactions to a music hall that he believed to have been penetrated by "seedy Jewish sensuality and vile Negro sensuality"[43] (although Coeuroy avoided these kinds of lurches). Molded, too, by the rationalist teachings of this Third Republic that he had begun to loathe, he undertook to establish what we would now call its "traceability," the different steps of its transformation." Bonnard writes:

> In the eighteenth century, this brilliant and sinister period when the impoverishment of humankind was announced through the excitation of the individual, the number of chansons did not decline, but their nature altered and deteriorated. They shifted away from a focus on singing. Once carefree, they became malevolent, with more wings than they needed to transport their poisonous sting. Their wickedness was already evident long before the Revolution came along. Under the Restoration, Béranger's songs were like ugly flies sullying the nobility of the last remaining lilies. Under the Third Republic, the ignoble, innuendo-filled chanson prevailed at first, as the bawdy eighteenth-century spirit breathed its last in Paris. But the audience has changed. In place of the bourgeoisie, who wanted to mingle with the riff-raff, we now have a drunken mob that is increasingly made up of foreigners and stuffed with half-breeds. Seedy Jewish sensuality and vile Negro sensuality exert their power over this formless people. Mischievous excitation has thus given way to torpid eroticism. A softly bellowed romance floods fallen souls with its feral nonsense. We must drag ourselves out of this mire to return to the true song, the one that leads people to life and makes them healthier, purer, and more honest, the one that makes love the brightest of all their feelings.[44]

We can see here all the ingredients—individualism, the critical mindset, bitterness, the mark of the foreigner, degradation, unashamed moralism—of the pro-Nazism that Bonnard clearly displayed in 1941 in *Je suis partout*. He continues: "Last year, at that terrible moment when France was struck by a thunderbolt, when the French, taken by surprise, showed a moment of naked vulnerability, many were astonished to hear the German troops entering the cities singing a pure and sober song. There was more than just one of us who felt we might perhaps envy in our enemies a disposition that we would do well to rediscover for ourselves."[45]

Coeuroy and Bonnard were not alone in singing the praises of folklore. Indeed, Céline's voice was far more thunderous: "we just have to change people's ideas and prioritize music, choral singing, painting, composition (especially), good individual dance ideas, some of the rigodons, everything that gives life its color, its 'guillerette jolie.'"[46] The Célinian rigodon represented dance, joy, movement, the France of yesteryear[47]: "France remained happy while we had the rigodon. We will never dance in a factory, we will never sing again."[48] Folklore made the spirit thrive: "The world no longer has a melody. We are still lulled by folklore, the last whispers of our folklore. When that has gone, and night comes, so will the Negro's tam-tam."[49] Coeuroy sent *La Musique et le peuple en France* to Céline, whose response is as follows:

> Absolutely in awe of your book. I was becoming quite optimistic, but the bitterness nevertheless prevails. How the evil goes deeper even than you describe it in your book.
>
> We would need an Aryan Shinto for folk art to flourish here again, a creative feeling, a passion, an enthusiasm, a fervor, a heart that beats to its rhythm and melody. It is not that a thousand small choral societies are necessarily constipated or shrunken ... [illegible], *with no mystical purpose*, which can recreate nothing at all. *Good intentions equal zero.*
>
> It is not in Freemasonry that the light is found. That's a whole different matter.
>
> As for Honegger and Delannoy, so deeply Jewish and Jewified. They are a million miles away from understanding everything. Their new thing now is Human Rights—the committee, arms and legs wide open, just got laid by King David. Colleague—absolutely not! I think that we ultimately, above all, need torpedo men.
>
> Music will come quite naturally then.
>
> Céline[50]

Clearly, neither Céline nor Cœuroy expected anything from public initiatives, from what we would now call cultural policies. Needless to say, this whole gloss on the effects of music appears quite unreal to us today. Music, a weapon of mass identity destruction? For Coeuroy, Bonnard, and Céline, this postwar transition period, perhaps because it followed a defeat, did not permit any irony.

Conclusion

This discourse on music at a time of defeat in France highlights the traits of the members of the nonconformist nebula who engaged in collaborationism. The contours of this discourse are yet to be delimited. It also depicts a French society whose moderate fringes could voice their disgust at the music hall. Coeuroy's complaint that "there is only one work song, 'Le métier de Prosper,' left [in France]"[51] was subsequently echoed by the family of the writer François Nourissier. More than sixty years on, he still remembered the disgust felt by his bourgeois family in Saint-Germain-en-Laye that the radio in the dining room was imperceptibly transforming into Prosper-Yop-la-Boum's passive accomplices. François Nourissier tells how politically moderate French people, concerned about good education, were revolted by this popular song which praised prostitutes, pimps, cheaters and could, by reaction, be led to choose La Révolution nationale promoted by Pétain and Laval.[52]

Philippe Gumplowicz is Emeritus Professor of Musicology at the University Paris-Saclay (Évry-Val d'Essonne) Among several articles on musical taste, political imaginary, the history of jazz, and popular music, he has notably authored or coauthored the following books: *Faiseurs d'histoire, Pour une Histoire indisciplinée*; *Les Résonances de l'ombre, Musique et identités de Wagner au jazz*; *La Catastrophe apprivoisée, Regards sur le jazz en France*; *Le Roman du jazz, première époque, 1893–1928*; *Le Roman du jazz, t. II, 1928–1942*; *Le Roman du jazz, t. III, Les modernes*; *Les Travaux d'Orphée, 150 ans de vie musicale amateur en France*).

Notes

1. This chapter was translated from French by Clare Ferguson.
2. It may seem somewhat surprising to view the armistice request of 16 June 1940 as the beginning of a postwar transition period. The war was still ongoing outside France (especially for the United Kingdom), and within France few agreed with General de Gaulle's declaration on 18 June that the country may have lost a battle but it had not lost the war. In his 17 June radio address, Pétain urged his compatriots to "stop fighting" and "put an end to hostilities" ("cesser le combat" and "mettre un terme aux hostilités," respectively). On 10 July, eighty of the eight hundred and fifty deputies and senators voted against full powers for Marshal Pétain. Until the tipping point came internationally at the end of 1941, France was, despite its prisoners and early pockets of resistance, still able to nurture the impression (or illusion perhaps) that it was in a postwar transition period.
3. Bloch, *L'Étrange défaite*; Bernanos, "Les causes de la déroute"; Maurois, *Tragédie en France*; Morize, *France été 1940*.
4. Loubet del Bayle Loubet del Bayle, *Les Non-conformistes des années 30*.
5. See Céline, *Les Beaux Draps*; Rebatet, *Les Décombres*; Fabre-Luce, *Journal de la France*; Jouvenel (de), *Après la Défaite*.
6. "Depuis la victoire [de 1918], l'esprit de jouissance [l'avait] emporté sur l'esprit de sacrifice."

7. Maxence, *Histoire de dix ans*, 365. "La France épuisée de tant de sursauts, secouée de tant de colères vaines, brisée de tant d'espoirs déçus. Comme les grands malades, elle ne bouge plus, ne parle plus guère. Elle attend, pâle, lasse, lasse à faire peur. Les événements déferlent sur elle. Elle ne se dresse plus."
8. Bernanos, "Les causes de la déroute," 67.
9. Jacques Chardonne (real name Jacques Boutelleau, 1884–1968) was a collaborationist during the war, particularly through his publishing. Coeuroy, *La Musique et le peuple en France*, preface.
10. Coeuroy, *La Musique et le peuple en France*, 6.
11. Faure, *Du Néoclassicisme musical,* 204. "Il faudra d'abord connaître les causes de la ruine, . . . La catastrophe ne se laisse pas déduire de fautes individuelles ou d'accidents techniques. La santé de la France était minée dans tous ses organes."
12. See Coeuroy, op. cit.; Chailley, *Petite histoire de la chanson populaire française*; Davenson, *Le Livre des chansons*; Dufourcq, *Petite Histoire de la musique en Europe*; voir Yannick Simon, "Le "francisme" musical sous l'Occupation" (unpublished article).
13. Davenson; Ibid., *Le Livre des chansons*, 42.
14. This conception of traditional music, which is said to be the conservatory of the memory of a collective people as delimited by territory, appeared at the end of the eighteenth century in the writings of the pastor Livre Johann Gottfried Herder. See Gumplowicz, *Les Résonances de l'ombre*.
15. Cafés with popular live entertainment.
16. Philippe Roussin has developed at length this question of the modernist cut-off between authentic art and mass culture. See Roussin, *Misère de la littérature, terreur de l'histoire*, 252.
17. Céline, *Bagatelles pour un massacre*, 191: "Le monde n'a plus de mélodie. C'est encore le folklore, les derniers murmures de nos folklores, qui nous bercent . . . Après ce sera fini, la nuit . . . et le tam-tam nègre."
18. A right-wing political and literary weekly newspaper founded in 1928, *Gringoire* became openly antisemitic and xenophobic from 1936 onward. Its antibellicosity and hostility toward the Left prompted Coeuroy's collaborationism.
19. Coeuroy, *La Musique française moderne*, 5.
20. Coeuroy, *Panorama de la musique contemporaine*, 9: "Longtemps l'on a cru que la musique n'était qu'un langage international. Mais chaque race a son style musical."
21. On Jacques Chailley, see Gribenski, "L'exclusion des juifs du Conservatoire (1940–1942),")"; Iglésias, *Musicologie et Occupation* . . . ; Le Bail and Buch, "Les résonances contemporaines de Vichy dans le milieu musical."
22. Renoliet, *L'UNESCO oubliée*, 10.
23. "la chaîne fidèle des générations."
24. Coeuroy, *La Musique et le peuple en France*, 8: "La musique populaire, la chanson, toutes ces mélodies que l'on dit éternelles et que de doux rêveurs recueillent dans des volumes et des archives . . . La chanson populaire existe encore dans les textes. Elle n'existe plus dans les têtes. Rien, zéro, néant . . . Les farandoles, les pastourelles, cela n'est plus que de l'opéra-comique?"
25. International Institute of Intellectual Cooperation, *Musique et chanson populaires*.
26. de Certeau, Julia and Revel, "La beauté du mort," 54.
27. Coeuroy, *La Musique et le peuple en France*, 62: "sociétés chantantes où le bourgeois venait pousser sa romance ou écouter celle du voisin: école d'individualisme." The quotations that follow come from the same work (61, 63, 69, 70): "l'esprit démolisseur"; "bourgeoisisme jouisseur . . . dont nous avons

crevé"; "chansons humanitaires à revendications enrouées"; "goguettes de la monarchie de Juillet"; "serinettes . . . , refrains d'opérette, vogue d'Offenbach, cabarets de Montmartre"; "divertissements de gens bien nés qui [avaient] la prétention de résumer l'élégance parisienne et l'esprit français"; "la chanson du café-concert qui fait ce qu'elle croit être son art avec le manque de tout: le manque de souffle, le manque de grâce, le manque de ligne, le manque de gout."

28. *La Musique et le peuple en France*, 49. "Les bergers poètes ne composaient pas pour les paysans; ils étaient eux-mêmes ces paysans et se reconnaissaient entre eux."
29. *La Musique et le peuple en France*: "La musique qui sort du peuple continue de vivre avec le peuple, et celle-là est la plus vraiment "Populaire" qui répond, à chaque instant donné, aux exigences de la vie de chaque jour."
30. *La Musique et le peuple en France*, 65: "l'origine de notre abaissement."
31. *La Musique et le peuple en France*, 34: "savent ce qui plait . . . Ils misent sur la bassesse et gagnent à tout coup."
32. *La Musique et le peuple en France*, 29: "nullité dans laquelle le peuple est tombé depuis plus d'un demi-siècle."
33. *La Musique et le peuple en France*, 29: "substance musicale de la France."
34. *La Musique et le peuple en France*, 29: "Avec le début du vingtième siècle, sous l'influence des expositions universelles, surtout celle de 1900, l'apport étranger devient menaçant. À l'abêtissement interne se joint un abêtissement externe: tangos, maxixes, cake-walk—non méprisables en soi; mais, transplantés, ils perdent tout leur sens—; on n'enn'en saisit que le coloris populacier, et les rythmes proprement français disparaissent."
35. Maurras, *Mes Idées politiques*, 264.
36. Coeuroy *(with G. Clarence), Le Phonographe*.
37. Coeuroy, *Panorama de la radio*, 12: "Ce n'est plus le clocher du village qui donne l'heure aux campagnes: ils règlent leurs pendules sur le carillon de Westminster. Ils dansent, ces villageois, au son de l'orchestre nègre d'un palace. Paris, Londres, les capitales lointaines qui, pour eux, n'étaient volontiers qu'unqu'un mot, se rapprochent et sont entrevues. Le bourg est transformé en salle de bal ou de concerts, grâce à l'énorme diffuseur placé au coin de la boutique désuète, . . . c'est au son de la marche funèbre de Chopin que la brave aïeule n'ayant jamais connu la joie d'entendre une note de musique s'endormira de l'éternel sommeil."
38. André Coeuroy, *Gringoire*, 5 May 1936: "bas produits d'une civilisation citadine [qui abaissaient] un goût qui [allait] en s'intoxicant."
39. Coeuroy, *La Musique et le peuple en France*, 75: "Musique populaire, seule capable de régénérer l'inspiration musicale menacée par les formules et les manies intellectuelles."
40 Ibid.. *La Musique et le peuple en France*, 76. "Paysannerie faite art."
41. *La Musique et le peuple en France*, 160: "Pour le dire en gros et sans nuances, nous sommes et nous restons des paysans. L'art français, si subtil et si délié qu'il puisse être, se rattache à la terre. Il ne reste autant dire rien d'un Gossec, d'un Lesueur et toutes les musiques sociales de ce temps-là; mais aucune des chansons que recueillit Gérard de Nerval n'a péri."
42. Gumplowicz, "Debussy. Un nationalisme au miroir du Cake-Walk," 64.
43. "La louche sensualité juive et la lâche sensualité nègre."
44. Abel Bonnard, "Chanter," *Je suis partout*, 29 May 1941: "Le XVIIIe siècle, dans ce moment brillant et sinistre où l'appauvrissement de l'homme s'annonce par l'excitation de l'individu, le nombre des chansons ne diminue pas, mais leur caractère change et s'altère; elles rompent avec le chant; de gaies, elles de-

viennent malignes et ont plus d'ailes que ce qu'il en faut pour transporter leur dard venimeux. Bien avant la Révolution, leur méchanceté est atroce. Sous la Restauration, les chansons de Béranger sont de vilaines mouches qui souillent la noblesse des derniers lys. Sous la Troisième République règne d'abord l'ignoble chanson à sous-entendus, où l'esprit grivois du XVIIIe siècle vient expirer dans l'esprit parisien. Mais déjà le public change; à des bourgeois qui demandent qu'on les mette en train, se substitue une foule alourdie par l'alcool, de plus en plus remplie d'étrangers, farcie de métis; la louche sensualité juive, la lâche sensualité nègre étendent leur pouvoir sur ce peuple informe [nous soulignons]. Alors, une excitation polissonne cède le pas à un érotisme torpide. Une romance mollement beuglée inonde de sa niaiserie bestiale des âmes déchues. C'est de cette bourbe qu'il faut nous tirer pour revenir au vrai chant, qui mène les hommes vers la vie, qui les rend plus dispos, plus purs et plus francs, et qui fait de l'amour le plus clair de leurs sentiments."

45. Bonnard, "Chanter": "L'an dernier, au moment terrible où la foudre a frappé la France, quand les Français surpris offrirent un moment une sensibilité nue, beaucoup d'entre eux furent étonnés lorsqu'ils entendirent les troupes allemandes entrer dans les villes en chantant un chant grave et pur. Plus d'un sentit que nous pouvions envier à nos adversaires une disposition qu'il serait bon de retrouver."
46. Céline, *Les Beaux draps*, 172: "Y a qu'à bouleverser les notions, donner la prime à la musique, aux chants en chœur, à la peinture, à la composition surtout, aux trouvailles des danses personnelles, aux rigodons particuliers, tout ce qui donne parfum à la vie, guilleretterie jolie."
47. Hardy, "Rigodon," 45.
48. Céline, *Les Beaux draps*, 148: "La France est demeurée heureuse jusqu'au rigodon. On dansera jamais en usine, on chantera plus jamais non plus."
49. Céline, *Bagatelles pour un massacre*, 191; Part 9: "Le monde n'a plus de mélodie. C'est encore le folklore, les derniers murmures de nos folklores qui nous bercent . . . Après, ce sera fini . . . la nuit et le tam-tam nègre."
50. Letter from Céline to Coeuroy (Bibliothèque Nationale de France—Département de la Musique—André Coeuroy, Correspondance reçue, NLA 15): "Émerveillé par votre livre. Je devenais déjà tout optimiste, mais tout de même l'amère fortement triomphe. Que le mal est encore plus profond que vous le décrivez dans votre ouvrage. / Il nous faudrait un shintoïsme aryen pour que refleurisse ici un art populaire, un sentiment créateur, une fougue, une ferveur, un cœur qui bat de son rythme et sa mélodie. Ce ne sont pas mille petites sociétés chorales forcément constipées, ratatinées . . . [illisible], *sans but mystique*, qui peut recréer rien du tout. *Bonne volonté* égale *zéro*. / Ce n'est pas de ce côté maçonnique que se trouve la lumière. C'est tout autre chose. / Quant à Honegger, Delannoy, si profondément juifs et enjuivés. Ils sont à mille [lieues] de tout comprendre. Le neuf pour eux, c'est les Droits de l'Homme et le comité bras ouverts tira un coup de Roi David. Mon confrère—absolument non ! Je crois qu'au fond, nous avons surtout besoin d'hommes torpilles. / La musique vient là-dessus tout naturellement. / Céline."
51. Coeuroy, *La Musique et le peuple en France*, 70.
52. Nourissier, *À Défaut de génie*, 83–84: "La France de 1935, je la vois aujourd'hui comme un vaste bastringue où on faisait un triomphe aux marlous et aux filles. Rappelez-vous—car ces musiques et ces paroles-là ont pénétré au plus profond de notre mémoire collective: Prosper, le chéri de ces dames; et le héros de *Comme de bien entendu*, glorifié pour avoir mis sur le trottoir cette fille qui était

jeune et belle ... Comment appelait—on cette lippe que les chanteurs gonflaient, de profil, pour détailler les paroles graveleuses, comme un cul pousse ses pets? Oui, la gouaille, le sourire gouailleur, qui assurait le succès des Chevalier, Préjean, Milton, Alibert, ah, j'en passe! J'en passe! ... N'y a-t-il pas eu, et chez des Français de qualité honorable, un dégoût, et ce dégoût n'a-t-il pas justifié chez les plus naïfs d'entred'entre eux la confiance faite à Vichy, du moins les premières semaines, dans l'ahurissement d'une défaite pourtant si prévisible. J'exagère? Il peut y avoir eu l'espoir d'un changement de ton. Comment oublier qu'elle fut, cette chanson, l'hiver 39–40, un des succès du Théâtre aux Armées? Il ne se trouva donc aucun officier, ni aucun ministre pour éprouver une nausée et interdire les fanfaronnades poisseuses dont se gorgeaient les Français?"

Bibliography

Bernanos, Georges. "Les causes de la déroute," article published in Portuguese in Rio de Janeiro on 9 August 1940. Reprinted in Georges Bernanos, *Le Chemin de la Croix-des-Âmes*. Paris: Éditions du Rocher, 2017.

Bloch, Marc. *L'Étrange défaite* [1940]. In *L'Histoire, la guerre, la Résistance*, edited by Annette Becker and Étienne Bloch, 516–653. Paris: Gallimard, 2006.

Burrin, Philippe. *La Dérive fasciste Doriot, Déat, Bergery, 1933–1945*, Paris : Le Seuil, 1986,

Céline, Louis-Ferdinand. *Les Beaux Draps*. Paris: Nouvelles Éditions Françaises, 1941.

———. *Bagatelles pour un massacre*. Paris: Éditions Denoël, 1941.

Certeau, Michel (de), Dominique Julia, and Jacques Revel. "La beauté du mort." In *La Culture au pluriel*, edited by Michel de Certeau, 55–94. Paris: Union Générale d'Éditions, 1974.

Chailley, Jacques. *Petite Histoire de la chanson populaire française*. Paris: PUF, 1942.

Coeuroy, André. *La Musique et le peuple en France*. Paris: Editions Stock, Delamain et Boutelleau, 1941.

———. *La Musique française moderne*. Paris: Delagrave, 1924.

———. *Panorama de la musique contemporaine*. Paris: Simon Kra, 1928.

———. (with G. Clarence). *Le phonographe*. Paris: Kra, 1929.

———. *Panorama de la radio*. Paris: Kra, 1930.

Davenson, Henri. *Le Livre des chansons* or *Introduction à la chanson populaire française*. Neuchâtel: Éditions de la Baconnière, 1944.

Faure, Michel. *Du Néoclassicisme musical*. Paris: Klincksieck, 1997.

Gribenski, Jean. "L'Exclusion des juifs du Conservatoire (1940–1942)." In *La Vie musicale sous Vichy*, edited by Myriam Chimènes, 363–81. Paris: Editions Complexe, 2001.

Gumplowicz, Philippe, *Les Résonances de l'ombre*. Paris: Fayard, 2011.

———. "Debussy. Un Nationalisme au miroir du Cake-Walk." In *Regards sur Debussy*, edited by Myriam Chimènes and Alexandra Laederich, 69–86. Paris: Fayard, 2013.

Hardy, Alain. "Rigodon." *Cahiers de l'Herne* 3 (1963): 147–60.

Iglésias, Sara. *Musicologie et Occupation*. Paris: MSH, 2014.

International Institute of Intellectual Cooperation. *Musique et chanson populaires*. Paris: IIIC, 1934.

Le Bail, Karine, and Buch, Esteban. "Les résonances contemporaines de Vichy dans le milieu musical." In *La Musique à Paris sous l'Occupation*, edited by Myriam Chimènes and Yannick Simon. Paris: Fayard/Cité de la musique, 2013.

Loubet del Bayle, Jean-Louis. *Les Non-conformistes des années 30: une tentative de renouvellement de la pensée politique française*. Paris: Seuil, 2001 (1st ed. 1969).

Maurois, André. *Tragédie en France*. New York: Éditions de la Maison Française, 1940.

Maurras, Charles. *Mes Idées politiques*. Paris: Fayard, 1937.

Maxence, Jean-Pierre. *Histoire de dix ans, 1927–1937*. Paris: Gallimard, 1939.

Morize, André. *France été 1940*. New York: Éditions de la Maison Française, 1941.

Nourissier, François. *À Défaut de genie*. Paris: Gallimard, 2000.

Rebatet, Lucien. *Les décombres*. Paris: Denoël, 1942.

Renoliet, Jean-Jacques. *L'UNESCO oubliée, la Société des Nations et la coopération intellectuelle (1919–1946)*. Paris: Publications de la Sorbonne, 1999.

Roussin, Philippe. *Misère de la littérature, terreur de l'histoire*. Paris: Gallimard, 2005.

Winock, Michel. *Nationalisme, antisémitisme et fascisme en France*. Paris : Le Seuil,1982.

Chapter 7

POSTWAR TRANSITIONS AND USES OF MUSIC IN A CENTRAL EUROPEAN BORDERLAND REGION
Tyrol and the Aftermath of Two World Wars, 1900–2010s

Michael Wedekind

At midnight on 20 April 1941, the Munich Reich's radio transmitter broadcast a concert live from Kufstein in Tyrol[1] to mark Adolf Hitler's (1889–1945) fifty-second birthday.[2] The instrument played was the Heldenorgel (heroes' organ), the world's largest outdoor organ, which had been installed in the Kufstein Fortress ten years earlier to commemorate the victims of the Great War. The press did not consider it necessary to provide any details of the work that was played, even though it had been commissioned for the occasion from the German composer Gottfried Rüdinger (1886–1946). Instead, they focused on the man performing the piece: the pianist and composer Emil Berlanda (1905–60),[3] who had taken up playing the keyboard for his "Führer" and was keen to make a name for himself among party officials. Indeed, three years earlier, on the occasion of Hitler's forty-ninth birthday, he had sent a composition to the Reich Chancellery in Berlin based on a poem that glorified the hierarchical relationship between the Führer and "his people."[4]

In the Tyrolean musical circles of the interwar period, Berlanda was not the only musician to feel unjustly ignored for political and aesthetic reasons. Sensing they were being sidelined because of their traditional musical orientations, a number of artists came together

---

Notes for this section begin on page 149.

between 1934 and 1938, at the time of the Austrofascist regime, to form a group called the Arbeitsgemeinschaft Tiroler Komponisten (Tyrolean Composers' Working Group).[5] This private circle included musicians, composers, and musicologists: Josef Eduard Maria Ploner (1894–1955)[6] (the group's main representative), Josef Gasser (1873–1957), Artur Kanetscheider (1898–1977), Karl Koch (1887–1971), Peter Marini (1878–1954), Albert Riester (1906–75), Anton Schiechtl (1881–1953), Karl Senn (1878–1964), and Emil Berlanda. Based on shared *völkisch* ideological interests, the group set out to exert an influence on Austria's cultural and political life. They sought to defend and promote their artistic and financial interests and foster a "renewal of art and culture rooted in the people."[7] Their aim was directly to counteract what was considered to be a dominant Jewish cultural influence. Similar goals had already been pursued by the Steirischer Tonkünstlerbund (Styrian Musicians' Union), founded in 1927 in Styria, a region in southeast Austria.

In 2010 a publicly funded program of recordings, rereleases, and concerts (in some cases under the patronage of the Tyrolean regional government) was launched featuring works composed by the Arbeitsgemeinschaft Tiroler Komponisten. The program had two fundamental objectives. One was to ensure that the group's "outstanding creative work should again be accepted as an indisputable part of regional music life."[8] The other, as a consequence, was to contribute to ensuring these composers would be "rightly" regarded as "Tyrolean national composers"[9] because of the elements of folk music and references to Tyrol in their compositions. Public approval of the group's music and works obviously presupposes the existence, or creation, of core national values and norms among the audience. As Benjamin Curtis noted:

> In order for music to be eventually "received" as national, . . . there first must be a public that is nationalized. The public has to, on some level, be aware of and accept the theses on the constitutive characteristics of their national communality. And before there can be a national public that receives works as national, there must be a project to construct that national public.[10]

The above-mentioned revaluation of the works of the *Arbeitsgemeinschaft Tiroler Komponisten* initiated a broad public debate on cultural policy[11] both in Austria (particularly in Tyrol and Salzburg[12]) and in Italian South Tyrol. The efforts to isolate personalities with a compromising past from their historical context have been questioned during the course of this debate. Scholars such as Ernst Gellner have pointed out that decontextualization can be used as a means to heroize such individuals and to integrate them into the process of national or regional identity building.[13] This chapter presents a regional case study of the uses made of traditional and folk music after the world wars in the Austro-Italian borderland region of Tyrol. It analyzes continuities and discontinuities not just in musical themes and styles but also in identity building through music. It therefore primarily focuses on the relationships, both before and after 1945, between the music world and policymakers.

Like many humanities subjects during the interwar period, Austro-German musicology was primarily based on national criteria. This period of crisis saw a further reinforcement of conservative prewar cultural positions and a rejection of the numerous processes of heterogenization that were underway in modern societies. These developments were countered with ideas grouped around concepts such as social cohesion, togetherness, and synthesis. German music historiography had been grounded in nationalist orientations long before 1933. Musicology presented a convergence with Nazi ideology that manifested, way beyond mere political agreement, in an active collaboration.[14] Austro-German musicology's shift toward Nazism was a voluntarist "internal consequence"[15] of musicologists' political opinions, although it is important to note that the complex and divergent array of individual attitudes in evidence toward the regime ranged from the highly conservative to Nazi sympathizers.

Within a general context of the politicization of music in the twentieth century, musicology underwent a major reevaluation under the Nazi dictatorship.[16] The Nazi era was characterized by considerable financial support from the State and the Party, which led to an expansion in musicological institutions, research areas, and public offices assigned to individuals from the music world. Additionally, the Reich ministry of education centralized non-university-based musicology through the founding of the Staatliches Institut für deutsche Musikforschung (State Institute for German Music Research) in 1935. The regime's interests and objectives became closely associated with the predominantly antidemocratic, reactionary, and antisemitic scholarly world of German musicology. This combining of interests materialized in a Nazi appropriation of music, resolutely supported by the cooperation of an "Aryanized" musicology, which was focused primarily on a search for all that was "German in German music."[17] Musicology played a considerable role (as did musicians) in the deindividualization, construction, and historical-cultural legitimation of the Volksgemeinschaft (a racially unified people), both in its aesthetic staging and in the sacralization of the regime and the representation and symbolization of power. This process took place through a reinterpretation of "Nordic-Germanic" traditions; a rejection of all that was foreign based on research studies of racial ideology; attempts to establish the *Blut und Boden* (blood and soil) ideology in music history; and, particularly in Austria, the affirmation of a "pan-Germanic cultural unity in music"[18] (which had to be proved also through the collection and publication of folk songs[19]).

There was no research conducted until the 1970s either on musicology's political commitment to, and collusion with, the politics of the Third Reich or on the ideological, methodological, and individual continuities of this commitment after 1945. By 1990 only a handful of studies on this topic had been published. This lag was due to the adoption of various resistance and prevention strategies by the "musicological establishments"[20] themselves. Indeed, after World War II, they had endeavored to maintain their positions and institutions and to rehabilitate by minimizing both their own involvement and that of musicians more generally in the Nazi regime. Most musicologists did not seek an "ideological conversion"[21] or a scientific reorientation. Reflecting on this delayed analysis of the past (which is also evidenced in many related domains), some musicologists have criticized their discipline's silence and lack of sincerity, citing an extraordinarily deep-running and resolute commitment from scholars (as well as some composers and performers) to the Nazi regime and its crimes.[22]

Research on regional music has also contributed little to ending this silence and filling the gaps in musicological research due to a number of specific methodological shortcomings. An often-dominant interest in conducting an "evaluation of the supraregional significance" or "'value' of this music"[23] has resulted in an absence of comparisons between regional musics and a lack of reflection on their role in the music of the era as a whole. Worse still, the structural, social, cultural, and ideological histories of regional music have been neglected in favor of biographical and monographic approaches. Partly intentional and partly linked to scientific negligence and dilettantism, these methodological orientations have only served to prolong this repression.

Rejecting the Present, Evoking the Past

Returning to the regional scene in Tyrol during the interwar period, while the members of the Arbeitsgemeinschaft Tiroler Komponisten may have come from different generations, they were united in their nationalist convictions. Many had been quick to join the Nazi Party, which was banned in Austria between 1933 and 1938. Ploner and Kanetscheider had become members shortly after the Nazis had seized power in Germany. It is thought Karl Senn became a secretly sworn Nazi Party member in 1937. Berlanda, who had displayed early Nazi sympathies and been a member of the Reichsmusikkammer (Reich Music Chamber) since 1937, joined the Party in 1938, briefly after the annexation of Austria, along with Marini and Riester. A number of the group's members had family ties in the southern regions of Tyrol,[24] which had been ceded to Italy after the Great War. These men's roots lay in the geographical, linguistic, ethnic, and national borderland of the Habsburg monarchy. They were also "marginal men"[25] politically. They shared a very particular ideological background that had first been shaped in the border territories before World War I, when the German-speaking populations were keen to protect their privileges (access to income, resources, and the state's political decision-making bodies) against the emancipation attempts of other nationalities in the Austro-Hungarian Empire. This segregative ideology and its nationalist, xenophobic, and antisemitic elements became further radicalized in the trenches of the Great War and then during the interwar period with the traumatic experience of defeat and the huge territorial losses. For the Arbeitsgemeinschaft Tiroler Komponisten members as well as for a large part of the nationalist Austrian cultural world more generally, border and territorial claims became established as artistic themes and concerns. The border was seen as a fortress to be defended against external threats. Only those who had protected the homeland during the Great War and the postwar border battles were considered worthy, authentic guardians of the national spirit, capable of renewing and revolutionizing the fabric of the state and of cultural life more specifically. Alarmist references to external threats were heavily instrumentalized both for internal political purposes and to give more force and urgency to claims made in the sociopolitical and cultural fields.[26] As the words of former Nazi Party member Hermann Josef Spiehs (1893–1964) in 1965 show, this way of thinking continued to prevail even after World War II: "Tyrol is a borderland. Its art-life is therefore particularly endangered. This is another reason why we must specifically protect our Tyrolean artists, who carry the legacy of our extraordinarily talented ancestors. Let us be grateful . . . and let us try to show them understanding."[27]

This ideology was, generally speaking, rooted in the provincial educated middle classes and particularly in their reaction to the disruptions caused by successive waves of modernization in the province, which lagged behind Vienna as the political, economic, and cultural center of the country.[28] This reaction took the form of a rejection both of the supposed tendencies toward cultural "alienation" and of the new life forms often associated with what was seen as the destructive decadence of large cities (especially Vienna). Against the backdrop of these cultural pessimist and antimodernist countercurrents, humanity, with all its inherited cultural and natural environments (including anthropized landscapes and spaces), was subject to new interpretations and identity-building processes. These reinterpretations were characterized by a nostalgic, romantic return to cultural elements inherited from the past. They conveyed a patriotic and idyllic vision of the conservation not just of nature and the landscape but also of the homeland, its people, and its authentic cultural heritage, which had to be defended against the influences of a modern industrialized society.[29] This ideological conglomerate progressed easily to nationalist tendencies.[30] The comprehensive collections of folk songs, the initiatives to preserve folk customs and costumes and the antibourgeois escapist youth movements, such as the Wandervogel and the Jugendmusikbewegung (Musical Youth Movement) with their prefascist elements,[31] were all largely rooted in this *völkisch* ideological context. As a result of their interpretations and reinterpretations of folk culture, these manifestations of cultural heritage were introduced into the canon of national symbols, and folk culture was consequently instrumentalized for political purposes. At the same time, the pressures of modern society had prompted a more intense perception of the concepts of identity and social diversity within the provincial middle classes—a perception that was further radicalized during the Great War and sustained after the end of the conflict.

This ideology contributed greatly to the identity schema of the Arbeitsgemeinschaft Tiroler Komponisten. The contrast between the city and the province, fueled by the topos of cultural alienation, proved particularly persistent in Tyrol's conservative right-wing climate and more specifically in the region's musical circles, which were opposed to the largely social-democratic state cultural policy that had been developed in "red" Vienna. The Arbeitsgemeinschaft Tiroler Komponisten sought to increase its cultural and political influence through its actions, requests, and sometimes aggressive demands directed at the media, state officials, and the Reichsmusikkammer. The group's members, who made themselves known in Germany as committed antisemites, aimed at reorientating not only regional musical life but also the Austrian broadcasting cooperation RAVAG's music program. In 1937 Ploner quantified the "predominance" of Jewish music in Austrian broadcasting programs. Copies of his paper were sent to the Reichsmusikkammer as well as to a number of Nazi-friendly music critics and several German newspapers and broadcasting stations.[32] On 26 March 1938 he triumphantly wrote: "As you can imagine, a complete tidy-up is first of all needed in the field of culture too. After an initial radical cleansing, the 'AKM' [State-approved society of authors, composers, and music publishers] is, for example, also now clean of Jews."[33] The group also established contact with the Verein für das Deutschtum im Ausland (Association for Germandom Abroad), the Reichsministerium für Volksaufklärung und Propaganda (Reich Ministry of Public Enlightenment and Propaganda), and high-level representatives at the German broadcasting cooperation, whom they used to promote their compositions.[34] Although the Arbeitsgemeinschaft Tiroler Komponisten only briefly managed to make a name for itself at the supraregional level, it saw itself as an advocate of a "popular revival of art and culture."[35] However, the Austrian composer, pianist, and conductor Rudolf Kattnigg (1895–1955), a friend of Berlanda and a Nazi Party member since 1938, made a remarkable comment with regard to the group's creative music production between 1934 and 1938:

> I would advise you to compose delightful music rather than squabble with critics. In the latter case, the composer always gets the short end of the stick; "activist groups" and the like are no substitute for decent music and even less suitable for winning sympathies in the world of music. On the contrary!! Did Beethoven or Verdi or Brahms need an activist group!!! The mere fact that such a "fighting community" is needed and even exists is, in my opinion, already an expression of weakness! ... "Communities" endanger the free development of individualism, which composers need more than any other profession![36]

The musical work of the group's members, which had often been rejected in the past, had to play a key role in this process of renewal. It had to endeavor to be better perceived and recognized by the public. Ploner regarded his artistic role and work to be the "spiritual pillar" of the Nazi's "New Man." This phrase "spiritual pillar" was directly borrowed from Alfred Rosenberg (1892–1946), one of the main ideologues of National Socialism. It appears in a number of Ploner's publications.[37] The group's identity schema was marked by a racist ideology and characterized by patriotic conceptions of the land, its people, country romanticism, and defending the homeland.

Additionally, a virulent antisemitism ran through this ideological conglomerate, which the group had integrated into its aesthetic and political program. Indeed, its main objective was to "fight against Semitism in the arts. It is unacceptable that . . . here too the Jews are trying and even ultimately managing to achieve the predominance they have long coveted."[38] This assembly of beliefs corresponded perfectly with Nazi ideology.

Allegiance to the Führer

In 1938, as the Nazis seized power in Austria (*Anschluss*), the members of the Arbeitsgemeinschaft Tiroler Komponisten—which, along with all other existing associations, was dissolved by the new regime—hoped not only to see an "Aryanization" of music and of cultural life more generally but also to advance their individual careers and exert a major influence in cultural affairs. In November 1940, for example, Ploner applied to Gauleiter Franz Hofer (1902–75) for a position that would enable him to "better serve our people in the spiritual support of their way of life."[39] Several members of the group succeeded in obtaining official positions in the cultural domain: Ploner had already taken up a position in 1937 working for the Reichskulturkammer (Reich Chamber of Culture) as an approved trainer of composers in Tyrol, even though the Nazi Party was still banned in Austria at the time. In 1941 he began collaborating with the Tiroler Volksliedarchiv (Tyrolean Folk Song Archives). Marini became department manager within the head office of the Tyrolean branch of the Reichsmusikkammer. He was replaced in this role by Karl Senn in 1943. In 1939 Kanetscheider began serving as a consultant for music education in the Nationalsozialistischer Lehrerbund (National Socialist Teachers' Association). Marini, Riester, Senn, and Berlanda, who also lectured at the university of Innsbruck in 1943/44, were temporarily active as music critics for the Tyrolean Nazi newspaper *Innsbrucker Nachrichten*. These official titular positions do not of course fully convey the significance of their roles in the construction of the Volksgemeinschaft, dissemination of war propaganda, and creation of a Tyrolean regional identity.[40] They were important because they gave the actors direct access to regional political decision-makers and because they demonstrated their artistic, scientific, political, cultural, and propagandistic commitment.

The Arbeitsgemeinschaft Tiroler Komponisten members also contributed to reinforcing the Nazi Volksgemeinschaft ideology through their works. The pieces were mainly concert music, marches, and patriotic songs that had either been commissioned by the state or composed on the group members' own initiative.[41] These works glorified the regime and conveyed antisemitic, xenophobic, and revisionist sentiments. They contributed to idealizing the homeland and to aesthetizing mountain peasants, who were considered racially superior to urbanized populations. Traditional regional customs were divested of their religious components. Moreover, the works composed during World War II celebrated the conflict and promoted a true cult of heroes. This is exemplified by Ploner's 1941 cantata[42] *Opfersieg: Grenzland-Kantate*, op. 108 (Victory through sacrifice: Borderland cantata), which comprises three movements: Klage (complaint), Bereitschaft (determination), and Opfergang (sacrifice). Ploner also paid explicit homage to the Nazi regime in 1942 with his song *Bekenntnis zum Führer* (Allegiance to the Führer)[43] and, in the following year, with his *Tiroler Kantate für gemischten Chor, Jugendgesang und Orchester* (Tyrolean cantata for mixed choir, youth choir, and orchestra) entitled *Das Land im Gebirge*, op. 109 (Land in the mountains),[44] which he dedicated to the Tyrolean Gauleiter Franz Hofer.

Amnesty and Amnesia

In the public discourse of postwar Austria, 1945 was presented as a general cut-off point and the beginning of a completely new epoch. However, the country's post-1945 reality was instead characterized by the copresence of two opposing tendencies—namely political discontinuity, on the one hand, and cultural continuity, on the other. In the cultural world,[45] the end of the war was a "caesura without consequences,"[46] causing the "longevity of antimodernism."[47] Although 1945 marked the end of the Nazi dictatorship, it did not mark the end of one cultural era and the beginning of another.[48] The rebuilding of Austria, which refrained for a long time from fundamentally reappraising its Austrofascist and National Socialist past (a past that was ended by external intervention rather than by any internal resistance), was accompanied by a reconstruction of a "'culture' that had played a significant role in the victories of both fascisms."[49] This involved the promotion of a fundamentally conservative conception of culture that was in large part linked to the identity politics positions and codes of Austrofascism (1934–38). At the federal level, these positions and codes combined with an ideologized conception of Austria as the first victim of German expansionism. At the regional level, these tendencies were associated with Catholic and chauvinistic identity schemas, characterized once again by antimodern and antiurban positions. They combined with revisionist undercurrents, particularly on the question of South Tyrol, which had caused conflict between Austria and Italy since 1919.

Echoing the cultural policy promoted by Austrian fascism between 1934 and 1938, the compositions and musical aesthetics of the former Arbeitsgemeinschaft Tiroler Komponisten were perfectly in keeping with the cultural climate of the country's postwar years. The musicians were assured of exculpation, support, and even honors from regional politicians. For example, in 1952 Berlanda was awarded the Kunstpreis für Instrumentalmusik der Stadt Innsbruck (City of Innsbruck's Artistic Prize for Instrumental Music), receiving the title of honorary professor in 1960. Senn was awarded the Ehrenring der Stadt Innsbruck (City of Innsbruck's Ring of Honor) in 1953 and the Goldenes Ehrenzeichen des Landes Tirol (Land of Tyrol's Golden Badge of Honor) in 1956. A few years later, in 1962, Kanetscheider received the title of honorary professor. The Austrian ministry of education had failed to award the same title to Ploner in 1954 due to formal requirements. This overall favorable context also extended to the former representatives of folk music, who had been strongly supported by the Nazi regime in its day. On the whole, these musicians swiftly and sleekly managed to regain their former positions and have their musical aesthetics recognized.

Austria's so-called new start after 1945 was based on the mobilization of a specific agenda to externalize not just Nazi policy between 1938 and 1945 and its consequences but also the country's culpability. By brushing aside the period of dictatorship in this way, the very idea of Nazi ideology in Austrian culture and music was denied. It thus became possible to also deny any predisposition to Nazi thought within institutional folk culture. The Arbeitsgemeinschaft Tiroler Komponisten members consequently concealed their former role in devaluing the individual, glorifying the "New Man" idealized by the Nazis and promoting Nazi conceptions of the body, gender roles, and the enemy. As a result, music, especially folk music, was washed clean of its past service to the Nazi dictatorship and was once again pure, uncontaminated, innocent, and free of suspicion.[50] Denazification commissions considered Ploner (1946) and Berlanda to be "minderbelastet" (moderately burdened). Kanetscheider was suspended from office in September 1945 and permanently pensioned off in 1948. However, neither Berlanda[51] nor Kanetscheider[52] really engaged with the moral and political changes of 1945, although Berlanda—for obvious opportunistic reasons—did join the Vereinigung Sozialistischer Akademiker (Austrian Association of Socialist Academics) and the Österreichischer Gewerkschaftsbund (Austrian Trade Union Federation) shortly after the war. The music world was thus poised to contribute to the construction of a regional identity that had itself also remained largely unchanged after World War II.

Despite the differences in individual situations, the close and mutually beneficial relationship between the political and music worlds endured in post-1945 Austria, continuing to serve as a lever for the mobilization and promotion of musicians in the cultural politics of North and South Tyrol, especially in the field of "patriotic education." Various compositions by Ploner became choreographic fixtures at state celebrations, such as his *Land im Gebirge*, op. 81, and his compositions based on the poems of Tyrolean *Blut und Boden* writer Joseph Georg Oberkofler (1889–1962). His works, which had an open anti-Italian subtext, were performed, for example, at the ceremonial act of the Land of Tyrol to mark Oberkofler's 60th birthday in April 1949 and to commemorate the anniversaries of Tyrolian patriot Andreas Hofer's (1767–1810) birth and death. The folk music associations of North and South Tyrol did not adopt a critical stance with regard to the Arbeitsgemeinschaft Tiroler Komponisten composers.

The first research studies, which were mainly biographical, to emerge on the Arbeitsgemeinschaft Tiroler Komponisten were conducted in the 1960s by authors who came from the same artistic and ideological environment as the group's members[53] and used the same *völkisch* stylistic and lexical models. Often publicly funded, these studies were part of an attempt at mutual rehabilitation and marked the starting point for a discourse of exculpation. The majority ignored the composers' educational background and ideological and artistic orientations as well as the provenance and historical position of the musical themes and material that they mobilized and the ideological aims behind them. Most of the historical aspects of the region's musical life and institutions under Nazism were also overlooked, as were the group's objectives and initiatives. Its cultural and political involvement was generally seen as a "brief aberration"[54] in an otherwise coherent mission of covert opposition to Nazi dictatorship. Any internal discord within the regime as well as any personal clashes and conflicts of interests with local Nazi Party and state representatives were interpreted in an exculpatory manner as signs of an ideologically based opposition to Nazism. This specific "denazification" reaffirmed and revalidated the strongly illiberal, religiously sugarcoated, German-nationalism-derived "Tyrolean ideology" represented by Ploner's circle.

Given the positions adopted only recently by certain societal forces in the region with regard to the forms, actors, and survival phenomena of Nazi cultural policy, it is clear that amnesia, amnesty, exculpation, and decontextualization strategies are by no means confined to the years directly following World War II. Quite the contrary. Today's Tyrolean policymakers still view folk culture as an important contribution to societal cohesion and to strengthening regional identity. The concepts and policies they put forward in this regard have often been rooted in nationalist ideas. This is revealed through the fact that regional political elites contribute to promoting artists with a compromising past. Particularly notable in this regard were the 1959/60 commemorations of the 150th anniversary of the death of Andreas Hofer, which received 26 million Austrian schillings of state funding. Karl Senn was commissioned by the Tyrolean government to compose a "great patriotic" oratorio (*Andreas Hofer 1809*, op. 176, for four solo voices, one speaker, male, female, and mixed choirs, large orchestra, and organ). The commemorations, which lasted a whole year, ended in February 1960 with a *Requiem for vocal soloists, choir, orchestra, and organ* (op. 85) composed by Karl Koch, who had once set a distasteful anti-Italian poem written by Anton Müller (1870–1939) entitled "Dolomitenwacht" (Dolomite guard) to music. Koch's Requiem was performed again in the same place in 1984 on the 174th anniversary of Hofer's death. Another notable example was the resolute support shown by the Tyrolean government's cultural department of Kanetscheider's artistic work between 1957 and 1970.[55] A similar mindset was also demonstrated in the award presented to the composer Florian Pedarnig (1938–2022) by the Tyrolean regional government in 2013 in recognition of the importance of his work. Among his compositions is a march called "Dem Land Tirol die Treue" (Loyalty to the land of Tyrol), which has been very popular over the years not just in the world of folk music but also among the younger generation. It is regularly played at traditional festivals and nightclubs alike; it is predisposed to political readings because of its open allusions to nationalist and revisionist sentiments.

The end of World War II brought an end to a regime of unspeakable violence in the name of what was considered and justified as the perfection of human beings and their environment. The military defeat of Germany marked the definitive moral confutation of this regime and its ideology. With a reborn Austria developing the argument that it was the first victim of Nazi Germany's aggression and expansionism, there came an externalization of responsibilities and a halfhearted acceptance of the moral confutation. Rekindled borderland disputes and socioethnic conflicts further strengthened this position. The example of Tyrol shows that in the domain of folk music and dance, certain ideologies that had crystalized during World War II from a substratum of positions formulated in the aftermath of the Great War and during the period of Austrofascism far from disappeared in the years after the conflict; in fact, they persist to the present day. In order to understand how such sociopolitical continuities have been possible, one needs to examine the role not just of the protagonists but also of cultural policy, taking into account its underlying ideology, its structure, and the social circumstances that have conditioned its implementation. It is also essential to consider the clientelist exchanges established between the political sphere and folk cultural associations, where the political sphere provides the necessary state subsidies and, in exchange, the folk cultural associations guarantee their political support. This is how the political world lends its resources to the music world, and vice versa.

Michael Wedekind has been assistant professor at the Zentralinstitut für Kunstgeschichte (Munich) since 2016. His work focuses on the contemporary history of Germany, Austria, Italy, the Adriatic and Alpine area, and southeastern Europe (Slovenia and Romania). He is particularly interested in issues such as nationalism, international affairs and totalitarianism. His latest publications relate to these fields of research: *Contested Space—Contested Heritage: Sources on the Displacement of Cultural Objects in the 20th-Century Alpine-Adriatic Region* (with D. Levi); *La regione Trentino-Alto Adige/Südtirol nel XX secolo: L'oggetto popolazione* (R. Taiani); and: *Die Besetzung der Vergangenheit: Archäologie, Frühgeschichte und NS-Herrschaftslegitimation im Alpen-Adria-Raum, 1939–1945.*

Notes

1. Tyrol was a multicultural Habsburg crown land until 1918, comprising German-speaking territories north and south of the Brennero Pass and Italian-speaking territories (Trentino) along the Adige Valley. The crown land thus extended from the border with Germany in the North to Lake Garda and the border with Italy in the South. After World War I and the dissolution of Austria-Hungary (Treaty of Saint-Germain-en-Laye, 1919), the territories north of the Brennero

Pass came to constitute the *Land* of Tyrol (North Tyrol) within the newly established Republic of Austria, while the territories south of the Brennero Pass (i.e., South Tyrol/Alto Adige, with its center in Bolzano, along with the Trentino region, with its center in Trento) were attached to Italy. South Tyrol had a predominantly German-speaking population, although the number of Italian speakers increased significantly during the interwar period. Both South Tyrol and Trentino also have a Ladin-speaking minority.
2. The radio was frequently mobilized during Hitler's birthday celebrations.
3. On Berlanda, see Gitterle, "Emil Berlanda. Porträt eines Tiroler Komponisten." For Berlanda's autobiography, see Tiroler Landesmuseum Ferdinandeum, Innsbruck: FB 133.381. For his private archives, see Tiroler Landesmuseum Ferdinandeum, Innsbruck: Nachlass Berlanda, Privatkorrespondenz. Between 1981 and 2011 the Land of Tyrol awarded a music prize named after Berlanda. Since 2014, following observations presented by the author of this chapter, this has been called the Preis für zeitgenössische Musik (Prize for Contemporary Music).
4. We refer here to Berlanda's music and arrangement for a male voice choir and wind orchestra based on Josef Georg Blattl's (1897–1977) poem "Wir Kämpfer" (We, the fighters). See Josef Georg Blattl, "Wir Kämpfer," *Neueste Zeitung. Abendblatt der Innsbrucker Nachrichten*, 2 April 1938.
5. See Knapp, *Josef Gasser*; Chizzali, "'Ich bin 100 Jahre zu spät geboren'"; Chizzali, "Kompositorischer Konservativismus in Tirol," 157–81; Spiehs, *Josef Eduard Ploner*.
6. On Ploner, see Fastl, "Ploner, Josef Eduard."
7. Spiehs, *Josef Eduard Ploner*, 29. "Volkhafte Erneuerung von Kunst und Kultur."
8. Manfred Schneider in the supplementary booklet (page 10) to "Klingende Kostbarkeiten aus Tirol, 70: Artur Kanetscheider," Institut für Tiroler Musikforschung, Innsbruck, 2010, http://klangraumtirol.musikland-tirol.at/Arge/seite22.html; "[Dass dieses] hervorragende schöpferische Werk ... wie selbstverständlich im heimischen Musikbetrieb wieder akzeptiert wird."
9. Herrmann-Schneider: "Die klangliche Inszenierung des Mythos Tirol." "[sie haben] zu 'Recht' [als] Tiroler Nationalkomponisten [zu gelten]."
10. Curtis, *Music Makes the Nation*, 33.
11. In 2013 the author of this chapter was commissioned by the Tyrolean government to submit an official expertise on regional cultural policy. https://www.tirol.gv.at/fileadmin/themen/kunst-kultur/abteilung/Sonstiges/Gutachten_Wedekind_S._1-40.pdf, published in 2013 (hereafter Wedekind, *Expertise*), and https://www.tirol.gv.at/fileadmin/themen/kunst-kultur/abteilung/Sonstiges/Gutachten_Wedekind_S._41-81_Dez15.pdf.
12. For the similar case of the Salzburg musician Tobias (Tobi) Franz Reiser (1907–74), see Rathkolb, *Tobi Reiser*.
13. Gellner, *Nations and Nationalism*.
14. Eckel, *Hans Rothfels*, 330.
15. John 2001, "Legendenbildung und kritische Rekonstruktion," 462. "[Aus] innerer Konsequenz."
16. Schmid, "Volk, Nation, Stamm und Rasse."
17. John 1998, "Der Mythos vom Deutschen in der deutschen Musik." "[Nach allem] Deutschen in der deutschen Musik [forschen]."
18. Lach, "Die großdeutsche Kultureinheit in der Musik." "Großdeutsche ... Kultureinheit in der Musik."
19. Meyer, "The Nazi Musicologist," 649; John 2000, "Deutsche Musikwissenschaft."
20. Potter, "Musikwissenschaft und Nationalsozialismus: Der Stand der Debatte," 139. "Musikwissenschaftliche ... Establishments."

21. Idem., 136. "Weltanschauliche Konversion."
22. Gülke, "Die Nazis und der Fauxbourdon."
23. Loos, "Landesgeschichte und Kulturregion," 139. "Feststellung überregionaler Ausstrahlung oder . . . 'Geltung.'"
24. Berlanda's parents had immigrated to Innsbruck from Trentino. Kanetscheider's ancestry came partly from the Sudetenland and partly from the Val Pusteria (Pustertal) in South Tyrol and the Ladin-speaking region of the Dolomites. Marini was born in Bressanone (Brixen), and Ploner in Vipiteno (Sterzing).
25. Lerner, *The Nazi Elite*, 154.
26. Wedekind, *Nationalsozialistische Besatzungs- und Okkupationspolitik in Norditalien 1943 bis 1945*, 23–36.
27. Spiehs, *Josef Eduard Ploner*, 55. "Tirol ist Grenzland, sein Kunstleben daher besonders gefährdet. Auch aus diesem Grunde müssen wir unsere Tiroler Künstler, an denen das Erbe reich bedachter Vorfahren hängt, besonders schützen. . . . Danken wir . . . [ihnen] und versuchen wir, ihnen Verständnis entgegenzubringen." Although closely associated with the Ploner circle, Spiehs never became a member of the Arbeitsgemeinschaft Tiroler Komponisten. He was, however, a member of the Gau Tirol-Vorarlberg's regional Gauausschuss für Volksmusik (Nazi Committee for Folk Music) and the Reichsmusikkammer. In the late 1950s he began to promote Ploner's works in cooperation with the regional authorities.
28. Hanisch and Fleischer, *Im Schatten berühmter Zeiten*, 21.
29. This was the context in which the Heimatschutz (protection of the homeland) movement emerged in Germany (1904), Switzerland (1905), and Austria (1908). The first branch founded in Austria was in Innsbruck. Other branches were established in the years that followed. They were mainly supported by members of the small-town educated middle classes. The Tyrolean Heimatschutz drafted a regional identity concept that was based on patriotic ideals of agrarian Romanticism and centered on ideas of preserving nature, landscape, folklore, and folkdom. The Heimatschutz members developed a vision of protecting Tyrol entirely as a "reserve" or monumental complex composed of the space and people that made up their landscape. Shortly before World War I, it was proposed that Tyrol should designate itself entirely as a conservation area. See Ignaz Zangerle, "Der Inbegriff von Tirol," *Tiroler Wegweiser (Innsbruck)*, 1955, 3–5. The Heimatschutz movement initiated the collection of folk songs, the preservation and "revitalization" of customs and costumes. Additionally, a specific architecture emerged that was based on references to traditional rural elements.
30. Plattner, *Fin de siècle in Tirol*, 210–27.
31. John 1998, "Der Mythos vom Deutschen in der deutschen Musik," 65.
32. Minutes of the Arbeitsgemeinschaft Tiroler Komponisten meeting of 3 June 1937 (Tiroler Landesmuseum Ferdinandeum, Innsbruck, Bibliothek, FB 51.899).
33. Ploner to Josef Gasser, cited in Chizzali, "'Ich bin 100 Jahre zu spät geboren,'" 37. "Wie Du dir ja vorstellen kannst, muss auch auf kulturellen Gebieten zuerst vollständig ausgemistet werden. Die 'A.K.M.' z.B. steht nun nach der ersten Radikalsäuberung ebenfalls judenrein da."
34. Berlanda's autobiography, Tiroler Landesmuseum Ferdinandeum, Innsbruck: FB 133.381, 142; Minutes of the Arbeitsgemeinschaft Tiroler Komponisten meeting of 18 May 1937 (Tiroler Landesmuseum Ferdinandeum, Innsbruck, Bibliothek, FB 51.899).
35. Spiehs, *Josef Eduard Ploner*, 29. "Volkhafte Erneuerung von Kunst und Kultur."
36. Kattnigg to Berlanda, Berlin, 31 January 1935; see Tiroler Landesmuseum Ferdinandeum, Innsbruck: Nachlass Berlanda, Privatkorrespondenz.

37. See Josef Eduard Ploner, "Singende Volksgenossen," *Deutsche Volkszeitung (Innsbruck)*, 26 April 1928, and Josef Eduard Ploner, "Weltanschauung und Tonkunst: Zum Wirken des 'Innsbrucker Kammerchores,'" *Deutsche Volkszeitung (Innsbruck)*, 27 April 1938.
38. Minutes of the Arbeitsgemeinschaft Tiroler Komponisten meeting of 2 April 1937 (Tiroler Landesmuseum Ferdinandeum, Innsbruck, Bibliothek, FB 51.899).
39. See Tiroler Landesarchiv, Innsbruck: LSR-1086 "Ploner, Josef": Ploner to Gauleiter Hofer, Innsbruck, 26 November 1940. "Unserm Volke in der seelischen Untermauerung seiner Lebensführung ... besser dienen zu können."
40. See Wedekind, "Expansion und regionale Herrschaftsbildung."
41. See Drexel, *Klingendes Bekenntnis zu Führer und Reich*.
42. For a detailed study of Ploner's involvement with the Nazi regime, see Wedekind, *Expertise*, notes 28 ff.
43. Ploner, *Hellau!*; see also Drexel, *Klingendes Bekenntnis zu Führer und Reich*, 136–37.
44. See Drexel, *Klingendes Bekenntnis zu Führer und Reich*, 140–42.
45. In relation to the history of Austrian music specifically, see, for example, Eickhoff, "'Mit Sozialismus und Sachertorte.'"
46. Boeckel, "'Kulturnation Österreich,'" 34. "Zäsuren ohne Folgen."
47. Müller, *Zäsuren ohne Folgen*. "[das] lange Leben der Antimoderne in Österreich."
48. Baur, "Kontinuität—Diskontinuität," 117.
49. Dvořák, "Thesen zur soziokulturellen Entwicklung," 31. "Rekonstruktion jener 'Kultur,' die nicht unbeträchtlich Anteil an den Siegen der beiden Faschismen gehabt [hat]."
50. Wedekind, "Politisierungen von 'Volkskultur' im Tirol des 20. Jahrhunderts," 137–166.
51. See the sarcastic remarks in his autobiography; Innsbruck Ferdinandeum: FB 133. 381, f. 320–21.
52. See Kanetscheider, "Josef Pöll," 62. "Many personal wounds were inflicted by World War II and the vengeful postwar period." "Viele persönliche Wunden schlugen der Zweite Weltkrieg und die rachedurstige Nachkriegszeit."
53. Wilhelm Lackinger, "Erinnerungen an Josef Eduard Ploner," In *Tiroler Tageszeitung*, 23 June 1960, 5; Holzmann, "Söhne der Heimat," and Spiehs, *Josef Eduard Ploner*.
54. Spiehs, *Josef Eduard Ploner*, 65. "Kurzzeitige Verirrung."
55. Kanetscheider, *Erinnerungsblätter*, 29–30.

Bibliography

Baur, Uwe. "Kontinuität—Diskontinuität: Die Zäsuren 1933–1938–1945 im österreichischen literarischen Leben. Zum Problem des Begriffs 'literarische Epoche.'" In *Literaturgeschichte: Österreich: Prolegomena und Fallstudien*, edited by Wendelin Schmidt-Dengler, Johann Sonnleitner, and Klaus Zeyringer, 115–16. Berlin: Erich Schmidt, 1995.

Boeckel, Matthias. "'Kulturnation Österreich.' Bemerkungen zu ausgewählten Kunstereignissen 1934 bis 1948." In *Kunst in Österreich 1945–1995*, edited by Patrick Werkner, 32–42. Vienna: WUV-Univ.-Verlag, 1996.

Chizzali, Michael. "'Ich bin 100 Jahre zu spät geboren': Studien zum weltlichen Musikschaffen des Tiroler Komponisten Josef Gasser (1873–1957)." PhD diss., University of Innsbruck, 2012a.

———. "Kompositorischer Konservativismus in Tirol: Das weltliche Schaffen von Josef Gasser (1873–1957)." In *Rudolf von Ficker (1886–1954)*, edited by Lukas Christensen, Kurt Drexel and Monika Fink, 157–81. Innsbruck: Innsbruck University Press, 2012b.

Curtis, Benjamin. *Music Makes the Nation: Nationalist Composers and Nation Building in Nineteenth-Century Europe*. Amherst, NY: Cambria Press, 2008.

Drexel, Kurt. *Klingendes Bekenntnis zu Führer und Reich: Musik und Identität im Reichsgau Tirol-Vorarlberg 1938–1945*. Innsbruck: Universitätsverlag Wagner, 2014.

Dvořak, Johann. "Thesen zur soziokulturellen Entwicklung in Österreich 1933 bis 1955." In *Kontinuität und Bruch 1938–1945–1955. Beiträge zur österreichischen Kultur- und Wissenschaftsgeschichte*, edited by Friedrich Stadler, 27–34. Vienna: LIT Verlag, 1988.

Eckel, Jan. *Hans Rothfels: Eine intellektuelle Biographie im 20. Jahrhundert*. Göttingen: Wallstein Verlag, 2005.

Eickhoff, Thomas. "'Mit Sozialismus und Sachertorte . . . ': Entnazifizierung und musikpolitische Verhaltensmuster nach 1945 in Österreich." In *Deutsche Leitkultur Musik? Zur Musikgeschichte nach dem Holocaust*, edited by Albrecht Riethmüller, 85–99. Stuttgart: Franz Steiner, 2006.

Fastl, Christian. "Ploner, Josef Eduard." Österreichisches Musiklexikon, 2002. Retrieved 22 September 2020 from https://www.musiklexikon.ac.at/ml/musik_P/Ploner_Josef_Eduard.xml.

Gellner, Ernst. *Nations and Nationalism*. Ithaca, NY: Cornell University Press, 1983.

Gitterle, Christine. "Emil Berlanda. Porträt eines Tiroler Komponisten." Salzburg: Hochschule Mozarteum. University of Innsbruck, term paper, 1979.

Gülke, Peter. "Die Nazis und der Fauxbourdon. Anfragen an nicht vergehende Vergangenheit: Heinrich Besseler." In *Musikforschung, Faschismus, Nationalsozialismus. Referate der Tagung, Schloss Engers, 8. bis 11. März 2000*, edited by Isolde von Foerster, Christoph Hust and Christoph-Helmut Mahling, 373–94. Mainz: Are Musik Verlag, 2001.

Hanisch, Ernst, and Ulrike Fleischer. *Im Schatten berühmter Zeiten: Salzburg in den Jahren Georg Trakls (1887–1914)*. Salzburg: Otto Mueller Verlag, 1986.

Herrmann-Schneider, Hildegard. "Die klangliche Inszenierung des Mythos Tirol: Tiroler Komponisten des 20. Jahrhunderts und ihre Hommage an das Land im Gebirge." *Vortrag, gehalten auf der Jahrestagung 'Synthese Österreich' der Österreichischen Gesellschaft für Musikwissenschaft in Kooperation mit der Kommission für Musikforschung der Österreichischen Akademie der Wissenschaften, Vienna, 03.12.2011.*

Retrieved 19 September 2020 from http://musikgeschichten.musik land-tirol.at/content/musikintirol/info/die-klangliche-inszenierung-des-mythos-tirol.html.

Holzmann, Hermann. "Söhne der Heimat—Berühmte Sterzinger." In *Sterzinger Heimatbuch*, edited by Anselm Sparber, 449–502. Innsbruck: Universitätsverlag Wagner, 1965.

John, Eckhard. "Der Mythos vom Deutschen in der deutschen Musik: Die Freiburger Musikwissenschaft im NS-Staat." In *Musik in Baden-Württemberg*, vol. 5, edited by Georg Günther and Reiner Nägele, 57–84. Stuttgart: J. B. Metzler Verlag, 1998.

———. "Deutsche Musikwissenschaft: Musikforschung im Dritten Reich." In *Musikwissenschaft—eine verspätete Disziplin? Die akademische Musikforschung zwischen Fortschrittsglauben und Modernisierungsverweigerung*, edited by Anselm Gerhard, 257–80. Stuttgart: J. B. Metzler Verlag, 2000.

———. "Legendenbildung und kritische Rekonstruktion: Zehn Thesen zur Musikforschung im NS-Staat." In *Musikforschung—Faschismus—Nationalsozialismus. Referate der Tagung Schloss Engers, 8–11. März 2000*, edited by Isolde von Foerster, Christoph Hust, and Christoph-Hellmut Mahling, 461–70. Mainz: Are Musik, 2001.

Kanetscheider, Artur. "Josef Pöll: Der Meister des mundartlichen Tiroler Volksliedes. Zur 20. Wiederkehr seines Todestages am 21. Juni 1960." In *Hundert Jahre Tiroler Sängerbund 1860–1960*, edited by Karl Leipert, 62. Innsbruck: Wagner Verlag, 1960.

———. *Erinnerungsblätter: Ein Leben für die Musik*. Innsbruck: Helbling Verlag, 1978.

Knapp, Ernst. *Josef Gasser. Ein Tiroler Komponist*. Brixen: A. Weger Verlag, 2001.

Lach, Robert. "Die großdeutsche Kultureinheit in der Musik." In *Die Anschlussfrage in ihrer kulturellen, politischen und wirtschaftlichen Bedeutung*, edited by Friedrich Kleinwächter and Heinz von Paller, 294–95. Vienna: Braumüller, 1930.

Lerner, Daniel. *The Nazi Elite*. Stanford, CA: Stanford University Press, 1951.

Loos, Helmut. "Landesgeschichte und Kulturregion—keine selbstverständliche Übereinstimmung: Das Beispiel Mitteleuropa." In *Niedersachsen in der Musikgeschichte. Zur Methodologie und Organisation musikalischer Regionalforschung. Internationales Symposion Wolfenbüttel 1997*, edited by Arnfried Edler and Joachim Kremer, 139–45. Augsburg: WißnerVerlag, 2000.

Meyer, Michael. "The Nazi Musicologist as Myth Maker in the Third Reich." *Journal of Contemporary History* 10 (1975): 648–65.

Müller, Karl. *Zäsuren ohne Folgen. Das lange Leben der literarischen Antimoderne Österreichs seit den 1930er Jahren*. Salzburg: Otto Müller Verlag, 1990.

Plattner, Irmgard. *Fin de siècle in Tirol. Provinzkultur und Provinzgesellschaft um die Jahrhundertwende*. Innsbruck: Studien Verlag, 1998.

Ploner, Josef Eduard, ed. *Hellau! Liederbuch für Front und Heimat des Gaues Tirol-Vorarlberg. Im Auftrag des Gauleiters und Reichsstatthalters Franz Hofer*. Potsdam: Verlag Voggenreiter, 1942.

Potter, Pamela, "Musikwissenschaft und Nationalsozialismus: Der Stand der Debatte." In *Nationalsozialismus in den Kulturwissenschaften, Band 1: Fächer—Milieus—Karrieren*, edited by Hartmut Lehmann and Otto Gerhard Oexle, 129–41. Göttingen: Vandenhoeck & Ruprecht, 2004.

Rathkolb, Oliver. *Tobi Reiser und der Nationalsozialismus*. Salzburg: Verlag des Salzburg Museums, 2016.

Schmid, Birgitta Maria. "Volk, Nation, Stamm und Rasse: Die Politisierung der deutschen Musik 1850–1945." PhD diss., University of Heidelberg, 1997.

Spiehs, Hermann. *Josef Eduard Ploner: Ein Tiroler Komponist*. Innsbruck: Universitätsverlag Wagner, 1965.

Wedekind, Michael. *Nationalsozialistische Besatzungs- und Okkupationspolitik in Norditalien 1943 bis 1945: Die Operationszonen 'Alpenvorland' und 'Adriatisches Küstenland'*. Munich: Oldenbourg, 2003.

———. "Expansion und regionale Herrschaftsbildung in der 'Ostmark' am Beispiel des Gaues Tirol-Vorarlberg." In *Die NS-Gaue: Regionale Mittelinstanzen im zentralistischen 'Führerstaat'?*, edited by Jürgen John, Horst Möller and Thomas Schaarschmidt, 382–90. Munich: Oldenbourg, 2007.

———. "Politisierungen von 'Volkskultur' im Tirol des 20. Jahrhunderts: Von der Tracht und ihrer Unschuld." *Geschichte und Region—Storia e regione* 30/2 (2021): 137–166.

Part III
MEMORY, MOURNING, AND COMMEMORATION

Chapter 8

BÉRANGER'S NAPOLEONIC SONGS
Mourning, Memory, and the Future

Sophie-Anne Leterrier

Songs have long been used as a source of study by historians of the nineteenth century, especially when examining domestic political conflicts.[1] However, national conquests and defeats are also a frequent theme in songs, particularly those penned by France's famous "national chansonnier," Pierre-Jean de Béranger. Mourning past glory and denouncing a liberticidal peace, Béranger's songs were a form of commemoration at a time when the memory of war was still very present. In this chapter, I will first outline the context of 1815 and then analyze both the thematics of Béranger's songs and the rhetorical devices used by the chansonnier. In the final section, I examine his skillful use of timbres as a way of creating a network of ideas, associations, and values.

1815: The End of an Era

France was emerging from not just one war in 1815 but an almost uninterrupted series of wars that had begun in 1792 with the *levée en masse*. The French Revolutionary Wars had been followed by the campaigns of the French Directory and then the Napoleonic Wars. These "wars of freedom" had turned into wars of conquest, and with the loss of 1.3 million lives (from a total 30 million inhabitants in 1815), they came at an enormous cost to France.

Notes for this section begin on page 175.

France's Misfortunes

By 1814 the country had been left weary and numb with grief. The concern not to surrender territory to the enemy vied with the fear that fresh victories could trigger a never-ending war. In Louis XVIII the people saw an opportunity to make peace with Europe and to end this twenty-five-year-long period of warfare that had played out both internationally and domestically, ripping through and dividing families. This is evidenced in the French author George Sand's life story not to mention the fate of Victor Hugo's character Marius in *Les Misérables*. Ultimately, this "civil war" did not end until the 1880s, when the majority of the French people finally accepted the Republic.

Both of these "wars" had continued after 1814/15. In France the return of the Bourbons prompted an overt response, leading to resistance in Europe in the form of plots and Carbonarism. This culminated in the revolutions of 1848 and fueled the "republican" struggle right up to the Paris Commune of 1871 and the subsequent general amnesty for all Commune supporters in 1880. The postwar transition therefore happened in several stages over both the short term (i.e., 1812, 1814, and 1815) and the long term, and it involved diplomacy, economic development, and ideological "reunification."

First of all, the impact of the defeat was brutal, and peacetime conditions were catastrophic. On 1 January 1814, Napoleonic France was invaded by five hundred thousand Russian, Prussian, Austrian, and British soldiers. At the end of March that same year, one hundred thousand coalition soldiers besieged Paris. The capitulation was signed, and the emperor abdicated and bid farewell to his guard. On 30 May the peace agreement (Treaty of Paris) was signed. While this did not stipulate any indemnity or territorial occupation, France's borders were reverted to what they had been in 1792. On 4 June, a constitutional charter recommended "that the courts and citizens forget."[2] However, this return of the white flag triggered a reaction that manifested at different levels. The new regime immediately alienated much of the country, and so the Hundred Days began, concluding on 18 June 1815 with the Battle of Waterloo. This battle marked a turning point in the history of Europe; indeed, Hugo devoted a whole book to it in *Les Misérables*.[3] Napoleon abdicated a second time and quit France for good, this time accompanied by more than one million foreign soldiers. Weighed down by heavy war debt, the country experienced organized pillaging, including 10 million francs a month to maintain the army stationed in the territory and a one-off contribution of 100 million. The royalist reactionaries, the exiling of patriots, and the White Terror of 1815 aroused fear, consternation, despondency, and exasperation among the population. The new order was sealed by the Second Treaty of Paris, signed on 20 November 1815. However, it was immediately considered to be a yoke around France's neck. Its purpose was morally and politically to disarm the country, which was seen as a breeding ground for subversive ideas in relation to the European order. The brutality of the occupation and resulting close surveillance were accompanied by the stationing of foreign troops in the country, and these remained until 1818. France's national territory was reduced still further (reverting to the borders of 1790), and it had to pay an indemnity of 700 million francs plus occupation costs, which were set at 150 million a year. Both the army and the press remained under surveillance. With Napoleon's shadow looming in the background and the future scarcely visible on the horizon,[4] 1817 was a year of inanity and denial. Hugo summed it up as follows: "Louis XVIII . . . had two anxieties—Napoleon and Mathurin Bruneau."[5]

The Memory of Conflicts in Béranger's Songs

"Mathurin Bruneau," one of Béranger's songs, tells the story of a clog maker-cum-chansonnier who wants to become king. The chansonnier advises him to remain at his workbench and not to succumb to the sirens of glory. In 1817, Béranger turned song into a weapon in the fight for liberalism. As part of the revolutionary tradition, he became France's national chansonnier. Because poetry had little impact on people at the time and because the political press only addressed an educated and wealthy elite, song was the most effective way of spreading liberal ideas by evading censorship. It was to be the vehicle for remembering events, battles, emotions, bereavements, and hope. Béranger's "glory" came from the part he played in maintaining this memory. In his own words:

"So that my country may know how grateful I am, above all, for having given myself over to the kind of poetry that I judged most useful to the cause of liberty, when I could have attempted more solid success in the genres that I had first cultivated (. . .) But I have used my life as a poet, and that is my consolation. The people needed a man who would speak to the people in the language they understand and love, and who would create imitators to vary and multiply the versions of the same text. I was that man."[6]

Born in Paris on 19 August 1780, Béranger had not participated in the French Revolution. During the Empire, he wrote the occasional song, which he would sing in private clubs and to private audiences. In 1813 "Le Roi d'Yvetot" helped him gain access to some celebrated bourgeois singing companies. In 1815 he met Jacques-Antoine Manuel, a lawyer and prominent member of the Liberal Party, with whom he developed a close friendship. Béranger's songs became increasingly politicized, with some being published by the liberal newspaper *La Minerve*. His second collection of songs cost him three months in prison and 500 francs following a trial in 1821. A second trial in 1829, this time in a criminal court, led to a sentence of nine months and a fine of 10,000 francs for another collection of songs. The chansonnier's fame was at its height. In 1830 the liberal cause triumphed, and Béranger bid adieu to song. He ceded all his future work, which was to be published posthumously, to his publisher in return for a lifetime annuity. He would no longer play an active political role, at least not until his death in 1857.

Béranger was a true creative artist. He had dragged song out of the gutter of bawdiness and given it values that were new, national, and liberal. The success of his songs was due not only to their lyrics, which were highly classical in form and in keeping with the prevailing sentiments of the time (nostalgia for bygone national greatness, loathing of the clerical reaction, and voicing of democratic aspirations), but also to their musical dimension and the emotions they conveyed. Almost all his songs were a reflection on the meaning of France's recent history. They spoke either implicitly or explicitly of the Revolution of 1815 and the Bourbon Restoration as well as the wars of freedom. For example, in "Mathurin Bruneau" (or "Le Prince de Navarre," a title full of hidden meanings, which was set to the tune of "Air du Ballet des Pierrots"), he wrote: "Sad tricks with us our friends have played: / 'Tis now for foreigners our lot— / Not for ourselves—to boil the pot."[7] He specifically alludes, for example, to the White Terror of 1815 ("How badly Nismes was served of old"[8]) and the war debt demanded by the Allies ("Their grasping League, from day to day, / Dear, and more dear, would make thee pay"[9]), which had been increased in 1815.

In "Le Grenier" (to the tune of Meissonnier's "Air du Carnaval"), one of Béranger's most popular songs, he sings about his youth, which had vanished along with all his sweethearts, and about an age of glory and joyful illusion:

Once as we feasted—'twas unwonted cheer—
Whilst loud the chorus of my comrades pealed,

> A shout of triumph reached us, up even here—
> "Napoleon conquers on Marengo's field!"
> The cannon thunder—we, in homage paid
> To deeds so great, another song essay;
> The soil of France kings never shall invade!
> That garret-life, at twenty, 'tis so gay![10]

In a subtle interplay with censorship and with a shrewd use of dissemination methods (oral and print), Béranger's songs thus conveyed the memory of conflicts at a time when the regime was coming to terms with and trying to bury the memory. The Restoration tried to make people forget the revolutionary past, to pretend that it had never existed. This is why those who considered themselves to be the children of the Revolution, on the contrary, have multiplied tributes and evocations of heroic times (including wars).

The precise dating of some of his songs alters their meaning. Most of the songs are undated. Only the collection in which they appeared and the chansonnier's correspondence give us a clue as to when they were composed. However, Béranger used a publishing strategy that transferred part of the content into the paratext to guide interpretation. We can see this, for example, in the paratext to "La Cocarde Blanche": "These verses are supposed to have been written for a dinner, at which certain royalists celebrated, on the 30th of March, 1816, the anniversary of the first entry of the Austrians, Russians, and Prussians into Paris."[11] Similarly, the paratext to "La Sainte Alliance des Peuples" reads: "In the month of October, 1818, the Duc de la Rochefoucauld gave a grand entertainment at Liancourt, to celebrate the evacuation of the French territory by the Allied armies."[12] The print versions of his songs contain many explicit references to 1814 and 1815. There is no other period in Béranger's work with so many precisely dated songs (with the exception perhaps of the songs he wrote in prison[13]). Some are commentaries on specific contemporary events. "Le Convoi de David," for example, alludes to Napoleon:

> —Soldier, his eyes until death
> Turned toward the homeland.
> He defended its glory
> From the depths of an exile that honored him;
> Through him our greatness
> Radiates still from the canvas.[14]

The defeat of 1815 was catastrophic. In "Le Cinq Mars," Béranger avoids any celebration of the event: "On such a day, we see our empire fall, / We see the foreigner bring us back in chains, / We see our people smile pusillanimously at them. / His name will never taint my songs with sadness."[15] The defeat was considered an injustice, a misfortune, a betrayal. It was never seen as the result of error or excess. This is clearly exemplified in "Mathurin Bruneau":

> Think'st thou as warrior to be great?
> Know that 'tis oft the Conqueror's fate,
> To find the laurels of the day
> By some rude General snatched away:
> An English Chief, by Tartar's aid,
> Low in the dust proud standards laid.[16]

It is also evident in "L'Exilé": "Betrayed by victory, / This outcast, in our woods, / Anxious for his honor, / Flees the hatred of kings."[17] And again in "Les Enfants de la France": "Queen of the world! O France, my country, now / At length lift up thy cicatrized brow: / Though soiled and rent thy children's standard lies, / Their glory rests untarnished in thine eyes."[18] However, Béranger also denounced the marshals' betrayal, which he often contrasted with the loyalty of France's noncommissioned soldiers. For example, in "Le Vieux Sergent": "To ennoble themselves, from the ranks are they lured: / And with mouths blackened still by the cartridge, prepare, / Basely fawning on tyrants, their homage to swear. / Freedom, too, with her arms has deserted—they turn / From one throne to another, fresh prizes to earn."[19]

Thematics

Béranger's songs constructed national legend, denounced the decadence and degradation of the times, sympathized with the patriots' misfortunes, and accused the enemy.

The National Legend

Recalling a glorious epic, his songs centered on Bonaparte (as opposed to Napoleon). "Le Vieux Sergent" tells the story of a Grande Armée soldier who is on the brink of death but still full of the same spirit of sacrifice and heroism as that demonstrated by the *va-nu-pieds* at the Battle of Valmy:

> "Who," pursues the old hero, "shall give us anew,
> On the banks of the Rhine, at Jemappes, at Fleurus,

Peasants, such as of yore the Republic could rear,
Sons who swarmed at her voice to defend her frontier?
Starving, barefooted, deaf to all coward alarms,
How they marched, keeping step, to seek glory in arms![20]

In this sense, Béranger's songs were the musical equivalent of Raffet's imagery (Raffet painted the chansonnier's portrait). These magnanimous old soldiers were, both literally and figuratively, the founders of a new community. They were the exiles depicted in the song "Champ d'Asile." In his song about this settlement, Béranger recalls the campaign in Egypt (verse 3), Napoleon's absolute power (verse 4), his fall and the exodus of his followers (verse 5) and the glory that accompanied them, which turned them into the missionaries of a new vision: "(The glory) still horrifying to kings, / And banished us from our humble thatched cottages / Whence, forced out to avenge our rights, / We have quashed twenty kingdoms."[21] Napoleon was somehow vindicated by this glory. As Sudhir Hazareesingh's book *The Legend of Napoleon*[22] shows, the fall of the tyrant was also his redemption. The son of 1789 had been resurrected:

Lofty in mind, in genius lofty, why,
Why on a sceptre stooped he to rely?
Towering above the thrones of Earth, it seemed
From this bare rock as though his glory beamed:
A world that's new—a world that's all too old—
Both, like a light-house, might its rays behold.[23]

This explains why Napoleon was the hero in Béranger's most famous song, "Souvenirs du Peuple"[24]: "Ay, many a day the straw-thatched cot / Shall echo with his glory / The humblest shed, these fifty years, / Shall know no other story."[25]

The chansonnier, just like the fallen emperor, "records for posterity all the great things" the French had done. This legend was rooted in a certain vision that France had of its role in the world. It saw itself as the standard bearer of the principles of 1789: liberté, égalité, fraternité (freedom, equality, fraternity).

With names of infamous renown that epoch hath been fraught;
But then, in youth's unconscious age, I could not judge of aught:
In spelling, with my childish tongue, our *country*—tender word—
The thought of foreigners and foes my soul with horror stirred.
All was in agitation then; all armed them for defence;
All, all were proud, but Poverty to pride made most pretence.
Ah, give me back! ah, give me back my childhood's joyous sense,
Goddess of Liberty![26]

Béranger was a close friend of Michelet in the 1840s, and many of their texts are similar, especially in this respect. Béranger spoke out in favor of the 1789 Revolution, as we can see from the extract from "La Déesse."

Decadence and Degradation

Béranger's songs were also, however, a virulent criticism of the Restoration. They contained bitter complaints and violent attacks leveled at the reign of the "old fogeys," the "pipsqueaks," the "midgets."[27] In "Couplets sur la Journée de Waterloo," for example, Béranger berated: "The giant sinks—the dwarfs, forgetful, swear / In slavish yoke the universe to tame; / Alas for glory, doubly cheated there! / Ne'er shall my verse be saddened by that name."[28] In "La Déesse," too, he railed against the Restoration:

> As some volcano quenched beneath its ashes, heap on heap,
> This people, after twenty years, was lulled again to sleep:
> 'Twas then the alien brought with him his balance in his hold,
> And twice could say to them, "O Gauls! come, weigh us out
> your gold!"
> . . .
> Be re-assured; the car, the flowers, the altar as of yore,
> Youth, glory, virtue, grandeur, hope, and pride, are now no more:
> All, all have perished; thou art not a Goddess as before,
> Goddess of Liberty![29]

After the happy epoch that had popularized "La Marseillaise" and "Le Chant du Départ," song took on the mantel of a lament. This explains the tendency toward bitterness in Béranger's songs. This trend is clearly manifested in "Les Adieux à la Gloire," for example, which was written in 1820: "Sing we to Beauty and to Wine, / For all the rest is naught: / Mark, mark, how soon mankind forgets / The hymns that Freedom taught!"[30] The theme is revisited in "Les Esclaves Gaulois": "A fig for stupid fools, who for their country die! / Come, let's get drunk!"[31]

The Patriots' Misfortunes

Béranger was the bard of France through all its decadence, trials, and tribulations. He dedicated many of his songs to the patriots' misfortunes. In 1814 Louis XVIII's government disregarded the enormous human and emotional legacy of Napoleon's former Grande Armée. Many of Béranger's songs commemorated these figures, their loyalty, and their humiliation. For example, "Les Deux Grenadiers," a dialogue between two grenadiers getting ready to follow the emperor to the island of Elba, condemns the betrayals of the aristocrats and some military officers. "Le Vieux Drapeau," too, tells the story of the French tricolor that an old soldier has hidden under his straw mattress, wondering when he will be able to wave it again.

As Sylvie Aprile[32] has demonstrated, the nineteenth century was the century of the exile. The figure of the exile is polarized in Béranger's account of history. On the one hand, we have the emigrants' return and all the many stereotypes created by the chansonnier, such as "Le Marquis de Carabas" and "La Marquise de Prétintaille"; on the other, the valiant patriots. "Le Champ d'Asile" comments on one specific event, while the theme is dealt with more broadly in "Les Hirondelles."

The exiles' suffering was alluded to in many sublime songs. "Le Retour dans la Patrie," for example, talks about French exiles having to return to their mother country to die, even if this means leaving behind family and fortune. In "Le Prisonnier de Guerre," Marie, who dashes off to get the prisoners of war released, demonstrates that the exile question also allowed Béranger to highlight the solidarity that existed between ordinary people.

The Enemy

Béranger contrasted the patriots with the figure of the enemy, who was generally portrayed as an Englishman (although he is a Cossack in one poem). In "L'Opinion de ces Demoiselles," the enemy is lauded by the prostitutes from the Palais Royal (which is described as their "homeland" [*patrie*]). Their opinion is dictated solely by their own interests: "So there is no girl who does not cry out: / Long live our friends, / Our friends the enemy!"[33] The song alludes, too, to women from the "noble faubourg" who were also friendly to the enemy, even to the point of competing with the prostitutes and tolerating violence: "When we hear some houses are burned down, / Some people slain, / That's the least of our worries. / But how I'll laugh if I'm raped."[34] Barbarity was not only accepted but celebrated by these women.

He of the Battle of Waterloo and Congress of Vienna fame, is referenced many times in songs such as "La Faridondaine."

> File a report on *Mirliton*:
> The court finds it obscene.
> Report as well that *Malborough is dead*:
> It will disquiet his *Grace*.

> . . .
> May the throne be protected
> From our frivolous refrain
> By *God Save the King*.³⁵

The English were generally referred to in a negative way, as brutal, primitive beings. In "Les Boxeurs": "One against one—the fight is fair: / Such odds with Englishmen are rare. / . . . Pshaw! clap your hands! one's tapped a vein— / O Heavens! these English are humane!"³⁶

Great Britain was associated with industrialism and cosmopolitanism. It was seen as the antithesis of French heroic patriotism. Béranger systematically contrasted English gold and French glory, as for example in "Les Enfants de la France." Chauvinism is evident in many of his songs, including "Le Bon Français." The songs that date from 1814 and 1815 are particularly virulent. Béranger would annotate his subsequent collections to highlight the brotherhood of nations and the fact that his anti-English criticism was justified under the circumstances. The note to "Dieu des Bonnes Gens,"³⁷ for example, states:

> English critics, who have incidentally been very benevolent toward our author, have reproached him for the characteristics, both amusing and serious, he has attributed to their nation. They should remember that these attacks date back to the time of France's occupation by the foreign armies responsible for the Restoration. . . . The idea of harboring hatred between two nations goes completely against the grain for a man who, when our territory was evacuated, was the first to call all peoples to a holy alliance.³⁸

The note to "Le Cinq Mai" even refers to a rhetorical device: "of all the nations of Europe, the Spaniards have the fairest cause of complaint against Napoleon. In placing his soldier, therefore, on board a Spanish vessel, he designed to show to what degree the misfortunes of the 'Great Man' had caused the people of every country to look with complacency upon his fame."³⁹

One might argue that it was the violence of the emperor's disgrace that led Béranger to praise him.

The Chansonnier's Strategies and Rhetorical Devices

In the November 1815 preface to his first collection, Béranger wrote: "Song is by nature a form of resistance."⁴⁰ In a letter dated 12 October 1821, he declared to his friend Dupont de l'Eure: "The only reward I seek is to contribute, within my small sphere, to making the tyranny that weighs upon us more striking, that is to say more ridiculous, and to popularize further the patriotic and philosophical principles with which my popular ditties are imbued."[41] Béranger's accusers were fully aware of this strategy.

Song Choice

His advocate, Dupin, made the same argument (in support of his client of course): "Song, the lightest of all poems, must also be the freest."[42] But this freedom did not mean innocuousness. "Le Vieux Sergent" shows the usefulness of song as a way out of moral degradation:

> Here his daughter, to soothe him, was fain to break in,
> And in notes low and soft, without ceasing to spin,
> Sang the airs now proscribed, that were wont with a start
> To awaken all Kings, and chill Royalty's heart.
> "People," softly he murmurs, "ah! would that these songs
> Might in turn—for 'tis time—bid you heed to your wrongs!"[43]

Song used two weapons, satire and pathos, to raise an army of patriots. Béranger's songs ridiculed not just specific individuals but also the social categories that embodied the reaction—in other words, the kings, priests, and emigrants. However, as "La Petite Fée" demonstrates, his songs also conveyed nostalgia for a better time, for the golden age of the past and even of the future. This song evokes the fairy Urgande and her magical kingdom, where all is well: the country is prosperous, the laws respected, the government honest, the justice fair, the people united and devoted to their leader, the enemies repelled. All this describes Restoration by irony and antiphrasis.

Rhetorical Devices

Béranger made wonderful use of rhetoric, which was essential in this era but quite alien in the world of songwriting. The devices he drew on most frequently were metaphor, antiphrasis, and irony. Often, he would use the metaphor to confer a sense of intimacy on political affairs, as in "Traité de Politique à l'Usage de Lise" and "Plus de Politique." By communicating everything he celebrated and everything that now wearied Lise,[44] the chansonnier was setting out what he lamented in the ruined empire, namely a politics that would (according to the lyrics of his songs) "sling the abuses" and promote "works of Art," "Glory's offspring," "France, grown great," "soldier's pride,"[45] France, and freedom.

Antiphrasis is the ultimate principle underlying "La Cocarde Blanche," which is aimed at the royalists: "Let's sing that day, our fair ones' pride, / When monarchs, not a few, / Scourged—by success—the rebel French; / Saved all the good and true."[46] The device allowed Béranger to suggest betrayal: "The Aliens and their cohorts came, / Invoked by us; with ease / They forced an entry through our gates— / When we gave up the keys."[47] He recalls the royalists' Anglomania and lack of patriotism. He contrasts the glory of Henri IV with the disgrace of the kings restored solely through the enemy's military might: "Lastly—the flower of Henry's race, / For such rare pity shown— / Let's pledge the King who could, himself, / Take Paris—and his throne!"[48]

Béranger's use of satire was often ironic. We can see this clearly in "Requête pour les Chiens de Qualité," where the eponymous dogs ask: "Now we are sure that the tyrant's laid low, / Hinder us not; we would frolicking go."[49] This song describes everything that the "usurper" had forbidden but which had become possible again since the Restoration. Irony is also used to good effect in "Les Boxeurs ou l'Anglomane" and is employed with ferocity against the signatories of the Vienna treaties in "La Sainte Alliance Barbaresque." These kings "swear to act as one / Bravely always twenty against one."[50] "[They] Want us to read the Alcoran, / And the Bonald and the Ferrand. / But Voltaire and his coterie / Are on the *Index* in Barbary."[51] The monarchy was to introduce slavery throughout its empire and to renounce glory and its memory; as we can see, others were making sure it was not forgotten.

Selection of Timbres and their Associated Webs of Meaning

Béranger made very subtle use of the tunes to which he chose to set his songs. He selected them based on the following criteria: genre, meaning, and associated references. His main technique consisted in using "timbres," a French word which in this context refers to a known tune on which one sings (generally designated by the first lines of the original song). The timbre thus served as a subtext to the song, orienting the reading by indicating an intertextual connection, and more particularly a thematic continuity between the original song and the next. Béranger used this process but did not invent it. Béranger, who was not the first to use this process, always chose "timbres" in such a way that the meaning of the initial song would remain in the mind of the listener of his own song, while being inflected by the new lyrics.

Selection of Tune

Songs about the emigrants and the English were set to tunes with popular or even slangy titles. For example, "Requête pour les Chiens de Qualité" was set to the tune of "Faut d'la Vertu, Point Trop n'en Faut," and "Les Boxeurs" was set to "A coups d'Pieds, à coups d'Poings." These tunes were used extensively during the Revolution, which reinforced the inclusion of Béranger's songs in this aural and semantic tradition. Sublime tunes were strictly reserved for songs about the patriots. For example, "Les Deux Grenadiers" was set to "Guide mes pas ô Providence," a tune taken from the opera Les Deux Journées ou Le Porteur d'Eau, composed by Cherubini with Bouilly's libretto. "Le Convoi de David" was set to "Air de Roland," a lyrical tune from one of Lully's first musical tragedies with alternating verse and chorus, which in the song embodies the stoic and patriotic people of France.

While Béranger sometimes used opera arias, he rarely opted for romances. Generally speaking, romance and song were closely related rivals at this time.[52] When Béranger did opt for a romance, it was a conscious decision on his part, designed to move people and to lament France's misfortunes. There were only two examples of this in our corpus: "Les Hirondelles," which was set to the romance from Méhul's *Joseph en Egypte*,[53] and "Le Champ d'Asile," set to the romance from *Bélisaire*. Béranger retained the historical and pathetic character (but not the mawkishness) of the romance and applied it to contemporary France to promote democratic and national values.

Reusing Meaningful Tunes

When setting songs to timbres, the custom was to choose a tune based on the particular feeling with which it would generally be associated because of its rhythm or melody. However, Béranger's songs evidence associations with more varied motifs, including corresponding rhythm and register, exposition, variation or inversion of the original tune's meaning, and a continuity introduced between several songs set to the same timbre.

Béranger selected the tune according to the register his songs reflected. For example, he would use catchy, rhythmic tunes to allude to the professional dance teachers in France at the time (e.g., "Air des Petits Pâtés" for "Le Ménétrier de Meudon"). The practice of dance and its learning in the bourgeois classes was common, but dance masters were a product of the Ancien Régime. Béranger preferred to target this kind of character, which has a contextual meaning, as well as the paid informer or the missionary.

For political songs, he generally chose lively tunes, such as rounds (e.g., "J'ons un Curé Patriote" for "Le Sénateur," and "Le Ventru" of 1818), duple-time contradances (e.g., Tourterelle's "Halte-là" for "La Muse en Fuite"), hunting tunes (e.g., "Air de Chasse du Jeune Henri" for "La Double Chasse"), and marches (e.g., "Air de la Sentinelle" for "L'Ombre d'Anacréon"). Songs that were more personal or lyrical in nature, however, were set to simple tunes in a minor key that were reminiscent of a bygone era.

This practice of using timbres implies, by definition, an intertextuality of sound. This was not a tactic that was specific to Béranger, however. Under the ancien régime, there were innumerable crossovers between the sacred and the profane. Sometimes, Béranger would choose a timbre as a kind of camouflage. For example, "Le Vieux Drapeau" was set to the tune of an old round called "Elle Aime à Rire, Elle Aime à Boire." Béranger generally used playful tunes to convey liberal ideas. He chose songs that expressed a conventional, shared morality that was applicable to all individuals to promote civic notions. However, the coupe and the scansions could give old tunes a new form. This was the case with "Le Vieux Drapeau"; while its text is generally plaintive, the catchy, cheerful tune gives it a swaggering tonality. Above all, as the German musicologist Herbert Schneider[54] has highlighted, the question mark at the end of its chorus ("Ah! when shall I shake off the dust / in which its noble colors rust?"[55]) that then disappears in a perfect cadence gives it an affirmative, warlike character.

Using a timbre conjured up the content of the original lyrics and the feelings and ideas associated with them. The new song, then, provided a kind of variation on this. The original meaning could simply be applied to the new song, as for example in "Vieux Habits, Vieux Galons." The same principle applied to the songs he set to the timbre "Te souviens-tu?," thus reviving a very famous melody composed by Émile Debraux, who had played a major role in the popular cult of the emperor. Presented as a dialogue between a captain and "a veteran begging for bread,"[56] it recalls the military successes of Napoleon's campaigns (in Italy, Egypt, and Russia), the occupation, and finally France's decline, and it calls on its listeners never to forget. Many songs were subsequently to follow this model, including two from Béranger, "Le Vieux Sergent" and "Le Tombeau de Manuel," both of which were a reflection on patriotic loyalty.

The device becomes even more apparent when Béranger's revisited the timbres he had used. For example, in 1817 his famous song "Dieu des Bonnes Gens" was set to a new tune, composed by

Doche.⁵⁷ This song was a kind of profession of faith. As is often the case with Béranger's work, the first few, relatively anodyne verses lead into a scathing attack on France's kings (3) and enemies, (4) followed by a mockery of the clergy (5) and a complete dismissal of their gloomy prophecies. Béranger would use the same tune again for "Le Coin de l'Amitié," and more importantly for "La Sainte Alliance des Peuples." This Holy Alliance, sharing the same vision presented in the song, namely that the time for fighting was over and that all the former enemy nations must now join forces, promised to be a great success. In other examples, Béranger's use of the timbre allowed him to both vary and enrich their initial meanings. For example, "La Faridondaine" was coupled up with the old satirical song "À la façon de Barbari."

> The English want, they say,
> To take back Grenada
> To the valiant Admiral Byron
> Who was apparently unwell.
> Everyone looked like a dragoon
> Boom boom boom
> He had courage too.
> Biribi.⁵⁸

While both songs are about fighting the enemy (the English in one case, the police in the other), they are nevertheless lighthearted. In Béranger's song, the subject matter has been transposed and updated. He attacks ad hominem the Paris prefect of police, Anglès, the enemy of the *goguettes*,⁵⁹ and presents a joyful satire of justice, which was aimed at the English because they had pursued the patriots.

Béranger's choice of timbre wove webs of significance around his songs, conveying the meaning not only of the lyrics associated with the original timbre but also possibly of the lyrics in subsequent uses of the tune. This was the case with "La Sainte Alliance Barbaresque," which was set to "Air de Calpigi." This tune was taken from Salieri's opera *Tarare* (1787), which was based on a libretto by Beaumarchais. The original lyrics tell of the misfortunes of Calpigi, who is a eunuch and prisoner of the barbarians. They are punctuated by the ritornello that alternates between "ahi, povero Calpigi!" and "ah, bravo, caro Calpigi," which is repeated in the chorus. This timbre was used for the lyrics of a 1792 song entitled "Le Nouveau Joujou Patriotique," which tells the story of the ancestor of the yoyo—in other words, the emigrant or *émigrette*—and plays on the double meaning of the word (i.e., a child's toy and the figure of the emigrant). Like Calpigi, the emigrant in question is impotent, his migration is pointless, and ultimately he is fooled and dominated by his opponent (here, the revolutionary Frenchman played by the bandit). This tune would have therefore conjured up two types of associations for Béranger's contemporary audience. One would have been barbarism and powerlessness; the other the emigrants, who had returned "from abroad in wagons" still enemies of the brave French people. It was therefore perfectly suited to the message that the chansonnier wanted to convey. Béranger was to use this tune again for the song, "Nebuchadnezzar" (1823), which tells the story of an ox who becomes king only to be betrayed by his unscrupulous ministers, and for "Les Orangs Outangs" (1839 collection), which is Béranger's reflection on human beings as the failed monkey imitators. We can see, then, that the choice of tune (whether the timbre was correctly cited or not) was far from arbitrary.

In summary, what are Béranger's songs all about? The postwar transition? Or resuming the war (against the tyrants)? The focus in reality was more on a successful outcome than on a transition. The war against the enemies continued through satire. Derision was a good way to bring them down—it was less bloody and more lasting. Béranger generally combined his sharpened arrows with calls for fraternal unity, as in "La Sainte Alliance des Peuples" and "Les Enfants de la France." By writing and circulating these songs, Béranger sought to teach the people of France about their history, not in a boring, chronological way but through the nation's lyrical epic, casting the recent past through a Revolutionary light. Unscrupulously accepting the testimony, the songs oversimplified and poetized events. Song brought history to life. It was moving. It was a purely oral form of teaching, based on images and short stories, where the characters were made to speak. It paved the way for a form of common memory, of commemoration,[60] that emerged from the real time of war and entered the imaginary time of epic and legend.

Sophie-Anne Leterrier is a professor of contemporary history at the Université d'Artois. She is a specialist in nineteenth-century cultural history, focusing in particular on the history of music from the perspective of practices and representations. She has most notably published *Le Mélomane et l'historien*; "Le Chant national au XIXe siècle, entre folklore et patrie," a contribution to the catalog *Europe en hymnes, des hymnes nationaux à l'hymne européen*; *Béranger—Des chansons pour un peuple citoyen*; "Les concerts au front," in *Entendre* *la guerre. Sons, musiques et silence en 14–18*; and "Choral Societies and Nationalist Mobilization in Nineteenth Century France," in *Choral Societies and Nationalism in Europe*.

Notes

1. This chapter was translated from French by Clare Ferguson.
2. "Recommande l'oubli aux tribunaux et aux citoyens."
3. Victor Hugo, *Les Misérables*, translated by Isabel F. Hapgood (New York: Thomas Y. Crowell & Co., 1887), Volume II, Book I, "Waterloo."
4. Hugo, *Les Misérables*, Volume I, Book III, Chapter 1, "The Year 1817."
5. Hugo, 123.
6. *Œuvres complètes de Béranger*, Paris, Fournier, 1840, 1833 Preface, p. XIV-XV.
7. "Nos amis nous ont fait capot. / C'est pour que l'étranger la mange / Que nous mettons la poule au pot." Translation taken from Young, *Béranger*, 131.
8. "Les malheurs de Nîmes." Young, 130.
9. "De jour en jour leur ligue avare / Augmenterait le prix des baux." Young, 130.
10. "À table un jour, jour de grande richesse, / De mes amis les voix brillaient en chœur, / Quand jusqu'ici monte un cri d'allégresse: / À Marengo Bonaparte est vainqueur! / Le canon gronde ; un autre chant commence; / Nous célébrons tant de faits éclatants. / Les rois jamais n'envahiront la France. / Dans un grenier qu'on est bien à vingt ans!" Young, 321.
11. "couplets censés faits pour un dîner où les royalistes célébraient l'anniversaire de la première entrée de Russes, des Autrichiens et des Prussiens à Paris." Young, 101.
12. "chanson chantée à Liancourt pour la fête donnée par M. le duc de la Rochefoucauld, en réjouissance de l'évacuation du territoire français." Young, 133.
13. Leterrier, "Béranger en prison."
14. "Soldat, ses yeux jusqu'au trépas / Se sont tournés vers la patrie. / Il en soutenait la splendeur / Du fond d'un exil qui l'honore; / C'est par lui que notre grandeur / Sur la toile respire encore."
15. "Un jour pareil voit tomber notre empire, / Voit l'étranger nous rapporter des fers, / Voit des Français lâchement leur sourire. / Son nom jamais n'attristera mes vers."
16. "Quand tu combattrais avec gloire, / Sache que plus d'un conquérant / Se voit arracher la Victoire / Par un général ignorant. / Un Anglais, aidé d'un Tartare, / Foule aux pieds de nobles drapeaux." Young, *Béranger*, 130.
17. "Trahi par la victoire, / Ce proscrit, dans nos bois, / Inquiet de sa gloire, / Fuit la haine des rois."
18. "Reine du monde, ô France! ô ma patrie! / Soulève enfin ton front cicatrisé. / Sans qu'à tes yeux leur gloire en soit flétrie, / De tes enfants l'étendard s'est brisé. (*bis.*)" Young, *Béranger*, 150.
19. "Pour s'anoblir nos chefs sortent des rangs; / Par la cartouche encor toute noircie / Leur bouche est prête à flatter les tyrans. / La Liberté déserte avec ses armes; / D'un trône à l'autre ils vont offrir leurs bras." Young, 234.
20. "Qui nous rendra, dit cet homme héroïque, / Aux bords du Rhin, à Jemappes, à Fleurus, / Ces paysans, fils de la république, / Sur la frontière à sa voix accourus? / Pieds nus, sans pain, sourds aux lâches alarmes, / Tous à la gloire allaient du même pas." Young, 234.

21. "[La gloire] épouvante encore les rois, / Et nous bannit des humbles chaumes / D'où, sortis pour venger nos droits, / Nous avons dompté vingt royaumes."
22. Hazareesingh, *The Legend of Napoleon*.
23. "Grand de génie et grand de caractère, / Pourquoi du sceptre arma-t-il son orgueil? / Bien au-dessus des trônes de la terre / Il apparaît brillant sur cet écueil. / Sa gloire est là, comme le phare immense / D'un nouveau monde et d'un monde trop vieux." Young, *Béranger*, 194–95.
24. The song evokes the meetings of an old peasant woman and Napoleon Bonaparte several times, but only at the time of the Empire (his wedding, the coronation and the last Campaign). However, it is always the man (straightforwardly in his relationships with the people) and not the monarch who is evoked.
25. "On parlera de sa gloire / Sous le chaume bien longtemps. / L'humble toit, dans cinquante ans, / Ne connaîtra plus d'autre histoire." Young, *Béranger*, 312.
26. "De noms affreux cette époque est flétrie; / Mais, jeune alors, je n'ai rien pu juger; / En épelant le doux mot de patrie / Je tressaillais d'horreur pour l'étranger. / Tout s'agitait, s'armait pour la défense; / Tout était fier, surtout la pauvreté. / Ah! rendez-moi les jours de mon enfance, / Déesse de la Liberté." Young, 267.
27. "Barbons," "myrmidons," and "nains," respectively.
28. "Le géant tombe, et ces nains sans mémoire / À l'esclavage ont voué l'univers. / Des deux côtés ce jour trompa la Gloire. / Son nom jamais n'attristera mes vers." Young, *Béranger*, 154.
29. "Volcan éteint sous les cendres qu'il lance, / Après vingt ans ce peuple se rendort; / Et l'étranger, apportant sa balance, / Lui dit deux fois: "Gaulois, pesons ton or." / . . . Rassurez-vous: char, autels, fleurs, jeunesse, / Gloire, vertu, grandeur, espoir, fierté, / Tout a péri; vous n'êtes plus déesse, / Déesse de la Liberté." Young, 267–68.
30. "Chantons le vin et la beauté: / Tout le reste est folie. / Voyez comme on oublie / Les hymnes de la liberté." Young, 179.
31. "Nargue le sot qui meurt pour la patrie! / Enivrons-nous!" Young, 238.
32. Aprile, *Le Siècle des exilés*.
33. "Aussi point d' fille qui ne crie: / Viv' nos amis, / Nos amis les enn'mis!"
34. "Quand y aurait queuqu's maisons d' brûlées, / Queuqu's gens d'occis, / C'est l' cadet d' nos soucis. / Mais j' rirai bien si j' sommes violées."
35. "Sur *Mirliton* fait un rapport: / La cour le trouve obscène. / Dénonce aussi *Malbrouck est mort*: / A sa *Grâce* il fait peine. / . . . Que le trône soit preservé / De faridondaine / Par le *God Save*."
36. "Ils doivent se battre un contre un; / Pour des Anglais c'est peu commun. / . . . Le sang jaillit . . . battez des mains. / Dieux! que les Anglais sont humains!" Young, *Béranger*, 83–84.
37. The note in question appears in most editions of Béranger's complete works, notably that of 1840 by Fournier and that of 1847 by Perrotin.
38. "Des critiques anglais, très bienveillants d'ailleurs pour notre auteur, lui ont reproché les traits plaisants ou graves dirigés contre leur nation. Ils auraient dû se rappeler que ces attaques remontent au temps de l'occupation de la France par les armées étrangères, qui avaient fait la Restauration. . . . L'idée d'entretenir la haine entre deux nations a toujours été loin du cœur de celui qui, à l'évacuation de notre territoire, fut le premier à appeler tous les peuples à une sainte alliance."
39. "Des peuples d'Europe, les Espagnols étaient ceux qui avaient les plus justes plaintes à former contre Napoléon. En plaçant son soldat sur un vaisseau de

cette nation, l'auteur eut la pensée de faire voir à quel point les malheurs du grand homme avaient réconcilié tous les peuples avec sa gloire." Young, *Béranger*, 193.

40. Béranger, *Œuvres complètes*, vol. 2, 13. "La chanson est essentiellement du parti de l'opposition."
41. *Lettres inédites de Béranger à Dupont de l'Eure*, 1820–1854. "La seule récompense à laquelle j'aspire, c'est de contribuer, dans ma petite sphère, à rendre plus éclatante, c'est-à-dire plus ridicule, la tyrannie qui pèse sur nous, et à populariser davantage encore les principes patriotiques et philosophiques dont j'ai imprégné mes ponts-neufs."
42. *Note sur le procès fait aux chansons de M. de Béranger*, 139. "La chanson, le plus léger de tous les poèmes, doit être le plus libre."
43. "Sa fille alors, interrompant sa plainte, / Tout en filant lui chante à demi-voix / Ces airs proscrits qui, les frappant de crainte. / Ont en sursaut réveillé tous les rois. / 'Peuple, à ton tour que ces chants te réveillent: / Il en est temps!' dit-il aussi tout bas." Young, *Béranger*, 234.
44. Lise is at once an imaginary woman whom Béranger addresses in the song; however, she is at the same time a representation of Napoléon. Lise, here, was Napoleon.
45. "Frondant les abus," "Des arts," "enfants de la gloire," "France agrandie," "rois vaincus," "fiers soldats." Young, *Béranger*, 96–97.
46. "Chantons ce jour cher à nos belles, / Où tant de rois, par leurs succès, / Ont puni les Français rebelles, / Et sauvé tous les bons Français." Young, 101.
47. "Les étrangers et leurs cohortes / Par nos vœux étaient appelés. / Qu'aisément ils ouvraient les portes / Dont nous avions livré les clés!" Young, 101–2.
48. "Enfin, pour sa clémence extrême, / Buvons au plus grand des Henri, / À ce roi qui sut par lui-même / Conquérir son trône et Paris." Young, 103.
49. "Puisque le tyran est à bas, / Laissez-nous prendre nos ébats." Young, 67.
50. "Jurent de se mettre en commun / Bravement toujours vingt contre un."
51. "[Ils] Veulent qu'on lise l'Alcoran, / Et le Bonald et le Ferrand. / Mais Voltaire et sa coterie / Sont à l'*index* en Barbarie."
52. The romance, music of the heart, of the feeling, is (re)considered in the 1830s as "salon music," then in the 1850s as "industrial music." In all its forms (successively mawkish song, bourgeois song, commercial song), it appears as the opposite of the "committed" song: in a way, "the opium of the people" in terms of song.
53. *Joseph en Egypte*, libretto by Alexandre Duval, music by Etienne Méhul, "drama mixed with songs" (*drame mêlé de chants*) in three acts, first performed on 17 February 1807, at the Opéra-Comique in Paris.
54. Schneider, "Les mélodies des chansons de Béranger," 121.
55. "Quand secouerai-je la poussière / qui ternit ses nobles couleurs?" Young, *Béranger*, 161.
56. "Un vétéran qui mendie son pain."
57. The tune was then published in a collection of Doche's tunes entitled *La Musette du Vaudeville*, which Béranger made great use of.
58. "Les Anglais ont voulu dit-on / Reprendre la Grenade / Au vaillant amiral Biron / Qui paraissait malade. / Chacun avait l'air d'un dragon / La faridondaine, la faridondon / Il avait du courage aussi / Biribi."
59. The goguette was a popular meeting place where people went to drink, sing, and have fun.
60. See Ozouf, "Célébrer, savoir et fêter," 327.

Bibliography

Aprile, Sylvie. *Le Siècle des exilés, bannis et proscrits de 1789 à la Commune*. Paris: CNRS Editions, 2010.

Béranger, *Œuvres complètes*. Paris: Perrotin, 1834.

Démier, Francis. *La France de la Restauration (1814–1830), l'impossible retour du passé*. Paris: Gallimard, Folio Histoire, 2012.

Hazareesingh, Sudhir. *The Legend of Napoleon*. London: Granta Books, 2004.

Leterrier, Sophie-Anne. "Béranger en prison: 'Mes fers sont prêts; la liberté m'inspire; Je vais chanter son hymne glorieux.'" *Criminocorpus, Musique et Justice, Les musiciens face à la justice*, 2013. http://journals.openedition.org/criminocorpus/2594

———. *Béranger, des chansons pour un peuple citoyen*. Rennes: PUR, 2013.

Locke, Ralph P. "The French Chanson." In *La Musique à Paris en 1830–1831*, edited by François Lesure. Paris: Bibliothèque nationale de France, 1983.

Ozouf, Mona. "Célébrer, savoir et fêter." In *1789, La Commémoration*, 318–54. Paris: Gallimard, 1999.

Schneider, Herbert. "Les mélodies des chansons de Béranger." In *La Chanson française et son histoire*, edited by Dietmar Rieger, 111–48. Tübingen: G. Narr (Études littéraires françaises, no. 39), 1988.

Young, William. *Béranger: Two Hundred of His Lyrical Poems, Done into English Verse*. New York: George P. Putnam, 1850.

Chapter 9

"WILL WE RETURN UNSCATHED?"
Paul Hindemith's *Minimax* and the Trauma of War

Lesley Hughes

At the 1923 Donaueschingen Chamber Music Festival, the members of the Amar String Quartet posed for a very unusual photograph. In it, they stand at attention, holding their bows as if presenting arms, and sport paper helmets.[1] The inspiration for the photo was the premiere of composer Paul Hindemith's string quartet *"Minimax": Repertorium für Militärorchester*, which parodies a military band concert.[2] The work's six movements replicate standard wind band repertoire, including two marches, an overture, a character piece, an intermezzo, and a waltz (table 1). Moreover, each movement is a parody of a specific piece, imitating the form and style of the original. The movement "Ouvertüre zu 'Wasserdichter und Vogelbauer'" (Overture to "Watertight and Birdcage"), for example, spoofs Franz von Suppé's famous overture *Bauer und Dichter* (*Poet and Peasant*, 1846), reproducing—in ridiculously truncated form—von Suppé's slow, lyrical introduction, rollicking allegro section in 2/4 time, and final presto push to the end. *Minimax* also lampoons the performance of this music by military bands; wrong notes appear in all the movements and the final march awkwardly stumbles into 3/4 and 5/4 time signatures. In the first movement, the cello even imitates a tuba with a stuck valve, consistently playing a D-flat pedal tone in a C-major movement.[3] The greatest source of the work's humor, however, comes from the musical situation itself: the absurdity of a string quartet playing military music. As musicologist Elmar Budde

---
Notes for this section begin on page 188.

Table 9.1. The movements in *Minimax*. Table created by the author.

Movement	Title	Parodied Work
1	Armeemarsch 606 ("Der Hohenfürstenberger") (Army March 606).	*Hohenfriedberger March*, attributed to Frederick the Great.
2	Ouvertüre zu "Wasserdichter und Vogelbauer" (Overture to "Watertight and Birdcage").	Franz von Suppé, Overture to *Dichter und Bauer* (*Poet and Peasant*, 1846).
3	"Ein Abend an der Donauquelle." Intermezzo für zwei entfernte Trompeten (An Evening at the Source of the Danube. Intermezzo for Two Distant Trumpets).	Contains quotations of works by Beethoven and Wagner.
4	"Lowenzähnchen an Baches Rand." Konzertwalzer (Dandelions at the Edge of the Stream. Concert Waltz).	Unidentified.
5	"Die beiden lustigen Mistfinken." Charakterstück, Solo für 2 Pikkolo-Flöten (The Two Merry Dirtbags. Character Piece, Solo for Two Piccolos).	Henri Louis Kling, *Die beiden kleinen Finken, Konzert-Polka* (The Two Little Finches, Concert Polka, ca. 1880).
6	"Alte Karbonaden." Marsch (Old Cutlets, March).	Karl Teike, *Alte Kameraden* (Old Comrades, 1889).

observes, "The serious musical performance of a string quartet . . . mercilessly exposes the emotional appearance and sentimental kitsch of military bands."[4]

At first glance, *Minimax* appears to be a playful jest, poking fun at the wind band concerts popular in the nineteenth and early twentieth centuries. Yet the work has serious origins, as Hindemith based it on his own experience playing in a military band during World War I.[5] Although the recent centennial of World War I has prompted several investigations into the links between music and the war,[6] *Minimax*, which most closely reflects Hindemith's experience of that conflict, remains relatively unknown or is generally dismissed as a novelty and an example of his unique sense of humor.[7] In this chapter, I reevaluate *Minimax* within the context of Hindemith's military service during World War I, examining the work along different points of what Carolyn Williams describes as the "spectrum" of parody, ranging from homage to sharp critique.[8] While the quartet's repertoire echoes the soundscape of Hindemith's service, the incongruity between the string quartet and military music recalls his mix of musical and martial duties. Moreover, Hindemith's profound disillusionment with the war effort, expressed in his wartime diary and letters, suggests that *Minimax* can also be understood as a satire of German militarism. This satire falls in line with the widespread use of sarcasm, irony, and parody in music after the war as a means to puncture the lofty ideals of prewar Romanticism.[9] Finally, *Minimax* may represent one way Hindemith worked through the aftereffects of his experience of the war, an experience that included bombing raids and trench warfare. The fact that he composed the quartet nearly half a decade after the end of the war indicates that the sounds—and even trauma—of his military service continued to permeate his postwar life.

Like many of his generation, Hindemith initially supported the outbreak of hostilities in 1914, claiming that "the German people are fighting for a just cause."[10] His enthusiasm soon dampened, however, with the losses of friends and family, including his father, in the first years of the war. After several deferments, Hindemith himself was called up for military service on 13 August 1917 and began training with an infantry regiment in Frankfurt, receiving the rank of musketeer. Hoping to avoid the front lines, he applied for a transfer to a military band, believing that life there would be "decidedly more pleasant than in the trenches."[11] His application was approved, and in January 1918 he became the bass drum player for the regimental band of the 222nd Infantry, stationed in the Alsatian town of Tagolsheim. In the first few months of his service, Hindemith's prediction of a "more pleasant life" seemed to come true; despite being three kilometers from the front lines, the worst enemies he encountered were lice and boredom.[12] His days were filled with band rehearsals, performances for soldiers in military hospitals and recreation centers, and open-air concerts in towns around the region. Evenings were often spent carousing with band members or earning extra money by performing for officers. He even had time to compose and practice the violin. Best of all, he was able to perform in a string quartet with his fellow soldiers for the entertainment of his commanding officer, Count von Kielmansegg. As Hindemith reported to a friend, "I'm glad that I came to this regiment; I have a terrific existence here. . . . The service is not very strict; I have lots of free time and can work for myself on what I want. It's not that life-threatening here either."[13]

These feelings faded, however, when his regiment left the relative safety of Tagolsheim in April 1918 and traveled through France to Flanders. Hindemith now witnessed the horrors of modern warfare, recording in his diary on 27 May:

> Around evening 8 bombs were thrown in the vicinity. One hit a munitions convoy camped 10 minutes from us. We had a look at the damage: the 4 dead horses, the slain man. And 8 more wounded. A horrible sight. Blood, perforated bodies, brains, a torn-off horse's head, shattered bones. Terrible![14]

Hindemith himself had several brushes with death while in Flanders, as the regimental band increasingly came under enemy fire during rehearsals and performances and was finally ordered to man the trenches in the last months of the war—the very thing he had hoped to avoid.[15]

During these last months, Hindemith increasingly lost faith with the war effort, questioning notions of patriotism and expressing his "enormous disgust at it all, at comrades, the soldier's life, the entire present."[16] He began to lash out at the politicians whom he now described as "eager warmongers," writing to a friend:

> You have no idea how sick I am of this entire life. How long must this miserable existence go on? Will this stupid breed of idiots not stop this devilish war soon? . . . The damned people who keep this war going should be sent here for a few weeks of summer vacation; they would soon learn then.[17]

Hindemith also privately expressed a growing sense of melancholy, fearing that he would not live to witness the end of the war. One particularly poignant diary entry from 4 November reads:

> Why has the armistice still not come? [Why] does this goddamned war never end? Why do we have to hang around here in these cellars? Why are we the fools? Why can't one be at home now, enjoying the beautiful fall? Why can't one be at home working diligently? Why and for whom or what does one wait here patiently for a grenade? Why? Why? Why? If only we would march to Germany tonight!!![18]

The armistice finally came one week later on 11 November, and on 5 December his final diary entry would contain just one word: "Dismissed!" (*Entlassen*).[19]

Although Hindemith composed *Minimax* several years after his discharge, the work's evocation of bad musicianship and banal repertoire clearly stemmed from his firsthand experience with—and dim view of—the regimental band. Derogatory comments about the band littered the pages of his wartime diary, as he complained about "boring" (*langweilig*) rehearsals, "soul-destroying" (*geisttötend*) repertoire, the band's "horrible clangor" (*schauderhaft Getön*), and having to "blow march after march."[20] Yet the work's primary source of humor—a string quartet playing "lowbrow" wind music—also captures what Sylvie Gregg and Giselher Schubert have described as the "hard, unmediated simultaneity of absolutely contradictory elements" that characterized Hindemith's service.[21] The clash of musical tropes echoes his wildly disparate musical activities, as he juggled intimate performances of string quartets with open-air band concerts, often in a single day. Hindemith himself referred to the incongruity of these musical tasks, noting in one letter, "Officially I am a drummer in the regimental band, but my main task is playing quartets," and in another, "Here, we play only quartets and band music. I find the first kind very refreshing."[22] Furthermore, the absurdity of classical musicians playing the "wrong" kind of music in *Minimax* encapsulates Hindemith's frequent observations on the absurdity of a musician playing the part of a soldier.[23] As he wrote to one friend:

> I can hardly imagine most musicians as soldiers. Bach as a staff-sergeant (presenting a pair of too-large boots to a Musko), that would still work, but: Beethoven practicing rifle drill, Mozart throwing hand-grenades or standing guard in front of a barracks; Schubert as an air force lieutenant and Mendelssohn as a non-commissioned officer at a vehicle fleet convoy. That is inconceivable.[24]

In another letter, he sarcastically notes that he had been promoted to corporal "not because of my bravery or my other military virtues, but just because the last time we played quartets for our colonel, he amused himself by 'giving me a stripe.' If the war goes on long enough, maybe I'll end up a captain!"[25]

The quartet's absurdity also resonates with Hindemith's frequent observations on the senselessness of the war, especially in the final months of his service. His diary and letters described a world turned upside down: officers fighting, smashing bottles, and demolishing furniture in a drunken fit; himself and his fellow musicians crazily dancing and making music "as in a madhouse" (*wie in einem Narrenhaus*); or English prisoners of war festively attired like "Prince Karneval" at the funeral of one of their comrades.[26]

Scenes of bombed villages, decimated landscapes, and near-death experiences alternated with mundane entries about food, sleeping, or playing cards; as Hindemith noted after witnessing the gruesome aftermath of a bombing,

> How rough and indifferent one becomes. I don't think that earlier I could have calmly eaten or worked after such a sight—and now one sits again quietly at home, writes, chats, and eats good things—and doesn't think about how soon our own number could be up. It is becoming surreal here, bit by bit. Will we return unscathed???[27]

Hindemith's observation that "the most theatrical theater doesn't create such theatrical impressions as natural as reality" probably best captured the surrealism of his experience.[28]

These musings, coupled with Hindemith's disillusionment and anger, suggest that *Minimax* can be read as a satiric critique of German militarism. In his work on musical semiotics, scholar Raymond Monelle lists the values conveyed by military band music, such as heroism, patriotism, and masculinity.[29] Because of these extramusical meanings, satirizing military music ultimately satirizes the values associated with it. As musicologist Esti Sheinberg observes,

> A march is a musical topic that correlates with the military. If some elements of this topic are presented in a way that is incongruous with its stylistic norms, e.g. by their exaggeration, then not only the musical topic of the march will be satirized, but the whole ethics correlated with the military . . . will be highlighted in a derogatory light.[30]

In this way, Hindemith's off-key, off-kilter depictions of popular German marches, along with his caricature of bad playing and clichéd repertoire, subvert cherished ideals of German military—and musical—prowess.

Because Hindemith never disclosed the meaning or motivations behind *Minimax*, this interpretation of the quartet as a critique of German militarism remains conjecture. At least one audience member at the premiere, however, understood the work precisely this way. In her essay "Donaueschingen im Sommer 1923," Annette Kolb read an antimilitarist message not only in the music itself but in how the work was performed. As she recalled:

> On the last evening, when all the concerts were finally behind us, there was still the prospect of a few works by Paul Hindemith in store for us at the resort. We sat with wine or tea and cake, when the Amar Quartet approached with the humble request we might not serve [refreshments] for a while, as they intended to offer something else. . . . And

now, first of all, a military march rang out, a little military march I say, an adorable little march whose curly ritornellos, whose little curly tail of a ritornello was the funniest, wittiest, cockiest, and at the same time, juiciest derision of military arrogance and stupidity ever experienced. The composer got into it, [gesturing] with his round, merry head, and whenever the ritornellos arose from his bow, irresistible laughter went through the hall. Oh! If only we had listened to such Pied Pipers of Hamelin earlier![31]

Whether a lighthearted joke, a satire of militarism, or both, *Minimax*'s irreverence echoes several other works by Hindemith from the early 1920s that subverted established musical conventions. His comic opera *Das Nusch-Nuschi* (1920), for example, satirized Wagner's *Tristan und Isolde*, while his scandalous inclusion of a foxtrot in the finale of Kammermusik no. 1 (1922) undermined the aesthetics of chamber music.[32] This subversion, in turn, reflects the use of irony or parody by many musicians after the war in order to deflate the subjectivity, sincerity, and intense emotions associated with (German) Romanticism and Expressionism.[33] Indeed, Joel Haney has interpreted Hindemith's "hard turn from lofty sincerity toward irony" after the war as a way to distance himself from a now-tainted German cultural legacy.[34] As American composer George Antheil observed, the war had caused him "to house-clean out of me all the remaining old poesy, false sentimentalism, and over juicy over idyllicism. I now found, for instance, that I could no longer bear the mountainous sentiment of Richard Strauss or even what now seemed to be the fluid diaphanous lechery of the recent French impressionists."[35] Examples of this "debunking spirit" include Stravinsky's and Manuel de Falla's spoofing of Beethoven's iconic Fifth Symphony or the subversion of operatic conventions in works such as Prokofiev's *The Love for Three Oranges* (1919) and Weill's *Die Dreigroschenoper* (1928).[36]

An extreme manifestation of this cynicism was the Dada anti-art movement, an artistic and literary formation that emerged in Zurich in 1916 in reaction to the war. Dadaists used provocation, ridicule, and outlandish performances in their rejection of traditional values and aesthetics, nationalism, and militarism. Although Hindemith never self-identified as a Dadaist, several scholars have compared his lampooning of Romanticism in postwar works like *Das Nusch-Nuschi* to the Dadaists' use of satire and absurdity in their assault on prewar artistic conventions.[37] Moreover, Hindemith's subversion of military marches in *Minimax* resonates with the antimilitarist stance of the movement in Berlin, where artists such as George Grosz, John

Heartfield, and Otto Dix used caricatures of pompous officers and grotesque depictions of mutilated veterans in order to expose what art historian Matthew Biro calls "the patriotic myths that helped support the interdependent systems of capitalism, nationalism, and militarism in Germany in the 1910s and 1920s."[38]

Reexamining *Minimax* in connection with Hindemith's wartime experience reveals it to be a multilayered work, simultaneously serving as a flippant homage to his short career as a bass drummer, an echo of the soundscape of his service, a reflection of the absurdities of war, and a sharp critique of German militarism. This multivalence illustrates what literary scholars such as Linda Hutcheon and Carolyn Williams have identified as parody's ability to encompass a broad range of simultaneous and even conflicting motives.[39] As Williams observes:

> We should think of parody involving a spectrum of attitudes on the part of its creators and its audiences. At one extreme of the spectrum lies critique, but at the other lies a kind of homage. In any particular instance, these attitudes can be mixed, and thus parody can make fun of its object, humorously indicating that it is old-fashioned or long past, while affectionately, ruefully—or with any other attitude—preserving its memory.[40]

Conclusion

In preserving the memory of Hindemith's military service, the "spectrum of attitudes" apparent in *Minimax* captures not only the varied aspects of that service but arguably the complex mixture of emotions with which he regarded it. Despite his anger toward the war effort and later declaration that he "took precious little pride in wearing the Kaiser's nettlecloth tunic," he also appeared to retain some fond memories of the comradeship, hijinks, and even the music from his experience.[41] Conductor Rudolf Hartmann, for instance, recalled "an amusing evening with Paul Hindemith, with whom I sang . . . all the marches that we knew, to the great amusement of the two women who were there. We discovered a shared fondness for the 'Mussinan' march."[42] Carolyn Williams's statement is also a reminder that parody depends not only on the author's intentions but also on the audience's interpretation of those intentions. And indeed, the audience's reactions to *Minimax* in 1923 were mixed, ranging from Annette Kolb's antimilitarist reading, to Austrian critic Paul Stefan's approval of the "charming musical jokes" (*reizenden musikalischen Scherzen*), to English critic Edwin Evans's description of the work as simply "an amusing jest."[43] A statement by the conductor Hans Curjel illustrates the ambiguity of the quartet's parody, as he recalled how "the Amar Quartet presented itself as the military band 'Minimax,' armed with paper helmets and sticks. Was it an ironic treatment of militarism or childlike soldier-play? It is hard to decide."[44]

By the time of the 1923 Donaueschingen festival, Hindemith appeared to have put his military service firmly behind him. He had resumed his prewar position as concert master of the Frankfurt Opera orchestra and gradually established himself as one of Germany's leading young musicians, performing with the Amar Quartet and composing numerous works in a variety of genres.[45] Yet nearly five years after his discharge, the creation of *Minimax* indicates that the memories of his military service still lingered. Moreover, in the decades following the war, he returned to marches again and again in his compositions, to the extent that scholars have spoken of his "predilection" (*Vorliebe*) for the genre.[46] As with *Minimax*, he would frequently twist and distort those marches, creating a stumbling and even grotesque effect.[47] The final movement of Kammermusik no. 5 (1927), for example, a set of variations on the popular *Bayrischer Avanciermarsh*, featured wrong notes, wrong entrances, and a breakneck tempo, causing one critic to decry how Hindemith had "atonally distorted" (*atonal verzerrt*) a "cultural asset of the people" (*Kulturgüt des Volkes*).[48] The continued negative depiction of military music suggests that works like *Minimax* may represent one way in which Hindemith bore witness to—or even processed—the trauma of his experience. He had suffered the violence of mechanized warfare and what Joel Haney describes as the "shocking disjunction between prewar confidence and the devastation that followed," which "traumatically undermined a sense of connection with once-cherished ideals."[49] *Minimax*'s absurdity implicates the military band as a source of that trauma, as its music mobilized soldiers and civilians for war by evoking the myths of patriotism, heroism, and German cultural greatness. Ultimately, while Hindemith did manage to avoid any physical injury in the war, the satirical military tropes that echo in his postwar compositions indicate that he did not escape unscathed.

Lesley Hughes is assistant professor of musicology at Sam Houston State University. Her research explores the forces of politics, economics, and technology on the production of art music in interwar Germany. Her forthcoming book examines the commercial motivations behind Paul Hindemith's compositions of the 1920s and 1930s. Other research interests include music and the Great War, the use of modern music journals as propaganda for publishing firms, and the expansion of music criticism in the early twentieth century.

Notes

1. This photograph appears in Häusler, *Spiegel der neuen Musik*, 49.
2. The title "*Minimax*" refers to the German brand of fire extinguishers of the same name. It was also the nickname for the Donaueschingen festival's patrons, Maximilian von Fürstenberg ("Maxi") and his wife, Wilhelmine ("Minzi"). See Jacobi, "Zu Hindemiths *Minimax*-Komposition," 96.
3. For discussions of the parodied musical sources and how Hindemith created the humorous effects, see Jacobi, "Zu Hindemiths *Minimax*-Komposition," 93–114; Gruhn, "Wie heiter ist die Kunst?," 682–84; and Budde, "Humor, Witz und Parodie," 91.
4. Budde, "Humor, Witz und Parodie."
5. Haney, "The Emergence of a Postwar Musical Outlook," 301.
6. See Magee, "Music and the Great War"; Giesebrecht, *Musik und Propaganda*; and Gétreau, *Entendre la Guerre*.
7. See Jacobi, "Zu Hindemiths *Minimax*-Komposition," 102; and Ross, *The Rest Is Noise*, 182. Exceptions to this are Christian Münch, who attributes *Minimax* to "Hindemith's ambivalent experiences in the First World War" and Michael Saffle's characterization of *Minimax* as a "musical protest." See Münch, "Anklänge des Grotesken im Werk von Paul Hindemith," 7; and Saffle, "Military Music for America's Peacetime," 4–15.
8. I use Yayoi Uno Everett's definition of parody in musical discourse, which she describes as "a composer's appropriation of pre-existing music with intent to highlight it in a significant way." Everett, "Parody with an Ironic Edge," 5.
9. Joseph Auner notes that after the war, "the new fashion was for irony, sarcasm, parody, or simply no emotion at all." Auner, *Music in the Twentieth and Twenty-First Centuries*, 88.
10. Hindemith, *Briefe*, 35.
11. *Briefe*, 189.
12. Hindemith, "Notizen," 60.
13. Hindemith to Emmy Ronnefeldt, "Ich bin froh, dass ich in dieses Regiment gekommen bin, hier habe ich ein ausgezeichnetes Dasein. . . . Der Dienst ist nicht arg streng, ich habe viel freie Zeit u. kann für mich arbeiten, was ich will. So arg lebensgefährlich ists hier auch nicht." Hindemith, *Briefe*, 72.
14. Hindemith, "Gegen Abend werden 8 Bomben in die Nähe des Ortes geworfen. Eine trifft eine Munitionskolonne, die (10 Minuten von uns entfernt) biwakiert. Wir besehen uns den Schaden, die 4 toten Pferde, den erschlagenen Mann. Und noch 8 Verwundete. Ein entsetzlicher Anblick. Blut, durchlöcherte Körper, Hirn, ein abgerissener Pferdekopf, zersplitterte Knochen. Furchtbar!" Diary, 27 May 1918, in "Notizen," 103.
15. "Notizen," 130.
16. "Notizen," 91. "einem riesigen Ekel an allem, den Kameraden, dem Soldatenleben, der ganzen Gegenwart." See Joel Haney's discussion of Hindemith's disillusionment in "Emergence of a Postwar Musical Outlook," 133–37.

17. Hindemith. "Du glaubst garnicht, wie überdrüssig ich dieses ganze Leben bin. Wie lange muss dieses elende Dasein noch dauern? Hört denn diese blödsinnige Idiotenmenschheit nicht bald mit dem Teufelskrieg auf? . . . Die verfluchten Kriegsverlängerer sollte man doch einmal für einige Wochen nach hier in die Sommerfrische schicken, wie bald wäre denen geholfen." Hindemith to Emmy Ronnefeldt, 28 September 1918, in "Jugendbriefe," 204.
18. Hindemith, "Warum kommt der Waffenstillstand noch immer nicht? Warum nimmt dieser gottverfluchte Krieg kein Ende? Warum müssen wir uns hier in Kellern herumdrücken? Warum sind gerade wir die Dummen? Warum kann man jetzt nicht daheim sein und den schönen Herbst genießen? Warum kann man nicht daheim sein und fleißig arbeiten? Warum und für wen oder was wartet man hier geduldig auf einen Granatbrocken? Warum? Warum? Warum? Wenn wir doch noch heute Nacht nach Deutschland marschieren würden!!!" Diary, 4 November 1918, "Notizen," 148.
19. "Notizen," 158.
20. "Notizen," 74, 106, 127.
21. Gregg and Schubert, foreword to Hindemith, "Notizen," 55.
22. Hindemith to Carl Schmidt, 19 January 1918, in *Briefe*, 17; to Emmy Ronnefeldt, 6 February 1918, in *Briefe*, 72. "Ich bin ziemlich heraus, da wir hier nur Quartett und Blasmusik spielen. Ersteres erfrischt mich sehr."
23. The figure of Count von Kielmansegg embodied this simultaneity off or collapse of boundaries between the musical and martial as well. As the commanding officer, he frequently ordered Hindemith's quartet to play for him and his private parties. Yet this position also resembled the traditional role of musical patron, the sort that financially supported Hindemith before and after the war. The count's aristocratic background only reinforced this simultaneity, as both military officers and musical patrons traditionally came from this class.
24. Hindemith, May 1918, "Einberufung 1917," "Überhaupt kann ich mir die wenigsten Musiker als Soldaten vorstellen. Bach als Kammerfeldwebel, (einem Musko ein Paar zu große Stiefel überreichend), das ginge noch an, aber—: Beethoven, Gewehrgriffe übend, Mozart, Handgranaten werfend oder vor einer Kaserne Posten stehend; Schubert als Fliegerleutnant und Mendelssohn als Unteroffizier bei einer Fuhrparkkolonne. Das ist doch undenkbar."
25. Hindemith to Frau Ronnefeldt, 20 August 1918. "Ich bin Gefreiter geworden. Nicht wegen meiner Tapferkeit oder wegen meiner militärischen Tugenden überhaupt, sondern nur weil sich unser Oberst, als wir das letzte Mal bei ihm Quartett spielten, den Spaß machte, mich 'eins hinaus' zu setzten. Wenn der Krieg noch lange dauert, werde ich vielleicht noch als Hauptmann abgehen!" in "Jugendbriefe," 203.
26. Hindemith, "Notizen," Diary entries of 13 February 1918, 6 August 1918, 25 May 1918, 70, 103, and 123.
27. "Notizen." "Wie gemein und gleichgültig man wird. Ich glaube nicht, dass ich früher hätte ruhig essen oder arbeiten können nach solchem Anblick—und nun sitzt man schon wieder ruhig daheim, schreibt, unterhält sich und isst guter Dinge—und denkt nicht daran, wie bald auch unser Stündlein schlagen kann.— Es wird allmählich unheimlich hier. Ob wir unbeschädigt abrücken werden ???," 103–4.
28. "Notizen." "Das theatrischste Theater bringt nicht so theatrige Wirkungen so natürlich hervor wie die Wirklichkeit," diary entry of 25 May 1918, 103.
29. Monelle, *The Musical Topic*, 122.
30. Sheinberg, *Irony, Satire, Parody and the Grotesque in the Music of Shostakovich*, 25.

31. Kolb, "Donaueschingen im Sommer 1923," 122. "Am letzten Abend, als alle Konzerte glücklich hinter uns lagen, standen im Kurhaus noch einige Gelegenheits-Kompositionen Paul Hindemiths in Aussicht. Man saß bei Wein oder Tee und Kuchen, als das Amarquartett mit der bescheidenen Bitte aufzog, man möge eine Weile nicht servieren; sie gedächten noch einiges zum besten zu geben ... Und nun ertönte als erstes ein Militärmarsch, ein Militärmärschlein, sage ich, ein goldiges Militärmarschli, dessen geringelte Ritornelle, dessen Ringelschwänzchen von einer Ritornelle die ulkigste, witzigste, übermütigste und zugleich saftigste Verhöhnung war, welche militaristischer Dünkel und Stupidität jemals erfuhren. Der Komponist spielte in sich hinein, machte seinen runden, lustigen Kopf, und sooft die Ritornelle seinem Bogen entquirlte, ging unwiderstehliches Gelächter durch den ganzen Saal. Oh! Hätte man solchen Rattensängern von Hameln eher gelauscht!"
32. Haney, "Slaying the Wagnerian Monster," 356–64; Kemp, *Hindemith*, 10–11; and Hinton, *The Idea of Gebrauchsmusik*, 170. Martin Guerpin also interprets Hindemith's deformation of jazz in the piano work *Suite "1922"* as portraying "an ironic sound image of the crisis of German identity and civilization" after World War I. Guerpin, "Détournements savants du jazz en France et en Allemagne (1919–1922)," 76.
33. Other "deflation" techniques included the creation of unsentimental, emotionless, or "objective" music; the revival of baroque and classical forms and genres; and the use of popular music idioms. Auner, *Music in the Twentieth and Twenty-First Centuries*, 87–89; Taruskin, *Music in the Early Twentieth Century*, chapters 8–10.
34. Haney, "Slaying the Wagnerian Monster," 344.
35. Antheil, *Bad Boy of Music*, 29.
36. Stravinsky, *Souvenir d'une marche boche* (1916); De Falla, *El sombrero de tres picos* (1919). See Taruskin, *Music in the Early Twentieth Century*, 501–2, 532–37. While this "debunking" of Romantic ideals can already be seen in prewar works by Erik Satie such as the movement "De podophthalma" from *Embryons desséches*, no. 3 (1913) and his wartime ballet *Parade* (1917), Taruskin observes how it "spread widely after the war, when disgust at Germany translated into disgust at artistic pretentions to weight and significance, especially in music (the 'German' art par excellence, at least in its weightier manifestations.)" Taruskin, *Music in the Early Twentieth Century*, 506.
37. See Watkins, *Proof through the Night*, 404; Kemp, *Hindemith*, 11; and Hughes, "'A Special Sort of Mordent Humor,'" 50–54.
38. Biro, *The Dada Cyborg*, 181.
39. Hutcheon uses the concept of ethos as a framework for describing the functions or motivations of parody and satire, with satire in particular having a scornful or disdainful ethos. Hutcheon, *A Theory of Parody*, 43–44.
40. Williams, *Gilbert and Sullivan*, xiv.
41. Hindemith to Willy Strecker, 15 November 1932. "als ich mit herzlich wenig Stolz des Kaisers Brennnesselstoffrock getragen habe."
42. Trumpeter Carl Karl composed this march in honor of Ludwig von Mussinan (1826–1908), colonel and commander of the 4th Field Artillery Regiment in Augsburg. Hartmann, *Das geliebte Haus*, 9. "einen vergnügten Abend mit Paul Hindemith, mit dem zusammen ich im kleinen Nebenzimmer der Maximilianstuben alle uns bekannten Märsche sang (sehr zum Ergötzen der beiden anwesenden Frauen), wobei wir eine gemeinsame Vorliebe für den 'Mussinan'-Marsch entdeckten."
43. Stefan, "Donaueschingen: Musikfeste 1923," 240.

44. Curjel, "Hindemith vor Augen," 9: "Das Amar-Quartett präsentierte sich als Militärkapelle *Minimax* mit Papierhelmen und Stöcken bewaffnet. War es eine Ironisierung des Militarismus oder ein kindliches Soldatenspiel—es ist schwer zu entscheiden."
45. Skelton, *Hindemith*, 55–69.
46. Schubert, "Foreword," xxi.
47. Christian Münch notes that "the typical Hindemithian march has nothing in common with stalwart military music, but rather exaggerates and distorts the march, often parodistically." Münch, "Anklänge des Grotesken im Werk von Paul Hindemith," 37.
48. Welter, "Hindemith—Eine Kulturpolitische Betrachtung," 418. While Welter used this march as evidence to show how Hindemith could not be a representative of German music in the Third Reich, scholar Ian Kemp also describes the movement as "raucous and vulgar . . . a travesty of the march upon which they are based." Kemp, "Some Thoughts on Hindemith's Viola Concertos," 76.
49. Haney, "Slaying the Wagnerian Monster," 344.

Bibliography

Antheil, George. *Bad Boy of Music*. Garden City, NY: Doubleday, Doran & Company, 1945.

Auner, Joseph. *Music in the Twentieth and Twenty-First Centuries*. Western Music in Context: A Norton History. New York: W. W. Norton and Company, 2013.

Biro, Matthew. *The Dada Cyborg: Visions of the New Human in Weimar Berlin*. Minneapolis: University of Minnesota Press, 2009.

Budde, Elmar. "Humor, Witz und Parodie. Anmerkungen zu Mozart, Strauss und Hindemith." In *Das Lächeln der Euterpe. Musik ist Spaß auf Erden*, edited by Sabine Borris, 84–91. Berlin: Berliner Philharmonisches Orchester, 2000.

Curjel, Hans. "Hindemith vor Augen." *Hindemith-Jahrbuch* 3 (1973): 7–19.

Evans, Edwin. "Donaueschingen and Salzburg Festivals." *The Musical Times* 64, no. 967 (1 September 1923): 631–35.

Everett, Yayoi Uno. "Parody with an Ironic Edge: Dramatic Works by Kurt Weill, Peter Maxwell Davies, and Louis Andriessen." *Music Theory Online* 10, no. 4 (December 2004): 5. http://www.mtosmt.org/issues/mto.04.10.4/mto.04.10.4.y_everett_frames.html.

Gétreau, Florence, ed. *Entendre la Guerre. Sons, musiques et silence en 14–18*. Paris: Gallimard, 2014.

Giesebrecht, Sabine. *Musik und Propaganda: Der Erste Weltkrieg im Spiegel deutscher Bildpostkarten*. Osnabrück: Electronic Publishing Osnabrück, 2014.

Gruhn, Wilfried. "Wie heiter ist die Kunst? Semiologische Aspekte musikalischer Komik." *Österreichische Musikzeitschrift* 38 (December 1983): 677–88.

Guerpin, Martin. "Détournements savants du jazz en France et en Allemagne (1919–1922): *Adieu New-York!* de George Auric et le 'Ragtime' de la *Suite 1922* de Paul Hindemith." *Les Cahiers de la Société québécoise de recherche en musique* 14, no. 2 (Fall 2013): 69–77.

Haney, Joel. "The Emergence of a Postwar Musical Outlook: Hindemith's 'Hard-Edged Simplicity' 1919–1922." PhD diss., Yale University, 2006.

———. "Slaying the Wagnerian Monster: Hindemith, *Das Nusch-Nuschi*, and Musical Germanness after the Great War." *The Journal of Musicology* 25, no. 4 (Fall 2008): 339–93.

Hartmann, Rudolf. *Das geliebte Haus. Mein Leben mit der Oper.* München: Piper, 1975.

Häusler, Josef. *Spiegel der neuen Musik, Donaueschingen: Chronik, Tendenzen, Werkbesprechungen.* Kassel: Bärenreiter, 1996.

Hindemith, Paul. *Briefe.* Edited by Dieter Rexroth. Frankfurt: Fischer Taschenbuch Verlag, 1982.

———. "Jugendbriefe von Paul Hindemith aus den Jahren 1916–1919." *Hindemith-Jahrbuch* 2 (1972): 181–207.

———. "Notizen zu meinen 'Feldzugs-Erinnerungen.'" *Hindemith-Jahrbuch* 18 (1989): 55–159.

———. *Selected Letters of Paul Hindemith.* Edited and translated by Geoffrey Skelton. New Haven, CT: Yale University Press, 1995.

Hindemith-Institut. "Einberufung 1917." Accessed 11 July 2017. https://www.hindemith.info/de/leben-werk/biographie/1914-1918/

Hinton, Stephen. *The Idea of Gebrauchsmusik: A Study of Musical Aesthetics in the Weimar Republic (1919–1933) with Particular Reference to the Works of Paul Hindemith.* New York: Garland, 1989.

Hughes, Lesley. "'A Special Sort of Mordent Humor': The Role of the E-flat Clarinet in Hindemith's Quintet for Clarinet and Strings, Op. 30." DMA diss., University of Wisconsin–Madison, 2010.

Hutcheon, Linda. *A Theory of Parody: The Teachings of Twentieth-Century Art Forms.* New York: Methuen, 1985.

Jacobi, Erwin R. "Zu Hindemiths *Minimax*-Komposition (1923)." *Hindemith-Jahrbuch* 3 (1973): 93–114.

Kemp, Ian. *Hindemith.* London: Oxford University Press, 1970.

———. "Some Thoughts on Hindemith's Viola Concertos." *Hindemith-Jahrbuch* 35 (2006): 68–117.

Kolb, Annette. "Donaueschingen im Sommer 1923." In *Wera Njedin: Erzählungen und Skizzen*, 117–22. Berlin: Im Propyläen Verlag, 1925.

Magee, Gayle, ed. "Music and the Great War." *American Music* 34, no. 4, 2016.

Monelle, Raymond. *The Musical Topic: Hunt, Military, and Pastoral.* Bloomington: Indiana University Press, 2006.

Münch, Christian. "Anklänge des Grotesken im Werk von Paul Hindemith." *Hindemith-Jahrbuch* 38 (2009): 32–48.

Ross, Alex. *The Rest Is Noise: Listening to the Twentieth Century*. New York: Farrar, Straus, and Giroux, 2007.

Saffle, Michael. "Military Music for America's Peacetime: *Victory at Sea* and 1950s Post-War Television." *Journal of Musicological Research* 38, no. 1 (2019): 4–15.

Schaal-Gotthardt, Susanne. "Ausdruck ohne Emotion: Hindemiths Nachtstücke." *Hindemith-Jahrbuch* 30 (2001): 103–25.

Schubert, Giselher. "Foreword to *Konzertante Kammermusiken II* by Paul Hindemith." In *Paul Hindemith: Sämtliche Werke* 4, no. 2, edited by Giselher Schubert, ix–xxviii. Mainz: Schott Music, 2007.

Sheinberg, Esti. *Irony, Satire, Parody and the Grotesque in the Music of Shostakovich: A Theory of Musical Incongruities*. Burlington, VT: Ashgate, 2000.

Stefan, Paul. "Donaueschingen: Musikfeste 1923." *Musikblätter des Anbruch* 5 (1923): 240.

Taruskin, Richard. *Music in the Early Twentieth Century*. Vol. 4 of *The Oxford History of Western Music*. Oxford: Oxford University Press, 2010.

Watkins, Glenn. *Proof through the Night: Music and the Great War*. Berkeley: University of California Press, 2003.

Welter, Friedrich. "Hindemith—Eine Kulturpolitische Betrachtung." *Die Musik* 26, no. 6 (March 1934): 417–22.

Williams, Carolyn. *Gilbert and Sullivan: Gender, Genre, Parody*. New York: Columbia University Press, 2011.

Chapter 10

THE CONSTRUCTION OF A TRANSATLANTIC REPERTOIRE OF RESISTANCE AND MOURNING IN THE POSTWAR YEARS
Sources Collected by Shmerke Kaczerginski (Vilna, New York, Buenos Aires)

Jean-Sébastien Noël

Poet, publisher, and partisan Shmerke Kaczerginski (1908–54) was one of the leading collectors of songs written by resistance fighters and the Jewish victims of the genocide.[1] He participated in the cultural life of prewar "North Jerusalem" and, along with the famous Yiddish-speaking poet Avrom Sutzkever (1913–2010), was associated with the Yung Vilne (Vilna youth) movement. A member of the "Paper Brigade," Kaczerginski established himself as one of the key figures in the Vilna ghetto's cultural resistance. After escaping from the ghetto to the Lithuanian forests in September 1943, he continued his involvement with the partisan resistance. He contributed to the creation of a sung repertoire (he was unable to read or write music) both in liberated Vilna[2] and during a tour of displaced person camps with the Central Historical Commission (1945–48).[3] His most influential collection, *Lider Fun di Getos un Lagern*[4] (Songs from the ghettos and camps), which was published in New York by the Central Yiddish Cultural Organization (CYCO) in 1948, gave rise to a whole series of questions concerning how and where these traces should be safeguarded and documented.[5] Most of the sources in this

---

Notes for this section begin on page 204.

collection were accompanied by a critical apparatus providing information on the composers, performers, and production contexts. Particularly from the 1960s onwards, this collection substantially fed a repertoire for commemorating forms of Jewish resistance and the genocide, and was of considerable importance in Yiddish-speaking communities[6]. in the United States. It was by no means the only documentation available, however. Other efforts to collect and record survivor testimonies also contributed to preserving their voices— in other words, to preserving their own interpretation, as filtered through memory, of the songs they had heard or sung in captivity. For example, the recordings made by Ben Stonehill[7] in Manhattan in 1948 form an important collection of audio testimonies. In addition to Kaczerginski's tour de force, there was a raft of initiatives to link individual collections with institutional programs (such as those of the Central Jewish Historical Commission (CHC)and of archive centers such as the Yiddish Scientific Institute (YIVO) and Yad Vashem). These initiatives developed in a geography of refuge and exile (from displaced persons camps to new world metropolises of New York, Buenos Aires, Montreal, and Tel Aviv) and in a context of crisis that was marked by a resurgence of antisemitic violence (the Kielce pogrom in July 1946). The result was a set of collections and holdings that give an account of the life-and-death conditions in the ghettos and camps and contribute original dimensions to the memorial narratives produced by the survivors.

The Paper Brigade and the Mission to Salvage Vilna's Judaica

Kaczerginski came from a Yiddish background. He was educated at a Talmudic school for orphans (his parents died at the start of World War I), and he went on to work as a lithographer for a printing company. He became a well-known figure in the cultural life of Vilna in the 1930s and devoted his efforts to cultural and militant activities. A communist, he coordinated the Agroid organization (semi-legal and pro-Soviet) and worked as a local correspondent for the New York newspaper *Morgn Frayhayt* (Morning freedom), which was affiliated to the Communist Party. The historian Lucy Dawidowitz, who knew him in Vilna, wrote that "his main talent lay in organizing meetings, artistic exhibitions, excursions, parties."[8] She commended his ability to mobilize and lead the Yung Vilne group membership. Kaczerginski was a journalist, publisher, teacher, and poet in this city, where incidentally the YIVO was founded in 1925 by Max Weinreich and Elias

Tcherikower.[9] A committed intellectual, he was nevertheless critical of the censorship imposed by the Soviet occupation in September 1939 and, as a result, left Vilna to teach at Białystok. He returned to his hometown in 1940. On 26 June 1941, first the Wehrmacht and then Einsatzgruppen entered and occupied Vilna. The massacres began immediately (notably in the Ponar [or Ponary] Forest) and were followed soon after by ghettoization.

With the consent of the Judenrat and its president Jacob Gens, there was a reorganization of the cultural life in the ghetto in January 1942[10] with the opening of its first theater on Konska Street and then a second on Rudnicka Street.[11] However, the Nazi Reichsleiter Alfred Rosenberg's task force (called the Einsatzstab Reichsleiter Rosenberg), led by Johannes Pohl, set about destroying the city's Jewish cultural heritage and moving some of the collections from the main cultural institutions (including the Strashun and YIVO Libraries) to the Institut zur Erforschung der Judenfrage (Institute for Research on the Jewish Question) in Frankfurt.[12] Avrom Sutzkever (poet), Zelig Kalmanovitch (philologist and YIVO codirector), Herman Kruk (librarian), and Kaczerginski, together with other prominent figures in the city's cultural life, joined this forced labor unit. Made up of about forty members, it soon became known as the Paper Brigade. The group established a cultural resistance movement aimed at rescuing books, artifacts, and handwritten documents from the looting and destruction process by hiding them in the ghetto. With the liquidation of the ghetto on 23 September 1943, the Paper Brigade's activities ceased. Its members were either sent to a concentration camp or were murdered. However, Sutzkever and Kaczerginski, both members of the Fareynikte Partizaner Organizatsye (the united partisan organization led by Itzik Vitnberg and then, following his death on 16 July 1943, by Abba Kovner), managed to escape.[13] Reaching the forests around Lake Narach (to the northeast of Vilna), they joined a group of Soviet partisans.

Collection Method, Controversies, and Source Uncertainties

When Vilna was liberated by the Red Army in July 1944, Sutzkever and Kaczerginski dug up most of the Judaica they had managed to save. Among these "buried monuments,"[14] to use historian Shirli Gilbert's expression, the songs and poems collected represented a first-rate testimony that a cultural life had been maintained there. The

Soviet authorities in Lithuania had no intention, however, of supporting a museum dedicated to Jewish cultures in liberated Vilna.[15] Kaczerginski's disappointment with the USSR's attitude reveals the complexity of the relationships between the Jewish partisans (the defenders of Yiddish culture and language) and the Communist Party of the Soviet Union (CPSU).[16] After a brief stay in Moscow, Kaczerginski moved to Poland and settled in Lodz, where he worked for the Po'ale Tsiyon (Poale Zion)[17] press organization and became involved with the Central Jewish Historical Commission. In a context of increasing antisemitic violence (analyzed notably by Jan Gross and Audrey Kichelewski[18]), which culminated in the Kielce pogrom on 4 July 1946, Kaczerginski decided to emigrate to Paris, taking with him the documentation he had collected. In 1947 Kaczerginski contributed to the publication of two collections of Jewish songs from the ghettos, including the Vilna collection and partisan songs. The first, "Undzer Gezang" (Our singing), was produced by the composer Leon Wajner (1898–1979) and published in Warsaw through Kaczerginski's contacts in the Department of Culture and Propaganda at the Central Committee of Polish Jews. The second, "Dos Gezang fun Vilner Geto" (Singing from the Vilna ghetto), was published by Kaczerginski himself, this time in Paris, through the Association des Vilniens de France.[19] Because he was not able to read or write music, Kaczerginski called on the composers and arrangers Leon Wajner and David Botwinik (born 1920) to prepare the scores. Some of Kaczerginski's poems were set to music. (Wajner wrote the score for "Varshe" [Warsaw], and Botwinik wrote the score for the Zionist song "Khalutsim" [the pioneers].[20])

In November 1947 Kaczerginski embarked on a three-week tour, giving talks in seventeen displaced persons camps in Germany's US-occupied zone.[21] He collected new materials and recorded about sixty unaccompanied sung testimonies in Yiddish on a phonograph (personally recording nine of them). This sometimes-incomplete documentation (the singer's identity is not always known) was presented to the Jewish Historical Commission in Munich and deposited in its archives, which are now housed in the Yad Vashem in Jerusalem. Created in August 1944 under the aegis of the Central Committee of Jews, the Jewish Historical Commission and then, from December 1944 onward, the Central Jewish Historical Commission, directed by the historian Philip Friedman (1901–60), were responsible for collecting all documents and testimonies relating to the genocide from their main centers (Lublin, Lodz, Warsaw) and their twenty-five branches distributed over the Polish territory under Soviet control. Their modus operandi was methodical, with systematized collection and documentation procedures and protocols. Supported and funded by the Polish Academy of Sciences and (predominantly) the American Jewish Joint Distribution Committee, this initiative documented the life of European Jewish communities during the genocide. Notable among these efforts was the campaign organized by the periodical *Fun Letsten Khurbn* (the last destruction),[22] which ran between August 1946 and December 1948 under the joint leadership of Moses Josef Feigenbaum and Israel Kaplan. Recording testimonies on a gramophone, they were able to preserve several dozen songs, including different versions of the same song in some cases.

The text, whose author is mentioned along with the composer when known, is accompanied by a score that has been reduced to its simplest form, that is, to just the melodic line with no indications of tempo or dynamics. When Kaczerginski had additional information, he would include it in a footnote, generally citing his source (the name of the survivor and the place where he had met them).

Kaczerginski's work was criticized for transcription errors. In the preface to his *Lider fun di Getos un Lagern*, he mentions a letter he received from the former director of the Vilna theater Israel Segal (then head of the Yiddish theater in Munich). Segal had identified a number of inaccuracies in *Dos Gezang fun Vilner Geto* and had pointed out that the songs collected from Dora Rubin and Khayele Rozental, two artists who had performed in Vilna, had not been transcribed correctly. Moreover, the director offered to provide the authentic versions. Reluctant to accept the theater man's criticisms, Kaczerginski replied that the songs came both in their original form and in variations on the original: "We may therefore conclude that contemporary variations of certain songs are sung in different places. It is clear that as soon as this collection appears, I will hear from readers who maintain that I have incorrectly transcribed texts that they themselves created in the ghettos or camps."[23] It is thus interesting to note that the collector himself, when faced with criticisms of inauthenticity, highlighted the complexity of testimonies whose form was not fixed but which had evolved according to the collection context. It follows, then, that each of the songs was presented as a palimpsest and that each layer, each version, had to be historicized. Hence, this postwar transition period, which was marked by intense mobility and a flow of refugees, gave rise to authorship, and even copyright, problems.[24]

New York, 1948: Publication of the Kaczerginski and Stonehill Collections

Although based in Paris at the time, Kaczerginski made a three-month trip to the United States in 1948 to give talks in some thirty cities. During the summer months, he stayed at the Hotel Marseilles, located on the corner of West 103rd Street and Broadway. Following Congress's adoption of the Displaced Persons Act on 25 June 1948, the establishment welcomed European war refugees. Kaczerginski was in New York in September 1948 to attend the inaugural conference of the Altveltlekher Yidisher Kultur Kongres, or World Jewish Culture Congress, as a delegate from the federation's Paris branch.[25] His *Lider fun di Getos un Lagern* collection was published under the auspices of this organization by CYCO (located initially on 78th Street before moving to 21st Street), which became the main publishing house for the World Jewish Culture Congress. The Congress aimed to promote Yiddish through the press[26] and through authors of so-called classical (Isaac Leib Peretz[27]) and contemporary literature (Chaim Grade [member of Yung Vilne group], Isaac Bashevis Singer, and Leivick Halpern [known as H. Leivick]). It had offices in New York, Buenos Aires, and Paris, thus forming an international publishing network.

In his preface to the New York edition of Kaczerginski's collection, Leivick linked the work of collecting and publishing the songs with a process of mourning and commemoration:

> There are around a hundred of these songs, composed by our people with the help of our songwriters and sung in the ghettos and camps. But this is only a fraction of them. Who knows how many songs have been lost? They have not been written down and may never be known. Should we not say a eulogy for these lost songs like we say a eulogy for the dead? Should we not say the Yzkor for the souls of all the words, verses, and rhymes that have disappeared into the fire or gas chamber along with the lips that sang them.
>
> Yes, we should say the Yzkor for the murdered songs because by valuing them, the songs of our people who have been saved and continue to live will be all the more sacred and dear to us. Let us never forget the songwriters who were tortured and whose names we do not know.

The international renown of H. Leivick, a Bundist militant in Tsarist Russia before he immigrated to the United States in 1913, gives this preface particular weight. A Yiddish-speaking journalist, editor, and poet, he distinguished himself within the American avant-garde group *di Yunge* before finding international success in 1921 with his play (the author rather defined it as a "dramatic poem") *Der goylem* (*The Golem*). In his preface to Kaczerginski's collection, H. Leivick tends to essentialize the repertoire by homogenizing the authors through their status of victims, thus inventing a community of sorrow and mourning. Leivick continued:

> It is true that not all the songs from the ghettos and camps, which we look on as the work of our people, have the same value. Some call for a degree of critical reservation. They do not all possess the true qualities of our people's singing (volksgesangn), the purity of its wisdom, the simplicity of expression, the directness without the awkwardness, the personal, national or social lived experiences. Not all of them have its artistically naïve charm. However, it is difficult to take these songs that have emerged from the depths of hell and subject them to the usual literary criticism. There is no gauge on earth that can measure them. We do not have the heart, even with the most inept of songs, to say "it's bad."[28]

In his preface, Leivick thus underlines the specificity of this collection, choosing not to analyze each song from a formal and aesthetic point of view. In fact, the literary quality of the lyrics and the musical quality of the melody are therefore less important than their quality as testimony to situations experienced or described by the authors. Moreover, by considering in a holistic way a composite set of works composed in incomparable contexts, Leivick essentializes the songs collected by Kaczerginski by erecting them as emblems of the suffering of the Jewish people.

Structured in four parts[29] and incorporating a vast typology of songs, the collection itself is less essentialist than its preface. While it is not possible here to put forward an exhaustive analysis of the collection,[30] it is important to stress that only 100 of the 235 songs are accompanied by a melody. Just as he called on Wajner and Botwinik to provide the musical notation for his 1947 collections, Kaczerginski used the services of composer and teacher Michl Gelbart[31] (1889–1962) to put together the scores for this collection. Its geography reflects Kaczerginski's experience as a collector, which centered mainly on Lithuania and Poland. The collection comprises sixty-two songs from the Vilna ghetto (which came either from theater and cabaret programs or from Vilnian songwriters and composers), forty-eight from the Kovno ghetto, fourteen from the Warsaw ghetto, ten from the Białystok ghetto, and ten from the Lodz ghetto.[32] From a strictly historical perspective, the collection's documentary dimension (dated works, localizable situations) varies from one page to the next. The subject matter of the songs ranges from general in scope (i.e., they do not relate to any explicit context) to works that directly evidence specific places, situations, or prominent figures. In the latter case, the musical sources provide some significant historical analysis data. For example, they shed original light on the social inequalities that existed in the Kovno ghetto,[33] and they recount the everyday violence of the bodies that lay strewn across the streets of the Warsaw ghetto (in the lullabies composed by Paulina Braun, who was murdered in 1943 in Majdanek). Among Braun's lullabies, the famous "Hots Rakhmones Yidishe Hertser" (Have compassion Jewish hearts) uses a beggar's voice to describe the reality of the ghetto: "Surrounded by walls and barbed wire / The ghetto fights against death, / The people are small, no more than shadows, / Twisted bones, dry flesh."[34] This song by Paulina Braun was made famous (as others were) in the Warsaw ghetto by the singer Diana Blumenfeld (1903–61). A survivor of the liquidation of the ghetto along with her husband, actor Yonas Turkov (1898–1988), Blumenfeld played a major role in the revival of Jewish cultural life touring the displaced persons camps. She settled in New York in 1947 and, like Kaczerginski, was among the witnesses recorded by the self-taught amateur collector Ben Stonehill (1906–64) in the lobby of the Hotel Marseilles on Broadway in the summer of 1948.

Stonehill was born north of Białystok into a Yiddish-speaking Jewish family that had emigrated to New York in the 1920s. This employee of a household appliance store managed to build up one of the largest collections of Yiddish song recordings from among the refugees newly arrived on US soil. The thirty-nine hours of recordings (a total of 1,078 sung testimonies) are currently being transcribed and preserved by musicologist Bret Werb and linguist Miriam Isaacs.[35] Equipped with a wire recorder (a display model borrowed from his boss), Stonehill would go to the hotel lobby on the weekends and ask the refugees and guests to perform a song they remembered. This type of recorder allowed relatively long tracks to be recorded on the wire (fifteen to thirty minutes for standard models). These recordings along with the publication of Kaczerginski's collection turned New York into a hub for the expansion and mediation of European collections.

Kaczerginski settled in Buenos Aires in 1950 and continued to work as a poet, journalist, teacher, and organizer within different Yiddish cultural circles in Latin America. An unequivocal figure, he angered his communist comrades when he openly criticized the Stalinist regime[36] and the purges affecting prominent figures in Jewish cultural life (including the collector Moshe Beregovsky[37]). In 1954

Kaczerginski died in a plane crash while traveling for a lecture tour in Argentina.

Conclusion: Posterity, Homogenization, and the Risk of Dehistoricizing the Repertoires

The "regimes of historicity"[38] at play in the process of building this postwar transition repertoire are thus more complex than they initially appear. Forged by French historian François Hartog, the concept questions the ways in which individuals or societies think about time in a dynamic relationship between past, present and future, analyzing their system of representation. Whether in written or audio form, fragmentary or complete, original or variation, these musical sources responded to multiple, intertwined rhythms. Within the general chronology of the genocidal process, each place, each camp, each ghetto, and each killing center had its own chronology. In addition, the postwar transition period progressed according to different rhythms. The collection phase (in the displaced persons camps and emigration destinations) was followed by the publishing phase and finally the reappropriation phase, during which composers and arrangers reinterpret the melodies through aesthetics and artistic choices independent of the contexts of creation. Whether they were sung by professional performers during the tours or by amateurs in social community settings (e.g., Zionist circles, workers' clubs, religious meetings), these sources were malleable and alterable through music's performative dimension, and they evolved in both form and meaning in the period following the postwar transition, during which new processes of memorialization were underway. As a result, the large volume of Shoah music recordings released from the 1950s onward reveals three trends. The first was generalist in nature (recordings based on archival collections that did not distinguish between the songs of Jewish and non-Jewish victims[39]). The second was more monographic,[40] and the third focused on generic, decontextualized titles. One of these latter recordings, "The Unforgettable Songs of the Ghetto," sung by contralto Sarah Gorby (1900–80) and accompanied by an orchestra conducted by Jacques Lasry (1918–2014) and the French experimental band Structures Sonores, received an Académie Charles Cros award in 1976 in the "Document Historique"[41] (Historical document) category. Lasry's innovative technique, which was based notably on the use of the Cristal Baschet, colored the arrangements of these songs (drawn from Kaczerginski's repertoires) in a very particular way. Sarah Gorby's contralto voice is very resonant, along with the specific timbres of the Baschet brothers' instrument, played alone or in often dramatic orchestral arrangements, sometimes evoking Mahlerian lieder. The Cristal Baschet is made up of glass rods connected to metal rods of varying sizes. Large cones diffuse the sound without the need for electricity. The instrumentalist rubs the glass rods with his wet hands, producing a vibration projected by the cones and creating a ghostly timbre. This Gorby/Lasry collaboration, which is a highly accomplished example of the reconstitution and rearrangement of prewar songs (such as Mordechai Gebirtig's famous "S'brent" [It burns]) and melodies collected in the displaced persons camps, questions the process of folklorizing songs composed or performed in a concentration camp setting. As H. Leivick did in his preface to the New York edition of the Kaczerginski's collection, the use of "ghetto" in the singular in this compilation's title and its homogenized arrangements tend to foreground coherence in a repertoire that was nevertheless disparate and to downplay the specificities of the contexts attached to each song. For example, Hirsh Glik's resistance song "Zog nit keynmol" (Never say never) sits alongside the rather dark "Moyde ani" (I give thanks) with no critical apparatus provided. This musical production is therefore quite clearly a work of (re)creation since its dual memory/commercial dimension overrode any aspiration to act as a "Document Historique." This publishing process specific to the post-war period attests to a related phenomenon of the invention of tradition, which goes far beyond the specific chronology of musical "sorties de guerre."

Jean-Sébastien Noël is associate professor of contemporary history at La Rochelle University (France). He works on a cultural history of music in the Atlantic space (late nineteenth/twentieth century). His original field of research focused on the impact of musical repertoires, archives, and practices on memorial processes. He studied how mourning and rememorizing pogroms and the genocide in the Ashkenazi sociabilities was expressed through music from the late nineteenth century to the 1980s from Eastern and Central Europe, and the United States of America. His first book is the edited version of the research project *Le Silence s'essouffle. Mort, deuil et mémoire chez les compositeurs ashkénazes. Europe centrale et orientale, États-Unis*. He teaches Atlantic cultural history, history of cultural policies, and the cultural history of music (nineteenth/twentieth centuries).

Notes

1. This chapter was translated from French by Clare Ferguson.
2. This Lithuanian city, which the Jewish people called Vilne ("Vilna" in Polish), was home to a thriving Jewish community before the war, with prestigious religious schools (*yeshivot*), libraries, literary schools, theaters, youth movements, political parties, Zionists, anti-Zionists, and an institute for the conservation of secular Jewish culture.
3. The Central Historical Commission of the Central Committee of Liberated Jews in the US Zone was founded in Munich in December 1945.
4. For an analysis of the collection, see Werb, "Yiddish Songs of the Shoah," and Noël, "*Le Silence s'essouffle*."
5. The Central Yiddish Cultural Organization (Tsentrale yidishe kultur-organizatsye) was created in 1938 and is based in Manhattan. Its archives are deposited at the YIVO (Yidisher Visnshaftlekher Institut, or Institute for Jewish Research), holding RG 1148.
6. Noël, "*Le Silence s'essouffle*," 312-324.
7. Ben Stonehill collection, YIVO, Center for Jewish History, New York, RG 533.
8. Dawidowitz, *From That Place and Time*, 121–22.
9. Kuznitz, *YIVO and the Making of Modern Jewish Culture*.
10. For an analysis of cultural life in the Vilna ghetto, see Miron, and Shulhani, *The Yad Vashem Encyclopedia*, 878–89; Roskies, "Jewish Cultural Life in the Vilna Ghetto"; and Minczeles, *Vilna, Wilno, Vilnius*.
11. The music scene in the Vilna ghetto is well documented. Among the direct testimonies, Herman Kruk's diary describes in detail the activities of the music institutions; see Kruk, *The Last Days of the Jerusalem of Lithuania*. For a synthetic analysis, see the work of British historian Shirli Gilbert, *Music in the Holocaust*, 55–98.
12. Kuznitz, *YIVO and the Making of Modern Jewish Culture*, 182 ff.
13. The circumstances of this escape were described by Sutzkever himself in his book *Vilner Ghetto 1941–1944*. See also Porat, *Le Juif qui savait*.
14. Gilbert, "Buried Monuments," 107–28.
15. Fishman, *The Book Smugglers*, 160–62.
16. On this subject, see Cerovic, *Les Enfants de Staline*; Gitelman, *A Century of Ambivalence*; Murav and Gennady, *Soviet Jews in World War II*; and Zeltser, *Unwelcome Memory*.
17. Literally, "the workers of Zion," a leftist Zionist political party.
18. Gross, *La Peur*; Kichelewski, *Les Survivants*.
19. The material for these two collections (containing twenty-nine and thirty-seven songs, respectively) was used in the *Lider fun di Getos un Lagern*, which was published in New York by CYCO the following year.
20. Werb, "Yiddish Songs of the Shoah," 25.
21. Ouzan, "Rebuilding Jewish Identities"; Patt and Berkowitz, *"We Are Here"*; Frühauf, and Hirsch, *Dislocated Memories*.
22. The newspaper's full title was *Fun letstn khurbn: tsaytshrift far geshikhte fun yidishn lebn beysn natsi rezhim* (On the final destruction: A periodical for the history of Jewish life under the Nazi regime).
23. "Bamerkungen fun zamler" (collector's remarks). Kaczerginski, *Lider fun di Getos*, XV–XXVII. Translation taken from Werb, "Yiddish Songs of the Shoah," 106.

24. For example, Werb recounts the case of Sigmunt (Zygmunt) Berland, a musician from the Warsaw ghetto who took refuge in Paris around 1946 and who claimed authorship of the songs "S'vet geshen" (renamed "Exodus 47") and "Vu ahin zol ikh geyn?"
25. On the creation of the *Kultur-Kongress*, see Rojanski, "The Final Chapter."
26. The *Kultur-Kongress* thus resumed publication of the periodical *Di Zukunft* (The future), which was founded in 1892 by Avrom Walt Liessin (1872–1938).
27. Isaac Leib *Peretz* (1852–1915), one of the three founders of contemporary Yiddish literature. Georges Perec was one of his progenies.
28. "Dos folk zingt eybik" (The people sing eternally) by H. Leivick. Kaczerginski, *Lider fun di Getos*, XXVIII *et sq.* Translated into English from a French translation of the original provided by Simone Weissmann.
29. The first part, "Zog nit keynmol" (Never say never), takes its title from a poem by a Vilnian partisan Hirsh Glik (1922–44), which was set to a preexisting tune composed by the Pokrass brothers, who were Soviet composers of military marches and film music. This first part contains eighty-three songs, the second, "Geto lebn" (Life in the ghetto), contains forty-eight songs, the third, "Treblinke" (Treblinka), fifty-eight songs, and the fourth, "Kontratak" (response), forty-five songs.
30. For an analysis of the collection, see Werb, "Yiddish Songs of the Shoah."
31. Born in Ozorkow, near Lodz, Gelbart emigrated to the United States in 1912. As well as being a composer and a teacher in the New York Workmen's Circle schools, he wrote music reviews for several Yiddish periodicals, including the daily *Der Tog*. Before the war, Gelbart had also composed the music for the song "Di Nakht" (The night), whose lyrics were written by Aharon Domnitz. This song is included in the first part of the collection.
32. Kaczerginski, *Lider fun di getos*.
33. Set to preexisting music composed by Isaac Dunaïevski (1900–55), Nosn Markowski wrote the satirical song "Der Komitetshik" (The committee member), which denounced the Judenrat membership, who were accused of increasing inequalities and material difficulties within the population. Also writing in Kovno, Avrom Alselrod vehemently condemned the "yalos" (Yiddish slang for "bureaucrats"), playing on the contrast between his lyrics and the sweetness of the accompanying lullaby melody composed by Moshe Diskant. Noël, "*Le Silence s'essouffle*," 294.
34. Translated into English from a French translation of the original provided by Jean-Sébastien Noël.
35. Originally housed in the Library of Congress, the collection was acquired in 2006 by the United States Holocaust Memorial Museum in Washington. Copies of the recordings are also available in New York at the Center for Jewish History (Ben Stonehill Collection, YIVO, RG533).
36. Kaczerginski, *Tsvishn hamer un serp*.
37. Beregovski, *Old Jewish Folk Music*.
38 Hartog, *Regimes of Historicity*.
39. Aleksander Kulisiewicz Collection, United States Holocaust Memorial Museum, Washington DC. There is a commercial recording that provides an overview of the tapes contained in this collection: Aleksander Kulisiewicz, *Songs from the Depths of Hell*, FW37700/FSS 37700, Folkways Records, 1979.
40. Henry Sapoznik and Josh Waletzky, *Partisans of Vilna: The Songs of World War II Jewish Resistance*, Flying Fish, FLY 450, 1989.
41. Noël, "*Le Silence s'essouffle*," 320–24.

Bibliography

Beregovski, Moshe. *Old Jewish Folk Music: The Collections and Writings of Moshe Beregovski*, translated and edited by Mark Slobin. Syracuse, NY: Syracuse University Press, 2000.

Cammy, Justin. "*Tsevorfene bleter:* The Emergence of Yung-Vilne." *Polin*, no. 14 (2001): 170–91.

Cerovic, Masha. *Les Enfants de Staline. La guerre des partisans soviétiques (1941–1944)*. Paris: Seuil, 2018.

Dawidowitz, Lucy S. *From That Place and Time: A Memoir, 1938–1947*. New York: W. W. Norton, 1989.

Fishman, David E. *The Book Smugglers: Partisans, Poets, and the Race to Save Jewish Treasures from the Nazis*. Lebanon, NH: University Press of New England, 2017.

Frühauf, Tina, and Lily E. Hirsch, eds. *Dislocated Memories: Jews, Music, and Postwar German Culture*. Oxford: Oxford University Press, 2014.

Gilbert, Shirli. "Buried Monuments: Yiddish Songs and Holocaust Memory." *History Workshop Journal*, no. 66 (2008): 107–28.

———. *Music in the Holocaust: Confronting Life in the Nazi Ghettos and Camps*. New York: Oxford University Press, 2005.

Gitelman, Zvi. *A Century of Ambivalence: The Jews of Russia and the Soviet Union, 1881 to the Present*. Bloomington: Indiana University Press, 2001.

Gross, Jan T. *La Peur: l'antisémitisme en Pologne après Auschwitz*. Paris: Calmann-Lévy, 2010.

Hartog, François, *Regimes of Historicity. Presentism and Experiences of Time*. New York: Columbia University Press, 2015.

Kaczerginski, Shmerke. *Tsvishn hamer un serp: tsu der geshikhte fun der likvidatsye fun der yidisher kultur in sovetn-rusland*. Buenos Aires: Der emes, 1950.

Kaczerginski, Shmerke, ed. *Lider fun di Getos un Lagern*. New York: CYCO, 1948.

Kichelewski, Audrey. *Les Survivants: les Juifs de Pologne depuis la Shoah*. Paris: Belin, 2018.

Kruk, Herman. *The Last Days of the Jerusalem of Lithuania Chronicles from the Vilna Ghetto and the Camps 1939–1944*. New Haven, CT: Yale University Press/YIVO Institute for Jewish Research, [1961] 2002.

Kuznitz, Cecile Esther. *YIVO and the Making of Modern Jewish Culture: Scholarship for the Yiddish Nation*. New York: Cambridge University Press, 2014.

Minczeles, Henri. *Vilna, Wilno, Vilnius, la Jérusalem de Lituanie*. Paris: La Découverte, 1993.

Miron, Guy, and Shlomit Shulhani, eds. *The Yad Vashem Encyclopedia of the Ghettos During the Holocaust*. vol. 1. Jerusalem: Yad Vashem, 2009.

Murav, Harriet, and Estraikh Gennady, eds. *Soviet Jews in World War II: Fighting, Witnessing, Remembering*. Brighton, MA: Academic Studies Press, 2014.

Noël, Jean-Sébastien. *"Le Silence s'essouffle." Mort, deuil et mémoire chez les compositeurs ashkénazes. Europe centrale et orientale, États-Unis (1880–1980)*. Nancy: PUN – Éditions Universitaires de Lorraine, 2016.

Ouzan, Françoise. "Rebuilding Jewish Identities in Displaced Persons Camps in Germany." *Bulletin du Centre de recherche français à Jérusalem*, no. 14 (2004): 98–111.

Patt, Avinoam J., and Michael Berkowitz, eds. *"We Are Here": New Approaches to Jewish Displaced Persons in Postwar Germany*. Detroit: Wayne State University Press, 2010.

Porat, Dina. *Le Juif qui savait, Wilno-Jerusalem, la figure légendaire d'Abba Kovner*. Latresne: Le bord de l'Eau, 2017.

Rojanski, Rachel. "The Final Chapter in the Struggle for Cultural Autonomy: Palestine, Israel and Yiddish Writers in the Diaspora, 1946–1951." *Journal of Modern Jewish Studies*, no. 6–2 (2007): 185–204.

Roskies, David G. "Jewish Cultural Life in the Vilna Ghetto." In *Lithuania and the Jews: The Holocaust Chapter*, edited by Paul A. Shapiro and Carl J. Rheins, 33–44. Washington: United States Holocaust Memorial Museum, 2005.

Sutzkever, Avrom. *Vilner Ghetto 1941–1944*. Paris: Denoël, [1945] 2013.

Werb, Bret. "Yiddish Songs of the Shoah: A Source Study Based on the Collections of Shmerke Kaczerginski." PhD diss., University of California, 2014.

Zeltser, Arkadi. *Unwelcome Memory: Holocaust Monuments in the Soviet Union*. Jerusalem: Yad Vashem Publications, 2019.

Chapter 11

SINGING THE UNSPEAKABLE IN RWANDA IN THE SUMMER OF 1994
Music in the Context of the Genocidal Abyss through a Portrait of the Artist

Benjamin Chemouni and Assumpta Mugiraneza

In the second half of the 1950s, on the eve of Rwanda's independence, the political struggle for power pitted the Tutsi-majority elites, who were contesting Belgium's colonial authority, against a new nationalist Hutu movement led by the Parti du Mouvement de l'Émancipation Hutu (PARMEHUTU) party, which was anti-Tutsi and took a similar line to the colonial rulers.[1] In 1959 the party encouraged a peasant revolt against the Tutsi minority, who made up most of the country's national and local political establishment. With the Belgian authorities' approval, this revolt, which ultimately gave rise to the First Republic (1961–73), quickly turned into indiscriminate violence against the Tutsis. The violence led to many deaths and the exile of tens of thousands of Tutsis, who fled to neighboring countries such as Uganda, Zaire, and Burundi. In 1987 the Rwandan Patriotic Front (RPF) was created in Uganda with the main aim of returning refugees to their homeland. It launched an attack on Rwanda in October 1990, triggering a civil war that ended with the genocide campaign against the Tutsis from April to July 1994.

The war and the genocide disrupted and transformed all aspects of Rwandan life, not least the world of song. During the conflict (1990–94), song was used as a tool to support one side over the other. It became an integral part of the war effort, mobilizing

---

Notes for this section begin on page 223.

the Rwandan population both inside and outside the country's borders. This dynamic led to an unprecedented proliferation of compositions. Song was used by the regime to crow about the presidential camp's invincibility and foster fear in the enemy. Olivier Urbain has noted on the subject of the regime's songs that in the years leading up to the genocide, "creativity was used extensively to compose songs, record them, and broadcast them, but only to divide people, to strengthen and unite members of one group against all others. Musicking was ... [used] to galvanize one group to the detriment and for the destruction of another group of human beings."[2] A creative force also manifested itself among the RPF supporters. Aimed at raising awareness of the refugees' plight, the songs condemned the incumbent regime and recounted a fantasized past in which Rwanda was united, harmonious, and peaceful. The songs told of the diaspora's nostalgia for their country and their desire to return. One such song is the famous "Turaje" (We're coming home), composed in 1990 by the diasporic all-women band Isamaza: "We're on our way, we're coming home, we miss Rwanda so! / We're on our way, we're coming home, to serve our country with intelligence / We're on our way, we're coming home in our thousands, leaving nothing behind."[3]

The politically volatile context of the early 1990s thus resulted in an unprecedented dynamism in the music scene. People used song to defend or impose their points of view, demonstrate political loyalty, and give meaning to an extraordinary situation. What happened to this musical momentum when it was confronted with the genocide? What and how did the people sing when they came face-to-face with the unspeakable spectacle of a "genocide by proximity" during which neighbors killed neighbors? Who was singing in the years immediately following the RPF's victory, when genocide had become the new yardstick of Rwandan life?

Relatively little research has addressed these questions. Various studies have discussed Rwanda's current music scene, but few have looked at the immediate post-genocide period and its impact on song. Noteworthy among the exceptions are articles written by Paul Kerstens[4] and Rémi Korman. The study by Korman focused on the memory of the genocide through music.[5] Covering the entire period from the genocide to recent times, it examined mourning songs composed shortly after the event. Our chapter aims to complement this research by reflecting in particular on the continuities and discontinuities produced by the genocidal episode in the world of Rwandan song. To this end and in contrast to the works cited, we focus on the pivotal time from 1990–99. The chapter first devotes significant analysis to song landscape as it existed prior to the war before moving on to an examination of the impact of the outbreak of the conflict in 1990 since it is not possible to fully comprehend the consequences of the genocide on the Rwandan musical universe, both in terms of style and themes, without first a solid understanding of the musical scene before the event. The chapter then focuses on the immediate effects of the genocide on musical creativity and, conversely, on the role of music for people to navigate the immediate post-genocide era. In particular, we profile two emblematic singers who composed before and after the catastrophe, Suzanne Nyiranyamibwa and Mariya Yohana Mukankuranga. This biography-centered methodology allows us to trace in detail the influence of the genocide on artistic interests and to grasp the ways in which the genocidal experience affected the creative process.

1980s to the Genocide: Creative Abundance and the Politicization of Song

After independence in 1962, the traditional court song largely disappeared from the public space. This song genre consisted mainly of sung poetry, called *ibisigo*, which was elaborated by court poets (*abasizi*) and accompanied by a zither (called an *inanga*). It was a demanding genre in terms of lyrics, rhythm, and rhyme. The poems were always long and full of biographical or historical references, often with a strong esoteric content. They typically celebrated the power of a monarch or the royal constitutional order. It was said that the omission of a single verse during an abasizi's recitation could condemn him to death. The court song was not associated with any particular ethnic category until colonization, which, by establishing a broadly ethnic interpretation of Rwandan reality, linked court music to the Tutsi ethnic group.[6] With the court song's disappearance, Rwanda was left with just a repertoire of popular songs and one other specific genre, namely political and propaganda songs.[7] The relatively limited musical creativity of the 1960s and 1970s in the country gave way to a profusion of compositions in the 1980s. The entrenchment of the regime of President Juvénal Habyarimana, who came to power in a coup d'état in 1973, brought a certain stability to the country. As a result, its propaganda became more assertive: accessible and simple political songs that glorified the regime and its single party became commonplace, especially around the time of the festivities to mark the twenty-fifth anniversary of independence in 1987. Some famous names and bands celebrated the regime's achievements and the president's infallibility. These songs were widely aired in the public space through various channels, such as the weekly "propaganda sessions" (known as *animations politiques*) in civil service workplaces and schools. Propaganda songs also infiltrated people's homes through Radio Rwanda, the country's only national radio station.

At the same time, music was opening up to new rhythms (jazz and Congolese rumba, in particular) that introduced a touch of modernity. Among the artists renewing the Rwandan music scene were the Impala Orchestra and the Abamararungu band, both formed in the late 1970s, as well as, in the 1980s, the Nyampinga band from Butare, the Inono Stars, the Ingeri, and composers such as Cyprien Rugamba (whose music was performed by the Amasimbi n'Amakombe band),[8] François Nkurunziza, Masabo Nyangezi, Cassien Twagirayezu, Jean-Paul Samputu, Ben Ngabo (also known as Kipeti), and François Mihigo (also known as Chouchou). The beginning of the 1980s was also marked by political events that led to a discreet," almost hidden, politicization of a section of Rwandan song. On the one hand, the arrest in 1981 of people close to the president, including his head of intelligence, following rumors of preparations for a coup, called into question the regime's apparent cohesion. On the other, a civil war broke out in Uganda (1980–86) between Milton Obote's regime and Yoweri Museveni's rebellion. While Obote's regime harassed the Rwandan refugees, some of whom were to settle in northern Rwanda until the end of the war before being sent back to Uganda, Museveni's rebellion recruited them, offering military training and fostering a politicization that would ultimately lead to the creation of the RPF.

These events brought about a new political awareness. While those living in Rwanda discovered the existence of a large refugee community, the diaspora became aware that Juvénal Habyarimana's regime was never going to allow them to return. A discourse that was not aligned with the regime's propaganda main themes thus began to emerge in the songs of the diaspora and in the new fashionable songs within Rwanda. Although not entirely legal, their discourse was nevertheless not illegal: the apparent neutrality of the songs, the seemingly depoliticized nature of their topics, and at the same time the revival of old musical styles, was itself a political statement in the propaganda-saturated environment of the time. In the stifling context of the Second Republic (1973–94), where song was still very much oriented toward propaganda, the circulation of these particular songs was surprisingly widespread. Certain members of the diaspora also managed to make their voices heard in Rwanda. The compositions of refugee artists in Burundi, such as Annociata Batamuliza (also known as Kamaliza) and Evariste Musoni, were not aired on the radio, but they did circulate unofficially. They were even sometimes played in shared taxis. In addition, Cécile Kayirebwa, a refugee in Belgium, obtained the right to give concerts in Rwanda.

Exiled Rwandans were also reviving repertoires that had been almost completely forgotten in Republican Rwanda. Certain Rwandan families managed to procure cassettes of these productions and were thus able to listen to artists such as Florida Uwera, Mariya-Yohanna Mukankuranga, Athanase Sentore, and Jean-Marie Muyango and bands like Imitali, Utumanzi, and Ibihangange. These artists' songs nurtured a nostalgia for musical genres and an era that had largely disappeared. Within Rwanda, old songs from different eras such as "Mukamabano," originally from the 1950s, or "Imitoma" (an *igisigo*[9]) and "Nyiratunga," from the pre-colonial era, were recorded by bands like the Impala Orchestra and seemed to remind a section of the population of a common belonging that had been lost amid the postindependence violence.

Paradoxically, the start of the war in 1990, which was triggered by the RPF's attack from Uganda, and the introduction of a multiparty system the following year, saw an acceleration in the creative momentum that had begun in the 1980s. Given its centrality in the lives of Rwandans, song became a major political tool, but it lost its diversity in the process. Within Rwanda it was the vehicle of choice for showing political loyalty to the threatened regime, as demonstrated by Simon Bikindi's song "Nanga abahutu" (I hate these Hutus). The singer expresses his disgust for those who were not proud of their ethnic identity and who showed a lack of solidarity with their Hutu brothers in the face of the RPF threat. In his song "Bene Sebahinzi" (The descendants of Sebahinzi), Bikindi stirs up fears of a return of the Tutsi monarchy and, with it, forced labor.[10] Conversely, any reluctance to sing during the regime's innumerable "propaganda sessions" (*animations*) became a suspicious gesture, as did listening to the songs (even those that were apolitical) of exiled Rwandans.

The musical proliferation within the RPF rebellion was maintained by three main categories of composers. One comprised the groups of soldiers who informally drew on their war experiences. They sang about the much-anticipated victory and expressed their hopes for the future. The second category was represented by the

RPF's cultural troupe, Indahemuka, which raised funds, publicized the objectives of the rebellion, and lifted the troops' morale. The third and largest category was made up of members of the diaspora who were getting themselves organized as the conflict dragged on. The song "Iya Mbere Ukwakira" (The first of October) celebrates the eternal beauty and harmony of Rwanda, denounces the regime, and proclaims liberation from its yoke for the people. The songs also appealed to the listener's generosity for support for the war effort. "Girubuntu" (Express your humanity in an outpouring of generosity) is one of the most emblematic in this respect.[11]

In comparison, domestic production of pro-RPF songs was largely nonexistent due to its inherent risks. Singers who did not embrace the regime's radicalization either fled—for example, Jean-Paul Samputu and Benjamin Rutabana—or were harassed because they were suspected of being RPF sympathizers and killed during the genocide, like Loti Bizimana, Cyprien Rugamba, and Rodrigue Karemera. However, external production found its way into Rwanda through cassettes hidden in the luggage of travelers crossing the border and were then copied clandestinely—for example, onto audio equipment used during wedding ceremonies. These songs could be listened to on Radio Muhabura, the RPF radio station that broadcast from transmitters in the war zone, although listeners risked imprisonment if they were discovered.

July 1994–July 1995: Singing the Unspeakable

The war may have accelerated music production, but the sudden shock of the genocide stopped it in its tracks. As a Rwandan proverb says, "Umutima usobetse amaganya, ntusobanura amagambo" (a heart full of sorrow cannot disentangle the lyrics). Artists and bands who had been prolific a few months earlier, like Jean-Paul Samputu, Ingeri, Imitali, and Isibo y'Ishakwe, just shut down completely when confronted with the horror. The situation in Rwanda was of a particular nature. Unlike the Holocaust, for example, it was a "genocide by proximity," where individuals killed other individuals with whom they shared close ties of solidarity, friendship, and even marriage.[12] The difficulty of referencing the horror was thus reinforced by the personal nature of the massacres. For most artists, this difficulty resulted in silence. However, some composers, mainly women from the diaspora who had returned to Rwanda,[13] confronted the situation head-on. Indeed, it was mainly women who spoke out after the genocide. This phenomenon can be explained in part by the gendered dimension of the expression of emotions in Rwandan culture, where "Amarira y'umugabo atemba ajya mu nda" (a man's tears flow inward) is a common saying. In Rwanda, masculinity is associated with modesty, moderation, and discretion. The man is also the protector. Perhaps because they had failed to protect, the men were condemned to silence after the genocide. More broadly, their place in society was reduced after the disaster, although not in the military field. As a result, men found themselves the least able to sing about mourning. To do so would have been, for them, like "crying with the women."

In order to analyze this phenomenon and without claiming to be exhaustive, we profile the two best-known artists who were emblematic of the immediate post-genocide period, namely Suzanne Nyiranyamibwa and Mariya Yohana Mukankuranga. Other famous musicians of the period sang for the RPF, including Kamaliza, but did not compose songs with the specific theme of the genocide, while some, like Cécile Kayirebwa, tried their hand at composing on the subject but only some years after the event. By comparing Nyiranyamibwa's and Mukankuranga's compositions before and after the spring of 1994, our aim is to grasp the thematic changes brought about by the genocide. In addition, by presenting their careers, we hope to understand the transformation that took place in the very act of composition for these artists. Although their compositions never claimed any semblance to the court songs register, they nevertheless retained certain traditional aspects. The choice of rhythm, for example, differed from that found in the more recent political propaganda songs that had invaded the song space since Rwanda's independence. Their lyrics awakened an ancient Rwandan sensibility by depicting a complex world through traditional allusions or concepts. These songs were composed a cappella, which indicated a formal continuity with the tradition of the everyday Rwandan songs composed and performed within the family and restricted social circles. As the songs became more popular, they were supplemented, with varying levels of success, by often approximate musical accompaniments. Because of their thematic difficulty, however, they lent themselves particularly well to an a cappella solo arrangement or just a light accompaniment from either the inanga (Rwandan zither) or a discreet vocal counterpoint.

These songs were a spontaneous form of expression, initially intended just for close family and friends or small circles of likeminded people. Nyiranyamibwa's songs, for example, were amateurishly recorded on an audio cassette in Belgium for the first genocide commemoration in 1995 and not formally released as a CD until ten years later.[14] Mukankuranga's early songs were also recorded on audio cassette and thus circulated informally in Rwanda at the end of the 1990s. They were never released as part of an album.

Suzanne Nyiranyamibwa, Member of the Isamaza Band

Singer-songwriter Suzanne Nyiranyamibwa's story is closely intertwined with that of Rwanda. Her father, a civil servant trained by the colonial administration, was imprisoned and then killed during the violence of the independence period. Nyiranyamibwa fled the second wave of massacres in 1973, first to Zaire and then, in the early 1990s, to Belgium. In exile, she composed and sang for her loved ones.

Like many other refugees, between 1990 and 1994, she supported the return-home movement encouraged by the RPF. She expressed this support through song as part of the Isamaza band, which she had formed with friends (Susanne and Françoise Ruboneka, Jeanne Kaligirwa, Rosalie Mukamutara) who were also invested in the drive for a return to Rwanda. Famous songs such as "Nimuberwe Bakobwa" (Be elegant, my daughters), "Indege Irahinda" (The plane is vibrating, ready for take-off), "Uraho Rwanda" (Greetings, Oh Rwanda), and "Turaje" (We're coming home) filled the refugees with hope and the Habyarimana regime supporters with rage. These songs were striking both melodically and structurally because they were reminiscent of the singing style that had preceded the postindependence propaganda style but without the linguistic and stylistic complication of the old court songs. Their content was primarily a mixture of shared memories that expressed nostalgia for an idyllic Rwanda, celebrated for its eternal beauty, as exemplified in "Uraho Rwanda" (Greetings, oh Rwanda). The song "Nimuberwe Bakobwa" (Be elegant, my daughters) evokes the idea of return and reconciliation:

> When we return to our roots,
> Our home, our place of serenity,
> Let us come together as we sing in jubilation,
> Seated calmly, we will restore justice,
> We will blockade the road to hatred.
> We will exchange beauty treatments[15] in togetherness
> We, the people of the trinity,[16]
> Which shines with eternal goodness,
> Surrounded by fraternal love.[17]

In the summer of 1994, Nyiranyamibwa returned to Rwanda. Although she had been told that some of her family, including her mother, had been massacred, she was convinced that all she wanted was the RPF's victory. However, this notion of victory lost all meaning when she came into contact with the reality of the genocide. After a few weeks, she returned to her modest flat in Belgium, where she would tell visitors: "What I saw there, there's no more Rwanda, what I saw is impossible to imagine, it's the unspeakable that reduces people to silence."[18] It was nevertheless impossible for her to remain silent about the horror. Her compositions became both reportage and an attempt to understand, as is clear in her first song "Mbaze nde?" (Who should I ask?), composed in autumn 1994 and then, a few weeks later, in "Ibuka" (Remember) and the poem "Ndabaza" (I ask the Question). The latter was recited with a traditional accompaniment for this kind of poem that uses a spoken style of recitation. These very early post-genocide compositions are particularly striking in that most people were unable to imagine such violence or to find the words to describe it.

"Mbaze nde?" is reportage delivered in the first person. The composer positions herself as an eyewitness who is physically experiencing the horror, which is communicated through body language, a fairly typical process in the Rwandan language:

> I enter Rwanda and no longer recognize anything,
> It's as if its heart has been torn out,
> I'm dazed, disoriented, as if emptied of meaning,
> Then my chest tightens as if I were breastfeeding but I'm not,[19]
>   ayiweeeeee.
> Chorus:
> Ayiii, how and what can I do?
> Who can I ask? The one I should ask is no longer here.[20]

Her compositions reflect the idea that the Rwanda she had been dreaming of for so long had disappeared. The country was materially, humanly, socially, and culturally unrecognizable, especially since those who could tell its story were all gone. The artist thus offers snapshots of the annihilation of coexistence: "All the paths have been invaded by the bushland, / The beautiful hills of yesteryear are now covered with ruins, / There where the children used to play, scavengers now frolic, ayiii."[21] She goes on to present the survivors' suffering: "The crying of the orphans will keep you awake, / The mother who gave birth is forever reduced to a life without children. / So many widows sick with their unspeakable grief, ayeeee."[22] Women who cannot give birth and whose infants have been killed, inconsolable children: the source of life has dried up. The song's poetic language describes the end of history, where, on the ruined hills, only widows, orphans, and scavengers remain.

Nyiranyamibwa also describes the broken link with the sacred, a significant element in Rwandan culture. The churches were desecrated, turned into killing fields. This was a spectacle never seen before. During the postindependence violence, the churches had been used as places of refuge. The composer describes the killing of the Hutus who refused to take part in the massacres and the arbitrariness of death, a practice that continued even after the genocide as a result of the antipersonnel mines dotted throughout the country:

> God's churches are overflowing with corpses,
> The country is swarming with [antipersonnel] mines,
> When you survive the night, you're never sure you'll survive the day, ayiweeee.
> They drove human beings like they were beasts,
> Leading them to their death, these villains
> Having decreed that being Tutsi is an absolute crime, ayiweeee.
> And any Hutu who didn't kill didn't deserve to live,
> Declared an accomplice of the Inkotanyi [name for the RPF soldiers], he deserved to die,
> Few in his family have escaped death.[23]

Nyiranyamibwa endeavored to put the unspeakable acts into words without trivializing them and without descending into voyeurism or debasing the victims. The narrative in *Mbaze Nde* is a skilful balance between a language of truth and a duty to restore some modicum of dignity to the victims:

> They (the killers) had fun at their expense while they were only clothed in shame.
> They dispossessed them of everything on the hills,
> It was like the Way of the Cross to Golgotha.
> They tortured, debased, and killed them without a care,
> They boasted of their misdeeds like they were some glorious victory,
> Anyone not killed with the machete perished by a small, worn-out hoe,
> You had to pay to get a bullet,
> If you didn't buy your death, you were cut up into pieces
> It was unthinkable, no one could ever have imagined it.
> Their aim was complete extermination,
> Whether it was a mother the same age as their own,
> Or a baby with a smile of complete innocence, there was no reprieve,
> I begged the Lord that it would all be a nightmare, but there was no point, it was true.
> As I couldn't find anyone to cry to, I swallowed my tears.[24]

Song became a way of bearing witness and exposing the extreme breach of the social pact that the criminals were guilty of when they attacked innocence.

Finally, these songs were an opportunity to describe the efforts made not to descend into feelings of vengeance and anger toward the executioners, feelings that were difficult to contain, as is clear from the atrocity of the descriptions. In the song "Ese ngire nte bagenzi" (What can I do, my friends?), for example, the singer asks that the person who "created the emptiness"[25] be kept out of her sight lest "I ask him about these babies, these young men and girls he murdered, or I ask him to explain why he opened up the wombs of pregnant women to eject their embryos."[26] She ends by thanking "the government of unity, which has held me back and prevented me from taking revenge."[27]

Mariya Yohana Mukankuranga, Member of the Indahemuka Troupe

The genocide also profoundly affected Mariya Yohana Mukankuranga's musical output. Like Nyiranyamibwa, her songs in the immediate post-genocide period were rooted in the contrast between her arrival full of hope in a liberated Rwanda and the horror she encountered there.

The life of this nonagenarian, who is today famous throughout Rwanda, was closely intertwined with the country's tragic history. When Rwanda descended into violence around independence, Mukankuranga was forced to flee with her husband and baby to Uganda, where she lived in exile for thirty years. She earned her living first as a farm laborer and then as a teacher in a refugee camp. She composed songs for the children, singing of exile and nostalgia for their country, as in the song "Icyamara agahinda" (The thing that could heal my sorrow):

> I used to like sitting up with my grandfather,
> He told me wonderful things about Rwanda,
> He's the one who taught me this was our home.
> Chorus:
> Oh, the only thing that could heal my sorrow,
> Is to be shown where home is[28]

Like many other artists in exile, she campaigned alongside the RPF for the right to return. She first composed alone and then with friends before joining the RPF's Indahemuka troupe. Her most famous song, "Intsinzi" (Victory), recalls traditional divinatory practices to affirm that victory is inevitable and envisions the celebrated homecoming of those who had fought in Rwanda. The contrast between her long-anticipated joy at returning home with her husband and daughter and the atrocities she discovered when she got there is vast. It becomes impossible for her to sing of victory. Like Nyiranyamibwa, her compositions became reportage on the horrors that few dared to put into words. During the decade that followed, she published a series of compositions with her daughter, Angélique Garuka, including "Nyibutsa Nkwibutse" (Remind me so that I can remind you in turn), "Ese ngire nte bagenzi" (What can I do, my friends?), "Nkwibutse se kwibuka?" (Shall I remind you of the memory?), and "Wa munsi waje" (D-day is coming). These songs are presented as testimonies in the form of portraits of different categories of survivors, but they also question this "brother turned killer."[29]

While Nyiranyamibwa and Mukankuranga both addressed common themes (e.g., rape, child murder), the precision of Mukankuranga's portrayal, enhanced by the fact that she uses the victim's voice, is sometimes almost unbearable. This is illustrated in "Nyibutsa Nkwibutse":

> Remind me, so that I can remind you in turn, on this day when we remember,
> The last time I saw you, you were being stabbed with knives and machetes,
> I was raped and I lost my mind,
> I'm just waiting for my last day to come because I've been contaminated by the cursed evil [AIDS]
> . . .
> Wherever I go, wherever I am, I hear a voice calling me:
> Go my child, so they don't kill you before my eyes,
> It was my mother. . . She was raped by young men my age,
> From my new hiding place, I could see her, right in front of me, as she lay dying.
> I gave birth to many children, but I don't have one left to bring me a little water.[30]

Like Nyiranyamibwa, Mukankuranga's songs highlight the paradox of a "genocide by proximity," that tension between yesterday's social familiarity and today's executioner and victim, as in "Nyibutsa Nkwibutse":

> You, the person I'd shared everything with till then,
> Became a wild beast before my eyes, more savage than those of the forest,
> When I begged him to hide me, he replied: go join your own people,
> He told me straight: We live together yes, but you're so stupid!
> Do you not hear our father's instructions?

There's only one goal: "We're resolved to eradicate."
Get out of there quickly where I can see you or I'll finish you off myself.[31]

The songs also touch on the physical, psychological, and social consequences of the violence for the victims in the post-genocide era: "This person was born into a good family but he became a street child / This one has become a cripple, ruined by the machete forever / We three together present a snapshot of the survivors."[32]

Finally, the songs show a complicated relationship with the enemy and guilt. While they do not directly encourage forgiveness, they convey the idea that putting the horror into words is cathartic. For the composers, forgiveness and reconciliation is not possible without first attempting to verbalize the atrocities that have been perpetrated. This is illustrated in "Nkwibutse se kwibuka?" (Shall I remind you of the memory?): "We can never be reconciled over guilt and resentment, never / We cannot think of unity with irreparability at its core, / But the real truth is restorative, / Let us beg our Creator, that He may one day restore unity among us."[33]

In "Nyibutsa Nkwibutse," the chorus explains: "Ohhhh, reconciliation is an imperative so it seems, / It's not so much that I'm opposed to it, I'm just leaving it to the courts."[34] The song ends as follows: "Rwandans, all of us without exception, know what's happened here / Let's all pull together so that this never happens again."[35] While recounting what happened appears to have been a prerequisite for reconstructing the victims and Rwanda's social fabric, the unbearable acts portrayed in Mukankuranga's and Nyiranyamibwa's songs show just how difficult this task has been. The composers sometimes seem to doubt their own ability as well as that of the survivors to embrace reconciliation. Although "Nyibutsa Nkwibutse" describes reconciliation as "an imperative so it seems," this imperative has not come directly from the survivors but from the justice system, God, and the government.

Conclusion

Any discussion of post-genocide songs in Rwanda is first and foremost a discussion of the absence of song. Paralysis at the horror stopped the proliferation of the 1990s in its tracks. We could compile a long list of Rwandan composers who seem to have been struck dumb in the aftermath of the genocide. It seems songs were no longer the vehicle of choice even for the Hutu power, whose discourse of hatred continued, and negationism grew.

There were thus a number of different discontinuities in the world of song in the immediate post-genocide period. The main one was sociological. A generation of singers had been decimated. Most of those who survived had managed to flee the country during the war. The remainder, artists formerly close to the regime, had either stayed silent out of shame or fear or fled to neighboring Zaire. The only category of composers still active in the summer of 1994 and the months that followed was therefore made up primarily of women from the diaspora who were returning to Rwanda.

However, they may still have been singing, but they no longer sang about the same topic. There was thus also a thematic discontinuity; the genocide produced a depoliticization of song in the sense that it no longer supported one side or the other in the conflict, despite the fact that many perpetrators were on the run in Zaire and the war was relocating there. In addition, song did not celebrate the much-anticipated victory. It was too bitter. Song composition was instead transformed in order to respond to a number of needs. First, it had to let the world but most especially the Rwandans in the diaspora know what had happened. The composer turned into a reporter poet in order to expose the violence of the "genocide by proximity." Second, it had to open up, albeit tentatively, the possibility of mourning by speaking the unspeakable. Traditionally, Rwandan songs did not dwell on death—only on the grief it causes. The genocide thus introduced this new concept of singing about death and the way in which it had been inflicted, as if its omnipresence made its consignment to the domain of song a requirement for social survival. The songs composed in the months following the genocide sought to put into words the annihilation of the social pact, the crushed Rwandan culture, its desecrated relationship with the sacred, and an unprecedented level of sadism that most traumatized survivors are still not able to talk about today. These song lyrics, whose translation cannot do justice to the poetry and their anchoring in a specific sociocultural world, helped negotiate this transition between paralysis and the beginning of a process of mourning by giving an account of the facts.

At the same time, the songs of Mukankuranga and Nyiranyamibwa highlight the ambiguity of their relationships with forgiveness and reconciliation. Although these artists recognized these were necessary, they naturally found it difficult to come to terms with them.

This aspect is particularly interesting because it is typical of the songs composed in the immediate post-genocide period. The government was later to promote a "euphemization" and "deconflictualization" of the memory of the genocide in aid of policies of forgiveness and reconciliation.[36] A decade after the genocide, songs had been transformed in this sense. They had become officialized because they were "often commissioned by survivors' associations or the State."[37] Mukankuranga was thus to become a prolific artist, composing regularly for official commemorative ceremonies. Nyiranyamibwa followed a different path, however. She only returned to the theme of genocide in 2017 with a song about her mother, but this composition was no longer a direct commentary on the events. In general, songs became imbued with the style of the evangelical religious movements that had flourished in the post-genocide years and that "explained in particular the exhortations for forgiveness and the reconstruction of national unity" contained in their lyrics.[38] This "takeover" of the songs from the genocide, orienting them toward resilience and reconciliation, encouraged silence on some of its most disturbing aspects in the name of reconstructing the social pact of the new Rwanda. The immediate post-genocide songs sung by these women are so important because they mark a quite specific and pivotal time. Before an official normalization of the memory had a chance to emerge and in a context of disbelief at a horror that was inaccessible to the intellect, the artistic word thus took up the baton in the summer of 1994. These songs were rare, but they were nevertheless essential in the face of an injunction to speak the unspeakable.

Benjamin Chemouni is an assistant professor in development studies at the Université Catholique de Louvain in Belgium. His work is interested in postconflict dynamics of state formation as well as transitions of rebel movements to ruling parties in Africa's Great Lakes region, especially in Burundi and Rwanda. He is a former Early Career Leverhulme Fellow at the University of Cambridge, and a former Junior Research Fellow (JRF) at Wolfson College. He holds a PhD from the London School of Economics. His work has been published in a range of journals, including *African Affairs* and *World Development*.

Assumpta Mugiraneza is a Franco-Rwandan academic with degrees in Education Studies (Rwanda), Social Psychology, and Political Science from the Université de Paris VIII. Since 1994 her research has focused on genocide and extreme violence, particularly through discourse analysis, comparing the genocidal discourse of Hutu power to Nazi discourse. Since 2010 she has cofounded and directed the IRIBA Center for Multimedia Heritage, a center for Rwandan audiovisual archives spanning more than a century, freely accessible to all, at the intersection of academic research and practice. She is the author and coauthor of a range of articles on the topics of hate speech and propaganda, the teaching of history, the role of archives in state-building, and the deconstruction of ideologies of hatred.

Notes

1. This chapter was translated from French by Clare Ferguson.
2. Urbain, "A Statement of Values for Our Research on Music in Peacebuilding," 233, cited in Ubaldo and Hintjens, "Rwandan Music-Makers Negotiate Shared Cultural Identities after Genocide," 27.
3. Chemouni and Mugiraneza, "Ideology and Interests in the Rwandan Patriotic Front." "Turaje turukumbuye (Rwanda) / Turaje, turukorere buhanga / Turaje n'ibihumbi n'ibihubi" (translated from Kinyarwanda via French as all the following quotations).
4. Kerstens, "Amahoro. Chanter après le genocide."
5. Korman, "Indirimbo z'icyunamo. Chanter la mémoire du genocide"; Mugiraneza, "La langue blessée"; Mugiraneza, "Annexes: Chants du deuil."
6. On these aspects, see Mbonimana, *La Musique rwandaise traditionnelle*; and Mbonimana and Nkejabahizi, *Amateka y'ubuvaganzo nyarwanda*.
7. Gansemans, *Les Instruments de musique du Rwanda*.
8. On the richness of Rugamba's work, see Nyemazi, *La Poésie et la chanson de Cyprien Rugamba*; and Nsengimana, "Cyezamitima de Cyprien Rugamba."
9. *Igisigo* is the singular form of *Ibisigo*.
10. Cited in McCoy, "Making Violence Ordinary," 92.
11. On the RPF's songs, see Chemouni and Mugiraneza, "Ideology and Interests in the Rwandan Patriotic Front."
12. See Mugiraneza, "Rebuilding Rwanda." The expression "génocide de proximité" was coined by Jean Hatzfeld. On the mechanics of massacres "by proximity," see Dumas, *Le Génocide au village*; Fujii, *Killing Neighbors*.
13. Korman, "Indirimbo z'icyunamo. Chanter la mémoire du genocide," 352–54. Mention should be made of the women in the associations Benimpuhwe (an exiles association) and Avega (a mutual assistance association), which were created in the wake of the genocide. Another category of actors, made up of a number of young singers who had taken refuge abroad or fought alongside the RPF, such as Thomas Sankara, Ben Rutabana, and Dieudonné Munyanshoza, also sang about the genocide, often in a similar spirit of documenting what they had seen.
14. For example, one of the first CDs to be released was *Mbahoze nte?: 10 ans après le génocide rwandais*, JC. M Sounds Studio, 2004.
15. A reference to *guca imanzi*, which is the social practice of making small beautifying lacerations.
16. A reference to the three ethnic groups in Rwanda, Hutu, Tutsi, and Twa.

17. "Nitugera ku gicumbi / igicaniro cy'ituze / Muzaze tugweragwere / Tuzicara duce imanza / Urwango turuce icyuho / Turangize duce imanzi / Imbaga y'inyabutatu / Itamba ineza iteka / Dutamirije urukundo."
18. In Kinyarwanda, "ibyo mbonye hariya hantu, nta Rwanda rukiriho, ibyo mbonye ni agahomamunwa, nta cyo wabona uvuga, urumirwa." Personal communication to the author.
19. An image in Kinyarwanda that would prompt serious cause for concern.
20. "Ayiiiii, ngire nte, nkore iki? / Ese mbaze nde? / Ko uwo nabajije atakiriho Mpingutse i Rwanda, nyoberwa aho ndi / Umutima urankuka, mba igishushungwe / Maze amabere yikora ntonsa, ayiweeeee."
21. "Inzira zose zabaye ibigunda / Ya misozi myiza yuzuye amatongo / Ahakinaga abana, harakina inkona ayiweee."
22. "Amarira y'imfubyi ntatuma usinzira / Umubyeyi wabyaye bamugize incike / Abapfakazi benshi barwaye intimba, ayiweeee."
23. "Kiliziya z'Imana zuzuye imirambo / Mu gihugu ahenshi hatabye mine / N'iyo bucyeye, ntuba uzi ko bwira, ayiweeee / Bashoreye abantu boshye ibitungwa / Bajya kubica ba bagome / Ngo kuba Umututsi ni icyaha kibi, ayiweeee / Umuhutu utishe ngo ntakabeho / Ngo ni icyitso cy'Inkotanyi akwiye gupfa / Mu muryango we hasigaye ngererwa, ayiweeee."
24. "Babakiniyeho biteye isoni/ Barabacuje ku gasozi / Iyo nzira yabaye iya Gologota, ayiweeee / Babishe urubozo ntacyo bishisha/ Bivuga cyane babihiga / Utishwe n'umupanga, yazize ifuni, ayiweee / Kwicwa n'isasu ngo banza urihe, nutabagurira ucagagurwe / Iryo ni ishyano ryabize gihanura, ayiweeee / Intego yabo ni ugutsembatsemba / Ari umubyeyi ukwiye kubabyara/ n'igisekeramwanzi nticyarokotse, ayiweeee / Nambaje Uhoraho ngo bibe inzozi / Ariko biranga biba impamo / Mbuze uwo ndirira, ndayamira, ayiweee."
25. "Ese ngire nte bagenzi?"
26. "Ntamubaza impinja yahotoye / Nkamubaza abasore n'inkumi / Nkamubaza ababyeyi yafomoje."
27. "Leta y'Ubumwe, yo yankoze mu nkokora, kwihorera ikabimbuza."
28. "Nkakunda gutaramana na sogoluru / Akambwira ubwiza n'ibyiza by'u Rwanda / Ni we wansobanuriye ko ari ho iwacu / Umhhh, icyamara agahinda / ooohhh, ni icyanyereka iwacu."
29. "umuvandimwe wabaye umwishi or umwicanyi."
30. "Nyibutsa nkwibutse kuri uyu munsi twibuka / Naherutse ukubitwa ibyuma n'imipanga / Njye narabohojwe nkurizamwo guta umutwe / None nteze umunsi, nanduye nyagutsindwa / . . . Aho ngenda hose, numva ijwi rimpamagara / Ngo 'genda mwana, batakunsinda mu maso' / Uwo yari mama, abohozwa n'abo tungana / Aho nari nishishe, njye yapfuye mureba / Nabyaye benshi, mbuze uwo ntuma amazi."
31. "Mugenzi wanjye twasangiraga byose / yambanye inyamanswa, imwe iruta iy'ishyamba / Musabye ngo ampishe ati 'sanga benewanyu' / Yakomeje ambwira ati 'tubana uri igicucu / ese ubwo ntiwumva amabwiriza y'umubyeyi? / Umugambi ni umwe, twiyemeje gutsemba / Ndetse mva mu maso cyangwa nkwirangirize."
32. "We yavutse heza none ni mayibobo / Undi ni ikimuga cyashegeshwe n'imihoro / Uko turi batatu, ni twe twitwa abarokotse."
33. "Nta wiyungira ku nzika, kirazira / Nta n'ubumwe burimo inzigo / Ariko ukuri kurubaka / Dusabe Nyagasani, tuzunge ubumwe."
34. "Uuunhhmmm, ngo kwiyunga ni ngombwa / Simbirwanya, mbihariye ubutabera."
35. "Banyarwanda twese, tuzi ibyabaye iwacu / Dufatanye rero, bitazapfa bigarutse."

36. Korman, "La politique de mémoire du genocide." "Euphémisation" and "déconflictualisation," respectively). See also Gillou, *Au Rwanda, le pardon est-il durable?*
37. Korman, "La politique de mémoire du genocide," 7.
38. "La politique de mémoire du genocide," 7.

Bibliography

Chemouni, Benjamin, and Assumpta Mugiraneza. "Ideology and Interests in the Rwandan Patriotic Front: Singing the Struggle in Pre-genocide Rwanda." *African Affairs* 119, no. 474 (2020): 115–40.

Dumas, Hélène. *Le Génocide au village. Le massacre des Tutsi au Rwanda*. Paris: Le Seuil, 2014.

Fujii, Lee Ann. *Killing Neighbors: Webs of Violence in Rwanda*. Ithaca, NY: Cornell University Press, 2011.

Gansemans, Jos. *Les Instruments de musique du Rwanda: étude ethnomusicologique*. Leuven: Leuven University Press, 1988.

Gillou, Benoit. *Au Rwanda, le pardon est-il durable? Une enquête au Rwanda*. Paris: Édition François Bourin, 2014.

Kerstens, Paul. "Amahoro. Chanter après le genocide." In *Les Langages de la mémoire. Littérature, médias et génocide au Rwanda (textes réunis)*, edited by Pierre Halen and Jacques Walter, 89–104. Metz: Université Paul Verlaine, 2007.

Korman, Rémi. "Indirimbo z'icyunamo. Chanter la mémoire du génocide." *Les Temps Modernes* 4 (2014): 350–61.

———. "La politique de mémoire du génocide des Tutsi au Rwanda: enjeux et evolutions." *Droit et Cultures*, no. 66 (2013): 87–101.

Mbonimana, Gamaliel. *La Musique rwandaise traditionnelle*. Butare: Éditions de l'Université Nationale du Rwanda, 1971.

Mbonimana, Gamaliel, and Jean-Chrysostome Nkejabahizi. *Amateka y'ubuvaganzo nyarwanda kuva mu kinyejana cya XVII kugeza magingo aya* [The history of Rwandan arts from the seventeenth century to the present day]. Butare: Editions de l'Université Nationale du Rwanda, 2011.

McCoy, Janson. "Making Violence Ordinary: Radio, Music and the Rwandan Genocide." *African Music* 8, no. 3 (2009): 85–96.

Mugiraneza, Assumpta. "Annexes: Chants du deuil." *Histoire de la justice* 28, no. 1 (2018): 237–42.

———. "La langue blessée." In *Clinique du trauma*, edited by Ghislaine Capogna-Bardet, 123–40. Toulouse: ERES/Centre Primo Levi, 2014.

———. "Rebuilding Rwanda: Challenges in Education on the Genocide." In *Combating Intolerance, Exclusion and Violence through Holocaust Education*, 55–61. Paris: UNESCO, 2009.

Nsengimana, Joseph. "Cyezamitima de Cyprien Rugamba: tradition et modernité." *Études rwandaises* 1, no. 2 (1987): 138–44.

Nyemazi, Pascal. *La Poésie et la chanson de Cyprien Rugamba, Tradition et Modernité*. Saint Denis: Edilivre, 2011.

Ubaldo, Rafiki, and Helen Hintjens. "Rwandan Music-Makers Negotiate Shared Cultural Identities after Genocide: The Case of Orchestre Impala's Revival." *Cultural Studies* 34, no. 6 (2020): 925–58.

Urbain, Olivier. "A Statement of Values for Our Research on Music in Peacebuilding: A Synthesis of Galtung and Ikeda's Peace Theories." *Journal of Peace Education* 13, no. 3 (2016): 218–37.

Part IV
MUSIC FOR PEACE AND RECONCILIATION?

Chapter 12

PEACEMAKING AND FESTIVITIES AT THE CONGRESS OF PARIS, 1856

Damien Mahiet

Contemporaries approached the Congress of Paris (25 February–30 March 1856) as a chapter in a history that began with the Napoleonic Wars and the Congress of Vienna and that needed to be supplanted, if not erased. Edouard-Louis Dubufé's painting *Le Congrès de Paris* (1856-57), modeled after Isabey's seminal group portrait for the Congress of Vienna (*Le Congrès de Vienne*, 1815), captured a conception of the past as a palimpsest for the present. Both paintings, in the genre of conversation pieces, foreground the practice of multilateral diplomacy.[1] Centered on diplomats rather than sovereigns, they depict a moment of relaxation rather than an exchange at the negotiation table.[2] Yet the similarity of the paintings also makes a program of redress apparent. There is no counterpart, in Dubufé's painting, to the figures of Metternich and Talleyrand, who, with their gaze facing the viewer, held a prominent place in Isabey's composition; instead, the only gaze turned toward the viewer is that of Napoleon I, whose portrait hangs in the shadows where those of Austrian sovereigns once appeared.[3] Similarly, the bust of Napoleon III now replaces that of the eighteenth-century Austrian chancellor Kaunitz. At the edge of the scene, where the stance of a Russian diplomat actively engaged other participants in Isabey's painting, the Ottoman ambassador Mehmed Emin Âli Pasha now holds his hand up. It was precisely in the absence of the Ottoman Empire at the Congress of Vienna that the historian and political commentator Sirtema de Grovestins found fault: in his 1856 essay, he invited negotiators

---

Notes for this section begin on page 239.

to find in the "mirror of the past a guide to the present" to correct the "imperfect work" of the Congress of Vienna and the "disorderly power" of Russia.[4] In the end, Article 7 of the Treaty of Paris would grant the Ottoman Empire "its admission to the advantages of European public law and concert."[5]

This essay focuses on the meaning ascribed to peacemaking festivities in reports and accounts of the Congress of Paris, which, much like the composition of Dubufé's painting, advanced a bid for a reformed Concert of Europe. The Congress of Paris solidified the invention of a specific tradition that tied together multilateral negotiations with festivities. Press articles published during the Congress foreground a historiographical turn that, while highlighting the shortcomings of diplomacy at the 1814–15 Congress of Vienna, gave credence to the sustaining and prefigurative functions of festivities as performances and experiences of a world at peace. Music together with dance, costumes, and decorative arts served as a script and symbol of harmony that made the diplomatic concert audible and visible. Balls especially were a privileged site of concert politics that engaged diplomatic actors directly in a space implicitly filled and regulated by music. While foregrounding international ensembles, diplomatic festivities also mediated dissonance, difference, and competition. Far from opposing war to peace, they ritualized the sound of the cannon and the cries of the multitude as shared components of national and international community.

Peacemaking and Congress Festivities

Recent scholarship on the Congress of Vienna and on works composed for the occasion has reassessed the significance of aesthetic and social activity in the definition of international stakes and the perception of multilateral negotiations.[6] The debate over whether festivities pertain to or distract from the labor of diplomacy emerged early in the 19th century: the oft quoted (and misquoted) bon mot of Austrian diplomat Prince de Ligne portrayed the Congress as a place "for dancing rather than peacemaking" (le congrès danse, il ne marche pas). But this assessment was open for debate, and in 1820 the historian Gaëtan de Raxis de Flassan objected that "this witticism had no ground, for the Congress was moving forward."[7]

Flassan's take on the festivities as a practice that enabled diplomats to sustain difficult negotiations informed many a memoirist. Countess Bernstorff, for example, understood the entertainments to mitigate the Congress's heavy atmosphere.[8] In the memoirs of the Duchess of Abrantes, a misquotation of the bon mot—"at least the Congress dances, if it does not advance"—introduced a depiction of Vienna as a "place of enchantment and delights."[9] There, the magical unfolding of "perfumed golden pages where the eye only reads joy, festivities, love, happiness, ambition" numbed people until a "cabalistic word, Napoleon," brought an abrupt end to these voluptuous days.[10] If the Prince de Ligne remains a central figure of the Congress in *Festivities and reminiscences from the Congress of Vienna*, published in Paris and Leipzig in 1843 by Auguste-Louis-Charles de Messence, comte de La Garde-Chambonas, he is no longer portrayed as a witty critic of its proceedings.[11] Instead of the famed bon mot, La Garde-Chambonas highlights a different quotation on his title page that describes the Congress as "a political fabric all embroidered with festivities."[12]

In the work of La Garde-Chambonas, De Ligne becomes the privileged observer of a new mode of peacemaking: "Diplomacy and pleasure are almost always at war; [yet] in Vienna, one sees them walking hand in hand," La Garde-Chambonas has the prince declare toward the beginning of the Congress.[13] A few months later, the prince still holds the same view: "guided by pleasure, we advance gaily in the midst of balls, festivals, games, and carrousels to the great outcome of this wise assembly. The day will likely come when [this assembly] will allow us to know Europe's destinies."[14] Vienna offered Congress participants a continuous succession of "féeries," or festivities imbued with a sense of poetry and magic.[15] A performance of *Partant pour la Syrie*, with music by Hortense de Beauharnais (the mother of Napoleon III), offered the opportunity to highlight Prince de Ligne's appreciation for music, "a universal language" that "harmoniously relates life's sensations to all ears."[16] La Garde depicted the prince writing a bagatelle on the "Congress of Love" two weeks before his death: Cupid commands Minerva to surrender to pleasures and, having at long last exhausted them, agrees to peace and the conclusion of the Congress.[17] The verses convey some impatience, but they still dismiss critiques against an extraordinary mode of peacemaking.

"The memorable examples of Vienna in 1814 are not lost to the Paris of 1856, and it is well known that congresses move forward best when they dance," Philippe Busoni mused in the journal *L'Illustration* on 16 February 1856.[18] For the chronicler of diplomatic life, the pursuit of pleasures, music, and dance offered clues as to the advancement of negotiations otherwise kept secret. On 12 January already, Busoni noted the likely resurrection of diplomatic sociability:

> In high foreign diplomacy, which in the eyes of a certain world offers mostly balls and feasts, it was once customary to divide the week so that each power had its day of reception, and this conciliatory program may be about to start again. The ambassadors would, one at a time, open their salons to the grand European quadrilles, where one might for example see England inviting Prussia into the dance, and so forth.[19]

Two weeks later, Busoni returned to the topic: "In the high world, all kinds of munificence are getting readied. Is it not right to offer a ball bouquet to European diplomats in exchange for the olive branch they bring? The ladies are on the war path to bring forth peace, which never advances faster than to the tune of violins. . . . Each day in February will have its thousand and one nights."[20] Busoni pondered a dearth of balls on 1 March, but noted that the conclusion of negotiations should bring about the return of peace and of dance.[21] This was confirmed on 22 March:

> Even before closing the temple of Janus for good, the salons are being opened wide. . . . Russia itself, or at least its still all too rare representatives, do not lack politeness. Monday, concert at Madam the countess Pozzo di Borgo; Tuesday, another concert at Madam the Princess Bagration: such are the preludes of a happy accord that the wisdom of diplomats will well make definitive.[22]

The pace of social life was only compounded by the peace treaty: "the diplomatists," one could read in *The Morning Advertiser*, "dine and dance, like merry warsailors as they are."[23]

L'Illustration interspersed these reports with, on 23 February and 1 March, a two-part history of the Congress of Vienna that went a step further in affirming a prefigurative function of festivities while also observing that diplomats could fall short of their aspirational program. The author of this history, Paul Bruno, acknowledged that "it would be difficult to show the trace [of the ardent love of pleasure] in the decisions" made there, but he found it possible to "say without fear that it acted on the people who led [foreign] affairs."[24] Yet the outcome of the Congress of Vienna had been ambiguous, and Bruno bemoaned that "the contrasts between the greatness of events and the narrowness of ideas, and between the urbanity of social relations and the fierceness of greedy desires, formed a unique spectacle."[25] As a result, the very name of diplomacy had suffered from the Congress's shortcomings. "Up until then," Bruno found, "diplomats had formed a distinct and honored class, [but] from that time on, people got into the habit, which continues today, of denying their utility, expecting nothing good from their unending disputes, and ridiculing them."[26]

In contrast, the Congress of Paris offered festive diplomacy an opportunity to prove itself anew. In a history of the Congress published in 1857, Edouard Gourdon, a publicist who served the Second Empire in an official capacity, underscored the role of the government as a diplomatic host, the function of sociability in political communication, and the opportunities that "moments of distraction, one might even say recreation" afforded actors with no direct seat at the negotiation table.[27] At the first dinner and concert at the ministry of foreign affairs on 25 February, for example, women took advantage of social occasions to enter the diplomatic stage: in this instance, they "invade[d] the *Salon des Ambassadeurs*" and took up pens and paper from the negotiation table to write a "magical word"—and demand!—"peace."[28] Festivities also offered opportunities for informal yet visible conversations between plenipotentiaries and the French sovereign, Napoleon III.[29] Governmental festivities that Gourdon reports include dinners at the Tuileries to honor the plenipotentiaries of each country in turn as well as a vaudeville and musical divertissement, a dinner at the ministry of war, dinners and concerts at the ministry of foreign affairs, a ball at the ministry of finance, and a dinner at the ministry of interior, all in March.[30] Gourdon reports only two social occasions at foreign embassies, hosted by British and Austrian representatives.[31] But the volume of entertainments offered by embassies, private hosts, and musical entrepreneurs created sharp competition among them. In "a night worthy of the *One and Thousand Nights*," *L'Illustration* counted 37 concerts not including private occasions.[32] Festive peacemaking thus demanded a degree of endurance: "some stomachs protested," and "not all the honorable diplomats bore this life equally well."[33] As trivial as they may seem, reports of this physical toll also serve as a reminder that the performers of festive diplomatic life were not only the artists engaged for the occasion, but also the diplomats, sovereigns, and high society members who participated in and experienced these events.

International Compositions

Diplomatic festivities at the Congress of Paris were thus at once theatre oriented toward a public and ritual engaging the participants.[34] They created opportunities for the symbolic recomposition of international relations and community. For example, three balls held between February and April publicized, even before the publication of the treaty, a bid to incorporate the Ottoman Empire into the Concert of Europe.³⁵ While the record of the musical repertoire of balls is frequently lacking beyond the mention of its function as harmonious background, balls formed a significant site of the sensible politics of concert diplomacy, with music scripting the placement and motions of the diplomats' bodies into a concerted ensemble.³⁶ In this instance, the series of balls expanded the diplomatic space of the Congress to Constantinople where, in February, ambassadors of the United Kingdom and France hosted balls in the presence of the sultan. This was followed, in April, by the Ottoman ambassador's ball in Paris. The presence of the sultan in February signaled a historic moment characterized by the advent of a new diplomatic urbanity. In the words of the *Times* in London, "the presence of the Sultan at the fancy ball [at the English embassy] . . . was a remarkable event. It is looked upon as preliminary to a complete revolution in the etiquette observed hitherto at the palace of Tcheragan, which, for some time past, tends to the adoption of the usages observed in Western Courts."³⁷

The British and French press foregrounded in particular "the Ottoman emperor's acknowledgment of the reciprocity of social duties" as a symbol of the empire's entrance into the European concert.³⁸ The performance of this reciprocity took multiple forms, from ceremonial gestures to dress and décor.³⁹ Compliments and thanks were repeatedly exchanged in demonstratively "affable conversation."⁴⁰ At the French embassy, military music included the "Mahmudiye March" for Sultan Mahmud II by Giuseppe Donizetti, Gaetano's brother.⁴¹ At the Ottoman embassy in Paris, the décor, featuring flowers and shrubs, offered a pastoral frame for "one of the most brilliant fêtes of the season" and paid homage to the Napoleonic regime. The *Morning Chronicle* reported: "Besides the ordinary state rooms of the Hotel Forbin Janson, in which the Turkish Ambassador resides, numerous additional salons on either side of the garden were fitted up specially for this occasion. One of the drawing rooms, hung throughout with white silk, studded with golden bees, was particularly admired."⁴² Sovereigns and diplomats harbored honorific insignia recently awarded as a mark of alliance and recognition. At the Ottoman embassy, the emperor "wore the Ottoman order of Medjidie, and Aali Pacha, the Grand Vizier, wore the grand cordon of the Legion of Honour just given him by the Emperor."⁴³ More generally, guests appeared "in uniform or Court dress . . . in consequence of the sultan having lately attended a ball at the French embassy in Constantinople in military uniform."⁴⁴

Nonetheless, differences between the Ottoman Empire and France or the United Kingdom still remained. The costume ball of the British embassy fused British historical costumes—a lady of the reign of George III, a druidess, Mary Queen of Scots—with other regional and national costumes. A British guest could hardly contain her enthusiasm at the sight:

> for besides the gathering of French, Sardinian, and English officers, the people of the country appeared in their own superb and varied costumes. The Greek Patriarch, the Armenian Archbishop, the Jewish High Priest were there, in their robes of state. Real Persians, Albanians, Kourds, Servians, Armenians, Greeks, Turks, Austrians, Sardinians, Italians, and Spaniards, were there in their different dresses, and many wore their jeweled arms. Some of the Greek yataghans and pistols were splendid. Two Jewish ladies were almost covered with diamonds. There were Fakirs, and Pilgrims, and Knights in real chain-armor, and Dervishes, and Maltese ladies, and Roman Empresses, English Shepherdesses, and Persian Princesses, and Turkish ladies without their vails. Of course, there were also the usual oddities of a fancy ball; there was a Negro king, dressed in white and red feathers, and two gentlemanly Devils in black velvet, who waltzed with their long forked tails twined gracefully under their arms. Italian Bravos and Princes, Spanish Dons and Brigands, were of course plentiful. In fact, every costume in the known world was to be met with: queens and shepherdesses; emperors and caiquejees; Crimean heroes, ambassadors, attachés, and diplomatists.[45]

The fusion of the artificial and the real along with the proliferation of character types enhanced the fantastic appearance of this diplomatic microcosm and its fairy-tale aesthetic. The commingling of characters typically kept separate by time, geography, race, class, and gender offered a unique tableau. However, the very effect of the gathering depended on the continued awareness of differences. News reports emphasized the sultan's pleasure and delight, but also recorded his surprise, and even annoyance, at the sight of guests costumed as a Muslim dervish, a Sultan Selim, or (in an instance of both cross-culture and cross-gender acting) a Turkish woman.[46] In addition, while the *Sheffield Daily Telegraph* boasted that the United Kingdom was introducing "dancing, ball-going and merry-making among the Osmanlees," the sultan himself did not dance, but observed the "unknown entertainments" of the quadrille from a platform.[47] The distanced gaze of the Ottoman sovereign contrasted with Napoleon III's participation in the quadrille of honor at the Ottoman embassy's ball in Paris along with members of the French military and representatives of Sardinia, Belgium, and England.[48]

On such occasions, absences were also noted and their significance pondered; "it was remarked," one read in the *Morning Chronicle*, "that Count Orlov and Baron Brun[n]ow did not appear at the fête."[49] The absence of the Russian delegation raised questions about continued enmity, and the press offered contradictory interpretations. For the *London Evening Standard*, the absence "created quite a sensation, as no ground is even alleged for such an apparent slight upon Turkey."[50] The *Daily News* instead reported hearsay "that the reason for their absence was unconnected with politics."[51] But the *Times* conveyed sarcastic praise for the excuse presented by the Russian delegation:

> The Russian diplomatists have, it appears, sent an excuse for not being present; the reason assigned is, that one of the *attachés* has the measles. Who shall say that the Muscovites are a barbarous people, or that they are indifferent to human life? If the excuse be not a pleasantry—a stroke of Russian wit—nothing can be more deserving eulogy than this self-imposed restraint.[52]

Even after the conclusion of the negotiations, Dubufé's painting, which depicted the Russian diplomat Orlov looking away from his Ottoman colleague Âli, captured the slight of avoidance. Dubufé also left uncertain the relation between Orlov and his Austrian counterpart Buol: Orlov has his back to Buol, and while the latter casually holds the back of the chair on which Orlov sits, this may also be interpreted as a watchful if not restraining gesture. In his history of the Congress, Gourdon insisted on dispelling the idea that Orlov and Buol might have purposefully avoided one another at an evening hosted by the British ambassador.[53] He pointed instead to their "long," "lively," and "cordial" conversation the following day at the Tuileries: "The two diplomats, to be freer, stood slightly apart, behind the spectators; they were nonetheless noticed."[54] Whatever the case may have been, the interpretation of an absence as a possible slight points to the capacity of diplomatic festivities to mediate conflict as well as peacemaking.

Symbolic Recompositions of Space

Paradoxically, diplomatic festivities did much to blur the spatial and functional division between war and peace. Entertainments took place within a competitive economy of prestige, patronage, and gifts constitutive of cultural diplomacy from the sixteenth century onwards. A close examination of the chronology of musical programming in

1856 brings to the fore the use of the Opéra in January, during the allied Council of War that preceded the Congress.[55] Two gratis performances on 12 and 19 January, held to celebrate the return of the *Armée de l'Orient*, featured Auber's *Le Philtre* and the ballet *Le Diable à quatre*.[56] Willa Collins points to a third celebratory performance at the Opéra, this time featuring the ballet *Le Corsaire* only a few days after it premièred on 23 January.[57] (The press later reported the presence of the Russian diplomat Brunnow at a performance of the ballet in February.[58]) Adapted from Byron's poem, the libretto had been expunged of all traces of political conflict between Greek and Turk characters.[59] With the beginning of the Congress, the musical repertoire of official events expanded to an eclectic mixture of cosmopolitan genres, from Italian opera music by Donizetti, Verdi, and Bellini to a French comic opera by Aubert and Scribe. Performances featured artists from a broad range of institutions, such as the Paris Opéra, the Opéra-Comique, and the Conservatoire, as well as musical entrepreneurs and solo artists like the violinist Alard, the bass player Bottesini, the conductor Jules Pasdeloup, and the composer and theatre director Jacques Offenbach.[60]

As noted by Mark Everist, this pot-pourri of Parisian musical life, which included members of the Théâtre des Variétés and the Théâtre du Palais-Royal, suggests a more intimate and less ceremonial approach to entertainment than the performances initially hosted at the Opéra.[61] At the same time, this programming, with the work of Offenbach in particular, outlines a distinctive aesthetics crucial to the Second Empire's self-presentation and its hodgepodge of modernity and tradition.[62] *Les Deux Aveugles*, performed at the Tuileries on 28 February, and *Ba-Ta-Clan*, presented the following day to the diplomats by the president of the *Corps législatif*, Charles de Morny, celebrated Parisian life at the same time as they poked fun at the political and social roles individuals adopt through self-interest.[63] In this regard, the negative response recorded in the diary of the Austrian representative Hübner—"little, foul show" to describe *Les Deux Aveugles*, for example—reveals not only a difference in individual taste but also a gap between the diplomat's expectations and the program proposed by the French government.[64] Hübner took it to reveal a lack of judgment on the part of Félix Baciocchi, the man responsible for court entertainments, but the presentation of Offenbach's work could also be read as an aesthetic affirmation of the regime's distinctive and revisionist identity.[65]

In the early process of peacemaking, between February and April, festivities appeared to fill the void left by increasing "tranquility" on the "theatre of war."[66] As early as January, the *Morning Chronicle* noted that "the constant endeavours to destroy the *ennui* of camp life by theatricals, concerts, and champagne dinners weary by their repetition, and are scarcely consistent with the notions of a state of war."[67] With the birth of an heir to the French throne on 16 March and the news of the peace treaty signing on 30 March came expectations of festivities across enemy lines: "Leave has been asked by the Russian Officers of their Commander-in-Chief to be allowed to give a Ball to the Allied Armies, and the French are actually going to construct a Ballroom."[68] If the name of Napoleon and the sound of the cannon had disbanded the Congress of Vienna, they now signaled, on the contrary, the success of diplomacy. The birth of the prince provided the occasion to unify diplomatic, civic, and military spaces into one resounding festival. The 101 cannon shots that awoke Paris on 16 March were heard a week later in Crimea, according to military reports, and fired simultaneously by the French, British, and Sardinian armies.[69] The singing of the *Te Deum*, the celebratory cries, and illuminations completed the program that prefigured the return of peace, even if the performance of amity also proved taxing: a report from the "Camp before Sebastopol, 25 March," while extolling "many demonstrations of the *entente cordiale*" between the French and the British, qualified this account by noting that soldiers had done "their best to be 'happy together.'"[70] The 101 cannon shots were repeated for the proclamation of peace, and the *Times* special correspondent William Russell, who had often invoked the "roar" of the cannons in his narratives of battles, now also heard their "thundering voices" exulting in happy news.[71]

    The transformation of the significance of the cannon, from cry to "voice" and from chaos to celebration, completed the labor of symbolic recomposition.[72] Gourdon's narrative concludes on April 1 with the military parade at the Champ de Mars and elides the negotiations and festivities that continued that month. The "magnificent *fête*" of the military parade was a demonstration of power: France had, "without weakening itself domestically, sent 250,000 fighters to Crimea" and remained "wealthy enough in men to have nothing to fear."[73] In a striking metaphorical inversion, men took on a more primal quality than the cannon itself as the crowd's "cry of pride and enthusiasm" filled the Champ de Mars "better than the voice of the cannon."[74] Before the end of the month, the United Kingdom responded in kind with the Great Armament, a naval parade of steam ships, gunboats, and floating batteries that reaffirmed its claims over the oceans.[75] Beyond the harmonious accord of a plural world, or the communal silence of memorial ceremonies, the Concert of Europe restored by the Congress of Paris found in the sound of war the first element of international sonorous coexistence.

Damien Mahiet is director of academic programs at the Cogut Institute for the Humanities at Brown University. He coedited, with Rebekah Ahrendt and Mark Ferraguto, *Music and Diplomacy from the Early Modern Era to the Present* (Palgrave Macmillan, 2014). His articles have appeared in *Eighteenth-Century Music*, *Haydn-Studien*, *19th-Century Music*, *Dance Research*, *History of European Ideas*, and the *Journal of International Political Theory*. Trained in political thought (MA, Sciences Po Paris) and musicology (PhD, Cornell University), he is a former fellow of the Mahindra Humanities Center at Harvard University.

Notes

1. On the making and legacy of Isabey's painting, see Telesko, "Mundus concors?," 17–27, and "The Visual 'Afterlife,'" 372–81.
2. On the fictional moment captured in the painting, see Telesko, "Jean-Baptiste Isabey," 130–31.
3. See Felbinger, "French Art in Vienna," 167–71.
4. Grovestins de, *Le Congrès de Vienne*.
5. Adanir, "Turkey's Entry into the Concert of Europe," 414.
6. Among recent publications, the first three chapters of Brian Vick's admirable *The Congress of Vienna* give a rich account of the role of festivities and music in diplomacy while Nicholas Mathew's study of the *Political Beethoven* elucidates the musical composition of the moment. For a broader overview of the Congress's historiography, see Jonathan Kwan, "The Congress of Vienna: Diplomacy, Political Culture, and Sociability."
7. Raxis de Flassan, *Histoire du congrès de Vienne*, 156n1: "Cette saillie n'était pas fondée; car le Congrès marchait." On Flassan's argument, see Mahiet, "The Diplomat's Music Test," 116, and more broadly, Mahiet, "The Musical Diplomacy of Metternich."
8. Bernstorff, *Ein Bild aus der Zeit*, 148.
9. Junot, *Mémoires*, 314: "Vienne était à cette époque un lieu d'enchantement et de délices."
10. Junot, *Mémoires*, 314–15: "on était engourdi par une magie qui déroulait ses pages d'or parfumées où l'œil ne lisait que joies, fêtes, amour, bonheur, ambition."
11. The heavily amended 1901 edition dates the first publication to 1820, which is doubtful. The 1843 edition includes a dedication to the Prince de Ligne dated 1 September 1842. La Garde, *Fêtes et souvenirs du congrès de Vienne*. The work is also printed in Brussels with the same publication date. Vick (*Congress of Vienna*, 367n65) characterizes the memoirs as "notoriously unreliable." Hilda Spiel defends the partial value of La Garde as an eyewitness, in *Congress of Vienna*, 316–17. Harold Nicolson mentions La Garde's memoir and its "horrible

gusto" to deride the "unending series of drawing-rooms, balls, banquets and gala performances which took place" at the Congress. See Nicolson, *The Congress of Vienna*, 161.

12. La Garde, *Fêtes et souvenirs*, vol. 1, 3 and 29, and vol. 2, 3: "C'est un tissu politique tout brodé de fêtes."
13. *Fêtes et souvenirs*, vol. 1, 38: "La diplomatie et le plaisir se font presque toujours la guerre ; à Vienne, on les voit se donner la main et marcher en compagnie."
14. *Fêtes et souvenirs*, vol. 1, 421: "A bientôt me dit-il, puisque, guidés par le plaisir, c'est au milieu des bals, des fêtes, des jeux, des carrousels que nous avançons gaiment vers le grand résultat de cette docte assemblée. Le jour viendra probablement où elle nous permettra de connaitre les destinées de l'Europe."
15. *Fêtes et souvenirs*, vol. 1, 295 and 547.
16. *Fêtes et souvenirs*, vol. 1, 288: "La musique est une langue universelle : elle raconte harmonieusement à toutes les oreilles les sensations de la vie." The queen set some of La Garde's verses into music, which La Garde published in 1853, soon after the beginning of the Second Empire, along with a biographical sketch and personal memories; see La Garde, *Album artistique de la reine Hortense*.
17. *Album artistique de la reine Hortense*, vol. 1, 416–17.
18. Philippe Busoni, "Courrier de Paris," *L'Illustration* (16 February 1856), 103: "Les mémorables précédents de Vienne, en 1814, ne seront pas perdus pour le Paris de 1856, et l'on sait bien que les congrès ne marchent jamais mieux que quand ils dansent." On the journal's role in mediating court life to a broader audience, see Truesdell, *Spectacular Politics*, 9 and 22.
19. Philippe Busoni, "Courrier de Paris," *L'Illustration* (12 January 1856), 18: "Dans la haute diplomatie étrangère, laquelle, aux yeux d'un certain monde, représente principalement des bals et des festins, il était d'usage autrefois de se partager la semaine de manière à ce que chaque puissance avait son jour de réception; et ce programme conciliateur serait en voie de reprise. MM. les ambassadeurs ouvriraient à tour de rôle leurs salons à de grands quadrilles européens, où l'on verrait, par exemple, l'Angleterre faire danser la Prusse, et ainsi de suite."
20. Philippe Busoni, "Courrier de Paris," *L'Illustration* (2 February 1856), 72: "Dans la haute société, toutes sortes de magnificences se préparent en vue du congrès. N'est-il pas juste d'offrir le bouquet de bal aux diplomates européens, en échange du rameau d'olivier qu'ils nous apportent ? Ces dames se mettent à l'envie sur le pied de guerre pour accélérer la paix qui ne marche jamais plus vite qu'au son des violons . . . chacun des jours de février aura ses mille et une nuits."
21. Philippe Busoni, "Courrier de Paris," *L'Illustration* (1 March 1856), 134: "ce n'est pas seulement la paix, mais la danse qui doit sortir de leurs protocoles."
22. Philippe Busoni, "Courrier de Paris," *L'Illustration* (22 March 1856), 182: "Avant même que le temple de Janus soit fermé pour tout de bon, les salons s'ouvrent de plus belle . . . La Russie elle-même, ou du moins ses représentants encore trop rares, ne sont pas en reste de politesse. Lundi, concert chez Mme la comtesse Pozzo di Borgo, mardi autre concert chez Mme la princesse Bagration. Tels sont les préludes d'un heureux accord que la sagesse des diplomates saura bien rendre définitive."
23. *The Morning Advertiser* (10 April 1856), 5.
24. Paul Bruno, "Le Congrès de Vienne en 1814," *L'Illustration* (23 February 1856): 118. "Il serait difficile d'en montrer la trace dans les résolutions qui ont été prises . . . mais comme il était dans l'air que l'on respirait, on peut dire sans crainte qu'il agit malgré elles et à leur insu sur les personnes qui dirigeaient les affaires."

25. Bruno, "Le Congrès de Vienne: Suite et fin," 139: "D'ailleurs toutes ces passions et toutes ces intrigues, ces dissensions entre des hommes qui travaillaient à une œuvre commune, le contraste entre la grandeur des événements et l'étroitesse des idées, entre l'urbanité des relations sociales et l'âpreté des convoitises, formaient un spectacle unique."
26. Idem: "Jusqu'à ce moment les diplomates avaient formé une classe à part et honorée ; à partir de cette époque on prit l'habitude, qui dure encore, de nier leur utilité, de n'augurer rien de bon de leurs interminables disputes et de les tourner en ridicule."
27. Gourdon, *Histoire du congrès de Paris*, 487. On Gourdon, see Bruley, *Le Quai d'Orsay Impérial*, 165.
28. Ibid., 492.
29. Hübner records in his diary a number of conversations with Napoléon III at balls; see Hübner, *Neuf ans de souvenirs*, 378, 383, 386, and 389.
30. Gourdon, *Histoire du Congrès de Paris*, 495, 507–8, 520, and 526. Gourdon mentions the dinner honoring the Russian plenipotentiaries on 28 February 1856. The dinner offered to the Austrian plenipotentiaries on 24 February was followed by a small concert; see Comte de Hübner, *Neuf ans de souvenirs*, 396.
31. *Histoire du Congrès de Paris*, 507 and 511.
32. Philippe Busoni, "Courrier de Paris," *L'Illustration* (22 March 1856), 183.
33. Ibid., 511.
34. On the distinction and overlap, see Balzacq, "Rituels et diplomatie," 138–39.
35. On the ball as diplomatic relation, see for example Tyrrell, *The History of the War with Russia*, vol. 3, 116–18, and Candan Badem, *The Ottoman Crimean War*, 332–36. On the role of publicity in collective intention and Concert diplomacy, see Mitzen, *Power in Concert*, 42–46 and 102–41.
36. On the concept, see William A. Callahan, *Sensible Politics*.
37. "The Peace Conferences," *Times* (16 February 1856), 10.
38. Arthur Baligot de Beyne, "Le bal de l'ambassade française à Constantinople," *L'Illustration* (1 March 1856), 147. Baligot de Beyne served as a diplomat and journalist. A report of *L'Illustration* on the sultan's acceptance of the *grand cordon* of the Legion of Honour already made the point: "In the same way Turkey was, in certain aspects, outside the common law of nations, the sultan had prerogatives that would not have been tolerated in other courts." See "Remise du grand-cordon de la légion d'honneur par l'ambassadeur de France à Constantinople," *L'Illustration* (19 January 1856): 35–36.
39. *The Manchester Examiner and Times* (12 April 1856, 5) describes the presence of the French emperor at the Turkish embassy as made "in return for the presence of the Sultan at the ball of M. Thouvenel, the French ambassador at Constantinople."
40. Arthur Baligot de Beyne, "Le bal de l'ambassade française à Constantinople," *L'Illustration* (1 March 1856), 148.
41. Baligot de Beyne, "Le bal de l'ambassade française à Constantinople," 148. See also Einre Aracı, "Giuseppe Donizetti Pasha and the Polyphonic Court Music of the Ottoman Empire," *The Court Historian* 7, no. 2 (2002): 135–43.
42. *The Morning Chronicle* (14 April 1856), 6.
43. *The Daily News* [London] (14 April 1856), 5.
44. "Foreign Intelligence," *Times* (12 April 1856), 10.
45. Hornby, *In and Around Stamboul*, 218–19.
46. "The Sultan at the Ambassadors' Balls," *The Morning Chronicle* (18 February 1856), 6.

47. "Visit of the Sultan to the British Embassy," *The Sheffield Daily Telegraph* (18 February 1856): 2, and Baligot de Beyne, "Le bal de l'ambassade française," 148.
48. According to the *Morning Chronicle* (14 April 1856, 6), the quadrille was "composed of the Emperor with the Princess Mathilde; the Marquis de Villamarina, Sardinian Minister, with Lady Clarendon; Marshal Magnan with Madame Firman Rogier [the wife of the Belgian Ambassador]; and Marshal Canrobert with Lady Cowley." See also the *Illustrated London News* (12 April 1856), 2.
49. *The Morning Chronicle* (14 April 1856), 6.
50. *London Evening Standard* (14 April 1856), 2.
51. *The Daily News* [London] (14 April 1856), 5.
52. "Foreign Intelligence," *Times* (12 April 1856), 10.
53. Gourdon, *Histoire du congrès de Paris*, 507.
54. *Histoire du congrès de Paris*, 508: "Ce soir-là, le premier Plénipotentiaire Russe et M. de Buol, loin de s'éviter, causèrent longtemps ensemble avec une certaine animation, mais aussi avec cordialité. Les deux diplomates, pour être plus libres, s'étaient tenus un peu à l'écart derrière les spectateurs. Ils n'en furent pas moins très remarqués."
55. Everist, "The Empire at the Opéra," 24–31, and "Music, Theatre, and Diplomacy," 289–93.
56. Everist, "Opera, Soft Power, and Anglo-French Relations," 110,
57. Collins, *Adolphe Adam's Ballet* Le Corsaire, 152–59. I am grateful to Willa Collins for her kind answer to my query on the ballet.
58. "The Peace Conferences," *Times* [London, England] (16 February 1856), 10: "Baron de Brun[n]ow was present at the Grand Opéra on Wednesday night to witness the representation of the *Corsaire*."
59. Everist, "Opera, Soft Power, and Anglo-French Relations," 111.
60. Yon, "En marge des négociations," 180–84.
61. In a diary entry dated Rome, 20 March 1864, the diplomat Henry d'Ideville understands the success of French comic songs in Rome as a sign of the triumph of the "Parisian spirit" and the "immortal principles" of 1789. Ideville (d'), *Journal d'un diplomate*, 141.
62. See Schneider, "Du boulevard du Temple à la place du Châtelet," 224–25.
63. Yon, *Jacques Offenbach*, 164–65 and 171–72.
64. Hübner, *Neuf ans de souvenirs*, 398: "petit spectacle détestable."
65. Ibid., 399: "Décidément, ce pauvre Bacciochi n'est pas très heureux dans le choix des pièces." Jean-Claude Yon also points to the qualms of the minister of education, Hippolyte Fortoul, who enjoyed *Les Deux Aveugles* but wondered how appropriate it was to share the laugh with the "representatives of Europe"; quoted in Yon, "En marge des négociations," 183.
66. Paulin, "Histoire de la semaine," *L'Illustration* (2 February 1856), 70.
67. "Preliminaries of Peace," *The Morning Chronicle* (30 January 1856), 4.
68. "The British Army: Celebration of the Birth of a French Prince," *The Manchester Courier, and Lancashire General Advertiser* (12 April 1856), 4.
69. Hübner (*Neuf ans de souvenirs*, 403–4) writes that he was awakened on Sunday, 16 March, by the cannon of the Invalides. The report of Marshall Pélissier on the response of the armies to the news, dated 23 March, appears for example in the *Journal des débats politiques et littéraires* (30 March 1856), [1].
70. *The Constitution: Or, Cork Advertiser* (1 April 1856), 3.
71. Russell, *The British Expedition to the Crimea*, 467.
72. On the mediatization of the cannon and gunfire during the Crimean War, see the chapters by Peter McMurray, Gavin Williams, and Flora Willson in Williams, *Hearing the Crimean War*.

73. *Histoire du congrès de Paris.* Ibid., 527.
74. *Histoire du congrès de Paris.* Ibid., 527.
75. Tate, *A Short History of the Crimean War*, 153–55, and Lambert, *The Crimean War*, 336.

Bibliography

Adanir, Fikret. "Turkey's Entry into the Concert of Europe." *European Review* 13/3 (2005): 395–417.

Aracı, Einre. "Giuseppe Donizetti Pasha and the Polyphonic Court Music of the Ottoman Empire." *The Court Historian* 7, no. 2 (2002): 135–43.

Badem, Candan. *The Ottoman Crimean War (1853–1856)*. Leiden: Brill, 2010.

von Bernstorff, Elise. *Ein Bild aus der Zeit von 1789 bis 1835*. Berlin: Ernst Siegfried Mittler und Sohn, 1899.

Balzacq, Thierry. "Rituels et diplomatie." In *Manuel de diplomatie*, edited by Thierry Balzacq, Frédéric Charillon, and Frédéric Ramel, 129–141. Paris: Presse de Sciences Po, 2018.

Bruley, Yves. *Le Quai d'Orsay Impérial*. Paris: A. Pedone, 2012.

Hornby, Emilia. *In and Around Stamboul*. Philadelphia: James Challen & Son, Lindsay & Blakiston, n.d.

Callahan, William A. *Sensible Politics: Visualizing International Relations*. Oxford: Oxford University Press, 2020.

Collins, Willa. "Adolphe Adam's Ballet *Le Corsaire*, Paris Opéra, 1856–1868: A Source Study." PhD dissertation, Cornell University, 2008.

Everist, Mark. "Opera, Soft Power, and Anglo-French Relations in the Crimea (1855–1856)." In *Opera as Institution: Networks and Professions (1700–1914)*, edited by Cristina Scuderi and Ingeborg Zechner, 95–118109–10. Berlin: LIT-Verlag, 2019.

Everist, Mark. "Music, Theatre, and Diplomacy: The Paris Opéra during the Second Empire." *Diplomatica* 3 (2021): 278–301.

Everist, Mark. *The Empire at the Opéra: Theatre, Power and Music in Second Empire Paris*. Cambridge: Cambridge University Press, 2021.

Felbinger, Udo. "French Art in Vienna at the Time of the Congress." In *Europe in Vienna: The Congress of Vienna 1814–15*, edited by Agnes Husslein-Arco, Sabine Grabner, and Werner Telesko, 167–71. Vienna: Belveder and Hirmer Verlag, 2015.

de la Garde, Auguste. *Fêtes et souvenirs du congrès de Vienne: Tableaux de salons, Scènes anectdotiques, et Portraits 1814–15*. Paris: A. Appert and Leipzig: Brockhaus and Avenarius, 1843.

———. *Album artistique de la reine Hortense. Esquisse biographique sur le reine Hortense, Une visite à Augsbourg, Lettres*. Paris: Heugel, 1853.

Gourdon, Edouard. *Histoire du congrès de Paris*. Paris: Libraire nouvelle, 1857.

Grovestins de, Sirtema. *Le Congrès de Vienne en 1814 et 1815 et le congrès de Paris en 1856*. Paris: Dentu, 1856.

Hübner de, Alexandre. *Neuf ans de souvenirs d'un ambassadeur d'Autriche à Paris sous le Second Empire, 1851–1859*. Paris: Plon, 1904.

Ideville d', Henry. *Journal d'un diplomate en Italie: Rome, 1862–1866*. Paris: Hachette, 1873.

Junot, Laure. *Mémoires de Madame la duchesse d'Abrantès, ou Souvenirs historiques sur Napoléon: La Révolution, le Directoire, le Consulat, l'Empire et la Restauration*. Paris: Ladvocat, 1835.

Kwan, Jonathan. "The Congress of Vienna, 1814–1815: Diplomacy, Political Culture, and Sociability." *The Historical Journal* 60/4 (2017): 1125–46.

Lambert, Andrew D. *The Crimean War: British Grand Strategy, 1853–56*. Manchester: Manchester University Press, 1990.

Mahiet, Damien. "The Diplomat's Music Test: Branding New and Old Diplomacy at the Beginning of the Nineteenth and Twenty-First Centuries." In *International Relations, Music and Diplomacy: Sounds and Voices on the International Stage*, edited by Frédéric Ramel and Cécile Prévost-Thomas, 115–39. Cham: Palgrave Macmillan, 2018.

Mahiet, Damien. "The Musical Diplomacy of Metternich." *Diplomatica* 3 (2021): 244–77.

Mathew, Nicholas. *Political Beethoven*. Cambridge: Cambridge University Press, 2013.

Mitzen, Jennifer. *Power in Concert: The Nineteenth-Century Origins of Global Governance*. Chicago: The University of Chicago Press, 2013.

Nicolson, Harold. *The Congress of Vienna: A Study in Allied Unity*. New York: Grove Press, 1946.

Raxis de Flassan, Gaëtan de. *Histoire du congrès de Vienne par l'auteur de l'Histoire de la diplomatie*. Paris: Chez Treuttel et Wurtz, libraires, 1829.

Russell, William H. *The British Expedition to the Crimea*, new and revised edition. London: George Routledge and Sons, 1877.

Schneider, Corinne. "Du boulevard du Temple à la place du Châtelet, le Théâtre-Lyrique comme 'laboratoire de la musique.'" In *Les Spectacles sous le Second Empire*, edited by Jean-Claude Yon, 213–28. Paris: Armand Colin, 2010.

Spiel, Hilda. *Congress of Vienna: An Eyewitness Account*. Philadelphia: Chilton, 1968.

Tate, Trudi. *A Short History of the Crimean War*. London: I.B. Tauris, 2019.

Telesko, Werner. "Mundus concors? The Congress of Vienna and the European Iconography of Peace in the 19th Century," 17–27. In *Europe in Vienna: The Congress of Vienna 181415*, edited by Agnes Husslein-Arco, Sabine Grabner, and Werner Telesko, 130–31. Vienna: Belveder and Hirmer Verlag, 2015.

Telesko, Werner. "The Visual 'Afterlife' of the Congress of Vienna." In *Europe in Vienna: The Congress of Vienna 1814–15*, edited by Agnes Husslein-Arco, Sabine Grabner, and Werner Telesko, 372–81. Vienna: Belveder and Hirmer Verlag, 2015.

———. "Jean-Baptiste Isabey's Picture of the Congress of Vienna." In *Europe in Vienna: The Congress of Vienna 1814–15*, edited by Agnes Husslein-Arco, Sabine Grabner, and Werner Telesko, 130–31. Vienna: Belveder and Hirmer Verlag, 2015.

Truesdell, Matthew. *Spectacular Politics: Louis-Napoléon Bonaparte and the fête impériale, 1849–1870*. New York: Oxford University Press, 1997.

Tyrrell, Henry. *The History of the War with Russia*. London: London Printing Company, 1858.

Vick, Brian E. *Congress of Vienna: Power and Politics after Napoleon*. Cambridge, MA: Harvard University Press, 2014.

Williams, Gavin, ed. *Hearing the Crimean War: Wartime Sound and the Unmaking of Sense*. Oxford: Oxford University Press, 2019.

Yon, Jean-Claude. *Jacques Offenbach*. Paris: Gallimard, 2000.

———. "En marge des négociations: Mondanités et spectacles pendant le congrès de Paris." In *Le congrès de Paris (1856): Un événement fondateur*, edited by Gilbert Ameil, Isabelle Nathan, and Georges-Henri Soutou, 171–84. Paris: Direction des Archives, Ministère des Affaires étrangères et européennes, 2009.

Chapter 13

INTERNATIONALISM AND MUSICAL EXCHANGE IN POST–WORLD WAR I EUROPE, 1918–1923

Barbara L. Kelly

> "Music more than anything else offers a means of bringing nations to a better understanding of one another."
>
> —Arthur Eaglefield Hull[1]

This chapter focuses on a particular form of musical internationalism that asserted itself during the postwar transition at the end of the Great War between 1918 and 1923. Taking the allied countries of France and Britain as particular examples, it looks specifically at the International Society for Contemporary Music (ISCM), which was founded in 1922 and had its first official festival in 1923 in Salzburg, setting itself up as a musical League of Nations to promote international musical exchange, while purporting to remain detached from politics.[2] I am interested in exploring the people who became associated with the ISCM. While Edward Dent's central role has received necessary scholarly attention,[3] I am also interested in the network of musicians who actively sought to promote musical internationalism or who found themselves associated in some capacity as figureheads, activists, assessors, or performers. These include Arthur Eaglefield Hull (1876–1928), Edwin Evans (1874–1945), Eugene Goossens (1893–1962), and Edward Clark (1888–1962) in Britain, and Henry Prunières (1886–1942), André Caplet (1878–1925), Erik Satie (1866–1925), Darius Milhaud (1892–1974), and Charles Koechlin (1867–1950) in France. I pay particular attention to the organizations

---

Notes for this section begin on page 263.

that took on the function of the British and French Sections of the ISCM: the British Music Society (BMS) and London Contemporary Music Centre (LCMC) in Britain, and *La Revue musicale* and Concerts de *La Revue musicale* in France. A key theme is the overlapping commitment to national promotion and international exchange. While there are many similarities between the French and British contexts, there are also notable differences. I am also interested in how the "return" to internationalism as Europe emerged from war differed from the heyday of internationalism in music in the early 1900s. The chapter probes the aims and motivations of the societies and their key players in unpicking the tricky territories of post–World War I musical reconstruction, alliances, and cooperation.

Shortly before the end of the Great War in 1918, the organist and musical scholar Arthur Eaglefield Hull founded the BMS. The monthly adverts printed in *The Musical Times* from 1 August 1918 stated the aim of the society: "For the Fostering and Encouragement of British Music at Home and Abroad."[4] In an unsigned article "A New Music Society," the author describes "the British Music Society (National and International)" as "a missionary body" with "the highly laudable purpose of advancing the cause of British Music at home and abroad."[5] The BMS promised to be aesthetically open and unconnected to particular schools or publishers. The organization of the society was noteworthy; the article claimed that the committee of management would consist entirely of amateurs. Nonetheless, on 1 November 1918 the committee of management included some powerful musical figures such as the conductor Adrian Boult (1889–1983), composer and musicologist Edward Dent (1876–1957), and clergyman and early music scholar Rev. E. H. Fellowes (1870–1951). Two other figures stand out: an aristocrat and a politician, Lord Howard de Walden and Arthur Balfour. The president of the BMS, Lord Howard de Walden (1880–1946), was an important patron of the arts in London and Wales. Arthur Balfour (1848–1930) was the foreign secretary at the time, having previously served as prime minister between 1902 and 1905.[6] This was not the first musical organization to which he lent his patronage; in 1911 Balfour presided over the International Congress of Music in London, the aim of which was to promote contemporary British music to a foreign audience. The society sought powerful patronage, on the one hand, and grassroots participation, on the other. While professionals were welcome as members, the society was keen to attract widespread support in order to create momentum and proselytize on behalf of British music. Part of the vision of the BMS was to establish local centers in London, Manchester, Birmingham, Liverpool, and Glasgow, for example.[7]

Regional centers did indeed take off with some enthusiasm, with centers throughout Britain and even a branch in Victoria, Australia, initiated by Louise Dyer in 1921.[8] These became embedded within the existing cultural life of the places in question. The events often combined performance and lectures on British early and contemporary music, and folk traditions, as well as canonical figures such as Bach. A *Manchester Guardian* critic linked the international aims of the Society to local opportunities in Manchester:

> A British Music Society . . . must not forget, either in the sense of export or import, that music is an international art and one of the strongest intellectual links for binding the peoples together in a league of peace. Speaking locally, the time could not be more opportune for reconstructing the public spirit and organization of Manchester music. . . . It is to everyone's interest that the Manchester branch of the British Music Society should be brought into being strong and vigorous, and should strive on its strength.[9]

It is striking that he links the internationalism of the postwar transition to the reconstruction of local musical life. His description of a "league of peace" is particularly apt, given that the ISCM, to which the BMS would soon be affiliated, was regarded as a musical "League of Nations."[10] The League of Nations would come into being a few months later in January 1920.

Recognition of the importance of the regions for this "missionary work" was undoubtedly due to the director and secretary of the BMS, Arthur Eaglefield Hull.[11] Despite his national profile as a musicologist, biographer, and editor of journals such as *The Monthly Musical Record*, he formed the affiliated Huddersfield Music Club the same year, the first concert taking place on 20 November 1918.[12] His affiliation with the national society meant that he was able to ensure that works by contemporary composers, such as Bartók, were heard in Huddersfield, although he was sensitive to local tastes.[13] It is striking, though, that while performances of Debussy, Ravel, Scriabin took their modest place alongside contemporary British music and early and traditional British music, the Austro-German tradition was only represented by the "classics," until Richard Strauss was programmed on 30 March 1927. This sensitivity to contemporary Austro-German music as late as 1927 shows that wartime attitudes persisted well beyond the postwar transition period, and it makes interesting comparisons with France, where the wartime campaign for a ban on contemporary Austro-German music continued well into the 1920s.¹⁴ Most striking was the Music Club's ability to attract internationally renowned performers and British composer-performers, such as Joseph Holbrooke, Cyril Scott, Myra Hess, Carl Fuchs, Edith Robinson, Frank Merrick, Lionel Tertis, Marjory Kennedy-Fraser, Pablo Casals, and Jelly d'Arányi, and ensembles, including the Catterall String Quartet, the Hungarian Quartet, and the Capet String Quartet.¹⁵ This regional club in the Pennine Hills succeeded in connecting itself to musical activities in London and throughout Europe.

Hull's strategy on propaganda had a local and international dimension. He outlined the creation of special representatives of the society in major international cities, including Paris, Rome, Madrid, Stockholm, and New York, "who will be able to assist British musicians living abroad."¹⁶ The arrangement suggests an embassy-style support; the idea being to facilitate British musicians to take their place in musical life abroad. He also announced the publication of pamphlets by key musical figures on aspects of English or British music, two of whom were on the committee of management of the BMS.¹⁷ Hull presents an ambitious program of work and activism to address the core purpose of the society: to create the right conditions in order to place British music (past and present) on the map alongside its predominantly European counterparts. The outcome of the war and cessation of conflict undoubtedly stimulated this action in the domain of music.

Promotion of New Music

The BMS's commitment to promoting new music is beyond doubt. In addition to establishing a catalog of compositions,¹⁸ the BMS also initiated opportunities for new commissions.¹⁹ While the Society wasn't alone in seeking to stimulate an interest in contemporary music, it was the most prominent and arguably the most successful.²⁰ In January 1921 the BMS established the LCMC "for the express purpose of performing (first in private and then in public) little-known and unknown music in all forms (except orchestral), MS or unpublished, by living British composers," with performances taking place at public and private venues across London.²¹ A concert at the YMCA on 5 May 1922 shows that British contemporary music was performed alongside music by European contemporaries—in this case, with Honegger's *Sonatine for Two Violins*; it was followed on 3 July 1922 by a concert hosted by Walden, which included a cello sonata by Rupert Erlebach (1894–1978), a Butterworth song-cycle, and Ravel's very recent Sonata for Cello and Violin, only two months after the French premiere at the Société Musicale Indépendante (SMI, 6 April 1922).[22] These performances took their place within an increasingly vibrant London musical scene, in which contemporary British music was placed alongside European counterparts. Superficially, it marked a return to the now nostalgic prewar era, but the traces of war were never far from view. The new music heard at these events was by composers who had served in the war or, in the case of Butterworth, prematurely lost their lives, and the repertoire had either been written in the war years or had not yet been heard or published as a result of wartime restrictions. While Debussy and Ravel had made their mark on London concert life and in other major cities,[23] the postwar period saw the introduction of newer and more diverse European voices. The critic Leigh Henry places the BMS and LCMC concerts in the context of musical life in the capital in 1921, describing the "outstanding event" of the first concert performance of Stravinsky's *Rite of Spring* in Britain, just a week before the BMS Congress.[24] Stravinsky's infamous piece was placed alongside Ravel's first major postwar work, Ravel's *La Valse*, and two British works: Lord Berners's *Fantaisie espagnole* (1918–19) and John Ireland's *Forgotten Rite* (1913). The conductor was Eugene Goossens, who was to take up a role on the ISCM jury in 1924.

Henry also championed the activities of the then freelance conductor Edward Clark (1888–1962) in promoting contemporary European music in Britain.[25] Clark organized a series of four concerts at the Aeolian and Queen's Hall in April and May 1921. He studied with Schoenberg (1910–1912) and promoted his music in the United Kingdom, conducting the world premiere of the *Five Pieces for Orchestra* in 1912. In this series of concerts, Clark placed British, French, and Austro-German repertoires side by side in a way that had hardly been seen since the beginning of the war, but now with the addition of more recent repertoire that contributed to shaping a new postwar soundworld. Henry described the first concert, on 8 April 1921, as "magnificent"; it included Stravinsky's 1919 reorchestration with reduced orchestra of the *Firebird* suite, which was programmed beside Bliss's "Storm Scene" from *The Tempest* (1921) and Bax's *Bard of the Dimbovitza* (1914) at the Queen's Hall.[26] On 6 May 1921 Clark conducted the first British performance of Schoenberg's *Kammersinfonie*. The addition of Schoenberg in postwar London concerts mirrors activities in Paris, which did not pass without xenophobic and antisemitic comment, particularly in the French capital.[27] The fact that the concert series also included recent works by members of Les Six, confirms that these concerts reflected the most recent European music; the postwar transition was also a transition in concert programming. One can appreciate Leigh Henry's enthusiasm in reporting on such rich international exchanges in the British capital:

> The activity of the last month, particularly in the domain of orchestral music has been extraordinary. One feels that London has definitely developed into the hub of present-day musical life. The energy of the younger men seems to be culminating in a tide of fresh impulses which is suffusing the main stream of music. Everywhere one notes a new stimulus and impetus. This is not a "movement" in the limited coterie sense; it represents group-forces of feeling and thought in the historical sense, a cumulative phenomenon contributed to by diverse factors of all types.[28]

Clark's particular training and contacts made him an ideal person to bring together diverse European musical traditions in his international concerts. It is perhaps unsurprising that he became involved with the International Society for Contemporary Music from 1927, taking a lead in the 1931 ISCM Festival in London and Oxford and later becoming its president (1947–55).[29] He was also to play a major role in the BBC's London programming of contemporary music from 1927.[30] It is clear that this intensive musical activity was creating a network of British and mainly European composers who were being promoted by prominent conductors, critics, and musicologists in the dual causes of national promotion and international exchange.

Most significantly, the BMS and its associated London Contemporary Music Centre with its key musician activists were ambivalent about the balance between promoting British music (present and past) and celebrating contemporary foreign music in the immediate postwar period from 1918 until the establishment of the ISCM British Section in 1923 and even beyond. However, their instincts were arguably insular, with foreign music often welcomed according to wartime international relations between particular nations; Bantock's public protest when Richard Strauss was programmed at the first BMS Congress in 1920 revealed the persistence of wartime attitudes toward contemporary German music.[31] What began as an initial mission to stimulate interest in British music at home broadened to include an international agenda that was largely focused on promoting British music abroad. The establishment of the British Section of the ISCM represented a moment of confidence and one-upmanship that signaled that Britain was ready to be participants around the musical table with their European counterparts.

The decision, in August 1922, to make the London Contemporary Music Centre the headquarters for the British Section of the ISCM was an important step in realizing Hull's belief that "music is an international art and one of the strongest intellectual links for binding the peoples together is a league of peace."[32] It accorded with the founding principles of the ISCM. However, it was Edwin Evans, the British critic and advocate of contemporary music, who was appointed chairman of the British Section rather than Hull or Edward Clark. Evans and Dent had made the journey to Salzburg for the chamber music festival and had taken an organizational role in discussions concerning the new society's future. Encouraged by the American representatives, they offered the London office as the headquarters for the new society, only sorting it out with Eaglefield Hull on their return.[33] Their diplomatic, organizational, and linguistic skills stood out in Salzburg, making them a clear choice to lead both the whole organization (Dent) and the British Section of the new international society (Evans).

Evans used his newly acquired role to speak out in the press for British music to take its place alongside music of other nations, for instance, at the British Empire Exhibition in 1923. In his view it was acceptable to invite "some of the leading musicians of the Continent to exhibit their wares alongside our own. The whole point is that it must happen at our invitation. British music must be treated as the host, and not as a poor relation."[34] Evans's articles also betray a somewhat wary approach to internationalism, challenging notions of music as a universal language, most likely in response to attitudes held by prominent figures, such as Guido Adler, who asserted that the music from some nations were more universal than others.[35] Although Evans nuanced the commonly held view that art has no boundaries, he nevertheless believed in artistic boundaries drawn upon national lines, but hoped that British music would benefit from its more open and equitable circulation.[36]

In 1910 Evans delivered a lecture to the Musical Association (later to be known by its current name, the Royal Musical Association) on the topic "French Music of To-Day."[37] He noted that London's openness to German music meant that it was "in danger of missing important musical developments in France," which in his view constituted an important "new page of the history of musical evolution . . . from César Franck to Debussy."[38] He had another aim in arguing that French music is well positioned to take over from the "Pan-Germanic epoch in musical history," which he describes as a "phase."[39] In the immediate aftermath of the Great War, Evans published the translation of Jean-Aubry's *La Musique française d'aujourd'hui* (1916)[40] in which he advocated for a closer musical alliance with France. Evans and Jean-Aubry were united in actively seeking alternatives to the dominance of German musical traditions on first French and now "English" music: "The French have been our forerunners and are our companions. Hence the mutual esteem which has grown up between French and English musicians is neither fortuitous nor due to statesmanship. It is a natural effect of similar causes operating on both sides of the Channel.[41] Evans argues that Jean-Aubry (and himself by extension) laid the foundations for a kind of "musical internationalism," which seeks to revise international musical allegiances to take account of the allies and shape an alternative trajectory, which includes Britain, but with France leading the way.[42] Thus, the postwar transition period, building on recent military alliances, provided the opportunity for such a realignment of musical allegiances and leadership.

Music, Internationalism, and the ISCM in France

What made France such an attractive model for musical activists in Britain? France had gone through a comparable stage of reflection and soul searching not so much at the end of the Great War, but after the crushing defeat of the Franco-Prussian War. French music and musical life had been found wanting; its music was dominated by foreign influence, notably Wagner and Italian influences in opera and Austro-German instrumental traditions.[43] Organizations such as the Société nationale de musique (SNM), founded immediately after the defeat in 1871, consciously sought to encourage a French tradition of mainly chamber music. When the original focus of the SNM—to promote primarily French contemporary composers—changed under d'Indy's leadership, the SMI was formed in 1909 to present a more radical agenda that covered not only French music but also the latest musical trends from all over Europe, including Schoenberg. Thus, an international spirit of musical exchange was firmly in place before the outbreak of the Great War; the war years saw this perspective challenged, not least by the likes of Saint-Saëns, but also the League for the Protection of French Music, headed by Charles Tenroc. The postwar period presented an opportunity to recapture what was perceived as a golden age of French music, with a number of internationally acclaimed composers, notably Debussy, Fauré, and Ravel, who were supported by particularly dedicated spokesmen.

These included figures who traveled widely to proselytize on behalf of French music, notably Émile Vuillermoz, Louis Laloy, Michel-Dimitri Calvocoressi, Jean-Aubry, the latter two of whom spent considerable time in Britain. The French state also funded propaganda initiatives to promote music abroad, including Jean-Aubry's mission abroad and the Association Française d'Action Artistique, which was set up in initially in 1917 to promote the circulation of French artists abroad.[44] The challenge facing French music in 1918 was the aging and death of the generation that had reestablished France as a leading musical nation. Nor was there consensus about whether to embrace this spirit of internationalism or hold onto wartime musical protectionism.[45]

A comparative glance across the Channel in the immediate aftermath of the Great War reveals many parallels but also subtle differences. In France, the figures who rose to prominence in the postwar period in promoting internationalism built on their prewar and wartime experiences. The same names recur on various committees and initiatives, so that they form a network of activity, which, unlike Britain, was largely centrally rather than regionally based, with some notable exceptions. Prunières emerges as a key figure in postwar France with his initiative to establish *La Revue musicale*. Michel Duchesneau has persuasively argued that his ambitious project built on the prewar journal *La Revue musicale de la SIM* and took advantage of the international connections he had established during the war itself.[46] Prunières made the internationalist aims of the journal clear in a letter to the protectionist nationalist Léon Vallas: "I fully understand your point of view in wanting to protect French artists, but it is not mine, because I run a journal that is essentially international. I consider that my role is to make French music known abroad, and in order to achieve this, I need to deserve the reputation as a protector of foreign music in France."[47] It reads as a statement of faith and one that guided his actions during the 1920s. Yet Prunières looked to Vallas for advice when setting up his own concert series, the Concerts de *La Revue musicale*. In July 1921 Prunières wrote to Vallas: "I have decided to organize a series of around ten chamber music concerts at the Vieux-Colombier next winter. I want to do for Paris something analogous to what you have done so successfully in Lyon, and I would like your advice on this matter."[48] Subsequent letters show that Prunières's main hesitation was how to build an audience for his concerts to make them financially viable, particularly in the economically difficult postwar years.[49] However, Prunières did not waiver for long; barely a month later he published his announcement in his journal:

> La Revue musicale is organizing a series of seven chamber music concerts at the Vieux-Colombier . . . under Henry Prunières's direction. The concerts of La Revue musicale will not duplicate the numerous recitals that are advertised throughout Paris. . . . You will hear works chosen with greatest freedom from French and foreign composers, both past and present, and where possible, unknown, forgotten or very rarely played works.[50]

Prunières's concerts resembled Vallas's Lyon concerts in giving a central place to French music of Debussy and Ravel's generation and also relatively unknown music of the French past. In the first five years of the series (1921–26), Debussy featured in at least nineteen concerts and Ravel in at least twenty concerts.[51] While there are fewer concerts featuring Fauré, the music of this generation of French composers constitutes the core repertoire for the series, with Roussel, Schmitt, Caplet, Koechlin, and Magnard prominent, the latter regarded as a "war hero" after his untimely death in 1914. Prunières's aesthetic orientation is absolutely clear in the almost complete absence of d'Indy and the Franckistes school in the programs.[52]

Prunières is most innovative in the place he gives to the most recent contemporary music. The music of Satie and Les Six have their place,[53] but it is Prunières's active promotion of foreign music, from mainly European traditions, that is most striking and sets him apart from the likes of Vallas. In the early days of the series, he relied on his numerous international contacts; he also depended on a number of performing groups, including the Belgian quartet, Pro Arte, the Société Moderne d'Instruments à Vents, and performers such as Marya Freund, Jelly d'Arányi, Andrès Segovia, Ricardo Viñes, Henri Gil-Marchex, and André Hekking. The concerts featured some composers performing their own works, notably Bartók, Szymanowski, and a composer more familiar to Paris, Manuel de Falla. Bartók, as a result, was able to introduce his most recent chamber music, notably the *Sonata for Violin and Piano*, Op. 21 (1921), and the *Sonata No. 2 for Violin and Piano* (1923). Stravinsky's work was frequently represented; while Jean Wiéner's concerts included notable Stravinsky premieres (concert performances of *Mavra* and *Petrushka* as a *Sonata for Piano*), Prunières established Stravinsky's chamber music as part of the performing repertory. His concerts also worked in tandem with Jean Wiéner in programming Schoenberg's *Das Buch der hängenden Gärten* and the Paris premiere of the *Sechs kleine*

Table 13.1. Performances of selected contemporary foreign composers (Bartók, Szymanowski, Stravinsky, Schoenberg 1921–26). Table created by the author.

Composer	No of concerts
Bartók	5
Szymanowski	4
Stravinsky	4
Schoenberg	5

Klavierstücke around the time of the infamous performances of the Austrian's *Pierrot lunaire* in 1921–22, although his performances attracted less attention. In addition to these prominent names, many other contemporary composers were included in the concerts including Scriabin, Malipiero, Kodály, and Václav Stepán.

Prunières wore his internationalism as a badge of honor and as a way of luring his elite audiences. In an advertisement in his own journal, he projects an image of these concerts as an international hub:

> It is a bit like the tower of Babel. . . . In the Director's office, people are smoking, chatting in every dialect under the sun. Spanish, Russian, Polish, Italian, Austrian, Czech, Hungarian, Romanian, American, Dutch musicians are brought together. The French are in the minority. . . . In a corner, Albert Roussel speaks to Alexandre Tansman and Ségovia with Auric. They are interrupted from time to time to hear a performer playing in the adjacent room. There, everyone is completely absorbed by the music. . . . Nothing is planned in advance. The performers sing or play what they want and when it pleases them, happy to present an unknown work by a young French or foreign composer, to a public almost entirely made up of performers or passionate amateurs. Even if some events have only a moderate musical interest, there are also some that are memorable, and on those days, the conversations magically fall silent. When Andrès Ségovia brings his guitar, when Yora Guller, Robert Casadesus . . . [or] Gil-Marchex sit down at the piano, no one dreams of speaking.[54]

Prunières's headquarters are more than the formal concerts; they are an international club where passionate amateurs can rub shoulders with the greatest performers. The critic-director adopts a very different strategy to the BMS in drawing in an elite audience. The BMS called amateurs to action to make music on behalf of the Society. Prunières gives them a more passive role, but one that is potentially thrilling. In 1925 he announced his exclusive Association des Concerts de *La Revue musicale*, which entitled subscribers to attend "Concerts privés pour l'Élite."[55] This initiative had clear parallels with Schoenberg's Verein für musikalische Privataufführungen (Society for Private Performances), 1918–1921. Reflecting back on his efforts to promote contemporary music in the 1930s, Prunières explained that his strategy was to attract the elite to contemporary music as a first step toward making it more widely accepted by the public. In 1933 Prunières revealed his strategy in a report he delivered in Florence, a strategy that is evident in his advertisements for new music concerts in his journal:

> When finally the killing was over, there was a feeling of general curiosity among the elite for unknown works from other countries. Germany, Austria returned with the keenest interest in music that was far from their way of thinking: Debussy, Ravel, Stravinsky. While in Paris, concerts that were reserved at first for an increasingly influential elite, enabled the new works of Schoenberg, Webern, Alban Berg, Bela Bartók, Kodály, Szymanowski and soon the young Hindemith to be heard, sometimes causing an uproar, as well as the works of Casella, Malipiero, Respighi, Castelnuovo, Manuel de Falla, Holst, Bax, Vaugh. Williams, Willem Pijper, etc. etc.[56]

This approach differed strikingly from the grassroots initiatives of the BMS. Prunières was generally bolder in promoting new European contemporary music than his British counterparts, with the exception of Edward Clark's dazzling contemporary music concerts in 1921. However, both of these forebears of the ISCM were united in establishing a long-term strategy for developing an interest and—crucially—an audience for new music.

In the list of nationalities mentioned in the quotation above, there are some exceptions: German and British. The concert programs confirm this bias too. Whether by accident or design, Kurt Weill is alone in representing contemporary German music at these concerts, even though Schoenberg, Berg, and Webern are given due prominence.[57] French wartime calls to ban contemporary Austro-German music seem to have lingered even in the most open contexts. It is perhaps harder to explain the relative paucity of British music in the programs. There is a smattering of British music, and it is precisely the generation that featured in the programs of the BMS, the LCMC, and the British Section of the ISCM.[58] Goossens's music is most regularly played (at six concerts), followed by Bliss (two) and Scott (two).[59] In the concert of 10 March 1923, French and British traditions were brought together thanks to the collaboration of the Société Moderne d'Instruments à Vent, the French composer-pianist Daniel Lazarus (1898–1964), and British singer Dorothy Moulton (1886–1984). In contrast to Britain in this period where French music was very prominent, contemporary British music had yet to make its mark in French concert life.

The Concerts de *La Revue musicale* were but one important example of concert activity focused on European contemporary music in Paris. Other notable concert initiatives were Jean Wiéner's concerts—which mixed contemporary music of Stravinsky, Les Six, Schoenberg and his school, and jazz[60]—and Walter Straram's "Quatre concerts de musique moderne internationale" in April–May 1923, which featured Schoenberg, Webern, Bartók, Cassela, Malipiero, Krasa, and Stravinsky alongside Debussy, Ravel, Koechlin, Dukas, Roussel, and Honegger on the much larger stage of the Théâtre des Champs-Élysées. This paved the way for Straram's regular concert series in the late 1920s, in which contemporary music had a prominent place.[61] Straram became involved in the ISCM, conducting the "Trois Concerts symphonique de musique moderne" on behalf of the French Section in 1925 and sitting on the international jury in 1927.[62] Nevertheless, given Prunières's considerable influence as the director of *La Revue musicale*, as well as his ability to network and attract a diverse range of composers and performers to Paris, it is not surprising that the French Section of the ISCM was linked to his concerts. The wording of the announcement of the French Section in the journal is strikingly familiar, echoing Prunières's assertion to Vallas about the internationalist aims of his journal: "The goal of the French Section is to promote by every means and to the greatest possible extent the knowledge and availability of foreign music in France and French music abroad, at its social center in Paris, in the offices of the *Revue musicale*, the branch headquarters of the Society, 35–37 rue Madame."[63] The concerts continued largely as before, with a similar mixing of different musical traditions. One difference is evident in the setting up of a new subseries devoted to young contemporary European traditions (Jeunes Écoles Européennes). Rather than mixing traditions in the context of a single concert, these concerts, which were labeled ISCM concerts, tended to separate the repertoire according to nationality. For example, on 22 November 1924 the concert was devoted to "La Jeune École italienne" and on 6 December to "Œuvres françaises et Espagnoles."[64]

French Section of the ISCM

Prunières did not act alone; he served on the committee of the French Section in an administrative capacity. The more official positions fell to others who had also taken prominent roles in promoting foreign music and contemporary music in prewar and wartime France. The important question in setting up the Section française was agreeing the membership of the French Section committee and the music that should represent France abroad. Given the personnel involved, which included critics and composers who held diametrically opposed aesthetic positions, there was arguably less consensus here than in Britain. This was the case particularly between Vuillermoz, on the one hand, and Satie and Milhaud, on the other, and there were also significant tensions between Ravel and Satie and members of Les Six:

- Président d'honneur: Fauré
- Président actif, Dukas
- Vice-présidents, Ravel, Roussel
- Members of the committee: Satie, Vuillermoz, Schmitt, Louis Aubert, Koechlin, Stravinsky, Milhaud, Honegger, Roland-Manuel, Caplet, Robert Brussel
- Administration: Daniel Lazarus, Paul Clemenceau, and Henry Prunières[65]

Committee Membership

Francis Poulenc reports on the establishment of the French Section of the ISCM in a letter to Milhaud on 30 January 1923, giving a fascinating insight into the discord within the committee:

> What a delightful mix, isn't it? Of course, there are already some incredible stories. Vuillermoz didn't want you on the executive committee at any cost. He had a shouting match with Satie. Do you know the reason for this animosity? Quite simply, because you gave an anti-Ravel lecture in America. In order to appear magnanimous, Ravel insisted that you be one of the 15 elected members. I bet that this new SMI won't last more than 2 years. Stravinsky is now completely against it. Satie seems to be faltering since this quarrel. Only Pruneton [Prunières], with a big, ineffable smile, proclaims: the French Section is formed, music is saved.[66]

Poulenc's cynicism reveals the real tensions between members of the committee concerning musical aesthetics and the direction of French music. The critic Vuillermoz was particularly hostile to members of Les Six, notably Milhaud, whose trip to America in January 1923 caused controversy by placing Satie rather than Ravel as the figurehead of contemporary French music.[67] While Prunières's role on the committee appeared modest, his influence and power were real.

André Caplet was invited in 1922 as the national delegate for the French Section and a member of the international jury, alongside Ernest Ansermet, Herman Scherchen, and Egon Wellesz.[68] His nomination to serve on the first (1923) jury was no doubt influenced primarily by his reputation as a conductor. Roland-Manuel's letter to Caplet from August 1922 outlines his role more precisely and the aims of the ISCM:

> A few young musicians who want to form a truly active and freely exchanging concert society are asking you, through my intersession, whether you would be willing in principle to join them. The committee, divided into three sections, would share the work, would have representatives in each country, who would receive concert material from you and would collect for you the most significant foreign works. The society would be of limited duration in order to avoid the inevitable transformation into a retirement home.[69]

Roland-Manuel's letter captures the idealism of the "youth" taking action to promote "free exchange" or "free trade." He may well have been referring to the wartime xenophobic tendencies of Saint-Saëns, Charles Tenroc, and others who campaigned to ban Austro-German music not in the public domain, which mirrored similar initiatives in Britain;[70] such attitudes persisted well into the interwar period, as the scandal that erupted after the French premiere of Schoenberg's *Pierrot lunaire* attests. Caplet, Roland-Manuel, Koechlin, and Ravel were part of a network with links to the SMI and the Apaches, the prewar circle that surrounded Ravel; the individuals listed all took stances against xenophobic tendencies. Roland-Manuel's definition of youth may not have been quite accurate. The youthful generation who formed the SMI in 1909 were aging, with some suffering from the effects of war (particularly Caplet and Ravel); in Caplet's case it hastened his death, while Ravel experienced premature aging.[71] However, despite Vuillermoz's objections, they were able to put aesthetic differences aside to include the youngest generation of Honegger, Milhaud, and others in putting their ideals into practice for the "free exchange" of music between nations.[72] The benefit of participation was the chance to influence what was played on an international forum and who represented their country on the programs.[73]

Looking across the Channel, key British musical figures were very much part of this international network. Goossens, like Caplet both a composer and conductor, represented Britain in the ISMC, alongside Ernest Ansermet, Ildebrando Pizzetti, Hermann Scherchen, Oscar Sonneck, and Alexander von Zemlinsky.[74] A glance at the British press shows that it followed the development of the ISCM with interest, noting the unanimous election of the first jury and expressing pride in the fact that the headquarters were located at the Incorporated Society of Musicians in Berners Street, London.[75] Edward Dent's prominent role as president (1922–38) also ensured that Britain was fully part of the exchange, from which it would benefit by association.

Conclusion

This study of the origins of the British and French Sections of the ISCM reveals the real tensions between national and individual (self-) interest, on the one hand, and international (in this case largely European) postwar idealism, on the other. The Sections that were established in the early years of the ISCM reflected the nations that had recently been allies or enemies during the war, as well as newly formed nations, notably Czechoslovakia. Both France and Britain understood the opportunities that such cultural diplomacy could offer them as Europe was emerging from the Great War. The British Section was founded on a concert society that was primarily motivated to regenerate its own musical culture and to reflect this new energy and creativity on the European stage.

The equivalent French society, by contrast, was part of a movement to encourage and consume foreign music after wartime restrictions on the circulation of contemporary music; rather than representing a return to prewar musical exchange, the musical circulation that emerged after the Great War was different in reflecting new power relations between nations and new alliances stemming from the experience of conflict. At the same time, many of its activists wanted to promote and canonize a golden age of French music that was quickly disappearing. The tensions within the French committee concerned the inclusion of a new generation and what image of French music should be portrayed abroad. It is clear that key figures, such as Prunières, Hull, Evans, and Dent, represented a cultural commitment to internationalism that was also political and selective. As Giles Masters argues, "to label oneself 'international' in 1922, signified a moral-political commitment (an *internationalism*) and an associated subject position (as an *internationalist*)."[76] Writing about the 1924 ISCM Festival in Prague and Salzburg, Prunières asserted that the "the Assembly had re-elected its President, the eminent English critic unanimously" because his "devotion to the cause of artistic internationalism and firm and prudent politics had [helped him] succeed in overcoming the countless pitfalls he has encountered."[77] Dent for his part, claimed that the ISCM was only interested in music; "it has nothing to do with politics nor with the social doctrine of 'internationalism'."[78] While he conceded that music in wartime could be used for propaganda, it was not, in his view, the true function of art in peacetime. He outlined the ideal of the independent artist who functions and engages as an individual above the limitations of national traditions and concerns of "national representation," "national prestige," and "national egoism."[79] In his view, dividing the ISCM into national sections was purely practical and not an excuse to encourage musical hierarchies: "Great musical powers."[80] In upholding the principle that the ISCM was above politics and financial concerns, he asserted rather bluntly that the ISCM "doesn't even want to come to the aid of composers."[81] Despite the rhetoric, Dent's statement was deeply political, and his ideals inevitably fell short in practice.

Individual nations were all too conscious of how their country was being represented, as we have seen; national sections did limit who was eligible to "represent" a particular country, as Federico Lazzaro has shown in the case of the École de Paris;[82] the aim of curbing "great musical powers" (namely Austria and Germany) was entirely in keeping with the wartime attitudes and entrenched musical rivalries.[83] As Anne Shreffler has shown, Dent's belief in keeping music separate from state politics was seriously tested in 1935 when Dent resisted the pressure from composers Hanns Eisler, Hermann Reichenbach, and Alois Hába for the ISCM to become involved in aligning with either the National Socialists or the Soviet Popular Front in the controversy surrounding the Czech Festival.[84] Clearly, the musical internationalism of the ISCM and its related organizations had its limitations and contradictions, but this chapter has shown that it was also a significant catalyst for musical action, creativity, and exchange on national, local, and transnational levels in the transition from war to peace after World War I.

Barbara L. Kelly is professor of music and head of the School of Music at the University of Leeds. She was previously director of research at the Royal Northern College of Music (2015-22). She is also president of the Royal Musical Association. Her research focuses on French and European music (1870–1939). She has authored three monographs: *Music and Ultra-Modernism in France: A Fragile Consensus, 1913–1939, Tradition and Style in the Works of Darius Milhaud, 1912–*

1939, and *Accenting the Classics: Editing European Music in France, 1915–1925,* with Deborah Mawer, Rachel Moore, and Graham Sadler. She is contributing editor of *French Music, Culture, and National Identity, 1870–1939; Berlioz and Debussy: Sources, Contexts and Legacies,* with Kerry Murphy; and *Music Criticism in France, 1918–1939: Authority, Advocacy, Legacy,* with Christopher Moore, and *Debussy Studies 2* with David Code†. She is currently preparing a study of the singer Jane Bathori.

Notes

1. Arthur Eaglefield Hull, "A Society for British Music." *The Manchester Guardian,* 4 October 1919, 8.
2. See Dent, "Internationalisme et musique." See also Shreffler, "The International Society for Contemporary Music and Its Political Context."
3. Fauser, "The Scholar behind the Medal."
4. Advert, *The Musical Times,* 1 August 1918, 338.
5. Unsigned, "A New Music Society," *The Musical Times,* 1 Aug.August 1918, 351.
6. Balfour was appointed president of the Sociological Society in 1911. See Unsigned, "Mr Balfour and Sociology." *The Evening Standard and St. James Gazette,* 3 May 1911, Foundation of Sociology Archive, Keele University, GB172 LP/11/1/6. I am grateful to David Amigoni for bringing this to my attention.
7. Frontmatter, *The Musical Times* 60 (922), 1 December 1919, 652.
8. Davidson, *Lyrebird Rising,* 150. Arthur Eaglefield Hull includes the British Empire in his scope for the society. See Hull, "A Society for British Music." The British Music Society bulletins at the British Library show that there was also a branch in Bangalore. I am grateful to Kerry Murphy for pointing this out to me. Sarah Kirby is currently writing a chapter on the Victoria Branch of the BMS.
9. Unsigned, "British Music Society," *The Guardian,* 4 October 1919, 8.
10. Shreffler, "The International Society for Contemporary Music and Its Political Context," 60.
11. For more detail on Arthur Eaglefield Hull, consult Rachel Cowgill. See, for example, "Relations with the Enemy": Arthur Eaglefield Hull, "Musical Internationalism, and the Politics of Postwar Recovery," paper given at A Musical League of Nations symposium, Institute of Musical Research, Senate House, London, June 2018. Cowgill is PI on an AHRC-funded project on Arthur Eaglefield Hull and the British Music Society.
12. I am grateful to Hilary Norcliffe, archivist of the Huddersfield Music Society, for sending me listings of the society's programs.
13. http://www.huddersfield-music-society.org.uk.
14. See Esteban, "'Les Allemands et les Boches." See also Moore, *Performing Propaganda,* 11–13.
15. Huddersfield Music Society Archive.
16. Arthur Eaglefield Hull, "A Few Words," 71.
17. Hull, "A Few Words," 71. Hull identifies the titles as follows: Fellowes, "The Elizabethan Madrigalians"; Cobbett, "Modern British Chamber Music"; and Ernest Newman, "The Treatment of Metre and Stress by English Composers." Although no publications with these exact titles appear to have been published inde-

pendently, all three authors remained authorities on these particular musical topics.
18. Solman, "British Music Society's New Catalogue," 492.
19. See notice from Arthur Eaglefield Hull (in letters to the editor) highlighting the conductor Mr. Vasco Akeroyd's call to perform a new British orchestral and chamber work at each of the concerts of the Akeroyd Orchestra, Liverpool, in the following season. *The Musical Times* 60, no. 918, 1 August 1919, 418.
20. "Advisory Board for Composers," *The Musical Times*, 1 November 1920, 723. The thirst for new music from the continent would come from other quarters, including Chester Music publisher and journal *The Chesterian* and from individuals such as Edwin Evans, Jean-Aubry, Calvocorressi, and Edward Clark, who advocated on behalf of European music.
21. *The Era*, 1 December 1920.
22. "The British Music Society, Concert at Seaford House, *The Times*, 4 July 1922, 12. See BMS and LCMC concert programs, Royal College of Music Library. I am grateful to archivist Michael Mullen for making copies of these programs available to me.
23. See Kelly, "French Connections," 115–46.
24. Henry, "London Letter."
25. Clark was appointed assistant conductor to Webern at the theatre in Szczecin (Stettin) in 1914, but the outbreak of war meant that he was detained as a foreign national at Ruhleben Internment Camp. He returned to England in 1918, where he became a freelance conductor. He was assistant conductor for the London Season of Diaghilev's Ballets Russes in 1919. Leigh Henry was also detained at Ruhleben. See Forkert, "'Always a European,'" 52–53.
26. Henry, "London Letter." *The Chesterian* New Series, 15 May 1921, 467.
27. See Kelly, *Tradition and Style in the Works of Darius Milhaud*, 10–15; Fulcher, "The Preparation for Vichy," 458–75. See also Doctor, *The BBC and Ultra-Modern Music, 1922–1936*, 96–125.
28. Henry, "London Letter," 498.
29. See Forkert, "'Always a European,'" 62–70, about Clark's troubled association with the ISCM.
30. Doctor, *The BBC and Ultra-Modern Music, 1922–1936*, 80–144; and Forkert, "'Always a European,'" 55–62.
31. Bantock, "A Glaring Anomaly," 336. David Larkin provides an important context for Strauss's fall from favor in Britain during World War I. See Larkin, "Richard Strauss's Tone Poems in Britain," 100–104. For the French context, see Guerpin, "Le Courrier musical et le premier conflit mondial (1904–1923)."
32. *The Manchester Guardian*, 4 October 1919, 8.
33. Edward Dent, "Plans for Salzburg," *The Nation and Atheneum*, 3 February 1923, 696; Evans, "The Salzburg Festival, International Chamber Concerts," *The Musical Times* 63, no. 955, 1 September 1922, 629; Dent, "Looking Backward," in *Edward J Dent: Selected Essays*, ed. Hugh Taylor (Cambridge: Cambridge University Press, 1979), 276–77. See also Giles Masters, "New-Music Internationalism: The ISCM Festival, 1922–1939," PhD dissertation, Kings College, London, 2021. I am grateful to Karen Arrandale for discussing this issue with me.
34. Edwin Evans, "British Music for the Empire Exhibition, Why It Must Not Take a Back Place, Foreign Domination, 'Host' of the Show," *Pall Mall Gazette*, 3 March 1923, 7.
35. See Adler, "Internationalism in Music," 281–300. In an article, Dent also questioned the notion of "Great Musical Powers"; see "Internationalisme et musique," 60.

36. Edwin Evans, "The World Republic of Music." *Portsmouth Evening News*, 4 April 1927.
37. Evans, "French Music of To-Day," 47–74.
38. "French Music of To-Day," 47 and 49.
39. "French Music of To-Day," 47.
40. Jean-Aubry, *French Music of To-Day*.
41. Evans, "Translator's Preface." xviii–xix. Note that Jean-Aubry adds a chapter to his book entitled "French Music and German Music," which was motivated by the outbreak of war, which declares "a musical victory of Modern France over Modern Germany." See Jean-Aubry, *French Music of To-Day*, 15.
42. Evans, "Translator's Preface," xxii–xxiv. See also Bantock, "A Musical Repas," 11–12. It is interesting that Evans, Jean-Aubry, and others did not object to leadership from their political ally France; they admired the regeneration of the arts that had taken place after the Franco-Prussian defeat, which had consolidated a golden generation of French composers, including Fauré, Debussy and Ravel. They wanted to emulate this revival.
43. See Kelly, *French Music, Culture and National Identity, 1870–1939*, 1–9; and Duchesneau, *L'Avant-garde musicale et ses sociétés à Paris de 1871 à 1939*.
44. See Unsigned, "Manual of Modern French Music," in *The Chesterian*, 5 November 1916, 66. It became the Association française d'expansion et d'échanges artistiques from 1922. See Pistone, "La Musique comme ambassadrice?" 21–35; Anselmini, "Alfred Cortot et la diplomatie musicale française," 33–43; Duchêne-Thégarid, "Les élèves musiciens étrangers en France," 45–56.
45. The stance of Prunières, Jean Wiéner, and Ravel was fundamentally opposed to the xenophobic attitudes of Charles Tenroc and Léon Vallas, for instance. See Kelly, *Tradition and Style in the Works of Darius Milhaud*, 11–13; Kelly, "Common Canon, Conflicting Ideologies," 121–50.
46. Duchesneau, "Enjeux culturels dans la presse musicale française, 1900–1925," 19–34.
47. Letter of 2 December 1921, Archives Vallas, Ms Vallas 44 (Correspondance concernant *La Revue musicale*, H. Prunières), 1920–24: "Je comprends parfaitement bien votre point de vue pour la protection des artistes français, mais ce n'est pas le mien, car je dirige une revue essentiellement internationale. J'estime que mon rôle est de faire connaître la musique française à l'étranger et, pour faciliter cette expansion même, de me faire la juste réputation d'un protecteur de la musique étrangère en France."
48. Letter from Prunières to Vallas, 2 September 1921. Ms Vallas 44, Fonds d'Archives de Léon Vallas: "Je me décide à organiser, l'hiver prochain, au Vieux-Colombier, une dizaine de concerts de musique de chambre. Je voudrais faire pour Paris quelque chose d'analogue à ce que vous avez si bien réussi à Lyon, et je désirerais vous demander conseil à ce sujet."
49. Letter from Prunières to Vallas, 2 September 1921. Ms Vallas 44, Fonds d'Archives de Léon Vallas.
50. Advert, "Concerts de *La Revue musicale*," *La Revue musicale* 2, no. 11, 1 October (1921): ii: "*La Revue musicale* organise au Vieux-Colombier des Concerts de Musique de Chambre . . . Sous la direction de M. Henry Prunières. Les Concerts de *La Revue musicale* ne feront pas double emploi avec les innombrables récitals dont les affiches couvrent les murs de Paris. . . . On y entendra des œuvres choisies avec la plus grande liberté chez les auteurs, français et étrangers, du passé et du présent et, autant que possible, des œuvres inconnues, oubliées ou trop rarement jouées."

51. Kelly, "Common Canon, Conflicting Ideologies," 128–30.
52. See Kelly, "Common Canon, Conflicting Ideologies," 131.
53. Milhaud and Honegger were the most frequently performed composers out of Satie and Les Six, with seven and eight appearances in the concerts.
54. Advertisement, "Les Mardis de la *Revue musicale*," *La Revue musicale* 7, no. 4, 1 February (1926): 161: "C'est un peu la tour de Babel . . . Dans le bureau du Directeur, on fume, on bavarde, dans tous les idiomes de la terre. Musiciens espagnols russes, polonais, italiens, autrichiens, tchèques, hongrois, roumains, américains, hollandais se retrouvent là en pays de connaissance. Les Français sont en minorité . . . Dans un coin, Albert Roussel parle avec Alexendre Tansman et Segovia avec Auric. On s'interrompt parfois pour écouter un artiste qui joue dans le salon voisin. Là, on est tout oreilles à la musique . . . Rien de prémédité. Les artistes chantent ou jouent quand il leur plaît et ce qu'ils veulent, heureux de révéler l'œuvre inconnue d'un jeune français ou d'un étranger, à un public composé presque totalité d'artistes ou d'amateurs passionnés. Si certaines séances n'offrent qu'un faible intérêt musical, il en est aussi de mémorables, et ces jours-là, les conversations se taisent comme par enchantement. Lorsque Andrès Ségovia apporte sa guitare, lorsque Youra Guller, Robert Casadesus, . . . Gil-Marcheix s'installent au piano, nul ne songe à parler."
55. Advertisement, "Concerts privés pour l'élite," *La Revue musicale* 7, no. 1, 25 November (1925): i.
56. Prunières, "Des rapports artistiques internationaux considérées du point de vue de la musique, de la musicologie et des musiciens," 243: "Lorsqu'enfin la tuerie eût fin, il y eût chez les élites un élan de curiosité générale vers les œuvres inconnues des autres pays. L'Allemagne, l'Autriche reçurent avec le plus vif intérêt ce qui était le plus éloigné de leur mentalité; Debussy, Ravel, Strawinsky, tandis qu'à Paris des concerts réservés d'abord à une élite, mais de plus en plus importants, révélaient, non sans scandale parfois, les œuvres nouvelles de Schoenberg, Webern, Alban Berg, Bela Bartok, Kodaly, Szymanowski et, bientôt, du jeune Hindemith, en même temps que les productions récentes de Casella, Malipiero, Respighi, Castelnuovo, Manuel de Falla, Holst, Bax, Vaugh. Williams, Willem Pijper, etc. etc."
57. It is not clear why the performance of contemporary German music took longer to resume than Austrian, except to note that the reputation of Schoenberg and his school and the contacts he had made with French composers, notably Jean Wiéner, Milhaud and Poulenc, made it inevitable that his music would be visible and attract attention.
58. The music of this generation was not entirely new to Parisian audiences; the SMI had devoted concerts to them before the war, no doubt as a result of Ravel's contacts with Vaughan Williams.
59. In his review of the 1924 Salzburg ISCM Festival, Prunières regretted the absence of Goossens, Bliss, and Berners at the festival. Prunières, "Chroniques et notes," 247.
60. See Guerpin, "Adieu New York, bonjour Paris!" 750–64.
61. Demonet, "Les Concerts Straram (1926–1933)," 360.
62. These concerts took place at the Théâtre de l'Exposition des arts décoratifs, 4, 8 et 11 June 1925, mixing French, Russian, Hungarian, Italian, and even British traditions.
63. *La Revue musicale* 4, no. 8, 1 June (1923), back cover after 192: "La section française qui a pour objet de favoriser par tous les moyens et au plus haut degré possibles la connaissance et la pénétration de la musique étrangère en

France et de la musique française contemporaine à l'étranger, a son siège social à Paris, dans les bureaux de la *Revue musicale*, organe de la Société, 35–37, rue Madame."
64. See advertisement in *La Revue musicale* 11, no. 4, 7 November (1924): 98.
65. Poulenc, *Correspondance*, 188–89.
66. Poulenc, 188–89: "Quelle jolie salade n'est-ce pas ? Naturellement, il y a déjà eu des histoires incroyables. Vuillermoz ne voulait à aucun prix de toi dans le comité exécutif. Il s'est engueulé avec Satie. Sais-tu le motif de l'animosité de ce Basile ? Tout simplement que tu fais en Amérique une conférence anti-ravéliste. Ravel pour avoir le geste beau a exigé que tu fasses partie des 15 élus. Je ne donne pas 2 ans pour que cette nouvelle SMI avorte. Stravinsky est dès maintenant tout à fait contre. Satie depuis cette algarade semble flancher. Seul Pruneton avec un grand sourire ineffable hurle : la Section française est formée, la musique est sauvée."
67. Kelly, *Tradition and Style in the Works of Darius Milhaud*, 7–9.
68. See Cathé and Huneau, "André Caplet-Charles Koechlin," 163–64.
69. Roland-Manuel letter to Caplet, 17 August 1922, BnF-Mus, N.L.a.269 (728). Quoted in Soret, "Entre la création et l'interprétation," 48: "Quelques jeunes musiciens désireux de former une société de concerts réellement active et réellement libreéchangiste, vous demandent par ma plume si vous seriez disposé en principe à vous joindre à eux. Le comité divisé en trois sections qui se partageraient le travail, aurait des représentants dans chaque pays qui recevrait des éléments de concerts par vos soins et rassemblerait pour vous les œuvres étrangères les plus significatives. La société serait à durée limitée afin d'éviter l'immanquable transformation en maison de retraite."
70. See Ravel, *Lettres, écrits, Entretiens*, 156; and Larkin, "Richard Strauss's Tone Poems in Britain," 100. See also footnote 16.
71. Kelly, "Ravel's Timeliness and His Many Late Styles," 158–73.
72. This free exchange of music was in no way incompatible with Milhaud's communist sympathies.
73. Caplet submitted *Épiphanie* for consideration in 1924 but it was not successful that year. See letter from Koechlin to Caplet, 16 March 1924 in Cathé and Huneau, "André Caplet-Charles Koechlin," 177; it was performed as part of the French Section of the ISCM on 8 June 1925, two months after his death. *Le Miroir de Jésus* was performed posthumously at the international festival in Zurich in 1926. https://iscm.org/wnmd/1926-zurich/.
74. *The Sheffield Daily Independent*, 22 January 1922, 5. https://iscm.org/wnmd/1924-prague-salzburg.
75. "Selection committee nominated," *The Westminster Gazette*, 22 January 1923, 12.
76. Masters, "Performing Internationalism."
77. *La Revue musicale*, 1 October 1924, 244.
78. Dent, "Internationalism et musique," 58: "Edward Dent, dont le dévouement à la cause de l'internationalisme artistique et la politique ferme et prudente a réussi à triompher des embûches sans nombre semées sous ses pas." Prunières, "Chroniques et notes."
79. "Chroniques et notes," 59–60.
80. "Chroniques et notes," 60.
81. "ne veut même pas venir en aide aux compositeurs." "Chroniques et notes," 60.
82. Lazaro, *Écoles de Paris en musique, 1920–1950*, 264–78.
83. On a political level, the postwar period was dominated by the reparations imposed on Germany and the military occupation of the Rhineland and Ruhr

(1923–24). The ending of this transition period occurred when Germany joined the Société des Nations in 1925. Arguably, musical attitudes followed a similar trajectory, although it seems have taken even longer to cast off wartime attitudes.
84. Shreffler, "The International Society for Contemporary Music and Its Political Context," 64–80.

Bibliography

Adler, Guido. "Internationalism in Music." *The Musical Quarterly* 11, no. 2 (1925): 281–300.

Anselmini, François. "Alfred Cortot et la diplomatie musicale française." In *Littératures et musiques dans la mondialisation*, edited by Anaïs Fléchet and Marie-Françoise Lévy, 33–43. Paris: Publications de la Sorbonne, 2015.

Bantock, Granville. "A Musical Repas." *The Chesterian*, New Series 1, September (1919): 11–12.

———. "A Glaring Anomaly." *The Musical Times*, 1 May 1920, 336.

Cathé, Philippe et Denis Huneau.Buch, Esteban. "'Les Allemands et les Boches': la musique allemande à Paris pendant la Première Guerre mondiale." *Le Mouvement social* 208 (2004): 45–69. https://doi.org/10.2307/3780276.

Cathé, Philippe, and Denis Huneau. "André Caplet-Charles Koechlin: une relation prometteuse trop vite interrompue." In *André Caplet, compositeur et chef d'orchestre*, edited by Denis Herlin and Cécile Quesney. Paris: Société française de musicologie, 2020.

Davidson, Jim. *Lyrebird Rising: Louise Hanson-Dyer of Oiseau-Lyre, 1884–1962*. Carlton, Victoria: Melbourne University Press, 1994.

Demonet, Giles. "Les Concerts Straram (1926–1933)." HDR. Paris: Université Paris-Sorbonne, 2015.

Dent, Edward. "Internationalisme et musique." *La Revue musicale* 4, no. 10 (August 1923): 58–60.

———. "Plans for Salzburg." *The Nation and Atheneum*, 3 February 1923, 696–98.

———. "Looking Backward." In *Edward J Dent: Selected Essays*, edited by Hugh Taylor, 272–290. Cambridge: Cambridge University Press, 1979.

Doctor, Jennifer. *The BBC and Ultra-Modern Music, 1922–1936: Shaping the Nation's Tastes*. Cambridge: Cambridge University Press, 1999.

Duchêne-Thégarid, Marie. "Les élèves musiciens étrangers en France dans l'entre-deux-guerres." In *Littératures et musiques dans la mondialisation*, edited by Anaïs Fléchet and Marie-Françoise Lévy, 45–56. Paris: Publications de la Sorbonne, 2015.

Duchesneau, Michel. *L'Avant-garde musicale et ses sociétés à Paris de 1871 à 1939*. Sprimont: Mardaga, 1997.

———. "Enjeux culturels dans la presse musicale française, 1900–1925." *Revue musicale OICRM* 4, no. 2 (2017): 19–34.

Evans, Edwin. "French Music of To-Day." *Proceedings of the Musical Association* (1909–1910): 47–74.

———. "Plans for Salzburg." *The Nation and Atheneum*, 3 February 1923, 696.

———. "The Salzburg Festival, International Chamber Concerts." *The Musical Times* 63, no. 955, 1 September 1922, 628–31.

Fauser, Annegret. "The Scholar behind the Medal: Edward J. Dent (1876–1957) and the Politics of Music History." *Journal of the Royal Musical Association* 139, no. 2 (1914): 235–60.

Fléchet, Anaïs, and Marie-Françoise Lévy, eds. *Littératures et musiques dans la mondialisation*. Paris: Publications de la Sorbonne, 2015.

Forkert, Anneka. "'Always a European': Edward Clark's Musical Work." *The Musical Times*, Summer (2018): 47–72.

Fulcher, Jane. "The Preparation for Vichy: Anti-Semitism in French Musical Culture between the Two World Wars." *The Musical Quarterly* 71, no. 3 (Fall 1995): 458–75.

Guerpin, Martin. "Adieu New York, bonjour Paris! Les Enjeux esthétiques et culturels des appropriations du jazz dans le monde musical savant français (1900–1930)." PhD diss., Paris and Montréal: Université Paris-Sorbonne—Université de Montréal, 2015.

———. "Le Courrier musical et le premier conflit mondial (1904–1923). Propagande, mobilisation culturelle et sortie de guerre." *Revue musicale OICRM* 4, no. 2 (2017): 35–57. https://revuemusicaleoicrm.org/rmo-vol4-n2/courrier-musical/.

Henry, Leigh. "London Letter." *The Chesterian* 16 (June 1921): 498–99.

Hull, Arthur Eaglefield. "A Few Words about the British Music Society." *The Musical Times* 60, no. 912 (February 1919): 71.

Jean-Aubry, Georges. *French Music of To-Day*, translated by Edwin Evans. New York: Books for Libraries Press, 1919.

Kelly, Barbara L. *Tradition and Style in the Works of Darius Milhaud*. Aldershot: Ashgate, 2003.

"Ravel's Timeliness and His Many Late Styles." In *Late Style and Its Discontents*, edited by Gordon McMullan and Sam Smiles, 158–73. Oxford: Oxford University Press, 2016.

———. "Common Canon, Conflicting Ideologies: Music Criticism in Performance in Interwar France." In *Music Criticism in France, 1918–1939: Authority, Advocacy, Legacy*, edited by Barbara L. Kelly and Christopher Moore, 121–50. Boydell: Woodbridge, 2018.

———. "French Connections: Debussy and Ravel's Orchestral Music in Britain from *Prélude à l'après-midi d'un faune* to *Boléro*." In *The Symphonic Poem in Britain, 1850–1950*, edited by Michael Allis and Paul Watt, 115–46. Woodbridge: Boydell, 2020.

———., ed. *French Music, Culture and National Identity, 1870–1939*. Rochester: University of Rochester Press, 2008.

Larkin, David. "Richard Strauss's Tone Poems in Britain." In *The Symphonic Poem in Britain, 1850–1950*, edited by Michael Allis and Paul Watt, 80–114. Woodbridge: Boydell and Brewer, 2020.

Lazzaro, Federico. *Écoles de Paris en musique, 1920–1950*. Paris: Vrin, 2018.

Masters, Giles. "New-Music Internationalism: The ISCM Festival, 1922–1939," PhD dissertation. Kings College, London, 2021.

Masters, Giles. "Performing Internationalism: the ISCM as a 'Musical League of Nations.'" In *Roundtable Round Table: A "Musical League of Nations"?: Music Institutions and the Politics of Internationalism Between the Wars*, edited by Sarah Collins, Laura Tunbridge, and Barbara L. Kelly. *Journal of the Royal Musical Association*, 147.2 Autumn 2022: 560–71.

Moore, Rachel. *Performing Propaganda: Musical Life and Culture in Paris during the First World War*. Woodbridge: Boydell, 2018.

Pistone, Danièle. "La musique comme ambassadrice? L'Association française d'action artistique (1922–2006): bilans et enjeux," *Relations internationales*, no. 156 (2013–14): 21–35.

Poulenc, Francis. *Correspondance*, edited by Myriam Chimènes. Paris: Fayard. 1994.

Prunières, Henry. "Chroniques et notes, La musique en France et à l'étranger, Le Festival de la S.I.M.C. à Salzbourg." *La Revue musicale* 5, no. 12, 1 October (1924): 244–49.

———. "Des rapports artistiques internationaux considérées du point de vue de la musique, de la musicologie et des musiciens." *Atti del Primo Congresso Internazionale di musica (Firenze 1933)*. Florence: Le Monnier, 1935.

Ravel, Maurice. *Lettres, écrits, entretiens*, edited by Orenstein. Paris: Flammarion, 1989.

Shreffler, Anne. "The International Society for Contemporary Music and Its Political Context." In *Music and International History in the Twentieth Century*, edited by Jessica C. E. Gienow-Hecht, 58–90. New York: Berghahn Books, 2015.

Solman, Frank. "British Music Society's New Catalogue." *The Musical Times*, 60 no. 919, 1 September (1919): 492.

Soret, Marie-Gabrielle. "Entre la création et l'interprétation." In *André Caplet, compositeur et chef d'orchestre*, edited by Denis Herlin and Cécile Quesney, 23–50. Paris: Société française de musicologie, 2020.

Chapter 14

MUSIC: A WEAPON FOR PEACE?
The United States, UNESCO, and the Creation of the International Music Council, 1945–1953

Anaïs Fléchet

The United Nations Educational, Scientific and Cultural Organization (UNESCO) was created in London in November 1945 to transition out of war through art and culture and educate "the minds of men and women"[1] in order to avoid future conflict.[2] In pursuit of these same objectives, the International Music Council (IMC) was established four years later in the new UNESCO offices on Avenue Kléber in Paris.[3] Music, with its emotive power and ability to transcend borders, was henceforth to be used as a "weapon for peace."[4] UNESCO's director-general Jaime Torres Bodet cogently communicated this conviction:

> Music, a form of expression without words or concepts, is the preeminently international art. It is at once the proof and the embodiment of a certain unity of human sensibility beyond political frontiers and the bounds of language. Through music, men who cannot understand one another's tongues, and who might sometimes find a still greater gulf created between them by the ideas, beliefs, habits, and prejudices that words serve to express, find an immediate bond in that common capacity to be moved by harmonies.[5]

In the early 1950s, the IMC became the main provider of UNESCO's music program. The ideal of peace and universal harmony was coupled with more concrete objectives, such as support for contemporary creation, the development of music education, and the defense of traditional music. With a view to helping reconstruct a music sec-

---

Notes for this section begin on page 285.

tor that had been sorely tested by the war, the IMC was also charged with acting as "a liaison agency for national and international music organizations throughout the world"[6] in addition to promoting a joint reflection on musical creation, the place of music in societies, and the value of music as an art form. The IMC's founders intended it as a place of exchange between composers, performers, and musicologists, irrespective of cultural borders and political rivalries between nations.

However, the IMC was not immune to the conflicts of its time, and the shadow of the Cold War hung over it in its early years. Who were the actors and what were the networks that led to the creation of the IMC? What were its first strategic and ideological orientations in the dual context of the postwar transition period and the institutionalization of the Cold War? As a number of recent works on Germany and the United States have shown,[7] the relationship between music, propaganda, and diplomacy was reconfigured in this overlap between the two wars. International organizations played a specific role in these reconfigurations; while they were inevitably hosts to conflicting national interests, they also gave rise to new forms of multilateralism. The International Institute of Intellectual Cooperation (IIIC), which was created in 1924 following the founding of the League of Nations, had already defined the broad outlines of an international music program in the wake of World War I.[8] However, the creation of UNESCO and the United States' deployment of cultural diplomacy led to a scaling-up of financial resources, actions, and geographic expansion after 1945. There was a simultaneous focus on regeneration—not just of war economies but also of war cultures, which needed to be redeployed in the promotion of peace—and on mobilization in a new, ideological conflict that had symbolic qualities at its heart.[9]

This is what I will demonstrate here using the IMC archives,[10] UNESCO archives, the extensive documentation of the US State Department, and the private archives of musicologists Charles Seeger (1886–1979) and Luiz Heitor Corrêa de Azevedo (1905–92), two key figures in this new international music diplomacy.

Reconstructing Musical Life, Redeploying the War Effort

The reconstruction of education and cultural life in war-torn areas was UNESCO's primary mission, and a plan to this effect was drawn up in London at the 1944 Conference of Allied Ministers of Education.[11] While a specific department was set up in 1946 to implement and oversee the reconstruction, this was an organization-wide objective. This is clearly evidenced in the first program established for "music and visual arts," which stated that UNESCO must:

1. Encourage organizations to raise funds for the purchase of necessary materials and tools for creative artists in devastated countries.
2. Encourage organizations to raise funds for the travel of artists and musicians of devastated areas to other countries, particularly to the U.S.
3. Organize, particularly in big towns, concerts, dance, recitals, exhibitions, etc. for the benefit of artistic reconstruction in devastated countries.[12]

Because its budget was severely limited, UNESCO appealed to the United States, with all its financial power and philanthropic tradition, for help in successfully implementing this policy of "artistic reconstruction." According to the information that UNESCO transmitted to the US State Department in the spring of 1947, these war-torn countries were in great need.[13] For example, a request was submitted for 100 pianos, 127 grand pianos (including 4 concert pianos), 261 violins, 41 violas, 78 cellos, 11 double basses, and 160 wind instruments, along with bows, strings, gramophones, records, radios, and music paper for conservatoires and professional musicians in Holland. Poland, too, appealed for emergency aid to restore a musical life that had been destroyed by the Nazi occupation: "After seven years of privations imposed by the oppressor, as far as concerts are concerned, there is now a great appetite for good music in Poland. Unfortunately, we are hampered by a lack of good instruments, which have mostly been destroyed or looted by the Germans."[14] The fate of Polish composers was equally concerning: one source reported that "they have lost almost everything, not just their libraries and pianos but often also their finished manuscripts, which were being carefully preserved for publication after the war."[15]

The US State Department had already begun to address these matters even before it was approached by UNESCO, however. An internal document dated May 1944 stressed the importance of the cultural—and more specifically musical—dimension of reconstruction:

> Attention should be given to aiding the intellectual and artistic rehabilitation of Europe though a proper use of musical programs in countries devastated by war. The economic and political measures undertaken

by our government in the work of reconstruction can helpfully supplement a carefully planned and integrated cultural effort in which music would play an important part.[16]

In February 1945 the issue was included on the agenda of the Advisory Committee on Music, a body created to guide the US State Department's music policy during the war. Interventions in Europe, the Middle East, and the Far East were planned.[17] The issue gained momentum in the months that followed as more information on the human and material losses caused by the war came to light. British musicologist Edward Dent, who had played a major role in the reconstruction of European musical life after World War I, through the leadership of the International Society of Contemporary Music,[18] presented a pessimistic report in a letter to Mark Brunwick (then president of the American section of the ISCM) transmitted to the Music Advisory Committee on December 1946. According to this report, musical life had shrunk everywhere in Europe.[19] In addition to the shortages ("the paper shortage has been disastrous in musical life"), lack of musicians (who were either dead, displaced, or still on active duty), and general devastation, the programs were monotonous and the performance quality poor:

> Orchestras are much in demand everywhere all over the country, and there are not enough good players; many are still waiting for release from the Forces. The result is that the standard of orchestral playing has gone down and cannot compare with the best US orchestras; ours are perpetually traveling in horrible discomfort . . . they have no time to rehearse, and hate rehearsing; . . . so we have nothing but eternal repetitions of the works that can be played without rehearsal—Beethoven and Tchaikovsky symphonies and concertos, with a few Rachmaninoff too.[20]

In June 1946 the US State Department convened a meeting of experts in Washington to discuss UNESCO's future music program. Among the many subjects deliberated (standardization, copyright, tours and festivals, music education, etc.), reconstruction aid was "one of the most crucially significant jobs to be done."[21] Without it a long-term program was not possible.

But musical reconstruction aid was not just a simple philanthropic undertaking. The United States, UNESCO's main funder at the time (contributing up to 44 percent of the budget in 1947, compared with 14 percent for the United Kingdom and 7 percent for France—the USSR had refused to join the organization[22]), was also keen to defend its own strategic interests. If music was to be used to help UNESCO through its contribution to bringing nations closer together and thus to the fundamental objectives of peace and security, UNESCO must also help the United States by encouraging the removal of the barriers to the music industry that it was experiencing, promoting the distribution of US music, and combating the global spread of anti-US sentiment. Repeatedly reiterated, these objectives were a direct continuation of the musical propaganda that had been developed during the war by the US Office of War Information (OWI), the US Armed Forces, and the US State Department, as well as the Pan American Union (PAU).[23] This idea was undoubtedly best expressed by the conductor Leopold Stokowski. In response to the US State Department's request for his opinion on music at UNESCO, he proposed to organize tours of the best US orchestras in Europe: "It would be the most honest, powerful, and yet subtle propaganda, and would immensely help the whole situation. It would be a continuation of psychological warfare into psychological peace."[24]

In Washington the reconstruction was not therefore seen as a return to the prewar situation. Rather, it was based on a new expertise in the use of music that had developed during the conflict. This is clearly evidenced by the list of key figures consulted by the US State Department when UNESCO's music program was being drawn up in 1946. Among others, it included Roy Harris, composer and former OWI musical director; Charles Seeger, chief of the music division at the PAU; and Carleton Sprague Smith, musicologist, head of New York Public Library's Music Department, and chairman of the first Office of the Coordinator of Inter-American Affairs' Music Committee, who was behind the creation of the US State Department's Music Committee in 1941. There were also many wartime musical advisers on the list, including Carlos Moseley, future administrator for the New York Philharmonic, who had worked at the OWI; Harold Spivacke, head of the Library of Congress's Music Division and member of the Joint Army and Navy Committee on Welfare and Recreation; and Harrison Kerr, composer and US army officer in charge of the War Department's musical reorientation program.

The diplomatic correspondence and proceedings of meetings are replete with references to the war. This was the foundational experience that conditioned the way in which the United States' and UNESCO's music programs were to be envisaged. Hence, Harris stressed the need to "supply a greater proportion of our more serious music" (and less "popular music"), citing the many requests he had received when he was musical director at the OWI,[25] and Seeger proposed to draw inspiration from the PAU's scholarship system to develop an exchange program for young musicians at UNESCO.[26]

Having served the war effort, music must now be mobilized in the service of peace. This discourse was based on a widely shared belief in the mobilizing power of music. As Charles G. Child from the US State Department's Office of International Information and Cultural Affairs explained: "Music by itself cannot do the job, but an intelligent and broad use of music in its many aspects could help in bringing about a greater degree of understanding."[27] The IMC was born not just out of this effort to redeploy musical propaganda from wartime to peacetime but also out of the profound ambiguity of this "peace," which to a large extent incorporated US interests and already anticipated Cold War tensions.

An International Organization for Music

The idea of a world music organization was first introduced at UNESCO in 1947. The project was the brainchild of Charles Seeger, a pioneer of US ethnomusicology who had been very involved in his country's musical institutions. After working for the Works Progress Administration, which was created by Roosevelt to combat unemployment during the Great Depression, Seeger helped set up the music division at the PAU, where he was appointed chief in 1941. During his time at the PAU, he remained very active in the American Musicological Society (AMS), including serving as its president between 1945 and 1946.[28] In two lengthy interviews given toward the end of his life, Seeger explained that he had wanted to create a world music organization from the moment he had joined the PAU: Pan American Union:

> My idea was, taught by my experience in the Roosevelt administration, that I would form an inter-American music council and then hope that there would be a European music council, an African music council, an East Asian music council, and so forth, and that they would eventually come together in a federation of world regions and we would have a world music council.[29]

However, the creation of UNESCO prompted him to review his plans for direct action on a global level. An active contributor to discussions on music in Washington, he believed there were two forms of international relations in the field of music. One was state-driven and was based on aggressive propaganda and aimed at strictly national objectives. The other was mobilized by international organizations (e.g., Pan American Union, United Nations) and was based on cultural cooperation "in which the competitive elements of nationalist propaganda are reduced to a minimum."[30] Seeger felt that the US State Department should concentrate its efforts on the latter.

In December 1946 Seeger set up the International Relations Committee within the AMS. As its director and as a representative of the PAU, he attended the first meeting of the US National Commission for UNESCO[31] in Philadelphia in March 1947. He already had a fairly clear idea by this point of what UNESCO should do for music. In the report he submitted to UNESCO's director-general Julian Huxley, through his friend Gustavo Durán,[32] a Spanish musician exiled in the United States, Seeger championed two strong convictions.[33] The first was that music can only be used in the service of peace if it relinquishes all forms of naive idealism: "To be avoided here is the belief that music is *in itself* good for world peace. To the contrary, it is a highly competitive field and can be used as a medium for aggression as easily as any other."[34] The second was that UNESCO must develop a pragmatic approach in order to achieve its goals:

> Materials of all regions should be used without prejudice as needed, using the idiom—primitive, folk, popular, fine-art or any hybrid—most suitable to the audience addressed and the theme and occasion chosen. Note: to be avoided here is the belief that "good" music is good for world peace but that "bad" music is not.... The frame in which music is presented often determines the value. Thus, "poor" art in a politically "good" frame yields better political results than "good" art in a politically "poor" frame.[35]

In September 1947 Seeger presented a new version of his plan at the Chicago meeting of the US National Commission for UNESCO, which now included a panel on music. He advocated for the creation of an independent organization, which should be drawn from the private sector and subsidized by UNESCO. This "International Music Institute" or "International Musicology Institute" (at this stage he was still undecided between the two names) would aim to

> promote international, inter-regional, and inter-cultural relations among existing music organizations ... ; to strengthen professional and other music organizations where these are weak and to promote building of music organizations where these do not exist, so as to effect well-rounded music development throughout the world; ... to cooperate with government and inter-government agencies in the promotion of international peace and understanding.[36]

To carry out his plan, Seeger was counting on the support of Durán, who had joined the UNESCO Secretariat to set up its Arts and Letters Section, and on the presence in Paris of two former PAU colleagues; the North American Vannett Lawler, an administrator at the Music Educators National Conference, was hired as a consultant to the Arts and Letters Section in July 1947, and Brazilian musicologist Luiz Heitor Corrêa de Azevedo had come to Paris in the September at Durán's invitation to take part in an expert committee on philosophy and the humanities.[37] Coming highly recommended by Seeger, Azevedo was hired to roll out UNESCO's music activities in October 1947. The two men corresponded regularly, in both English and Portuguese. As demonstrated by this letter sent in November by Azevedo from Mexico City, where he was attending the second session of the UNESCO General Conference, their correspondence reveals their warm relationship and a great intellectual meeting of minds:

> You may rest assured, my dear Charles, that one of the main reasons I accepted UNESCO's proposal was the prospect of working closely with you and Miss Lawler and, through you both, with the entire music education system in the United States. The possibility of seeing tangible, far-reaching action as a result of this cooperation has had an enormous, elucidating influence on the way in which I see my future at UNESCO.[38]

Although he was immediately in favor of the creation of an international music institute, Azevedo doubted whether he could get the proposal, which had been submitted after the deadline had passed in Mexico City.[39] He did, however, manage to convince Helen White, an acquaintance of Seeger and member of the US delegation, to propose a motion to the working group on Arts and Letters. Although the suggestion of an International Theatre Institute[40] gave rise to some lively and lengthy discussions, the motion was unanimously adopted thanks to the support of musicians and musicologists from the various national delegations, including notably the Mexican composer Carlos Chávez. The Secretariat was instructed to carry out a preliminary review to clarify the purpose of and implementation procedures for the future music organization. The results of these consultations were endorsed by the third session of the UNESCO General Conference in Beirut in November 1948, which urged the director-general "to continue enquiries about the feasibility of an international organization for music."[41] It was envisaged that its headquarters would be located in Italy, or Rome to be precise, which met with indignation from the Florentine-by-adoption composer Luigi Dallapiccola:

> We know only too well the "Romans'" sense of opportunism, the fierce egoism of this merciless race. Yesterday's fascists are today's "progressives." ... Choosing Rome for the institute's headquarters would be a

disaster for the rest of Italy. Is it not possible for UNESCO to inform the Italian government that its location of *choice* would be Florence?[42]

Did Dallapiccola's misgivings influence the Secretariat's decision? Did the determination to keep the new organization at UNESCO's headquarters prevail? In any event, a committee of music experts met in Paris from 25 to 28 January 1949 to consider the creation of an international music council (the word "council" was ultimately preferred to "institute" because it conveyed a "more modest and elastic structure"[43]). The committee included representatives from the four existing international music organizations: Edward Clark and Maud Karpeles of Great Britain from the International Society for Contemporary Music and the International Folk Music Council, respectively; Marcel Cuvelier of Belgium from the Jeunesses Musicales International; and Paul-Henri Masson of France from the International Musicological Society. It also comprised members of the UNESCO Secretariat, namely Azevedo, the Chinese writer Lin Yutang (head of the Arts and Letters Section), and Frenchman Jean Thomas (head of the Cultural Activities Section), as well as members of the US National Commission for UNESCO's panel on music, namely Carleton Sprague Smith and Harrison Kerr, whose visit was sponsored by the US State Department. Charles Seeger was also "invited by the Director-General as a special consultant, owing to the large share he had taken in the development of the project since its inception."[44] The Italian composer Goffredo Petrassi (1904–2003) also took part, as did the musicologist and composer Roland-Manuel, who had been invited to balance out the committee's French contingent.[45] The discussions led to the passing of statutes for the newly formed IMC, whose first General Assembly was held in Paris from 30 January to 3 February 1950 with UNESCO's director-general Jaime Torres Bodet in attendance. Roland-Manuel was elected president of the IMC, and composers Arthur Honegger (for France) and Andrzej Panufnik (Poland) were elected vice presidents.

In addition to the purely institutional aspects, the debates surrounding the creation of the IMC allow us to trace its intellectual origins. Like UNESCO, the IMC was situated at the intersection of two filiations. On the one hand, it drew its inspiration from the IIIC's interwar music programs. In 1947, for example, UNESCO took over the "world catalog of recorded music" project, which had been launched by the IIIC in 1931, and the IMC subsequently became its main operator. The IMC also supported the work being done to notate folk music by the International Commission on Folk Arts and Folklore, which was founded under the auspices of the IIIC in 1928.⁴⁶ The IIIC's legacy can also be seen in the "French influence," which was emphatically denounced by Seeger:

> The result was that the International Music Council, like most international organizations that are domiciliated in France, became almost more French than the French, thoroughly under the influence of the French ideas of culture, French ideas of music, and French ideas of everything else.... The rest of the world would be told by this French-dominated clique what was music, and what they ought to do in the way of music.... The contacts of the UNESCO, far from trying to reach the people of the world would content themselves with reaching the ruling classes and the elite of the professional music group.⁴⁷

Seeger's observation reveals the crux of the criticism leveled by the "anglo-american faction" at the "Latin faction" during UNESCO's early years. As French historian Chloé Maurel clearly demonstrates, the former favored programs oriented toward education and mass cultures while the latter advocated a more elitist model of "intellectual cooperation" inherited from the IIIC.⁴⁸

Despite Seeger's disenchantment, however, the PAU had far more influence than the IIIC on the design of the IMC. While not overtly displayed, this intellectual filiation can be seen very clearly in the professional trajectories of its promoters. Seeger, Durán, Lawler, Smith for the United States, Azevedo for Brazil, and the Chilean composer Domingo Santa Cruz (who later became its president), every single one of them had passed through the PAU headquarters in Washington before joining UNESCO and the IMC. The IMC was forged from powerful inter-US networks and the strategic support of the US State Department. These foundations distinguished it from the—still very European—initiatives of the IIIC, because the early years of the IMC were played out in Washington as much as in Paris.

The Cold War Scores

From the very start, UNESCO was suspected of serving the interests of the United States. The Soviet Union refused to participate, prompting the withdrawal of the Eastern Bloc.⁴⁹ Criticism also came from the "free world," however, notably from France, whose minister of foreign affairs, Georges Bidault, declared in 1947: "Because of its international status, UNESCO is a great propaganda tool for spreading US culture and thought throughout the world."⁵⁰

In terms of music, an examination of the US State Department's archives largely confirms this diagnosis. As we have seen, the United States was already discussing UNESCO's future music program in 1946. Moreover, it was the United States delegation that put forward the proposal to create an international institute of music at the 1947 General Conference in Mexico City, a plan that had emerged from the PAU networks. The US State Department's involvement became firmly established in 1948. First, the composition of UNESCO's committee of experts (the one that led to the creation of the IMC in January 1949) was subject to strict scrutiny, but UNESCO's decision initially to limit the United States to two invitees, Charles Seeger and Carleton Sprague Smith, was challenged by Washington. The US State Department lobbied for the additional nomination of the composer, pianist, and conductor Howard Hanson (1896–1981) (chairman of the US National Commission for UNESCO's panel on music), or, failing that, the composer Harrison Kerr. A telegram sent by the undersecretary of state, Robert A. Lovett, to the United States ambassador to France, Jefferson Caffery, shows the importance attached to this campaign: "Choice of invitees extremely important to secure support for UNESCO program items by National Commission and by private national organizations in member state."[51] The message was received loud and clear by UNESCO, which ultimately invited Kerr because Hanson was not available.

Washington closely supported the International Music Fund, which had been set up by the US branch of the International Society for Contemporary Music to help European composers recover after the war. Financed by charity concerts, this fund was launched at Tanglewood on 3 August 1948 by Serge Koussevitzky and the Boston Symphony Orchestra. Many officials were in attendance, including Archibald MacLeish (US National Commission for UNESCO), Felix Frankfurter (Supreme Court), and the composer Aaron Copland. The money raised (US$10,000 from the first concert) was managed by a committee chaired by Carleton Sprague Smith and closely supervised by the US National Commission for UNESCO. Hence, working away behind the scenes of this ostensibly private initiative, whose objectives read like a Marshall Plan for music, was the US State Department. According to the manifesto that accompanied its founding, the aim was to aid the spiritual rehabilitation of Europe: "Much has been written and said of the urgent necessity for a physical and material rehabilitation in war-shattered areas of Europe, little is heard of the spiritual exhaustion, the psychic devastation, the despair that is attendant upon these conditions." Above all, it aimed to combat "a flood tide of materialism, prejudice, and suspicion that threatens to engulf all other values."[52]

The underlying driving force behind this action was the fight against communism, and money was its main weapon. At the end of August 1948, UNESCO was entrusted with the task of distributing the funds in Europe.[53] All that remained was to assess the needs of European composers and to set up a committee to distribute the US aid. The UNESCO Secretariat then decided to merge this initiative with the ongoing discussions on the creation of the future IMC.

Washington's influence remained significant until the early 1950s. The US State Department closely monitored the setting up of the IMC. In April 1951 secretary of state Dean Acheson personally inquired about the progress of Constantin Brăiloiu's *The World Collection of Folk Music*, which was released through the International Archives of Popular Music in Geneva and the IMC.[54] The UNESCO Secretariat, in return, frequently sought the opinion of the US National Commission for UNESCO on music matters. For example, in 1951 Azevedo asked Harold Spivacke (a member of the panel on music) for his thoughts on Alan Lomax's proposal to link UNESCO to a series of folk music records produced by Columbia Records.[55] While UNESCO was in favor, Azevedo was unsure how the United States would react (Lomax being suspected of being Communist or at least sympathetic to the cause): "Do you consider it desirable, possible or outright undesirable? I have been very vague in my conversations with Lomax, and I know that one of these days, he will be back in Paris and will bring the subject up once more."[56] Washington's answer was not retained in the archives, but Lomax did not obtain UNESCO's support for this particular project.

Furthermore, the use of the International Music Fund was closely monitored. On several occasions, composers selected by the IMC were rejected by the United States, forcing UNESCO to reconsider its position. The reasons, which varied, show that the dynamics of the Cold War had not entirely erased the memory of World War II. For example, ignoring the advice of his colleagues Carleton Sprague Smith, Howard Hanson, and Harold Spivacke, who were already experienced in Cold War propaganda, the fund's main promoter, Serge Koussevitzky, opposed the decision to divert scholarships initially planned for Polish composers (who were isolated following Poland's withdrawal from UNESCO) to West German composers in 1951 in anticipation of the Federal Republic of Germany's upcoming membership.[57]

These overlaps between the end of World War II and the start of the Cold War attest to the complexity of this postwar transition, which lasted until the early 1950s. The transition period came to an end between 1952 and 1953. The IMC, which had been granted consultative status by UNESCO, now benefited from regular funding and its own administration. In 1952 Jack Bornoff became its executive secretary. A former British intelligence officer who had worked on the "musical rehabilitation" program in occupied Germany in 1945 and 1946,[58] Bornoff contributed to anchoring the IMC in the free world camp. In 1954 he took John Evarts on as his deputy. Evarts was a former assistant to Nicolas Nabokov at the Congress for Cultural Freedom, which was a propaganda machine generously funded by the CIA to counter Soviet influence in Western cultural circles.[59] At the same time, McCarthyism led to a closing of ranks among the North Americans. Seeger was forced out because he was suspected of being Communist and too closely linked to the activities of his son, the protest folk singer Pete Seeger. In January 1953 Charles Seeger's passport was withdrawn on the eve of his departure for Europe, where he was to attend an IMC meeting in preparation for its international conference on music education in Brussels a few months later:

> I had been connected with too many dangerous, subversive organizations. By this time I think they had some kind of dossier on me. . . . I told the State Department that they were acting unconstitutionally, and would be found to be so presently when the McCarthy hysteria went over, but as one lawyer told me, "you have less chance of getting a passport than a snowball in hell", so I didn't fight it. It would have cost a great deal anyway, and I would have been black-listed, and my whole family would have gotten into trouble.[60]

Shortly after this, Seeger resigned from the PAU, where his dreams of international action had been shattered. By this time, UNESCO's music program was in any case moving away from the "defense of all music" position advocated by Seeger. With the exception of *The World Collection of Folk Music*, the IMC's actions were mainly aimed at promoting contemporary Western music (serialism, electroacoustic) through records, catalogs, concerts, and radio broadcasts. This program, which defended and illustrated the "freedom" of the so-called apolitical creative artist, albeit these artists were in perfect agreement with the United States' official line, was introduced at the same time as Zhdanovism was imposing the canons of socialist realism on Soviet composers. We can see here the same factors at play in the US administration's contemporaneous championing of the leading figures of abstract expressionism, including first and foremost Jackson Pollock. Pollock's success was due not just to the aesthetic quality of his work but also to the strategic objectives of the cultural Cold War.[61]

Conclusion

The IMC's funding sources, membership, staff recruitment, and music programs reveal an organization that was well rooted in the Western camp at the beginning of the 1950s. However, it would be a mistake to think it was merely a tool used by the United States in the cultural Cold War because the "Latin faction" still had significant influence throughout the first half of the 1950s in the form of key figures such as Roland-Manuel, Arthur Honegger, Marcel Cuvelier, and Henri Barraud. Moreover, after its initial enthusiasm, the United States began to express a certain mistrust of UNESCO and its staff, which it suspected had been infiltrated by communist agents. The development of Cold War cultural diplomacy,[62] which was directly led by US government agencies and organizations that were covertly funded by the CIA, such as the Congress for Cultural Freedom (which had the advantage of not being hampered by multilateralism), also contributed to this perspective. The USSR's entry into UNESCO in 1954 only added to this already complex equation. The East-West divide weighed heavily on the future of the international musical organization that Charles Seeger, Luiz Heitor Corrêa de Azevedo, and others had dreamed of as the world had transitioned out of World War II. Although the discourses, which centered on music and universal harmony and reconciliation, remained the same, the postwar transition period had come to an end, giving way to new symbolic struggles that created not just new borders—both cultural and political—but also new aspirations and exchanges that were aimed at transcending them.

Anaïs Fléchet is associate professor in international history at the University Paris-Saclay (UVSQ), and member of the research team Centre d'histoire culturelle des sociétés contemporaines. Her research focuses on music and international history, and Latin America music, and the circulation of artistic practices in the Global South. She is the author of *Si tu vas à Rio. La musique populaire brésilienne en France au XXe et XXIe siècle*; and *Villa-Lobos à Paris: un écho musical du Brésil*. She has also edited *Cultural History in France: Local Debates, Global Perspectives*; *Histoire culturelle du Brésil contemporain*;

Littératures et musiques dans la mondialisation; "Musique et relations internationals"; and *Une histoire des festivals XX^{e}XXIe siècles*. Since 2016 she has been a principal investigator on the joint research project "Transatlantic Cultures." She is currently preparing a book on the International Music Council of the UNESCO during the Cold War.

Appendix. List of organizations

American Musicological Society (1934–)
Conference of Allied Ministers of Education (1942–1945)
Congress for Cultural Freedom (1950–1979)
International Commission on Folk Arts and Folklore (1928–1964)
International Folk Music Council, now International Council for Traditional Music (1947–)
International Institute of Intellectual Co-operation (1925–1946)
International Music Council (1949–)
International Music Fund (1948–1951)
International Musicological Society (1927–)
International Society for Contemporary Music (1922–)
International Theatre Institute (1948–)
Jeunesses Musicales International (1945–)
League of Nations (1920–1940)
Music Educators National Conference, now National Association for Music Education (1907–)
Office of the Coordinator of Inter-American Affairs (1940–1946)
Office of War Information (1942–1945)
Organization of American States (1948–)
Pan American Union (1890–1948)
United Nations Educational, Scientific and Cultural Organization (1945–)
United States National Commission for UNESCO (1946–)
Work Progress Administration (1935–1943)

Notes

1. According to the Preamble to the Constitution of UNESCO, "since wars begin in the minds of men and women, it is in the minds of men and women that the defenses of peace must be constructed."
2. This chapter was translated from French by Clare Ferguson.
3. For a general history of the IMC, see Fléchet, "Le Conseil international de la musique."

4. Luiz Heitor Corrêa de Azevedo, "UNESCO to Use Music as Weapon for Peace," *UNESCO Courier*, April 1948, 7.
5. Speech delivered at the first IMC General Assembly, 30 January 1950. Reproduced in International Music Council, *Foundation, First and Second General Assemblies*, 2.
6. "Musicologists Create World Council," *UNESCO Courier*, March 1949, 4.
7. See, among others, Thacker, *Music after Hitler, 1945–1955*; Fosler-Lussier, *Music in America's Cold War Diplomacy*; and Gienow-Hecht, *Music and International History in the Twentieth Century*.
8. Sibille, "La musique à la Société des Nations."
9. Gienow-Hecht, "Culture and the Cold War in Europe"; Mikkonen and Suutari, *Music, Art and Diplomacy*.
10. My warmest thanks to Silja Fischer, secretary general of the IMC, and Davide Grosso for allowing me access to the IMC archives and for all the help they gave me when I consulted them.
11. UNESCO was referred to at the time as the United Nations Educational and Cultural Reconstruction Organization. The current name was not adopted until 1945. See Maurel, *Histoire de l'UNESCO*, 21.
12. National Archives and Records Administration, College Park, Maryland (henceforth NARA), NARA/RG84/France. Embassy Paris. Classified General Unesco Records 1946-1949/Box 8/Letter from Tent to McKeon, February 22, 1947. Compilation of the material submitted by the UNESCO secretariat as suggestions for action by the US National Commission, 14: "Music and Visual Arts."
13. NARA/RG84 UNESCO/Box 7/Musical Rehabilitation in War Devastated Countries. Report by Gustavo Durán (chief of Arts and Letter Section, UNESCO), 29 May 1947.
14. NARA/RG84 UNESCO/Box 7, 29 May 1947: "Après sept ans de privations imposées par l'oppresseur dans le domaine des concerts, un grand désir d'écouter de la bonne musique se manifeste en ce moment en Pologne. Il se heurte malheureusement au manque de bons instruments qui ont été détruits ou pillés par les Allemands."
15. NARA/RG84 UNESCO/Box 7, 29 May 1947: "Ils ont perdu presque tout, non seulement leur bibliothèque et leur piano, mais aussi, souvent, les manuscrits déjà terminés et soigneusement gardés afin d'être édités après la guerre."
16. NARA/RG59 Music UNESCO/Box 5/General statement on the music program of the Department, May 1944 (not undersigned).
17. NARA/RG59 Music UNESCO/Box 4/Agenda for meeting of Advisory Committee on Music to the Department, 23 and 24 February 1945.
18. See Barbara Kelly's chapter in this volume.
19. NARA/RG59 Music UNESCO/Box 4/Letter from Edward Dent to Mark Brunswick, London, 17 December 1945.
20. NARA/RG59 Music UNESCO/Box 4, 17 December 1945.
21. NARA/RG59 Music UNESCO/Box 5/Proceedings of the meeting of the Advisory Committee to the Department of State on a Music Program for UNESCO, Washington, State Department Building, 20 June 1946, 140.
22. Maurel, *Histoire de l'UNESCO*, 102.
23. See, in particular, Fauser, *Sounds of War*; and Palomino, "Nationalist, Hemispheric, and Global."
24. NARA/RG59 Music UNESCO/Box 5/Letter from Leopold Stokowski to Charles Thomson, Beverly Hills, 15 June 1946.
25. NARA/RG59 Music UNESCO/Box 5/Letter from Roy Harris to Charles Thomson, New York City, 18 June 1946.

26. NARA/RG59 Music UNESCO/Box 5/Proceedings of the meeting of the Advisory Committee to the Department of State on a Music Program for UNESCO, Washington, State Department Building, 20 June 1946, 68.
27. NARA/RG59 Music UNESCO/Box 5/UNESCO and the National Music Council. An Address to the IMC by Charles G. Child, Advisor on Arts and Humanities, Office of International Information and Cultural Affairs, Department of State, 27 December 1946.
28. Pescatello, *Charles Seeger*; Franzius, "Forging Music into Ideology."
29. Seeger, *Reminiscences of an American Musicologist*, 321.
30. NARA/RG59 Music UNESCO/Box 5/Letter from Charles Seeger to Howard Hanson, 14 January 1947.
31. This is a strictly consultative body that brings together some hundred private and public organizations. It was set up by the US Department of State to advise it on all matters relating to UNESCO.
32. A colonel in the Republican Army during the Spanish Civil War, he was the inspiration behind characters in Ernest Hemingway's *For Whom the Bell Tolls* and André Malraux's *L'Espoir* (Man's hope/Days of hope). Made a naturalized US citizen in 1942, he was hired by the US State Department and worked for the United Nations from 1946 onward.
33. Charles Seeger Archive, Bancroft Library, University of California Berkeley/Box 3/Item 52: "Suggestion for a Music Program for UNESCO."
34. Idem.
35. Ibid.
36. Azevedo's Collection, Library of Congress/Box 14(1)/Recortes III/"Towards the Strengthening of International Music Organization."
37. This invitation had been elicited by Azevedo, who had asked his "old friend Durán" at a congress in Lisbon on Luso-Brazilian folklore in the summer of 1947 to come up with a pretext for him to visit Paris. Azevedo, "Minha memórias da UNESCO." I would like to thank Carlos Sandroni for sending me this document and for all his valuable guidance throughout this research.
38. IMC/Structure 2.1/Letter from Luiz Heitor Corrêa de Azevedo to Charles Seeger, Mexico City, 17 November 1947: "Pode estar certo, meu caro Charles, que uma das razões mais fortes que me inclinaram a aceitar a proposta da UNESCO, foi a esperança de poder trabalhar em estreita colaboração com você, com Miss Lawler, e com todo o mecanismo de educação musical dos Estados Unidos, através de ambos. Essa perspectiva de uma ação real, de larga repercussão, que podermos ter resultando dessa cooperação, influiu muitíssimo para iluminar a parte que posso entrever, de meu uture na UNESCO."
39. Azevedo, "Minha memórias da UNESCO," 34–35.
40. Eventually founded in 1948.
41. *Records of the General Conference of UNESCO, Third Session, Beirut, 1948. Volume II: Resolutions.* Paris: UNESCO, 1949, 26, resolution 6.12.
42. IMC/Structure 2.1/Letter from Luigi Dallapicola, Florence, 28 December 1948. Original in French.
43. UNESCO Archives/AL/Conf.4/12/"Committee for examining the establishment of an international organization for music. 25–28 January 1949. Report from the Secretariat."
44. Azevedo, "Minha memórias da UNESCO," 39–40.
45. "Minha memórias da UNESCO," 39–40.
46. CIM/Réunions du bureau 1950-1956/AL/CIM/Bur./SR.2/Procès-verbal de la deuxième séance tenue à la maison de l'UNESCO, 19 avenue Kléber, mardi 21 juillet

1950. On the work carried out by the IIIC, see: Ducci, "Le musée d'art populaire contre le folklore."
47. Seeger, *Reminiscences of an American Musicologist*, 337.
48. Maurel, *Histoire de l'UNESCO*, 16–26.
49. Although Poland, Hungary, and Czechoslovakia had contributed to the creation of UNESCO, they stopped participating in 1949 and officially withdrew in 1952. Yugoslavia was the only remaining Eastern Bloc country during this period. See Maurel, *Histoire de l'UNESCO*, 113–4.
50. Cited by Maurel, *Histoire de l'UNESCO*, 96. Original in French.
51. NARA/RG84 UNESCO/Box 18/Cable from Lovett to Ambassy Paris, 2 November 1948.
52. IMC/International Music Fund 3.12.2/"A manifesto of the International Music Fund."
53. UNESCO Archives/AL/Conf.4/7/"Committee for examining the establishment of an international organization for music. 25–28 January 1949. The International Music Fund. Background Document."
54. NARA/RG84 UNESCO/Box 8/Cable from Dean Acheson to Ambassy Paris, 7 April 1951.
55. This was the Columbia Folk Library. Lomax proposed to associate UNESCO with this project in return for funding for recording trips to the Middle East.
56. NARA/RG84 UNESCO/Box 8/Letter from Azevedo to Spivacke, 2 March 1951.
57. IMC/International Music Fund 3.12.2/Letter from Azevedo to Koussevitzky, 25 May 1951.
58. Thacker, *Music after Hitler, 1945–1955*, 39–74.
59. Scott-Smith, *The Politics of Apolitical Culture*.
60. Seeger, *Reminiscences of an American Musicologist*, 343.
61. I refer here to Serge Guilbault's classic work *How New York Stole the Idea of Modern Art*.
62. In respect of the musical domain, the US State Department's Cultural Presentations Program became its main tool from 1954 onward. See Fosler-Lussier, *Music in America's Cold War Diplomacy*.

Bibliography

Azevedo, Luiz Heitor Corrêa de. "Minhas memórias da UNESCO (a música nas relações internacionais, 1947–1965)." In *Luiz Heitor Correia de Azevedo 80 Anos*, edited by Dulce Martins Lamas, 31–45. São Paulo/Rio de Janeiro: Sociedade Brasileira de Musicologia/FUNARTE, 1985.

Ducci, Annamaria. "Le musée d'art populaire contre le folklore. L'Institut International de Coopération Intellectuelle à l'époque du Congrès de Prague." *Revue germanique international* 21 (2015): 133–48.

Fauser, Annegret. *Sounds of War: Music in the United States during World War II*. New York: Oxford University Press, 2013.

Fléchet, Anaïs. "Le Conseil international de la musique et la politique musicale de l'Unesco (1945–1975)." *Relations internationals* 156 (2013): 53–71.

Fosler-Lussier, Danielle. *Music in America's Cold War Diplomacy*. Berkeley: University of California Press, 2015.

Franzius, Andrea. "Forging Music into Ideology: Charles Seeger and the Politics of Cultural Pluralism in American Domestic and Foreign Policy." *Amerikastudien/American Studies* 56, no. 3 (2011): 347–79.

Gienow-Hecht, Jessica, ed. *Music and International History in the Twentieth Century*. New York: Berghahn Books, 2015.

———. "Culture and the Cold War in Europe." In *Cambridge History of the Cold War*, vol. 1, edited by Melvyn P. Leffer, and Odd Arne Wesdtad, 398–419. Cambridge: Cambridge University Press, 2010.

Guilbault, Serge. *How New York Stole the Idea of Modern Art: Abstract Expressionism, Freedom and the Cold War*. Chicago: University of Chicago Press, 1983.

International Music Council. *Foundation, First and Second General Assemblie*. UNESCO: Paris, 1951.

Maurel, Chloé. *Histoire de l'UNESCO. Les trente premières années. 1945–1974*. Paris: L'Harmattan, 2010.

Mikkonen, Simo, and Pekka Suutari, eds. *Music, Art and Diplomacy: East-West Cultural Interactions and the Cold War*. New York: Routledge, 2016.

Palomino, Pablo. "Nationalist, Hemispheric, and Global: 'Latin American Music' and the Music Division of the Pan American Union, 1939–1947." *Nuevo Mundo Mundos Nuevos*, June 2015. Retrieved 26 April 2021 from http://journals.openedition.org/nuevomundo/68062

Pescatello, Ann M. *Charles Seeger: A Life in American Music*. Pittsburgh: University of Pittsburgh Press, 1992.

Seeger, Charles. *Reminiscences of an American Musicologist: Charles Seeger Interviewed by Adelaide G. Tusler and Ann M. Briegleb*. Los Angeles: UCLA, 1972.

Scott-Smith, Giles. *The Politics of Apolitical Culture: The Congress for Cultural Freedom and the Political Economy of American Hegemony 1945–1955*. London: Routledge, 2002.

Sibille, Christiane. "La musique à la Société des Nations." *Relations internationales* 155, no. 3 (2013): 89–102.

Thacker, Toby. *Music after Hitler, 1945–1955*. Aldershot: Ashgate, 2007.

Afterword

SURVIVAL, DESIRE, EMPOWERMENT, AND THE ABSENCE OF WORDS
Music in Postwar Transitions, 1800–1950

Jessica Gienow-Hecht

Postwar transitions are in vogue, more so now perhaps than at any other point in recent history. The long-term public indifference toward regional conflicts notwithstanding, Russia's 2022 invasion of Ukraine has triggered powerful memories of the postwar years in Europe and across the world, alongside military rearmament, frantic preparation efforts, and grave considerations regarding future energy supplies.[1] Debates regarding the viability of economic and humanitarian aid for Ukraine and the vista of the region's postwar future have occupied policymakers, political observers, and the media alike. On the news, in public panels, and in institutes of higher education, prominent voices such as the Ukrainian president Volodymyr Zelensky, the US ambassador to Germany, Amy Gutmann, and the German minister of finance, Christian Lindner, have all advocated a "new Marshall Plan" for the reconstruction of postwar Ukraine while European Commission president Ursula von der Leyen's initiative to rebuild Ukraine, tied to the country's EU admission, likewise echoes visions of extensive humanitarian aid.[2]

Few of these discussions have considered the significance of culture and the arts in the rebuilding of the country and the nation. This is all the more curious for two reasons: first, a significant part of the Marshall Plan both contained and was embedded in cultural considerations regarding political reeducation, workplace culture,

---

Notes for this section begin on page 297.

Americanization, and ideological integration. Indeed, while there is generally agreement that the postwar transition in Ukraine needs to be wedded to anticorruption measures, transparency, and some sort of structural reorientation, few seem to grasp the extent to which the nation's enormous sociocultural energy may generate challenges and promises that such a transformation may entail. Any war's end yields a change of time and temper typically unanticipated yet prompting vast and irretrievable changes in terms of mood, outlook, creativity, and visions of the future.

Second, the absence of any focus on the pivotal role of the arts in postwar transitions is puzzling since the role of music in wartime societies has been a nadir of scholarly investigation for a considerable amount of time. For example, M. J. Grant and Férdia J. Stone-Davis have analyzed the role of music in wartime broadcasting and addressed many themes informing the present book: the musicology of conflict, the music of justice, the music of propaganda, as well as the role of mediators and consumers.[3] J. Martin Daughtry has studied the act of listening in modern warfare experience, based on interviews with both Iraqi civilians and US soldiers.[4] Likewise, Kathleen Smith's examination of how "Tin Pan Alley goes to war" evaluates popular songs, finding that most of them were actually "escapist" rather than propagandistic (something that caught the attention of the Office of War Information, who felt the situation needed adjustment).[5] What is more, for the last fifteen years, individual authors have turned to postwar transitions, again, most specifically in the case of Germany. David Monod, Toby Thacker, Elizabeth Jannik, and others have examined in great detail the effort on the part of occupation authorities seeking (and failing) to include music in the policy of democratic reorientation.[6]

To invite an inclusive gaze and to alert us to the impact of music in the field of postwar transitions, really *postwar emotion*, is the foremost contribution of this book. Its central query is both simple and complex: What, the authors collectively ask, does it mean to demobilize the mind both in terms of the abolition of wartime musical production and in terms of postwar creativity? And when, exactly, is mental demobilization over? To this end, individual authors offer reflections on a series of interconnected themes, relating to the link between music and war, music and memory, music and migration (or exile), as well as music as a manifestation of political power and propaganda. Their focus is somewhat Eurocentric (if not Francophone), but the editors are to be commended for branching out across the globe to the extent that we find chapters on Latin America, central Africa, along with an equally diverse range of genres and repertory, involving classical, folk, pop music, and others. Equally wide-ranging, the present book does not merely limit itself to musical production and reception but also considers a broad array of actors and institutions in between with their proper and individual agency: cultural agents, publishers, critics, along with unions, state governments, and international organizations. In doing so, the editors retrace what they believe is a "functional diversity" in which, as they put it, "music can reflect the postwar transition processes as they happen and, at the same time, can play an active role in these processes. As such, it can contribute to accelerating or slowing down the return to peace," (p. 5) or even boycott reconciliation altogether.

No doubt, then, this is a farewell note—a strong farewell to the idea that music is a happy purveyor of peace, harmony, and understanding among the otherwise so combatant community of nations. Pitched as both a reflection and a driving force, musical sound emerges here as a Janus-faced dynamic, meaningless unless harnessed to specific goals or perceptions.

What is music, then, if not harmonious? The authors identify a variety of ways of grasping music's "functional diversity": they point to aesthetic, institutional, and political considerations revolving around the question of which sort of triggers in musical culture contribute or even induce change in postwar transformation. Lacombe, Palomino, Pestel, and Reibel all examine varieties of "aftermath culture," ranging from musical magazines and Bizet's political considerations following the Franco-Prussian War, in 1871, over Mexican musical life post-1910, to the international tours on the part of the Berlin and Vienna Philharmonics following V-E Day in Europe, in 1945. Collectively, the authors point to the need to insert trauma, challenge, as well as the search for both identity and national projection into the analysis of postwar transitions. The common denominator here, it seems to me, is not just aesthetic but also survival, more specifically the link between mechanisms of endurance, on the one hand, and the almost immediate quest for remedy, on the other. Where Bizet sought to embrace the psychological wound inflicted by war on France, the urge to protest (in France), to rally (in Mexico), and to export (in Austria and Germany) symbolized strategies to turn survival into revival, either by way of an improved version of the past or a different future altogether.

The authors also consider how, specifically, music may have served the cause of and, indeed, the spark for a return to peace. Guerpin, Gumplowicz, and Wedekind all analyze scenarios of cultural demobilization: French café-concert and music hall chanson; writers and musicologists' concerns regarding variety music after the 1940 armistice; as well as Tyrolean folk music repertoires since the 1900s. As much as the individual topics may vary, these chapters' common theme is also a search for unity and identity, if by strategies altogether different from the ones outlined for Bizet and others mentioned previously. Here, we encounter the crafting of strong enemy images after World War I and the urge to downplay the unsavory side of collaboration during World War II, in France, along with the fanaticism residing in both folk clothes and songs (Tyrol). In all three cases, it seems to me, self-empowerment—that is, re-emergent imagined regional identity—served a far more radical goal than survival and remedy. Self-empowerment served to morph self-examination and identity into instruments of recalibration for the self and the other, and in preparation for a situation squarely located in the distant future: that of France and that of Tyrol.

The authors likewise invite us to consider music as an emotional forum, a place to nurture memories, notably those pertaining to loss and destruction. Leterrier, Hughes, Noël, and Mugiraneza and Chemouni, all address moments of feelings and reflections, including songs created by the "national chansonnier" Bérenger in the post-Napoleonic period, a musical-specific work (Hindemith's *Minimax*, 1923); the conception of an Atlantic musical memory in honor of Jews who died in the Holocaust after World War II; and songs composed after the Tutsi genocide in Rwanda, after 1994. Next to registering the powerful role of songs, again, it seems that while the authors focus on emotions—triggered by both nostalgia and horror—the real link among their findings is speechlessness. Speechlessness signifies the inability or even unwillingness to prioritize spoken words to mediate recognition and experience. In the four cases delineated from the early to the mid-twentieth century, speechlessness invited either silence or alternative modes of nonverbal or only partly verbal expression.

In a gesture to what has become the perhaps best-established literature pertaining to music and international relations, the authors finally reflect on the use of music as an instrument of power and diplomacy following the conclusion of war. Their focus is on convention and institutions: the Congress of Paris negotiating peace following the Crimean War; the different postwar aspirations of the British and French sections of the International Society for Contemporary Music; UNESCO's efforts to reconfigure and, indeed, transform the arts into a larger (un)political forum. The common theme here, it seems to me, is desire: Mahiet, Kelly, and Fléchet all grapple with political leaders who believed that, somehow, music could be that fleeting instrument of dialogue, harmony, reintegration, and community that, in reality, music could never be, least of all on its own.

Survival, self-empowerment, desire, and speechlessness, then, are what unite the chapters in the book, beyond a common interest in both structure and response. They alert us to the legacy of destructive forces affecting not merely buildings, people, and landscapes but also of sound and the world of listening. Destruction, however, yielded renewal, either, and more typically, by way of departure from prewar legacies or, less often, by the effort to resuscitate the past. I agree with the authors' collective assessment that music's meaning in the postwar transition was flexible: it could either serve as a trigger or an echo. It could either revise or transform prewar institutional organizations. It could either extend or curtail the emotions associated with postwar transitions.

Still, I believe that the collection yields more than mere echoes and triggers. Frequently written off as a pastime of sorts, funded by the state only when the state had extra funds, music mattered because it enabled independent mechanisms of survival, of self-empowerment, while at the same time admitting visions of humanity and the desire to attain the same, without the very instrument that so often seemed to induce war: words. Music emerges in these contexts as a seismographic tool to live, to feel oneself, to express, and to hope; in doing so, it often contradicted or completely deviated from the sociopolitical discourses associated with the deep postwar transformations under examination here.

And then there is a larger picture: the extent to which postwar music continues to matter, beyond immediate transition and reconciliation, beyond the moment of peace and the return to normalcy. For if there is one thing historians of postwar periods agree on, it is that the world was never quite the same, that war did far more than temporarily disrupt societies, that there was no return, and that peace remained most fragile to those who had been exposed to war.

There is a slight bent to favor music's "benevolent" attributes in this book, and it may have to do with what postwar societies and their historians were (and are) vying for, the centrifugal forces of peace on all social levels. Yet to cite one example, Europe after

1945, so central in this book, did not experience peace and Germany only became part of a peace treaty in the Two-Plus-Four talks, in 1990.[7] Thus, music also digested violence, (dis)unity, the abrogation of human rights, the emergent bipolar conflict, so much of which marked the end of World War II and the immediate postwar period.

In this context, four themes or possible fields of examinations come to mind that may inform future investigations of music in postwar transitions, and they again appear to revolve around the themes outlined previously: survival, silence, speechlessness, desire. The first, survival, concerns the long-term legacies of music that became tangible in the immediate postwar period, such as shunning, reorientation, the breaking with the past, and the prohibition of specific artistic forms. We know, for example, that music simultaneously served as a form of suppression, propaganda, and as a coping mechanism under suppression (e.g., in POW and gulag camps).[8] How do we make sense of these postwar experiences of imprisonment and injustice that did not merely prolong the war for those detained but also generated specific sounds situated between two sorts of horror?

Second, and in a gesture to speechlessness and Kathleen Smith's work, we might consider music's profound ability to both deepen and gloss over wartime ruptures. As irreconcilable as they sound, amnesia and protest, it seems, were the most obvious forms of inspiration for postwar musical activity. Mugiraneza and Chemouni have shown in this volume that song in Rwanda ceased to be political after the 1994 genocide. Yet, in their analysis of patriotic choral music in Kenya, Doseline Kiguru and Ernest Patrick Monte go even further; they argue that postindependence state policy encouraged composers, performers, and audiences to forget colonial crimes. Officials believed that memory obstructed the creation of a new state and nationhood.[9] While the authors believe that such forgetting is impossible (and their evidence is convincing), it remains striking that authorities, artists, even ordinary people—in Kenya and elsewhere—believed that music could perform this feat in the first place.[10] A similar case could likely be made for the Republic of Cambodia, the country with probably the longest and richest pop music culture in Southeast Asia. Suppressed during the Khmer Rouge regime, pop emerged rapidly and with new vigor, contributing significantly to the country's policy of amnesty and silencing.[11] To what extent do these stories reflect music's failure or success in postwar processes of healing?

Furthermore, protest against silence and forgetting, in turn, has been the number one characteristic of Western rock and folk in Europe and North America after World War II. Self-empowerment was at the heart of the protests of both early postwar civil rights advocates and teenagers who experienced massive pressure underneath a patina of peace and returning normalcy. Both in Europe and North America, these groups often voiced deep frustration with the expectations of an older generation that strove to return to an irretrievable prewar order. The postwar globalization of jazz and rhythm and blues, for example, offered young people everything the elders loathed: protest, sexuality, wild music, flying hair, jumping around, Elvis the Pelvis—in short, challenge and dissent.[12] How do these stories of protest fit into the saga of postwar transitions?

Last but not least, there is the role of music in voicing desire in the form of political demands: demands for regime change, human rights, and the revival of visions of both humanity and the human. In the songbook of classical music, there is a long list of names and cases testifying to an engagement for human rights in the name of peace and decolonization in the immediate post–World War II era. In 1948, the year of the UN Declaration of Human Rights, Italian composer Luigi Dallapiccola published *Il prigioniero* (The prisoner), an opera addressing both torture and hope.[13] These tales differ significantly from Fléchet's more optimist account of Charles Seeger's vision of a better world in that they feared the worst was coming. What does it mean that these artists, in addition to the music they composed, conducted, and played, all manifested the horrors of war while simultaneously making a plea for what they hoped would be an era forever shunning torture and future military conflict?

In early April 2022 Volodymyr Zelensky addressed the audience at the Grammy Award ceremony in a prerecorded speech, shot in a Kyiv bunker. Prefacing John Legend's performance of "Free" with Ukrainian refugee artists Mika Newton, Siuzanna Iglidan, and Lyuba Yakimchuk, the hoarse-voiced president urged the musicians to "fill the silence with your music! Fill it today," continuing, "What is more opposite to music? The silence of ruined cities and killed people."[14]

There is no saying when and how Ukraine's postwar transition will occur. One thing we do know, however, is that whatever happens, the country will look very different from the way it did before, not only due to loss and destruction. The last few months have already witnessed a profound sociocultural change, starting with an estimated ten million refugees, many of whom at least temporarily left their country, learned foreign languages, watched foreign news, adapted to foreign customs, and sent their children to foreign schools. Many of them will return to Ukraine, Marshall Plan or not, to the silence of those ruined cities and perished loved ones. And for whatever it is worth, they will have access to all the instruments and reflections outlined in this book: instruments of survival, desire, self-empowerment, and, hopefully, modes to express the unspeakable, alas, once again.

Jessica C. E. Gienow-Hecht is chair of the Department of History in the John F. Kennedy Institute for North American Studies at the Freie Universität Berlin.

Notes

1. "Ukraine, Resistance and Reconstruction: Issues for the Post-war Recovery," Ukraine Solidarity Campaign, 28 May 2022, https://ukrainesolidaritycampaign.org/2022/05/28/ukraine-resistance-and-reconstruction-issues-for-the-post-war-recovery/.
2. At the same time, reservations abound, not only among individual states ambivalent about Ukraine's membership (such as Georgia or Moldova), but also among parts of the European Commission. "Ukraine Needs a 'Marshall Plan,' German Finance Minister Says," Reuters, 22 March 2022, https://www.reuters.com/world/europe/ukraine-needs-marshall-plan-german-finance-minister-2022-03-22/. See also Jessica Gienow-Hecht, "Laskavo Prosymo, Mr Marshall!" Blog, Contestations of the Liberal Script, https://www.scripts-berlin.eu/blog/Blog-58-Marshall plan_1/index.html.
3. M. J. Grant and Férdia J. Stone-Davis, eds., *The Soundtrack of Conflict: The Role of Music in Radio Broadcasting in Wartime and in Conflict Situations* (Hildesheim: Georg Olms Verlag, 2013).
4. J. Martin Daughtry, *Listening to War: Sound, Music, Trauma, and Survival in Wartime Iraq* (New York: Oxford University Press, 2015).
5. Kathleen E. R. Smith, *God Bless America: Tin Pan Alley Goes to War* (Lexington: University Press of Kentucky, 2003).
6. David Monod, Settling Scores: German Music, Denazification, and the Americans, 1945–1953 (Chapel Hill: University of North Carolina Press, 2005); Toby Thacker, *Music after Hitler, 1945–1955* (Burlington VT: Ashgate, 2007); Elizabeth Janik, *Recomposing German Music: Politics and Musical Tradition in Cold War Berlin*. (Leiden, Brill, 2005)
7. Marie E. Sarotte, *Not One Inch: America, Russia, and the Making of Post-Cold War Stalemate* (New Haven, CT: Yale University Press, 2021).
8. Inna Klausen, "Sergej Protopopov – ein Komponist im Gulag," *Die Musikforschung* 63, no. 2 (April–June 2010): 134–46; Klause und Christoph-Mathias Mueller, eds., *From the Gewandhaus to the Gulag: Symphonic Music by Aleksandr Veprik* (Wiesbaden: Harrassowitz Verlag, 2020).
9. Doseline Kiguru and Ernest Patrick Monte, "Music, Memory and Forgetting: Patriotic Choral Music in Kenya," *South African Music Studies: SAMUS* 36–37, no. 1 (2018): 110–28.

10. John Morgan O'Connell, *Commemorating Gallipoli through Music: Remembering and Forgetting* (Lanham, MD: Lexington Books, 2018); Dale Alan Olsen, *Popular Music of Vietnam: The Politics of Remembering, the Economics of Forgetting* (New York: Routledge, 2008).
11. Timothy Williams, "Remembering and Silencing Complexity in Post-Genocide Memorialisation: Cambodia's Tuol Sleng Genocide Museum," *Memory Studies* 15, no. 1 (2022): 3–19; Mark A. Rhodes, "Music Work: Traditional Cambodian Music and State-Building Under the Khmer Rouge," *Asia Pacific Viewpoint* 62, no. 1 (2021): 27–39; Stephen Mamula, "Starting from Nowhere? Popular Music in Cambodia after the Khmer Rouge," *Asian Music* 39, no. 1 (2008): 26–41.
12. Celeste Day Moore, *Soundscapes of Liberation: African American Music in Postwar France* (Durham, NC: Duke University Press, 2021).
13. Jessica Gienow-Hecht, "U.N. Sounds of Humanity: The Declaration of Human Rights Concerts Since 1949," unpublished manuscript, 2022.
14. Nicole Lyn Pesce, "President Zelensky Asks Grammy Viewers, 'Support Us in Any Way You Can . . . But Not Silence,'" 3 April 2022, https://www.marketwatch.com/story/watch-president-zelensky-asks-grammy-viewers-support-us-in-any-way-you-can-but-not-silence-11649039408.

Index

Abrantès, Laure Junot (Duchess of), 231, 244
Acheson, Dean, 282, 288
Adler, Guido, 252, 264n35, 268
Advisory Committee on Music, 274, 286n17, 286n21, 287n26
Âli Pasha, Mehmed Emin, 229, 241n41
Alsace-Lorraine, 111–12
Allied powers, 57, 61
Amar Quartet, 184, 187, 191n44
Americanization, 114, 177, 291
American Jewish Joint Distribution Committee, 198
American Musicological Society (AMS), 18, 188, 276–77, 285
Amiati, Thérèse, 111
Anschluss, 58–59, 144
Ansermet, Ernest, 260
Antheil, George, 185, 190n35, 191
Anti-Germanism, 105
Antisemitism, 144
Arányi, Jelly d', 249, 255
Aráoz, Jesús Reynoso, 45–46
Arbeitsgemeinschaft Tiroler Komponisten (Tyrolean Composers' Working Group), 138, 140–47, 151n27, 151n32, 151n34, 152n38
Aristocracy, 108
Art musical, L', 84–86, 88, 90–92, 96n5, 97n10
Association Française d'Action Artistique, 254
Attlee, Clement, 59–60, 73n27
Auber, Daniel-François-Esprit, 29, 86, 92, 99n44, 237
Audoin-Rouzeau, Stéphane, 3

Austria, 1, 55, 57–63, 67–72, 72n2, 73n26, 74n43, 107, 138, 140–41, 143–49, 149n1, 151n29, 152n45, 160, 163, 186, 229–30, 233, 235–37, 241n30, 256–57, 262, 266n57, 292
Austrofascism, 1, 145, 149
Austro-Hungarian Empire, 141, 149n1

Baciocchi, Felix, 237
Balfour, Arthur, 247, 263n6
Baqueiro Foster, Gerónimo, 39–40, 47
Barraud, Henri, 284
Barenboim, Daniel, 10
Batamuliza, Annociata, 212
Battle of Racławawa [Racławice], 23–24, 33n12
Battle of Sedan, 21, 107
Battle of Waterloo, 26, 160, 166–67
Bazaine, Achille, 107–8, 110, 116
Beauharnais, Hortense de, 231
Becker, Annette, 3
Beethoven, Ludwig van, 26, 28, 35n26, 60, 64, 66, 69, 143, 180, 183, 185, 189n24, 239n6, 274
Bellini, Vincenzo, 237
Béranger, Pierre-Jean de, 1, 8, 102, 110, 116, 117n2, 129, 133n44, 159, 161–74
  "Le Cinq Mars", 163
  "La Cocarde Blanche", 163, 170
  "Le Convoi de David", 163, 171
  "La Déesse", 166
  "La Faridondaine", 167–73
  "Le Grenier", 162
  "Mathurin Bruneau", 161–62 164
  "L'Opinion de ces Demoiselles", 167
  "Le Roi d'Yvetot", 162

"La Sainte Alliance Barbaresque", 170–173
"Souvenirs du Peuple", 165
"Le Vieux Sergent", 164, 169, 172
Berners, Lord, 250, 261, 266n59
Berg, Alban, 257, 266n56
Berlanda, Emil, 137, 138, 141, 143–44, 146–47, 150nn3–4, 151n24, 151n34
Berlin, 2, 5–6, 54–57, 63–66, 68–70, 74n49, 74n63, 75n72, 94, 100n55, 137, 185, 292
Berlin Philharmonic, 54–57, 63–65, 68–70
Bernanos, Georges, 122
Bernard, Charles, 87
Bertrand, Gustave, 83–94, 100n55
Bevin, Ernest, 60
Bikindi, Simon, 212
Bing, Rudolf, 57, 59, 67
Bizet, George, 1, 6, 21–32, 34n25, 35n26, 35n30, 35n41–42, 36n43–44, 36n53, 292–93
  Carmen (1875), 22, 29, 32–33
  Djamileh (1872), 22, 29–31, 92
  La Fuite (The Escape, 1870), 1, 22
  La Patrie (The Homeland, 1873), 25, 34n25, 35n30,
Bizimana, Loti, 213
Blum, Léon, 127
Blumenfeld, Diana, 201
Böhm, Karl, 58
Bonnard, Abel, 7, 128–30, 133n44, 134n45
Bottesini, Giovanni, 237
Botwinik, David, 197, 200
Boullard, Marius, 87
Boult, Adrian, 247
Boyer, Lucien, 113
Brahms, Johannes, 66, 143
Br iloiu, Constantin, 282
Braun, Paulina, 201
  "Hots Rakhmones Yidishe Hertser" (Have Compassion Jewish Hearts), 201
Britain, 2, 11, 55–57, 60–61, 64, 67, 69, 71, 75n72, 168 246–48, 250–51, 253–54, 257, 259–61, 279
British Arts Council, 59–60
British Music Society, 11, 247–48, 263n8
Bureau de la Censure du Ministère de l'Instruction Publique et du Sous-Secrétariat d'État aux Beaux-Arts, 104–5

Bussine, Romain, 30, 36n48
Bruckner, Anton, 64–66
Bruneau, Mathurin, 161–62, 164
  "Le Roi d'Yvetot", 162
Bruno, Paul, 232, 240n24, 241n25
Budde, Elmar, 179
Buenos Aires, 9, 43, 195, 199, 201
Busoni, Philippe, 231–32, 240nn18–22
Buxbaum, Friedrich, 60

Cabanes, Bruno, 3, 21, 33nn2–3
Cabaret, 5, 125, 128, 132n27, 200
Café-concert, 7, 102, 106–8, 110–12, 115–16, 123, 125, 128, 132n27, 293
Caffery, Jefferson, 281
Cake-walk, 126, 133n34
Calles Plutarco, Elías, 126
Calvocoressi, Michel-Dimitri, 254
Campos, Rubén M., 44
Canon (musical), 34n15
Canon (pantheon), 44, 46, 49, 55, 70, 142, 248, 261, 283
Canto Coral y Orfeónico, 45
Caplet, André, 246, 255, 259–60, 267n69, 267n73
Casals, Pablo, 249
Castañeda, Daniel, 42–44, 51nn11–14, 51n17
Celibidache, Sergiu, 64
Céline, Louis-Ferdinand, 7, 123, 128–30, 132n17, 134n46, 134nn48–50
Central Jewish Historical Commission (CJHC), 195, 197
Central Yiddish Cultural Organization (CYCO), 194–95, 199, 204n5
Certeau, Michel de, 125
Chailley, Jacques, 123, 132n12, 132n21
Chanson, 2, 5, 7, 102–116, 117n2, 118n33, 123, 125–26, 128–29, 132n24, 132n27, 133n41, 133n44, 134n52, 175n12, 177n40, 177n42, 293
  L'Appel à l'Allemagne 110–111
  Le Chant du Départ, 108–9, 166
  Les Cuirassiers de Reichshoffen, 108
  Entrevue de Sarah Bernhardt et de Guillaume II, 113
  Le Fils de l'Allemand, 111
  Ils n'en ont pas en Allemagne, 110
  La Marseillaise, 106, 108–9, 112–13, 166
  Marseillaise de la Victoire, 113

Les Mercantis, 109
À Montfaucon, 108–9
Le Régiment de Sambre et Meuse, 110
Chansonnier, 8, 102, 106–8, 110, 113, 159, 161–63, 165, 167–69, 174, 293
Chardonne, Jacques, 122, 132n9
Chávez, Carlos, 48, 278
Chemouni, Benjamin, 9, 293, 295
Child, Charles G., 276
Choudens, Antoine de, 24, 34n18
Clark, Edward, 246, 250–52, 257, 264n20, 264n25, 264n29, 279
Cœuroy, André, 7, 121–30, 132n18, 132n24, 132n27, 132n37–39, 132n50
Cohen, Henry, 23, 24n14
Cold War, ix–x, 10–11, 55, 58, 65, 67–70, 272, 276, 280, 282–85
Collins, John, 57, 65–66, 68
Comité de l'Album Patriotique des Grands Maîtres de l'Art Musical, 88
Comité des Arts [for the liberation of French territory], 88, 98n27
Commemoration, 3, 8, 26, 86, 148, 159, 174, 199, 215
Commercial music, 6, 47
Communism, x, 282
Concerts de *La Revue musicale*, 11, 247, 254, 256, 258, 265n50
Concert of Europe, 230, 239
Concerts Populaires, 23, 31
Congress of Paris (1856), 2, 229–30, 233, 239, 293
Congress of Vienna, 10, 167, 229–32, 238, 239n6, 239n11
Congress for Cultural Freedom, 283–85
Contemporary music, 11, 248–49, 251–52, 255, 257–58, 261, 274, 294
Copland, Aaron, 281
Corrêa de Azevedo, Luiz Heitor, 272, 278, 284, 287n38
Corridos, 43
  La cucaracha (The cockroach), 43
Cristal Baschet, 202–203
Critics, 5, 11, 28, 36n46, 40, 44, 46, 64, 86, 89–90, 94, 143–44, 168, 251, 259, 292
Curtis, Benjamin, 138
Cuvelier, Marcel, 279, 284

Dada/Dadaism, 114, 185
Dallapiccola, Luigi, 278–79, 296

Daniel, Salvador, 86
Daughtry, J. Martin, 291
Davenson, Henri (Henri-Irénée Marrou), 123
Dawidowitz, Lucy, 195
Debussy, Claude, 248, 250, 252–53, 255, 257–58, 263, 265n42, 266n56,
Delannoy, Marcel, 130, 134n50
Delormel, Lucien, 111
Demobilization, 3–4, 7–8, 55, 103, 106, 291, 293
  of the mind, 103, 106, 291
  cultural, 3–4, 7–8, 55, 293
Democratic reorientation, 291
Dent, Edward, 246–47, 252, 261–62, 264n35, 274
Díaz, Porfirio, 40
Digeon, Claude, 28
Diplomacy, cultural, 4, 10–11, 57, 62, 124, 160, 233–34, 236, 239n6, 241n35, 261, 272, 284, 293
Disarmament of minds, 4
Donaueschingen Festival, 187, 188n2
Donizetti, Giuseppe, 234, 237
Dower, John, 2
Dubufé, Edouard-Louis, 229–30, 236
Duchesneau, Michel, 30, 36n48, 254
Dufourcq, Norbert, 123
Duparc, Henri, 22
Durán, Gustavo, 277–78, 280, 287n37
Dyer, Louise, 248

École normale supérieure, 124 129
Edinburgh International Festival, 57
Entente cordiale, 103, 238
Escudier, Léon 85–86, 96n5
European, x, 9–11, 42, 44, 49, 51n9, 54, 56, 58, 64–65; 67–68, 69–71, 106, 117, 161, 198–99, 201, 230, 232, 234, 249–51, 255, 257–58, 261, 264n20, 274, 276, 281–82, 291, 297
Europeanizing, 56, 61
Evans, Edwin, 187, 246, 252–253, 261, 264n20, 265nn41–42
Everist, Mark, 237
Exile, 3–4, 7, 56–57, 59–60, 61, 67, 73n31, 87, 163–65, 167, 195, 208, 212, 215, 218, 223n13, 277, 291
Exoticism, 22

Falla, Manuel de, 185, 255, 257, 266n56
Fascism, 128, 145–46

Fauré, Gabriel, 253, 255, 259, 265n42, 30, 88, 98n27
Faure, Michel, 123, 132n11
Fellowes, E. H., 247, 263n17
Femmes de France, 89, 98n27
Ferrier, Kathleen, 61
First National Congress of Music, Mexico City, 42
Fléchet, Anaïs, 11, 294, 296
Folk music, 4, 5, 8, 44, 128, 138–39, 146–49, 279, 282, 293
Fortoul, Hippolyte, 242n65
Fosler-Lussier, Danielle, 10
Foujlds, John, 12
France, 1–2, 5, 7–8, 11, 21–22, 25, 27–29, 31–32, 35n41, 55–57, 69, 75n72, 83–84, 86–90, 93–95, 97n14, 98n27, 100n48, 100n55, 101nn56–57, 103–4, 106–7, 110–12, 114–16, 117n6, 121–26, 128–31, 131n2, 132n7, 132n11, 134n45, 134n48, 134n52, 159–66, 168–75, 175n10, 176n38, 177n45, 182, 197, 234–35, 238, 241n38, 246–48, 252–54, 258–59, 261, 265n42, 265n47, 266n63, 274, 279–81, 292–93

Gilbert, Shirli, 196, 204n11, 206
Gil-Marchex, Henri, 255–256
Glyndebourne Festival, 57, 59, 72n11, 76
Goossens, Eugene, 246, 250, 260, 266n59, 269
Gorby, Sarah, 202–3
Gounod, Charles, 23, 97n23
Gourdon, Edouard, 233, 236, 238, 241n27, 241n30, 242n53, 244
Grand Théâtre de Marseille, 99
Grant, M. J., 291, 297n3
Gregorian chant, 44
Gringoire, 127, 132n18, 133n38
Gross, Jan, 197, 204n18, 206
Gumplowicz, Philippe, 1–18, 121–36, 293
Guerpin, Martin, 1–18, 72n4, 76, 102–20, 190n32, 192, 264n31, 266n60, 269, 293
Guiraud, Ernest, 23, 26, 28, 35n26, 35nn41–42
Gutmann, Amy, 290

Habsburgs, 55, 141, 149n1
Habyarimana, Juvénal, 210–11
Halanzier, Olivier, 90

Halévy, Léonie, 1, 29, 35n37, 36nn43–44, 36n54
Halévy, Ludovic, 28, 35n40, 37
Halpern, Leivick (H. Leivick), 199–200, 203, 205n28
Haney, Joel, 185, 187, 188n5, 189n16, 190n32, 190n34, 191n41, 192
Hanson, Howard, 281–282, 287n30
Hanzl, Rudolf, 62, 73n30, 73n34–35, 73n39, 73n40, 74nn43–44, 75–76
Harris, Roy, 275, 286n25
Hartmann, Rudolf, 186, 191n42, 192
Hartog, François, 202, 205n38, 206
Healing, 26, 87, 95, 295
Hekking, André, 255
Henry, Leigh, 250
Herder, Johann Gottfried, 126, 132n14
Hess, Myra, 57, 66, 74nn61–62, 77, 249
Hindemith, Paul, 9, 74n49, 180–187, 188n3, 188n7, 188n10, 188nn12–14, 189n17, 189n18, 189nn21–26
  Kammermusik, 185–187
  Minimax: Repertorium für Militärorchester, 9, 179–93, 293
  Das Nusch-Nuschi
Historial de la Grande Guerre international research center, 2, 121
Hitler, Adolf, 64, 84n6, 79, 286n7, 288n58, 301, 297n6
Hofer, Andreas, 148
Hofer, Franz, 144–45, 152n39, 155
Holbrooke, Joseph, 249
Holmès, Augusta, 31
Holocaust, 71, 76, 79, 153, 204n11, 205n25, 205n39, 206–7, 213, 225, 293
Honegger, Arthur, 130, 134n50, 258–60, 266n53, 279, 284
Horne, John, 3, 13n11, 13nn25–26, 13n31, 16, 72n4, 88, 106
Hubner, Joseph Alexander von, 237, 241n29–30, 242n64, 242n69, 244
Huerta, Victoriano, 52
Hughes, Lesley 9, 179–93, 293
Hugo, Victor, 110, 160–61, 175nn3–5
Hull, Arthur Eaglefield, 246–49, 252, 261, 263n1, 263n7–8, 263n11, 263nn16–17, 264n19, 269
Hutcheon, Linda, 186, 190n39, 192
Hutu, 208, 212, 217, 221, 223, 223n16
Huxley, Julian, 277

Ideville, Henry d', 242n61, 244
Iglidan, Siuzanna, 296
Indahemuka (troupe), 213, 218
Indy, Vincent d', 123, 253, 255
Innsbrucker Nachrichten, 144, 150n4, 152n37
Institut zur Erforschung der Judenfrage (Institute for Research on the Jewish Question, Frankfurt, 196
Inter-American Affairs' Music Committee, 275
International Folk Music Council, 279, 285
International Music Council (IMC), 11, 271–72, 276, 279–83, 283n3, 286n5, 286n5, 286n10, 287n27, 287n38, 287n42, 288n52, 288n57, 289
International Music Fund, 281–82, 285, 288nn52–53, 288n57
International Institute of Intellectual Cooperation (IIIC), 47, 124, 132n25, 136, 272, 279–80, 288n46
International Society for Contemporary Music (ISCM), 246–48, 250–53, 257–62, 263n2, 263n10, 264n29, 264n33, 266n59, 267nn73–74, 267n84, 269–70, 274, 279, 281, 285, 294
Ireland, John, 250
Isaacs, Miriam, 201
Isabey, Jean-Bapiste, 229, 239nn1–2, 245

Jannik, Elizabeth, 291
Jazz, 43, 47, 114, 116–117, 118n34, 118n36, 119, 124, 131, 190n32, 192, 211, 269, 296
Jean-Aubry, G., 253–54, 264n20, 265nn40–42, 269
Je suis partout, 121, 124, 129, 133n44
Jewish emigrants/emigrés, 57
Jewish Historical Commission, 195, 197,
Jewish resistance, 9, 195, 205n40
Joint Army, 275
Joncières, Victorin, 25, 27, 34n22, 35n30
Journalism (or music criticism), 13n8, 16, 85, 89–95, 188, 263, 269

Kaczerginski, Shmerke, 9, 194–207
Lider Fun di Getos un Lagern, 9, 198–199, 204n19, 206
Kaligirwa, Jeanne, 215

Kanetscheider, Artur, 138, 141, 144, 146, 148, 150n8, 151n24, 152n52, 152n55, 154
Karemera, Rodrigue, 213
Karpeles, Maud, 279
Kattnigg, Rodolf, 143, 152n36
Kaunitz, Wenzel Anton von, 229
Kayirebwa, Cécile, 212, 214
Kelly, Barbara L., 1–18, 35n32, 37, 101, 246–70, 294
Kennedy-Fraser, Marjory, 249
Kerr, Harrison, 275, 279, 281
Kerstens, Paul, 209, 223n4, 225
Keynes, John Maynard, 60
Kichelewski, Audrey, 197, 204n18, 206
Kiguru, Doseline, 295, 297n9
Knappertsbusch, Hans, 58
Koch, Karl, 138, 148
Kodály, Zoltan, 256–57, 266n56
Kœchlin, Charles, 246, 255, 258–60, 267n67, 267n73, 268
Kolb, Annette, 184, 186, 190n31, 192
Korman, Rémi, 187, 209, 223n5, 223n13, 225, 225nn36–37
Koussevitzky, Serge, 281–82, 288n57
Krauss, Clemens, 55, 58
Kwan, Jonathan, 239n6, 244

Lacombe, Hervé, 6, 14, 21–38, 292
Lanôme, Paul, 94–95, 100n51, 101n58
Lalo, Édouard, 30
Laloy, Louis, 254
Largeaud, Jean-Marc, 26, 35n28, 37
Lasry, Jacques, 202–3
Latin America, 40, 42, 51n10, 51n29, 53, 71, 201, 289, 292
Lawler, Vannett, 278, 280, 287n38
Lazarus, Daniel, 257, 259
Lecaillon, Jean-François, 26, 35n27, 37
League of Nations, 124, 246, 248, 263n11, 270, 272, 285
Legend, John, 206
Leterrier, Sophie-Anne, 8, 117n3, 119, 159–78, 293
Library of Congress's Music Division, 275
Ligne de, Charles-Joseph, 230–31, 239n11
Ligue de la Délivrance Nationale, 88
Lindner, Christian, 290
Lithuania, 197, 200, 204n11, 206–7
Lomax, Alan, 282, 288n55

Louis XVIII, 160–161, 166
London, 5, 11, 56–57, 60, 62–64, 66–67, 69, 73n26, 73n32, 74n57, 74n61, 75, 127, 234, 236, 241n43, 242n48, 242nn50–51, 242n58, 247–52, 261, 263n11, 264nn24–26, 264n28, 269, 271–72, 286n19
London Contemporary Music Centre (LCMC), 11, 247, 249–52, 257, 264n22
Lovett, Robert A., 281, 288n51
Lyre et palette group, 123

Ma, Yo-Yo, 10
MacLeish, Archibald, 281
Madero, Francisco, 40
Magnard, Alberic, 255
Mahiet, Damien, 10, 14n40, 229–45, 294
Mahler, Gustav, 61, 203
Malipiero, Gian Francesco, 256–58, 266n56
Manchester Guardian, 75n69, 248, 264n32
Manuel, Jacques-Antoine, 162
Marches, 47, 145, 172, 184–87, 205n29
Marchangy, Louis-Antoine, 102, 119
Marini, Peter, 138, 141, 144, 151n24
Marshall Plan, 281, 290, 297, 297n2
Massenet, Jules, 23, 33n13, 36n50
Masson, Paul-Henri, 279
Mathew, Nicholas, 239n6, 244
Maurel, Chloé, 280, 286n11, 286n22, 288nn48–50, 289
Maurras, Charles, 127, 133n35, 136
Maxence, Jean-Pierre, 122, 132n7, 136
Mazower, Mark, 2, 13n9, 17
Memorialization, 202
Memory, 1, 3, 8–9, 13n10, 13n22–23, 16–18, 21, 23, 25–27, 30, 36n51, 71–72, 75, 77, 79, 95, 102–3, 108, 114–116, 118n35, 119, 122, 132n14, 157, 159, 161, 163, 170, 174, 186, 195, 203, 204n16, 206–7, 209, 219–20, 222, 234, 282, 291, 293, 295, 297n9, 298n11
Ménestrel, Le, 27, 83–84, 87–94, 96n2, 96n4, 97n12, 97nn14–15, 97n20–21, 98nn24–27, 98nn30–31, 99nn41–42, 99n45, 100n46, 100nn48–49, 100n52, 100n55, 117n7
Menuhin, Yehudi, 10
Merrick, Frank, 249
Mexican Revolution, 39–40, 42

Mexico, 6, 39–53, 278, 281, 287n38, 292
Migration, 4, 18, 43, 56–57, 59, 61, 63, 72, 78–79, 173, 202, 291
Mihigo, François, 211
Milhaud, Darius, 13, 16, 246, 259–60, 262, 264n27, 265n45, 266n53, 266n57, 267n67, 267n72, 269
Military bands, 6, 39, 47, 179–80
Military choirs, 44–45
Minerve, La, 162
Monod, David, 72n56, 77, 297n6
Monte, Ernest Patrick, 295, 297n9
Monter, Mathieu de, 87, 91, 94, 96n8, 99nn36–37, 100n53–54, 101n57
Montgarde, Armand de, 91, 93, 99n40, 99n44, 100n50
Monthly Musical Record, The, 260
Moore, Celeste Day, 298n12
Moore, Christopher, 263
Moreau, Edmond, 87
Morning Chronicle, 234, 236, 238, 242n42, 242n46, 242nn48–49, 242n67
Morny, Charles de, 237
Moseley, Carlos, 275
Mourning, 1–3, 8, 18, 25, 64, 86, 157, 159, 194–207, 209, 214, 221
Mugiraneza, Assumpta, 9, 208–26, 293, 295
Mukamutara, Rosalie, 215
Mukankuranga, Mariya Yohana, 1, 9, 210, 212, 214–15, 218–22
Museveni, Yoweri, 211
Music bands, 39
Musical branding, 42
Music criticism. *See* Journalism
Musical Times, The, 191, 247, 263nn4–5, 263n7, 264n19–20, 264n33, 268–270
Music hall, 7, 102–20, 123, 126–30, 293
Musicology, 8, 17, 32, 96, 102, 107, 131, 139–40, 187, 239, 277, 291
Musoni, Evariste, 212
Muyango, Jean-Marie, 212

Napoleon III, 1, 21, 28, 107–8, 110, 118n33, 229, 231, 233, 235, 241
Napoleonic Wars, 2, 159, 229
National Guard, 22–23, 26
Nationalism, 1, 5, 7, 27, 30, 39, 46, 50, 92, 124, 127, 133n42, 136, 148–49, 150n13, 153, 175, 185–86
National music, 44–45, 49, 69, 287n27

National Popular School of Music (Mexico), 46
National Socialism, 55–56, 58–59, 61–63, 67–68, 71, 74n46
Nationalsozialistischer Lehrerbund (National Socialist Teachers' Association), 144
Navy Committee on Welfare and Recreation, 275
Nazi regime/Nazi Party/Nazism, 1, 6–7, 56–64, 68, 78, 129, 139–41, 143–49, 150n19, 151n22, 151n25, 151n27, 152n42, 153–54, 196, 204n22, 206, 223, 273. *See also* National Socialism
Nerval, Gérard de, 128, 133n41
Newton, Mika, 296
New York, 9, 72n16, 73n21, 192, 194–207, 249, 266n60, 269, 275, 286n25, 288n61, 289
Ngabo, Ben, 211
Nietzsche, Friedrich Wilhelm, 32
Nikisch, Arthur, 55
Nkurunziza, François, 211
Noël, Jean-Sébastien, 9, 194–207, 293
Nourissier, François, 131, 134n52, 136
Nyangezi, Masabo, 211
Nyiranyamibwa, Suzanne, 1, 9, 210, 214–15, 217–22

Obote, Milton, 211
Obregón, Alvaro, 40
O'Connell, John Morgan, 2, 12n4–5, 17, 298n10
Offenbach, Jacques, 28, 85, 91–93, 99n38, 99n45, 100n50, 125, 133n27, 237, 242n63, 245
Office of War Information (OWI), 275, 285, 291
Opéra-Comique, 23, 90, 92, 97n23, 99n41, 99nn43–45, 100n50, 125, 177n53, 237
Opéra National de Paris, 90, 98n32, 99
Orfeónes, 44
Orphelins de la Guerre, 88
Österreichischer Gewerkschaftsbund (Austrian Trade Union Federation), 147
Ottoman Empire, 229–30, 233, 235, 243

Palomino, Pablo, 6, 292
Paper Brigade, 194–96

Paris Commune, 21, 83, 117
Pasdeloup, Jules, 23, 25, 33, 37–38, 87, 237
Pasdzierny, Matthias, 56–57, 72, 78
Patriotism, 5, 21, 36, 94, 108, 112, 168, 170, 182, 184, 187
Peacemaking, vii, 10, 229–30, 233, 236–37
Pears, Peter, 61
Perelli, Genaro, 86, 97
Pétain, Marshal Philippe, 122, 131
Petrassi, Goffredo, 279
Pfeiffer, Georges, 31
Pigot, Charles, 24, 34, 37
Piketty, Guillaume, 3, 13, 15, 21, 33, 37
Paulus (Jean-Paulin Habans), 106, 118, 120
Perrin, Jules, 108
Phonograph, 127, 197
Planquette, Robert, 110
Ploner, Josef Eduard Maria, 138, 141, 143–47, 150–55
Poland, 26, 197, 200, 273, 279, 288
Polish Academy of Sciences, 198
Police bands, 39
Political exile, 56
Pougin, Arthur, 87, 97
Popular music, 4, 14–15, 43, 46, 49, 51–52, 110, 114, 116, 121, 125–26, 131, 190, 275, 282, 298
Popular Front (Front Populaire), 262
Price, Aimée Brown, 26, 32, 35
Propaganda, 4, 10, 11, 55, 57, 74, 77, 143, 144, 188, 192, 197, 210–15, 223, 249, 254, 262, 263, 270, 272, 275, 276–77, 280, 282–83, 291, 295
Protest, 55, 58, 74–75, 188, 251, 283, 292, 295–96
Prunières, Henry, 246, 254–59, 261, 265–67, 270
Prussia, 22, 94, 232
Public Library's Music Department, 275
Publishers (music), 5, 43, 117, 143, 247, 292

Radio, 44, 46, 48–49, 64, 123, 127–28, 131, 131n2, 134 n37, 137, 211–13, 283
RAVAG (Austrian broadcasting cooperation), 143
Ravel, Maurice, 248, 250, 254, 255, 257–260, 265 n42, 265 n45, 266n56, 267n66

Raxis de Flassan, Gaëtan de, 230
Reappropriation, 202
Reich, The, 58, 63, 74n49, 137, 139–41, 143–44, 191n48
Reichskulturkammer (Reich Chamber of Culture), 144
Reconciliation, 3, 8, 56, 61, 65–66, 68, 215, 220, 222, 284, 292, 294
Reconstruction, 3, 4– 6, 9, 27, 41, 49, 70, 85, 87, 94, 101n57, 107, 145, 222, 247–48, 272–75, 290
Reeducation, 4
Regeneration (musical), 89, 94–95, 101n57, 110, 265n42, 272
Regnault, Henri, 31, 37n51
Reintegration, 294
Renner, Karl, 62
Revenge (revanchism), 9, 127, 94, 101n57, 107, 114, 115, 218
Revolutionary music, 39
Revue et gazette musicale, La, 84, 86–88, 91, 94, 96n6
Revue musicale OICRM, 117
Revue musicale, 11, 122, 124, 247, 254, 255, 258, 265 n47, 265n50, 266 nn54–55, 266n63
Reyer, Ernest, 28, 35nn35–36
Rhythm and Blues, 266
Riester, Albert, 138, 141, 144
Robinson, Edith, 249
Roland-Manuel, 259–60, 267n69, 279, 284
Rolland, Romain, 32, 36n58
Roth, François, 116
Roussel, Albert, 255–56, 258–59, 266n54
Rousso, Henry, 121
Ruboneka, Françoise, 215
Rüdinger, Gottfried, 137
Rugamba, Cyprien, 213
Rutabana, Benjamin, 213
Rwanda, 208–23
Rwandan Civil War, 208–23
Rwandan Patriotic Front (RPF), 208

Saint-Saëns, Camille, 30, 36n48, 91, 253, 260
Salzburg, 246, 252, 261
Salzburg Festival, 59
Samputu, Jean-Paul, 211, 213
Satie, Erik, 259
Satire, 9, 113, 169, 170, 173–74, 181, 185, 187

Schiechtl, Anton, 138
Schmitt, Florent, 255, 259
Schneider, Herbert, 172
Schoenberg, Arnold, 1, 250, 253, 255–258, 260, 266n56
Scott, Cyril, 249
Scribe, Eugene, 237
Seeger, Charles, 11, 272, 275–81, 283, 284, 287n36
Segovia, Andrès, 255, 256, 266n54
Self-empowerment, 293, 294, 296–97
Senn, Karl, 138, 141, 145–46, 148
Sentore, Athanase, 212
Sheet music, 103–4, 111, 112n6
Siege of Metz, 107
Siege of Paris, 21, 22, 87
Silence, 140, 175, 213–14, 216, 222, 239, 263, 295
Six, Les, 45, 60, 123, 251, 255, 257, 259–60
Smith, Carleton Sprague, 275, 279, 281–82
Smith, Kathleen, 291, 295
Société des Auteurs, Compositeurs et Éditeurs de Musique, 88
Société Nationale de Musique (SNM), 6, 30, 253
Société Internationale de la Musique Populaire, 125
South Tyrol, 5, 138, 146–47, 150 n1, 151n24
Soviet blockade, 55, 63, 65, 68
Speechlessness, 293–95
Strauss, Johann [not Straub – typo], 46, 49
Strauss, Richard, 185, 248, 241
Spivacke, Harold, 275, 282
State Department, 272–75, 277, 279, 281–83
Stone-Davis, Férdia 199, 201
Stonehill, Ben, 199
Straram, Walter, 258
Stravinsky, Igor, 255–59, 267n66
Styrian Musicians' Union (Steirischer Tonkünstlerbund), 138
Sumpf, Alexandre, 106
Suppé, Franz von, 180
Survival, 148, 187, 221, 292–95, 297
Sutzkever, Avrom, 194, 196
Szymanowski, Karol, 255–57, 266n56

Tango, 47, 50
Tansman, Alexandre, 256, 266n54

Tenroc, Charles, 254, 260, 265n44
Thacker, Toby, 291
Tertis, Lionel, 249
Théâtre-Italien, 87, 89–90, 93n30–31
Théâtre-Lyrique, 87, 92, 97n23
Third Republic, France, 110, 112, 121, 129
Thiers, Adolphe, 83, 105
Thomas Ambroise, 92, 99n44
Thomas, Jean, 279
Tiroler Volksliedarchiv (Tyrolean Folk Song Archives), 144
Torres Bodet, Jaime, 271, 279
Toscanini, Arturo, 58
Tradition, 44, 58, 161, 171, 203, 214, 230, 237, 248, 253, 273
Trauma, 3, 9, 32, 83–84, 94, 111, 113–14, 137, 181, 187, 292
Treaty of Frankfurt, 93, 103, 105, 108
Treaty of Paris, 160–61, 230
Treaty of Versailles, 103, 112, 115
Tutsi, 1, 208, 211–12, 217, 293
Tutsi genocide, 9
Twagirayezu, Cassien, 211
Tyrol, 5, 125, 138–141, 144, 146–149, 149 n1, 150n3, 151n24, 151n29, 293
Tyrolean folk music, 8, 293

Uganda, 208, 211–13
Ukraine, 290–91, 297
United Kingdom, 66, 131n2, 234–35, 239, 250, 274
United Nations Educational, Scientific and Cultural Organization (UNESCO), 124, 271–72, 274–75, 273, 276– 282, 283–85, 287n37, 288 n38
Uwera, Florida, 212

Václav Stepán, 256
Vallas, Léon, 254, 258, 266n47
Verdi, Giuseppe, 22, 27, 143, 237
Vereinigung Sozialistischer Akademiker (Austrian Association of Socialist Academics), 147
Viardot, Pauline, 95
Vichy regime, 123
Vick, Brian, 240

Vienna, 5, 7, 10, 54–66, 68, 72,142, 167, 170, 239–41, 233
Vienna Philharmonic Orchestra, 2, 69–71
Villemer, Gaston, 110, 111
Viñes, Ricardo, 255
Violence, 2, 4, 22, 32, 40, 93, 106, 148, 167, 182, 195, 197, 201, 208, 212, 216–18, 220–21, 223, 295
Vuillemin, Louis, 107
Vuillermoz, Émile, 254, 259, 267n66

Waldheim, Kurt, 63
Wagner, Richard, 28, 29, 65, 66, 92, 93, 160n50, 131, 180, 253
Wagnerism, 1, 27, 92, 93
Wajner, Leon, 197, 200
Walden, Lord Howard de, 247, 250
Walter, Bruno, 7, 56, 57, 58–61, 67–68
War/peace continuum, 2
War in peace, 4
Weber, Johannès, 25
Webern Anton, 257–58, 266n56
West-Eastern Divan Orchestra, 10
Weill, Kurt, 257
Werb, Bret, 201
Wiéner, Jean, 255, 258, 265n45, 265 n57
Workers choirs, 44
Wolff, Albert, 24
World Jewish Culture Congress (Altveltlekher Yidisher Kultur Kongres), 199
World War I (or First World War), 3, 55, 103, 106, 107, 108, 112–15, 141, 149n1, 151n29, 181, 195, 247, 272, 274, 293
World War II (or Second World War), 6, 9, 11, 54–55, 58, 63, 140, 142, 145, 147–49, 283–84, 293, 296

Yad Vashem, 195, 197
Yakimchuk, Lyuba, 296
Yiddish Scientific Institute (YIVO), 195–96
Yung Vilne (Vilna Youth), 194–95, 199

Zaire, 208, 215, 221
Zelensky, Volodymyr, 290, 296
Zemlinsky, Alexander von, 261

www.ingramcontent.com/pod-product-compliance
Lightning Source LLC
Chambersburg PA
CBHW071149070526
44584CB00019B/2723